REVOLUTION

REVOLUTION
INTERNATIONAL DIMENSIONS

Mark N. Katz, Editor

George Mason University

CQ PRESS

A Division of Congressional Quarterly Inc.
Washington, D.C.

CQ Press
A Division of Congressional Quarterly Inc.
1414 22nd St. N.W.
Washington, DC 20037

(202) 822-1475; (800) 638-1710

www.cqpress.com

Printed in the United States of America

05 04 03 02 01   5 4 3 2 1

Cover design: Karen Doody
Cover Illustration © Teofilo Olivieri

∞ The paper used in this publication meets the minimum requirements of the American National Standard for Information Sciences--Permanence of Paper for Printed Library Materials, ANSI Z39.48-1992.

LIBRARY OF CONGRESS CATALOGING-IN-PUBLICATION DATA

Revolution : international dimensions / edited by Mark N. Katz.
         p. cm.
      Includes bibliographical references and index.
      ISBN 1-56802-553-X (alk. paper)
      1. Revolutions.   2. International relations.   I. Katz, Mark N. II. Title.
   JC491 .R48656 2000
   303.6'4--dc21

                                                                              00-010482

To
Winnie and Milton Yinger

CONTENTS

Preface   ix

The International Dimensions of Revolution:
An Introduction   1

   1 An Analytical Framework   9
      Jack A. Goldstone

Part I   Revolution and International Conflict   30

   2 A Theory of Revolution and War   32
      Stephen M. Walt

   3 War and Revolution   63
      Fred Halliday

   4 The U.S. and Third World Revolutionary States:
      Understanding the Breakdown in Relations   75
      Robert S. Snyder

Part II   Counterinsurgency and Revolution   114

   5 The Role of Military Power   116
      Timothy P. Wickham-Crowley

   6 Learning to Eat Soup with a Knife: British
      and American Army Counterinsurgency
      Learning during the Malayan Emergency
      and the Vietnam War   154
      John A. Nagl

Part III   Democratization and Revolution   167

7   Preempting Revolutions: The Boundaries of U.S. Influence   169
   Robert A. Pastor

8   Guerrillas and Elections: An Institutionalist Perspective on the Costs of Conflict and Competition   198
   Matthew Soberg Shugart

Part IV   The Transformation of Revolution   239

9   Revolution and World Order: The Revolutionary State in International Society   241
   David Armstrong

10   The Embourgeoisement of Revolutionary Regimes: Reflections on Abdallah Laroui   250
   Mark N. Katz

Part V   The Future of Revolution   270

11   Is the Age of Revolutions Over?   272
   Jeff Goodwin

12   Same as It Ever Was: The Future of Revolution at the End of the Century   284
   Eric Selbin

Suggestions for Further Reading   299

Index   303

PREFACE

I became interested in the international dimensions of revolution when I was a student in the 1970s. It was a period of great revolutionary upheaval in many areas of the developing world, including Southeast Asia, the Middle East, Africa, and Latin America. What struck me then was the profound influence that revolution in poor, weak countries like Afghanistan, Angola, and Nicaragua had on Soviet-American relations and world politics generally. Although strategic arms control and détente in Europe and Northeast Asia were far more important to Washington and Moscow than was revolution in the developing world, the latter not only distracted the superpowers from these more central concerns but often halted their efforts at cooperation in them.

From the beginning of the cold war in 1945 through the late 1970s, revolution in the developing world appeared to help the USSR and hurt the United States. Most of the revolutions during this period were of a Marxist or anti-Western variety. I was among those, however, who argued that revolution in the developing world would ultimately be as much of a military burden for the Soviet Union as it was for the United States. Several originally pro-Soviet revolutionary regimes (most notably communist China) had already become anti-Soviet. The Iranian Revolution of 1979 promulgated a revolutionary doctrine—Islamic fundamentalism—that was as anti-Soviet as it was anti-Western. The mounting burden of defending several weak Marxist revolutionary regimes in the developing world—most notably Afghanistan—eventually led the Soviet reformist leader Mikhail Gorbachev to abandon these regimes and allow them to fall. The Soviet brand of communism then succumbed to democratic revolution in Eastern Europe in 1989 and in the USSR itself in 1991. In retrospect, it appears that revolution in many parts of the world played an instrumental role in bringing about the demise of communism, the Soviet Union, and the cold war system of international relations.

Despite the spread of democratization and the increasing reach of globalization, revolution remains a salient feature of the international relations of the post–cold war era. Islamic revolutionary movements are active in the Middle East, Central Asia, and several predominantly Muslim countries in other parts of the world, where there happen to be large petroleum reserves on which the rest of the world is dependent. "Nationalist" revolutionaries (such as the Chechens in Russia, the Kashmiris in India, the Uighurs in China, and the East Timorese in Indonesia) threaten to inspire other such movements in the large multiethnic states in which they are active. Despite the downfall of communism, Marxist revolutionary movements pose varying degrees of threat to fragile democratization and economic development efforts in Colombia, Mexico, and Peru. Finally, there is also a possibility that peaceful democratic revolution will overthrow the Chinese government and other authoritarian regimes.

Revolution in the post–cold war era would affect not only the countries in which it occurs but also international relations generally. Islamic fundamentalist revolution in an oil-rich state such as Saudi Arabia could lead to a dramatic rise in the price of oil, jolting the world economy. The success of "nationalist" revolutionaries in seceding from multiethnic states could sharply diminish the latter's international importance. For example, a Russia shorn of its Muslim regions—where much of the country's petroleum reserves are located—would be an even less powerful actor on the international stage than it was after the breakup of the USSR. The success of Marxist revolutionaries anywhere in Latin America might galvanize the many people elsewhere in the region who feel impoverished by their countries' efforts to integrate their economies with those of America and the West. A democratic revolution in China obviously would have enormous influence on its relations with the rest of the world.

Structure of the Book

The potential impact of revolution on the international relations of the twenty-first century makes this a subject well worth studying. Ironically, though, the literatures on revolution and international relations often do not examine the relationship between them. There is, however, a small but rich body of scholarship that is sensitive to these linkages. I have selected from this literature twelve particularly insightful readings. Each selection, written by an accomplished scholar in the field, met three criteria: it explored an important aspect of the relationship between revolution and international relations from a theoretical or comparative perspective; it was written in an accessible and engaging style to facilitate comprehension by students and other readers; and it showcased a perspective in contrast with other selections, in order to provide starting points for discussion and debate in the classroom and other settings.

The book begins with an introduction that briefly examines the ways in which revolution has affected international relations historically and that discusses key terms to help students and others read and analyze the selections. The core of the book is divided into five parts; each part showcases readings that do not necessarily agree with one another on an important aspect of the relationship between revolution and international relations. The readings in Part I, for example, present differing arguments on why revolution and international conflict are linked and how the linkage occurs. The selections in Part II examine why counterinsurgency efforts to suppress revolution succeed or fail, and the essays in Part III discuss how democratization efforts might or might not preempt revolution. Part IV explores various theories about why revolutionary regimes eventually want to normalize relations with status quo powers. And, last, Part V presents two contending views on the future of revolution.

A number of features are employed in this collection to foster informed reading. Each part begins with an introduction that discusses the importance of the subject and alerts readers to the principal differences in argument or approach among the selections. In addition, each selection is preceded by a headnote that provides background information as well as several "critical questions" designed to assist the reader in analyzing the selection. Instructors might find them useful as the basis for exam questions. An annotated list of suggested readings appears at the end of the book as a guide for additional research and study.

Since the readings cover a range of cases from a variety of time periods and explore a number of theoretical debates, this book can be used for courses on revolution offered by political science, history, and sociology departments. This volume would also be an ideal text in general international relations courses where the instructor would like to explore the role of revolution in international relations. The book should also be of interest to policy makers, the analysts who serve them, and country or area experts seeking to place "their" revolution in a broader context.

Acknowledgments

I received help from many people at different stages of this project. There were two sets of external reviewers. Hanna Freij of Kent State University, Jack Goldstone of the University of California at Davis, and Timothy Wickham-Crowley of Georgetown University provided excellent advice when this project was at the conceptual stage. Neither Goldstone nor Wickham-Crowley, I should note, were aware that I would later include selections by each of them here. In addition, Ronald Cox of Florida International University, Rodger Govea of Cleveland State University, and Alan Liu of the University of California at Santa Barbara reviewed a full version of the reader and made many outstanding suggestions about how to improve it.

Thanks are also due to the people at CQ Press who worked with me on this project. I am especially grateful to Charisse M. Kiino, who guided this project from beginning to end with sage advice and gentle humor. Julianne C. Rovesti ably organized the marketing for this book, while Belinda Josey skillfully managed production. I would also like to thank my manuscript editor (and former student) Jerry A. Orvedahl for his patient persistence in polishing my prose. They have been a wonderful group to work with.

Finally, I would like to express my appreciation to Professor David Mozingo. His brilliant course on comparative revolutions, which he taught while a visiting professor at the University of California at Riverside in the spring of 1975, first inspired my interest in this fascinating subject.

The International Dimensions of Revolution: An Introduction

For years, Angola was a sleepy Portuguese colony in Africa where nothing ever seemed to change and about which outside powers did not concern themselves. As a result of the revolution that culminated there in 1975, however, Marxist Cuba and white-ruled South Africa each sent thousands of troops to Angola, which would be an arena of Soviet-American competition for the next fifteen years.

In the late 1960s and early 1970s, Ethiopia was allied to the United States while neighboring Somalia was allied to the Soviet Union. As a result of the Marxist revolution that took place in Ethiopia in the mid-1970s, however, Ethiopia became allied to the USSR and Somalia to the United States.

Despite its claims to some islands in the Persian Gulf, Iran under the shah did not seek the downfall of other governments in the Middle East. The Islamic revolution that occurred there in 1979, however, brought to power a government that called for just this. Not only did the United States fear that Iran under the ayatollahs could spread its revolution across the Gulf to conservative oil monarchies such as Saudi Arabia, but the USSR feared Iran too, since Tehran also called for Islamic revolution against leftist governments allied to Moscow.

These three examples illustrate the three basic effects that revolution can have on international relations. First, revolutions can magnify the importance of the countries experiencing them, even if the countries are relatively small and weak (as Angola demonstrated). Second, revolution can upset existing alliance patterns (as shown by Ethiopia and Somalia). Third, other countries usually fear—often justifiably—that revolutionary regimes will attempt to export their revolution (as occurred with Iran).

Not every revolution has affected international relations in each of these three ways. However, every revolution of the past two and a quarter centuries has affected international relations in at least one of them.

The American Revolution of the late eighteenth century transformed thirteen small British colonies into one large, independent state. Although the United States may have played only a minor role on the international stage when it was newly independent, the American Revolution greatly magnified the importance of the former thirteen colonies, which previously had been unable to play a large role. Except for failed attempts in Canada during the American Revolution and the War of 1812, the newly independent United States did not attempt to export its revolution. Nevertheless, the American Revolution would inspire other revolutionaries seeking to transform colonies into independent states as well as to replace authoritarian with democratic rule.

The French Revolution of the late eighteenth century had all three international effects. It transformed France from a declining power into an energized great power. Further, French revolutionary governments assisted the spread of "republican" revolution to other countries—and would dominate them afterward. In addition, the French Revolution induced many other European governments to put aside their quarrels with one another and work together against the French.

The Russian Revolution of the early twentieth century also had all three international effects. Russia, too, would be transformed from a declining power before its revolution into an energized great power afterward. The new communist rulers of Russia declared their desire to see their brand of revolution spread throughout the rest of the world. Moscow would eventually succeed in implementing its desires through the forcible imposition of communist regimes in Eastern Europe at the end of World War II and through support to the wave of Marxist revolutions that occurred in the developing world during the cold war. After World War II, many countries in several parts of the world would ally with the United States in an effort to halt the spread of communism.

Several other revolutions of the early twentieth century—including ones in China, Ireland, Mexico, and Turkey—had more modest international effects. Like other anticolonial revolutions, the Irish Revolution sought to transform a colony into an independent state. The Chinese, Mexican, and Turkish Revolutions were aimed at removing various forms of unwanted foreign influence. The new regimes that arose in these countries, however, did not seek to export their revolutions.

The mid-twentieth-century Chinese Communist Revolution, though, had all three international effects. Unlike the Manchu dynasty, which was overthrown in 1911, and the Nationalist government, which was ousted in 1949, the new communist government was able to transform China from a declining, dependent power into an assertive, independent great power. Communist China also sought to spread its brand of revolution elsewhere in the developing world, for awhile. When the communists first came to power, they ended China's alliance with the United States and entered into one with the USSR. Beijing and Moscow would later turn against each other, and China would become a de facto ally of the United States in the early 1970s and remain one through the end of the cold war.

Marxist revolutions also occurred in a number of small, mainly developing, countries during the cold war era. These included ones in Albania and Yugoslavia in the 1940s; Cuba and North Vietnam in the 1950s; the Congo and South Yemen in the 1960s; and Afghanistan, Angola, Cambodia, Ethiopia, Grenada, Guinea-Bissau, Laos, Mozambique, Nicaragua, and South Vietnam in the 1970s. Many of these revolutions transformed colonies into independent states. Some revolutionary regimes—such as those in Cuba, Nicaragua, North Vietnam, and South Yemen—vigorously attempted to export revolution. Others did not. Virtually all went from being part of the Western sphere of influence to being part of the Soviet one. Like China, Yugoslavia and Albania would also leave it. Cambodia was something of an exception: the brutal Khmer Rouge regime, which came to power there in 1975, allied with China against Vietnam and the USSR, but an invasion by Vietnam in 1978 ousted the Khmer Rouge regime and replaced it with a regime friendly to Hanoi and Moscow.

There were, of course, other types of revolutions besides Marxist ones after World War II. Arab nationalist revolution swept through several countries during the 1950s and 1960s: Algeria, Egypt, Iraq, Libya, North Yemen, Sudan, and Syria. All these revolutions were anti-Western and anti-Zionist. Where monarchies had been in power, the revolutions were also antimonarchical. The most ambitious goal of the Arab nationalist revolutionaries was to export their brand of revolution throughout the Arab world, creating one vast Arab state, which would necessarily play a much more important role in international relations than could the many small Arab states, which the revolutionaries saw as the artificial creation of European imperialism. All of the states where Arab nationalist revolution occurred left the Western sphere of influence and, to a greater or lesser extent, entered the Soviet sphere.

The 1979 Islamic revolution certainly raised Iran's international profile, transforming it from an ally of the United States into an aspiring great power that challenged both the United States and the USSR. In addition, as was mentioned at the outset, the Iranian revolutionary leadership was initially hopeful—and many other governments were fearful—that Tehran might be able to export its Islamic revolution. Similarly, the Islamic revolutionary regime that came to power in Sudan in 1989 also sought to export its revolution. On the other hand, the Taliban, the Islamic revolutionaries who seized most of Afghanistan in 1996, have not attempted to export theirs so far, perhaps because they have not yet eliminated all their domestic rivals. Other governments—most notably those of Russia and Uzbekistan—very much fear that the Taliban will try to export revolution if and when they do triumph at home.

Revolutionary activity has continued into the post–cold war era. Islamic revolutionary movements are active in many countries of the Middle East, Central Asia, and elsewhere in the Muslim world. Despite the apparent collapse of communism between 1989 and 1991, Marxist revolutionary movements are currently active in Colombia, Mexico, Nepal, Peru, and other countries. And while West European colonialism has essentially ended, nationalist revolutionary movements are fighting to wrest independence for what are now regions of larger states. Such activity is occurring in Chechnya, Xinjiang, parts of Indonesia, the Tamil regions of Sri Lanka, Kashmir and other parts of India, southern Sudan, and many other places.

These Islamic, communist, and nationalist movements threaten either to weaken or overthrow the governments they are fighting against. Although a successful revolution in some of these countries would have little international impact, a successful one in others might have great significance. America and the entire world would certainly be affected if Islamic revolution in any of the oil-rich states of the Middle East led to a dramatic rise in the price of oil.

Not only has revolution strongly affected international relations in the past, but it could well do so again. The relationship between revolution and international relations, then, is clearly a subject that is well worth studying.

Key Terms

Four terms are crucial for understanding the selections reprinted in this volume: *revolution, revolutionary movement, revolutionary regime,* and *status quo power.* The authors of the selections do not necessarily define these terms, and some use the terms differently. There is no universal agreement on what these terms mean. The following, therefore, are not authoritative definitions but guidelines to keep in mind as these or similar terms are encountered in this book and elsewhere.

Revolution

What constitutes revolution has been and continues to be widely debated. Some scholars insist that the only true revolutions involve the downfall of a dominant social class as a result of mass uprisings against it, as occurred in the French Revolution of the late eighteenth century, the Russian Revolution of the early twentieth century, and the Chinese Revolution of the mid-twentieth century. Other scholars see revolution as being any sudden, violent replacement of one type of regime by another type. The Arab nationalist revolutions of the 1950s in Egypt and Iraq, for example, occurred not as a result of mass uprisings but through military coups instead. Nevertheless, these revolutionary regimes proceeded to radically transform their societies. Still other scholars do not see violence as a necessary component of revolution, pointing to the largely peaceful uprisings that led to the downfall of communism in most East European countries in 1989.

Although definitions of it may vary, revolution is generally seen as involving two parts: 1) the downfall of an old regime through nonlegal means (that is to say, not via elections) and 2) its replacement by a new regime that attempts (whether successfully or not) to establish a new political, and perhaps also socioeconomic, order. The nonlegal downfall of an old regime does not alone constitute a revolution, especially if the new regime is similar to the old one, as when a coup d'état leads to the replacement of one military regime by another.

Revolutionary Movement

A revolutionary movement is a group, however organized, that seeks to bring about revolution but has not yet done so. Revolutionary movements have one principal goal: to overthrow the regimes they oppose and seize power themselves. Most do not succeed at this extremely difficult task.

Examples of twentieth-century revolutionary movements that succeeded in overthrowing governments and seizing power include the Russian Bolsheviks, the Chinese Communist Party, the Popular Movement for the Liberation of Angola, and the Sandinista National Liberation Front of Nicaragua. Examples of revolutionary movements that were militarily defeated—either by the status quo powers or other revolutionary movements—include the Russian Mensheviks, the Front for the National Liberation of Angola, the Popular Front for the Liberation of Oman, and the New People's Army of the Philippines. Still other revolutionary movements have failed to overthrow the regimes they fought against yet acquired some degree of legitimate political power through peace settlements that democratized or otherwise transformed their countries. Examples of these movements include the South West Africa People's Organization in Namibia, the African National Congress in South Africa, the Palestine Liberation Organization, and the Farabundo Marti National Liberation Front in El Salvador.

Revolutionary Regime

A revolutionary regime is a group that takes power after the downfall of an old regime. The new revolutionary regime may be drawn entirely from a single revolutionary movement or from a coalition of disparate revolutionary, and perhaps even nonrevolutionary, groups. Such governments may be deeply divided, as were the revolutionary coalitions that first seized power in Ethiopia, Iran, and South Yemen. A power struggle among the revolutionaries soon resulted in these and in many other cases.

Revolutionary regimes, especially when they are new, often attempt to spread their brand of revolution to other countries. Revolutionary France, for example, attempted to spread its revolution throughout Europe. The Soviet Union sought the spread of communism throughout the rest of the world. The Islamic Republic of Iran supported Islamic fundamentalist revolutionary movements elsewhere. It is this "export" of revolution that status quo powers have found highly threatening and have sought to halt.

The principal goal of revolutionary regimes, though, is the same as that of governments in status quo powers: to remain in power.

Status Quo Power

A status quo power is a government that feels threatened—for whatever reason—by the occurrence of, or even just the potential for, revolution in other countries. A status quo power, of course, can be the target of revolutionary movements itself. If the government of a status quo power is overthrown, it is usually referred to as the old regime. The new revolutionary regime that replaces it usually finds itself at odds with the status quo governments of other countries. The status quo powers most frequently referred to in this book are the Western great powers, especially the United States and the United Kingdom.

It needs to be borne in mind, though, that there is a certain slipperiness about the terms *revolutionary regime* and *status quo power.* Sometimes, revolutionary regimes behave like status quo powers. During the cold war, for example, the Soviet Union—the quintessential revolutionary regime—behaved as a status quo power insofar as it sought to uphold the communist status quo that it had established in Eastern Europe at the end of World War II. In addition, status quo powers sometimes assist revolutionaries. The French monarchy—a status quo government that would itself soon be overthrown by revolution—aided the American revolutionaries during the late eighteenth century in order to weaken a rival status quo power, Great Britain.

Recurring Patterns

Despite the great variation among revolutions in terms of time, place, and ideology, certain recurring patterns are observable in relations between status quo powers, on the one hand, and revolutionary movements and revolutionary regimes, on the other. This book identifies and analyzes some of them.

The foremost of these recurring patterns is examined in Part I: Revolution and International Conflict. Many scholars have observed that revolution within a particular country is usually associated with war between it and others. It is the linkage between these two phenomena that makes status quo governments so fearful of revolution. Yet, while the existence of a linkage between revolution and international conflict is widely acknowledged, scholars do not agree as to why the linkage exists, how it occurs, or who is mainly "to blame"—as the selections in Part I demonstrate.

Fearing that successful revolution will adversely affect them, status quo powers have often attempted to prevent its occurrence through forceful means—another regularly recurring pattern, which is examined in Part II: Counterinsurgency and Revolution. Although externally assisted counterinsurgency efforts have sometimes succeeded, they have sometimes failed spectacularly—as did the American effort in Vietnam and the Soviet effort in Afghanistan. The selections in Part II examine the conditions under which counterinsurgency aimed at suppressing revolution succeeds and fails.

In recent decades, Western, democratic, status quo powers have also sought to preempt revolution through working to transform the authoritarian regimes at which revolutions are aimed. This newly emerging pattern is explored in Part III: Democratization and Revolution. These selections explore how and why such efforts either succeed or fail.

No matter how much new revolutionary regimes may at first seek to overturn the existing system of international relations, scholars observe that, sooner or later, they stop trying to subvert the system and become status quo powers themselves. This regularly recurring pattern is the focus of Part IV: The Transformation of Revolution. The selections in Part IV offer different explanations as to why this process occurs.

Finally, a debate about whether revolution will be as prominent in the international relations of the post–cold war era as it has been in the past is presented in Part V: The Future of Revolution. The differing viewpoints advanced here stem from a basic disagreement about the impact of the recent wave of democratization in the poorer countries of the world.

Before examining any of these recurring patterns in the international relations of revolution, however, it is necessary to say something about an even more basic issue: Why do revolutions occur? This is a subject on which there are many different views. It is not the purpose of this book to discuss all of them. Instead, we reprint one essay by Jack Goldstone, who seeks to identify the features common to all revolutions, despite their many differences.

1

An Analytical Framework

Jack A. Goldstone

Jack A. Goldstone is the author of Revolution and Rebellion in the Early Modern World *(1991)—a book that greatly influenced the study of revolution. In that book, Goldstone applied demographic as well as political and economic analysis to revolution. Another noted student of revolution, John Foran, praised* Revolution and Rebellion *highly when he wrote, in* Debating Revolutions *(1995), "the book does alter the way future scholars will think about past events. It will stand as a synthesis of major proportions, and a storehouse of provocative leads and arguments" (p. 120).*

In Revolution and Rebellion in the Early Modern World, *Goldstone argued that the inability of fiscally mismanaged states to respond effectively to the challenges posed by prolonged, rapid population growth was what led to revolutionary crises in preindustrial states. He later extended his analysis to contemporary states in the developing world in an essay entitled "Population Growth and Revolutionary Crises," which appeared in* Theorizing Revolutions *(1997).*

In the following selection, Goldstone observes that modern revolutions in small states of the developing world differ in many respects from the classic revolutions in large countries such as France, Russia, and China that occurred earlier. Despite the differences, Goldstone argues that certain processes are common to all types of revolution. These common processes involve "basic patterns of state breakdown, the nature of revolutionary contention, and the challenges of state rebuilding." Because these processes are essentially the same in all revolutions, Goldstone contends that his process model of revolution has forecasting implications.

With regard to the international dimensions of revolution, Goldstone suggests that status quo powers may be able to preempt revolution through addressing the conditions that contribute to it. Once a revolution has occurred, however, Goldstone suggests that it is extremely difficult for status quo powers to alter the new regime's preferences and priorities.

Critical Questions

1. What three elements does Goldstone describe as being common to state breakdowns that give rise to revolution?

2. What typically happens to revolutionary coalitions when they succeed in overthrowing the old regime?

3. What does Goldstone identify as the challenges to state rebuilding that all revolutionary regimes confront?

4. How useful do you think Goldstone's process model is for predicting future revolutions?

Revolution—the forcible overthrow of a government followed by the reconsolidation of authority by new groups, ruling through new political (and sometimes social) institutions—is a complex process. Although the fall of a government may be sudden, the causal trends leading up to that fall, the ensuing struggle for power among contenders, and the reconstruction of a stable state often span decades.

Many factors implicated in revolutions in the late twentieth century—such as dependent development and superpower competition—are quite different from those faced by the major preindustrial European states. Yet I wish to suggest that if one focuses on causal processes and on how revolutions develop over time rather than on individual causes or specific events, the basic patterns of state breakdown, the nature of revolutionary contention, and the challenges of state rebuilding remain largely the same. I therefore believe it is possible to distill from earlier theoretical work, although with some modification, principles for understanding contemporary revolutions.

This chapter presents a process model of revolutions. The model has both forecasting and policy implications; although in some respects, the policy implications are that certain processes, once begun, are unlikely to be altered or deflected. For analytical purposes, I divide the process of revolution into temporal stages, even though in reality these stages overlap and interpenetrate. I first discuss the origins of state breakdown, then examine features of the ensuing struggle for power, and finally consider the factors that affect state reconstruction.

The Origins of State Breakdown

In my work on early modern revolutions (Goldstone 1986, 1988, 1991), I identify three conditions whose *conjunction* led to state breakdown: fiscal distress, elite alienation and conflict, and a high potential for mobilization of the populace. Although the particular forces that create these conditions may be quite different in contemporary societies than in earlier ones, I believe these conditions remain central to the development of revolutionary crises.

Conditions of State Breakdown

The first condition is a decline of state resources relative to the state's expenses and commitments, and relative to the resources of potential domestic and international adversaries. Historically, when the revenues of a state become, over time, insufficient to pay the standing army and bureaucracy, award pensions and favors to supporters, and meet the costs of building roads, ensuring the supply of grain to cities, maintaining order, enforcing justice, and overseeing local administration, the authority of the state wanes. The state is then forced to seek new sources of income. Early modern and contemporary Third World states have turned to borrowing, new taxes of dubious legality, and simple corruption—demanding payment for offices, honors, and the right to do business. When expenses still outrun revenues, as debts mount and funding for the military grows strained, the loyalty of the commercial community and of the army grows tenuous. As corruption increases, elites' loyalty to the state becomes more something to be purchased than something offered as a matter of course. The bureaucracy and military become less efficient instruments of the state and more centers of personal advance and peculation. As money becomes both more essential and harder to find, the state grows more dependent on maintaining the goodwill of its creditors, and its freedom of action diminishes. Both the ability to project military force abroad and the ability to control domestic opponents decline. Eventually, a final straw—a war, a collapse of state credit, or superpower pressure—leads the government to yield initiative to the country's elites. It was this dynamic that led to the calling of the English Parliament in 1640 and the French Estates General in 1789, the opening acts of the English and French revolutions.

Yet such a resource crisis is not invariably fatal to states. Elites—individuals who are exceptionally influential owing to their wealth, religious or professional positions, local authority, or celebrity—may, if they are loyal, rally around the government and continue to support it. In France in 1715, the leaders of the regency government developed a plan for recovery from the bankruptcy of Louis XIV. In Prussia, after its defeat by Napoleon at Jena, elites did not abandon the monarchy. Through the support of a conservative military nobility, and the efforts (though only partially successful) of loyal reform ministers to alter and strengthen the army, bureaucracy, and educational and status systems, the monarchy in Prussia emerged stronger in 1815 than before. A crisis of state resources is fatal only when it is accompanied by severe elite alienation. Elite alienation from the government creates resistance to the need for new state revenues and institutional reforms, and thus blocks recovery.

Furthermore, revolutionary struggles arise only when elites are severely divided—a united elite, opposed to a government that is weak in resources, can simply stage a coup d'etat and then alter government policies (Burton 1984; Burton and Higley 1987). Indeed, the near-total withdrawal of elite support, especially when accompanied by popular demonstrations, has sometimes persuaded rulers that they have been abandoned, leading them to flee: e.g., James II in England in 1688, Charles X in France in 1830, and Louis Philippe in France in 1848. In these cases, substantial elite unity prevented widespread struggles and civil war; there was no wholesale renovation of institutions or destruction of elites. Only when, in addition to widespread alienation from the state, elites are sharply divided over the future direction of institutional change is a revolutionary struggle likely to arise. Thus, a second key condition in the genesis of state breakdown is a certain set of attitudes among the elites—unsupportive of the government yet deeply divided over the degree to which existing institutions need to be merely shored up, moderately altered, or radically overhauled.

One key to this set of attitudes lies in patterns of social mobility. When social mobility is low and the composition and size of elites are stable, there is generally little conflict. However, when social mobility rises, as new groups acquire skills, gain middle-class and professional positions, while social and political institutions still *deny* them higher status and full political participation, conflicts generally arise. These conflicts may pit new aspiring elites against older, dominant elites; they may pit different new elites against each other; and—most important—they may pit a variety of elites against the state, if all groups come to blame the state for the increased insecurity and conflict over elite positions. Thus, it is often precisely when new or oppressed groups seem to be improving their position—as when non-nobles increased their wealth and bureaucratic positions in Old Regime France; when technical professionals increased their importance in modernizing Iran; or when blacks increasingly became skilled workers and township merchants and businessmen in South Africa—that revolutionary pressures increase.

Of course elite disunity is a double-edged sword. Elites who are fragmented into numerous competing and disarrayed groups are unlikely to pose a threat to a regime, much less overthrow it and succeed in reconstructing a stable state. When elites have varying degrees of loyalty to the state and multiple conflicts with each other, the state can play off elite factions against each other and keep the elites divided and weak. A primary policy of absolute monarchies was to promote new men and manipulate court factions to this end. In addition, early modern elites were frequently divided by regional loyalties, by rural versus urban orientation, by religion, by trends in social mobility that advantaged some and disadvantaged others, and in multi-ethnic states such as Austria-Hungary, by race and ethnicity. Indeed, it was such divisions that long sustained absolute rule. It is thus a particular trend in elite divisions that increases the risk of revolution. When, despite their divisions, *many* elite groups are sufficiently alienated from the state that broad anti-state coalitions emerge, *then*—if the state is weaker than its adversaries—revolution becomes increasingly likely. Furthermore, when divided elites begin to polarize into sharply opposed anti-state and conservative coalitions a revolutionary contest becomes almost inevitable. These two phases in elite dynamics—a broad anti-state coalition of elites followed by polarization into sharply opposed factions—are evident in both early modern and twentieth-century revolutions.

In some twentieth-century situations, such as Turkey in 1921, Peru in 1968, and Egypt in 1952, radical elites who are already in control of powerful state institutions, such as military-based reformers, might triumph over the government and conservative elites in a coup or a brief intra-elite struggle and stage a "revolution from above" (Trimberger 1978). But elites seeking radical change who are not already in influential positions in the state administration rarely can overcome the state and conservative elements in the armed forces without mobilizing support among the populace. Thus, a third necessary condition for revolution is urban or rural popular groups that can be readily mobilized against the state and against counterrevolutionaries. This generally means peasants or urban workers who have grievances against the economic or political regime and who have the autonomy and organization—whether through village communities or urban neighborhoods—to act (Skocpol 1979). A high mobilization potential is generally produced by the combination of adverse trends, such as shrinking access to land or falling real wages, *and* local community structures that give popular groups some freedom of action versus local authorities as well as a basis for organization in support of community goals. Popular support for change, and a willingness to act through demonstrations, riots, and enlistment in revolutionary militias, often makes the difference in the dismantling of existing regimes.

Each of these conditions—state resource failures, elite alienation and divisions, and popular mass mobilization potential—may create political problems and disturbances by themselves. Peasant revolts, urban uprisings, elite rebellions and succession struggles, and state bankruptcies litter early modern history. Yet only when all these conditions *come together* do they have sufficient force to shatter existing institutions and create a revolution.

I have therefore suggested that efforts to forecast political instability leading to revolution should not use an additive framework, simply listing causes that lead to state difficulties, because the key factor is not any one individual source of problems but the *conjunction* of difficulties in several sectors of the society. Thus, I have suggested a model that behaves *interactively*. The risk of revolution should not be seen to rise greatly only if state debt increases, or only if elite alienation and polarization are rising, or only if access to land or real wages in autonomous popular communities falter, but if all three of these elements are rising together, then the risk of revolution increases very rapidly indeed.

I believe this model forms a useful guide to the origins of revolutions in both modern and contemporary states. However, the forces that lead to a decline in state resources, elite alienation, and popular grievances may be quite different in the late twentieth century than in preceding eras, since the composition and aspirations of states, elites, and populations have undergone considerable change.

Forces for Revolutionary Conjuncture

What forces, then, may cause these elements to arise? The answers are as varied as the kinds of resources and tax systems used by states, the status and economic systems that support elites, and the means by which the populace earns its living. Generally, it is some combination of new dynamic forces—that is, some forces that have changed markedly over time—with existing institutional structures that respond poorly to such changes that undermines a manageable status quo.

Two forces that may have either positive or negative impact are price inflation and population growth. Mild inflation may boost government revenues and raise commodity prices for basic producers. If the real economy expands as well, providing jobs and avoiding a drastic fall in popular living standards, inflationary periods may be politically stable. Yet rapid inflation, or inflation in the context of institutions that adjust poorly, may lead to problems. Government obligations and debt may expand too rapidly, and real income may fall for many segments of the elite and the populace. Such conditions are destabilizing. Similarly, population growth may have benefits or drawbacks. If the economy is expanding, population growth can produce a new generation of workers whose successful socialization stabilizes the polity. Yet if the economy is stagnant, population pressures can lead to falling living standards and to downward mobility for members of the elite, whose numbers may increase faster than the growth of positions commensurate with their aspirations and status. In this case, population growth may breed a new generation of discontented radical opponents of the state. In short, there is no simple answer to the question of whether rising population, or rising commodity prices, or any single factor is destabilizing or not. The analyst seeking to assess the likelihood of revolution must be skilled in judging the impact of varied forces on a given society, and be aware of their impact on state resources, on elite composition and aspirations, and on the prospects for the population as a whole. The question is not whether a particular economic or demographic trend is present and in what degree. Instead, the question is one of the *interaction* of such trends with the existing structure of a particular society, and whether this interaction is creating, in conjunction, the conditions whose combination leads to state breakdown.

A third, similarly Janus-faced, factor to consider is the impact of the international political and economic environment. Support from international allies may strengthen states, but pressures from foreign allies may also lead states to take actions that alienate domestic elites. International economic trends may strengthen or weaken state finances, either supporting debt or imposing stringent conditions for credit. International firms may invest and increase employment, or drain resources and block the development of an indigenous skilled and managerial class. Again, the political analyst needs to be aware of what impact this factor is having at a particular time on particular groups in the society under consideration before pronouncing a verdict on its stabilizing or destabilizing effects.

Nationalist and ethnic identification can also be a double-edged sword for regime stability. A regime may gain strength, in the form of elite or ethnic sentiment, from such identification, but any number of state policies—obtaining massive aid or loans from other nations, allying with other nations for military or economic gains, favoring particular ethnic groups, or attacking the culture of such groups—can lead to a loss of a regime's nationalist or ethnic credentials. In such cases, regime support can rapidly erode and give way to sharp opposition.

To continue with the list of factors that can lead to revolutionary pressures in modern societies would create a laundry list of factors that, by themselves, may be innocuous or occur in many nonrevolutionary situations. For example, traditional elites may become alienated if their prerogatives are threatened by newly emerging professional groups. Excessive corruption or concentration of power may alienate elites who feel entitled to participate in economic and political decision making. Regional or ethnic rivalries, and orientation toward international markets or toward domestic development, may provide the basis for a polarization of elites. Shifts in commodity prices, export patterns, and land control may greatly affect the real income of large portions of the population, creating widespread grievances. The same factors can also affect state revenues. It is useful to keep such factors in mind, but the critical issue is whether, in a given society, such factors are occurring in isolation, or in a conjunctural pattern that creates multiple threats to the government. Only in the latter case is a revolution likely to occur.

This reasoning suggests that effective strategies to avoid revolution in the face of mounting pressures may be selective. For example, even when popular economic or political grievances are high, a state that has a strong resource base, or has the support of a unified elite, such as South Africa prior to 1990, may be able to weather storms of popular protest. Or a state that has diminishing resources may wish to concentrate them on providing positions for the elite in order to maintain their support. Thus blunting the rise of one essential condition may help a state escape revolution. But an awareness of trends in all three conditions—state obligations and resources, elite alienation, and mass mobilization potential—is necessary. Leaders who have believed themselves secure because they were surrounded by a small circle of supporters and ignored broader elite alienation, or who have believed themselves financially sound because their current income was high and ignored the broader macroeconomic consequences of their fiscal policies (such as Marcos in the Philippines and the shah in Iran), have paid for their oversight.

I thus would argue that approaches to the origins of revolution that pose the simple question, What are the *causes?* and seek a list of items that have destabilizing consequences in most states are misguided and not terribly helpful. As noted above, such factors as population growth, price inflation, and superpower influence may have widely different effects in different so-cieties. Thus, at the level of discrete causal factors, generalizations about consequences for political stability may not be possible. A more productive approach is to examine a particular society and ask, Are there any forces in this particular society that are straining the state's resources, alienating and dividing the elites, or increasing the potential for the mobilization of the populace against the existing regime? It is such a study of *processes* and *conjunctures* that I believe is necessary to forecast revolutionary crises.

Ideological Change and the Process of Revolution

New ideological movements are sometimes also heralded as a cause of rev-olutions. Yet such an identification again is the result of a search for discrete causes rather than paying close attention to interactions and long-term trends. New ideologies do not suddenly appear—the Enlightenment, liber-alism, communism, and fundamentalist Islam were evident for generations before becoming identified with revolutionary activity. Instead, existing ide-ologies become revolutionary when they are seized on and used by groups that are dissatisfied with their circumstances or with regime performance.

The conditions that give rise to state breakdown—state fiscal distress, usually accompanied by increasing demands on taxpayers, corruption, and military failures; problems among the elite and aspirants to elite status in achieving positions commensurate with what they feel they deserve; and problems of land scarcity, unemployment, falling wages, and associated unrest among the populace—also give rise to a widespread perception that something has "gone wrong" in society. This perception is expressed as complaints about specific conditions and state actions and through more general diagnoses and prescriptions for society's ills. When the state is perceived as strongly influenced by "foreign" ideas, such ideas are often the target of complaint.

Initially, reactions to such problems are conservative—complaints that traditional rights are being violated or general attacks on "injustice." Yet such conservative complaints can, as Calhoun (1983) has shown, spur revolutionary action, for peasants and artisanal communities may be prompted to seek to rectify injustice themselves by food riots, land seizures, or attacks on landlords. Such "conservative radicalism" was an important element in the French and Russian revolutions.

But some elites also voice their sense that society has gone astray by offering various plans for the renewal of the state. They diagnose current state and social institutions as not merely corrupt and in need of rectification but as being fatally flawed and in need of replacement by a new order. As the state's authority weakens, diverse elements in society each press their own cause without consciously attempting to unite with other groups. Elites seek reforms or resist state authority, artisans stage food riots, and peasants stage land invasions or withhold rents or tithes—all without any further thought than taking advantage of propitious times to rectify personally felt injustices.

Yet all of these actions precipitate further discussions of injustice and social ills. Elite groups seeking change begin to identify themselves with a more "truly just" order and moral reform. As Arjomand (1986), following Walzer (1965), has remarked, "The fact that [revolutionary] social movements are reactions to social dislocation and normative disorder explains the salience of their search for cultural authenticity and their moral rigorism" (Arjomand 1986: 402). Seventeenth-century English Puritans, eighteenth-century Jacobins, and twentieth-century Bolsheviks and Iranian mullahs all responded to perceived social problems by seeking to project greater identification with national aspirations and greater moral rigor than the reigning state.

Once the state's fiscal and political woes reduce its authority further, the situation changes. Instead of merely pressing demands for reform, of resisting state authority, elites (and sometimes the populace, when local control depends on the central government) find themselves with new opportunities and new rivals. The new opportunities appear because of the state's loss of initiative and inability to enforce its views, allowing elites new scope for action. The new rivals appear in the form of competing elite segments and various regional and popular demands seeking to shape the social and political order to replace the current regime.

Taking advantage of the new opportunities requires building coalitions and mobilizing support among the social and political fragments set free by the collapse of the state. It is at this point that revolutions characteristically have a flood of pamphlet literature and popular demagoguery. Instead of particularistic complaints, sweeping social programs come to dominate discourse. New symbols are developed to represent various viewpoints and factions competing for popular allegiance. New enemies are defined, vilified, and condemned in order to sharpen differences among and strengthen support for parties competing for power. The revolutionary struggle has begun.

The rapid spread of radical ideologies is thus an evident symptom of the decline of state authority. It indicates that genuine concrete problems have undermined the belief that the state is capable of maintaining order and balancing the needs of varied groups in the society. Generally, therefore, attempts to combat opposition ideologies merely through counterpropaganda, attacks on opposition leaders, and the like do not succeed, for the appeal of the radical ideologies is rooted in concrete social problems, not merely the rhetoric of a particular leader. Unless the state is able to take actions (or benefit from happy circumstances) that reverse the trends underlying the shift in elite and/or popular perceptions, ideologies opposing the current regime continue to spread.

The Unfolding of Revolutionary Crises and the Struggle for Power

Once the state's authority has lapsed, the specific problems that undermined the state's power become less important than the contest among contending groups for the allegiance of the populace. The ideological element of this contest then takes on greater importance, for radical ideologies, even if they, of themselves, "cannot account for the collapse of the societal structure of domination to any significant degree," may yet "shape the political order installed by the revolution to a significant extent" (Arjomand 1986: 384).

Complex societies typically comprise many diverse elements: religious, military, landlord, professional, and commercial elites; urban shopkeepers, artisans, and laborers; and rural peasants ranging from the well-to-do to the desperate. Within each of these "class" designations, segments may be sharply divided by local origin, family background, relation to the state, degree of wealth or status, education, and religious beliefs. Thus, any contender seeking to establish authority in the wake of state breakdown needs to build a "dominant coalition"—that is, a group with sufficient solidarity and resources to defeat all possible combinations of opponents.

It should be clear that the formation of such a coalition is by no means a foregone conclusion. Historically, when such a coalition has not formed—the prime examples in early modern history are the Fronde in seventeenth-century France and Germany in 1848—the old regime has recovered its authority by playing off various social elements against each other. In modern cases, the failure to build such a broad antiregime coalition can lead to a "stalled" revolution as in Afghanistan. To form such a coalition, it is critical to take the various particular complaints, and the various elite and popular ideologies, and forge them into an ideology that has broad appeal.

In the first months following the fall of a government, diverse groups are usually united by the hope that their individual complaints will be rectified and their individual goals realized. This stage is what Brinton (1965) has called the "honeymoon" period of exuberance and superficial unity, which follows the realization that the old state has lost its force and draws on the belief that positive change is on the way. Yet the honeymoon cannot last, for the problems that initiated state breakdown—international pressures, fiscal crisis, elite competition, popular deprivation—do not automatically disappear and still require some solution. As popular groups almost invariably have only local concerns and goals, the task of building a dominant coalition to address these issues falls to members of the elites. Behind the various ideologies that have played a role in revolutions—Puritanism, Jacobinism, constitutionalism, communism (in its Bolshevik, Maoist, Sandinist, and other national variants), Islamic fundamentalism—we can discern three broad themes that have been utilized in the task of mobilization of revolutionary coalitions: rectification, redistribution, and nationalism. Revolutionary struggles are, for the most part, the story of how elite segments seek to appropriate and dominate one or more of these themes while defeating similar attempts by their opponents.

Of course, such struggles are not waged merely in the abstract realm of ideas. It is not merely the content but also the organization that carries an ideology that is responsible for its success or failure. To dominate a revolution, an ideology needs a well-organized carrier able to interpret that ideology for a mass audience. The ideologies of transformation that have dominated Western revolutions—Puritanism, Jacobinism, bolshevism— were only strongly held by a small minority. These individuals played a dominant role in large part by being better organized than their opponents and competitors.

For example, in the decades before the English revolution of 1640, there arose a close-knit network of leading families with Puritan sympathies. They knew each other, they socialized and intermarried, and they corresponded about the political and religious problems of the day (Hunt 1983). When conflict with the king broke out in 1640–1642, and people sought to build new alliances amid the breakdown of the monarchy's traditional patronage network, it was the Puritan leaders who were already equipped with a network for communication and action. Throughout England, while most people sought chiefly to defend their local interests, only the Puritans were able to offer a national program to oppose the king, a program based on defense of "authentic" English law and religion. It should be no surprise that the Puritans, just as many modern revolutionaries, then turned to symbols of foreign threat: the need to throw off the "Norman yoke" of subjugation, the need to defend the "ancient constitution," the need to fight off "papists." This is a typical ideological progression, in which elites seek to mobilize popular support by identifying themselves as custodians of a more "authentic" and truly "national" tradition than their opponents. Only thus can "a movement originally concerned with issues of doctrine . . . be broadened out to become a cultural orientation arousing the emotions of large numbers of people" (Fulbrook 1983: 10). Similarly, in France the Jacobins sought to identify themselves as being the custodians of French "national virtue," as the true voice of the French "nation." They were able to do so, albeit briefly, in large measure because their national network of clubs in major towns allowed them to dominate the news from the capital and offer a coherent program during a time of chaos.

Why, as Brinton noted, do revolutions characteristically show a drift to greater radicalism in the course of the revolutionary struggle? The answer lies in the ensuing ideological conflicts for popular allegiance. Groups that are better organized than their rivals have an advantage in taking a leading role in governance immediately after a revolution. Such groups are usually not the most radical, for the latter have often been suppressed by the former government or have yet to gain a reputation. Instead, articulate professionals who are mostly moderate—the Puritans in the 1630s and the Jacobins in 1789 were moderate, not radical; their radicalization developed later (Cliffe 1984; Kennedy 1982)—and who have been advocating rectification and some redistribution of opportunities and assets, are best placed to initially assume authority.

Nonetheless, their success in dominating the polity, given the lack of accepted institutions and of adequate military force, rests on their ability to win the allegiance of key groups, which means appealing to desires for rectification of injustice, redistribution, and/or national authenticity. Rectification of formal grievances—reducing ostentation in government, purging corrupt old retainers and unpopular laws, creating a new constitution, and accepting greater popular participation in politics—can usually be quickly accomplished, to the credit of the new authorities. Yet rectification of material grievances usually requires more than mere formal and procedural changes. Generally, it means that a measure of redistribution of assets held by formerly privileged groups is required. This need in turn either forces those groups seeking popular support toward greater radicalism or gives an advantage to groups who espouse more radical measures. Struggles over the pay of the New Model Army in England and over the disposition of church lands in the French Revolution led to the radicalization of the Long Parliament and the National Assembly. On the other hand, the failure of the Provisional Government in Russia to adopt more redistributive measures to favor workers and peasants created an opportunity for the more radical Bolsheviks.

As the struggles by contending groups to achieve political primacy usually take the form of a growing identification and pursuit of "enemies," a period of terror is generally a part of the revolutionary process. This seems to be not merely a regrettable error or an avoidable "excess" but an essential part of the manner in which groups competing for authority in postrevolutionary situations operate. After all, radical redistributive measures, whether undertaken or resisted by the new government, are divisive, and counterrevolutionaries are still around. The collapse of state authority also generally lets social divisions—regional, ethnic, class, factional—that had been submerged initially by the power of the former state, and later by the united struggle against the state, emerge as overt conflicts. These antagonisms then generally become entangled with the revolutionary struggle. Repeated contests between revolutionaries and their opponents thus lead the former to push the revolution to the point where there can be no turning back, and to purge slackers from their midst. The new leadership "ordinarily [has to] establish 'structures of repression' as the instrument of retaining power in the face of renewed challenges" (Gurr 1986a: 150).

It should also be clear why military dictatorship or militarism toward neighbors is often the outcome of revolution. The weakened institutions left in the wake of the fall of the old government are often insufficient to resolve the strife among competing factions that follows. Radical appeals often further divide the polity. Thus, a nationalist policy, involving strong leadership and action against external "enemies," is often the key to restoring national unity and order.

In such cases, even authoritarian leadership is often initially welcomed. It can be seen as a "plebiscitary" dictatorship, and it appropriates the symbols that the revolution developed to embody national pride. It is thus generally not seen as a revival of the old regime; instead, it embodies the fervent nationalism that is the common denominator to which most revolutions are eventually reduced.

Indeed, much the same struggle—to win allegiance and mobilize on the basis of loyalty to the "nation" rather than the old regime—takes place in the armed forces of a nation during a revolution as takes place in the country at large. As Adelman (1985) has shown, recruitment and promotion in revolutionary armies take on a new principle, emphasizing talent, but also rectification of abuses, redistribution of authority, and national service. The armies of revolutionary states thus embody the state's ideology; their eventual dominance is not merely a triumph of strength but a victory of the revolution, albeit in authoritarian form.

In short, many of the characteristics of revolutions reflect the conditions of revolutionary struggle per se. It is for this reason that revolutions often follow a similar course, despite having diverse origins and espousing ideologies of diverse content.

State Reconstruction and Revolutionary Outcomes

Once a new ruling group begins to consolidate its authority, usually through the forging of revolutionary armies, internal repression, and assertive nationalism, the task of reconstructing stable political institutions looms large. The manner in which postrevolutionary elites approach this task is usually conditioned by three factors: the class and economic structures of the prerevolutionary society, the international context of the revolution, and the experiences of the new elites under the old regime and in the revolutionary struggle.

The class and economic structures of the prerevolutionary society set certain constraints on postrevolutionary state building. For example, when there is a substantial commercial and industrial middle class and major economic assets are privately held, building a successful coalition for taking state power generally requires maintaining private property. Thus, the American, English, and French revolutions were unlikely to move in the direction of socialist state reconstruction. (The failure of the French Jacobins to stay in power was largely owing to their failure to build a supporting coalition bridging the urban poor and the commercial middle classes.) On the other hand, when commercial classes are small and weak and major industrial assets are already held by the state, revolutionary leaders can simply seize these assets and, relying on the support of peasants and/or workers and dismissing the middle classes, establish state socialist economies, as occurred in Russia in 1917 and in China in 1949 (Skocpol 1979).

The international context includes both the pressures of distant great powers and the opportunities and threats posed by nearby neighbors. The drift toward an assertive nationalism plays a major role in both respects. To the extent that a country has been dependent on aid or support from a foreign power, the new regime generally seeks to break those ties. Thus, England and France, after their revolutions, broke old alignments and forged new alliances. Other countries, such as Russia, have sought to maintain a nonaligned status. In the contemporary world, however, smaller countries, with a greater need for foreign assistance, may explicitly switch their allegiance to another foreign power, if such a move seems a way of manifesting their new control of foreign policy. For this reason, revolutions in superpower client states often create geopolitical shifts that have implications for strategic rivalry. Moreover, the combination of sudden shifts in external alliances and assertive nationalism often leads to international wars. Even when overt aggression is not immediately chosen, new regimes still lay stress on arming for defense against external threats. Thus, new revolutionary regimes are usually more formidable and more threatening to their neighbors and to international peace than were the prerevolutionary regimes.

This situation is not always the case. Nationalistic and revolutionary fervor may be directed inward, against internal enemies, as the Russians did against kulaks in the 1920s and 1930s and the Chinese did against "capitalist roaders" in the 1960s. To a large degree, the difference depends on how the new revolutionary elites see the world. When the fear of obstruction of the revolution from within is greater, terror may remain primarily internal. Gurr (1986b) has suggested that the deeper the divisions in the domestic society—particularly regional and ethnic divisions—and the greater the resistance faced by the new revolutionary elites in their struggles with internal competitors, the more likely is a high and lasting degree of internal terror.

Regarding internal reconstruction, the choice of a capitalist or a socialist economy, and of a religious or a secular orientation, often reflects deeply held beliefs on the part of new elites. Skocpol (1979) has stressed that revolutionary leaders are generally drawn from groups that were "marginal elites" under the old regime. Marginal elites are groups that have had an upper-class education and have access to national debates over political and social issues; however, they are also restricted—by their personal circumstances or treatment by the government that is unrelated to their merit— from any prospect of active participation at the highest levels of government or society. These groups are, in some ways, discriminated against, excluded, or punished by regimes, and generally resent their treatment. Thus, when they come to power they have a missionary zeal to correct the aspects of the system that wronged them. For example, religious leaders—whether Puritans or Islamic mullahs—who have been marginalized under an old regime are likely to seek to make the role of religion primary. Revolutionaries from the relatively poor intelligentsia, if snubbed by the wealthy and influential, are naturally drawn to an abolition of private property. Revolutionaries who suffer and sacrifice to achieve the overthrow of foreign domination, or overturn a capitalist regime in the name of restoring land to the peasants and freedom to labor, are willing to take extreme measures and demand great popular sacrifices in order to stamp out foreign influence or attain their social goals.

The nature of the revolutionary struggle also influences the shape of postrevolutionary states. Skocpol (1979) has pointed out that when faced with the difficulties of mobilizing economic resources and achieving political ends, revolutionary leaders are liable to turn to the same methods they utilized in initially gaining power—the forcible mobilization of populations in an ideologically extreme and heightened battle to combat particular enemies. It is thus hard for postrevolutionary regimes to tolerate a "loyal opposition." As Gurr has noted, "The first generation of leaders who have seized power by violence are particularly likely to be habituated to its political uses, and to perceive a threat of violent displacement in the actions, even the existence, of potential challengers" (Gurr 1986b: 54). Postrevolutionary states generally become one-party states, and when a significant threat from internal challengers is perceived, they often become police states. This outcome is not merely the product of a particular ideology, such as communism—the biblically inspired English revolution became a military state under Oliver Cromwell, as did Enlightenment France under the Jacobin dictatorship and modern Shi'ite Iran under the mullahs. Rather, the pattern of the revolutionary struggle—and the resulting fear of internal competitors and violent displacement—affect the style of state reconstruction. Only when revolutions are fought primarily against external opponents—e.g., anticolonial revolutions in which there are few strong loyalists or collaborators, as in the United States and Algeria—are postrevolutionary regimes able to reconstruct their states without great fear of attack from internal adversaries and hence exhibit less of a "garrison" mentality.

Thus, it may be naive to assume that a moderate intervention—in the form of aid or threat of withholding some support—will cause a postrevolutionary elite to take a particular direction in state reconstruction. Certain directions and prejudices, having been forged by past discrimination, humiliation, or punishment or in the heat of revolutionary struggles, are liable to be set firm. Actions taken in the belief that there are "moderate elements" in the postrevolutionary Iranian government, or that Sandinista leaders might change the direction of their policies under moderate military pressure, are therefore likely misguided and unproductive from the outset. Such actions ignore the nature of revolution as a process, in which the impact of past experience and struggles is not easily altered.

Summary: An Analytical Framework for Understanding Modern Revolutions

The preceding framework offers a partial guide for understanding the development of revolutions. The key originating factor is a *conjuncture of several conditions:* declining state resources relative to expenses and the resources of adversaries, increasing elite alienation and disunity, and growing popular grievances and autonomy. These conditions, however, may be produced by a variety of forces depending on how they interact with the institutions and structures in particular societies. Forecasting revolutions thus requires that an analyst pay attention to the particular details of the society under study and ask whether current trends are likely to produce those conditions that threaten the state. This framework also suggests that since these conditions work *interactively* to undermine a state, interventions to forestall revolution may be successful if they can effectively counter one of the critical conditions, even though the others may still be present. Thus, this causal model has both forecasting and policy implications.

Once a government has lost the initiative—as evidenced by the wide spread of ideologies advocating radical changes and the emergence of anti-state coalitions of elites whose resources and popular support surpass those of the state—a number of different factors come into play. The chief of these are the organization and ideology of groups competing with the state for authority. Groups that are highly organized at the outset of a revolutionary crisis, and can more effectively deploy their resources to take advantage of opportunities, have a better chance of defeating other contending groups. In addition, groups that develop an attractive, synthetic ideology are likely to gain resources and supporters. In particular, radical and nationalist ideologies are liable to be more successful in this regard than moderate, merely formal rectification programs. One can thus predict that in a state on the edge of collapse, those groups that are the best organized will have an initial advantage. In addition, the group that is able to gain ideological primacy by capturing the aspirations and allegiance of the largest portion of the population is likely to dominate the revolutionary struggle. When moderates are able to capture the ideological high ground as true nationalists, responding to the needs of the population, they may survive. However, when the radicals are able to capture this high ground, they are likely to emerge as the dominant force in the successor regime. This observation suggests a strategy for moderate groups seeking to survive in the postrevolutionary melee. Thus, this model of revolutionary struggle, too, has both forecasting and policy implications.

This framework also, regrettably, suggests that a period of terror and the emergence of coercive and aggressive regimes are likely outcomes of revolutions. The deeper the divisions in the society, and the greater the degree of internal struggle and resistance accompanying the emergence and consolidation of revolutionary leadership, the more severe internal terror and coercion are likely to be. The greater the reliance on aggressive nationalism to cement the postrevolutionary regime, the more likely is the "pursuit of enemies" to spill over into arming against external threats or undertaking military engagements.

I have noted that certain features of the prerevolutionary society—the class structure and the concentration and ownership of industrial assets—can constrain the directions of postrevolutionary change. In addition, it is important to examine the experiences of the new postrevolutionary elites under the old regime. Elites that were, in some respect, marginal—owing to discrimination, neglect, or lack of some qualification—are likely to rebuild society in a manner that forcefully overcomes the source of their former marginality. Thus, groups that were discriminated against for their religion may seek to rebuild a state that is guided by, or favors, that religion. Groups that were marginalized because of lack of property or traditional status are likely to abolish such status divisions or property holding. Groups that felt oppressed by the influence of a foreign power are likely to be extremely hostile to that power. This observation suggests that the direction of state reconstruction can be partially forecast from an examination of the dominant postrevolutionary elites—their former positions and grievances. It also suggests that if new elites have emerged from a marginal position and won power through a heated struggle, later policy intervention aimed at changing the direction of state reconstruction is liable to be fruitless, given the deeply held formative experiences of former marginalization and discrimination and the hardening of these beliefs in conflicts against the old regime and other opponents. Thus, this last portion of the model again has both forecasting and policy implications.

Although I have presented this model in general terms, I have stressed that its concrete application to particular cases requires a skilled analyst, one who is capable of examining how varied forces and trends have developed in particular societies. Its value therefore depends on the extent to which it can usefully guide, rather than inhibit, the skill of the area specialist in understanding specific instances of revolution.

REFERENCES

Adelman, Jonathan R. 1985. *Revolution, Armies, and War: A Political History.* Boulder, Colo.: Lynne Rienner.

Arjomand, Said Amir. 1986. Iran's Islamic Revolution in Comparative Perspective. *World Politics* 38:383–414.

Brinton, Crane. 1965. *The Anatomy of Revolution.* Rev. ed. New York: Vintage.

Burton, Michael G. 1984. Elites and Collective Protest. *Sociological Quarterly* 25:45–66.

Burton, Michael G., and John Higley. 1987. Invitation to Elite Theory: The Basic Contentions Reconsidered. In G. William Domhoff and Thomas R. Dye, eds., *Power Elites and Organizations,* pp. 133-143. Beverly Hills, Calif.: Sage.

Calhoun, Craig. 1983. The Radicalism of Tradition: Community Strength or Venerable Disguise and Borrowed Language? *American Journal of Sociology* 88:886–914.

Cliffe, J. T. 1984. *The Puritan Gentry.* London: Routledge and Kegan Paul.

Fulbrook, Mary. 1983. *Piety and Politics.* Cambridge: Cambridge University Press.

Goldstone, Jack. 1986. State Breakdown in the English Revolution: A New Synthesis. *American Journal of Sociology* 92:257–322.

_____. 1988. East and West in the Seventeenth Century: Political Crises in Stuart England, Ottoman Turkey, and Ming China. *Comparative Studies in Society and History* 30:103–142.

_____. 1991. *Revolution and Rebellion in the Early Modern World.* Berkeley and Los Angeles: University of California Press.

Gurr, Ted Robert. 1986a. Persisting Patterns of Repression and Rebellion: Foundations for a General Theory of Political Coercion. In Margaret Karns, ed., *Persistent Patterns and Emergent Structures in a Waning Century,* pp. 149–168. New York: Praeger.

_____. 1986b. The Political Origins of State Violence and Terror: A Theoretical Analysis. In Michael Stohl and George A. Lopez, eds., *Government Violence and Repression: An Agenda for Research,* pp. 45–71. Westport, Conn.: Greenwood Press.

Hunt, W. 1983. *The Puritan Moment: The Coming of Revolution in an English County.* Cambridge: Harvard University Press.

Kennedy, M. L. 1982. *The Jacobin Clubs in the French Revolution: The First Years.* Princeton: Princeton University Press.

Skocpol, Theda. 1979. *States and Social Revolutions: A Comparative Historical Analysis of France, Russia, and China.* Cambridge: Cambridge University Press.

Trimberger, Ellen Kay. 1978. *Revolution from Above.* New Brunswick, N.J.: Transaction Books.

Walzer, Michael. 1965. *The Revolution of the Saints.* Cambridge: Harvard University Press.

I

Revolution and International Conflict

Revolution profoundly affects a country both at the time of its occurrence and afterward. Revolution, though, is not always contained within a single country. If it spills beyond a state's borders (or if other states think it might), revolution can affect many other countries or even the entire international system.

The French Revolution of 1789, for example, led to a conflict between France and most of the rest of Europe which did not end until 1815. The Russian Revolution of 1917 was followed by several abortive attempts by external powers to suppress it; several abortive Soviet attempts to foment communist revolution in Europe, China, and elsewhere during the interwar years; and, following the brief Soviet-Western alliance against a common foe during World War II, a cold war between East and West lasting over four decades involving a nuclear arms race, preparation for war in Europe, and a series of proxy wars in the developing world. The Chinese Communist Revolution of 1949 was followed by conflict between Chinese and American forces in Korea in the early 1950s and, after the rupture between Moscow and Beijing, armed conflict along the Sino-Soviet border in the late 1960s. The Iranian Revolution of 1979 was followed by the 1980–1988 Iran-Iraq war, which many feared could engulf other parts of the Middle East.

Although many scholars have observed this connection between revolution and international conflict, they disagree about how and why it occurs. The three selections reprinted in Part I present differing views about this issue. Stephen Walt sees conflict between revolutionary states and status quo powers as being caused by both parties. By contrast, Fred Halliday sees the status quo powers as responsible for these conflicts, whereas Robert Snyder contends that revolutionary regimes are responsible for them.

Although these three theories may appear to be mutually exclusive, it must be borne in mind that none of them may be always right or always wrong. Conflicts between revolutionary regimes and status quo powers have occurred in so many varied circumstances that none of these three theories can explain them all.

Whether in these selections or elsewhere, each of these three authors acknowledges that one theory does not fit all circumstances. Although Walt seeks to explain why revolution leads to war, he recognizes that it does not always do so. The American, Mexican, and Turkish Revolutions, for example, "did not lead to all-out war" (Walt 1996, 269). While Halliday argues that status quo powers are primarily responsible for the wars that follow revolutions, he also argues that war can precipitate revolution. Finally, Snyder makes his claim that revolutionary regimes are responsible for tension only when the status quo power in question is the United States. He also acknowledges that such tension does not always arise.

In reading these selections, it is important to weigh their relative merits when they are examining the same phenomena and to recognize when they are analyzing somewhat different phenomena.

REFERENCE

Walt, Stephen M. 1996. *Revolution and War.* Ithaca: Cornell University Press.

2

A Theory of Revolution and War

Stephen M. Walt

Stephen M. Walt is one of the foremost theorists of international rela-
tions. He is the author of The Origins of Alliances *(1987) and* Revolution and War *(1996). The following selection is drawn from the*
latter. Walt writes in the realist tradition of international relations the-
ory. Realist IR theories focus on states as the primary actors in interna-
tional relations. Realists see the international environment in which
states act as anarchic and hostile. Furthermore, realists tend to see in-
ternational organizations, such as the United Nations, as being ineffec-
tive at maintaining order. Such organizations, they argue, act effectively
only if the most powerful states in them want them to. When a threat to
a state arises, then, realists see that state as having to respond to the
threat with its own resources as well as those of its allies. And allies, of
course, cannot always be counted on. The realist approach, in short,
views the world rather pessimistically.

In the following selection, Walt seeks to explain why revolution in
one state often leads to war with others. Walt posits that states are al-
ways sensitive to threats from each other. One state's perceptions of
threat stem not only from an assessment of other states' capabilities, but
also from an assessment of their intentions and of the "offense-defense"
balance between states. Revolutions, Walt argues, have an especially
negative impact on "balance-of-threat" assessments.

Even when they are rivals, governments that have been in existence
for a long time have established relationship patterns that are usually
predictable. However, when one of these governments is overthrown
and replaced by a revolutionary regime, the stability of these long-
established relationship patterns can be shattered, especially when
the revolutionary regime advocates a political ideology that is hostile
not just to the old regime that it overthrew but to other status quo

governments as well. It is under these circumstances, Walt argues, that war can easily result.

Critical Questions

1. What is the sequence of events that Walt sees as giving rise to war between status quo powers and revolutionary regimes?

2. What calculations impel status quo governments to go to war with revolutionary regimes?

3. What calculations impel revolutionary regimes to go to war with status quo powers?

4. How realistic do these calculations usually prove to be?

5. Does revolution always lead to war between the revolutionary state and status quo powers?

Why do revolutions intensify security competition among states and markedly increase the danger of war? My explanation is laid out in three steps. I begin by setting aside the subject of revolution to consider how states interact in the international system, focusing on those factors that account for security competition and war. To this end, I offer a simple theory of international politics, which I call balance-of-threat theory. I then analyze the revolutionary process in some detail, in order to identify how revolutions affect the states in which they occur. Next, I bring these two lines of analysis together and show how revolutions affect international politics. Specifically, revolutions alter the main elements of threat identified by balance-of-threat theory, thereby encouraging states to favor the use of force. . . .

Balance-of-Threat Theory

Like all realist theories, balance-of-threat theory begins by recognizing that states dwell in an anarchic environment in which no agency or institution exists to protect them from each other. Security is thus the highest aim of states, and foreign policy decisions will be strongly influenced by how national leaders perceive the external environment and by how different strategies are expected to affect their relative positions.[1]

Where neorealist balance-of-power theory predicts that states will respond primarily to changes in the distribution of capabilities, however, balance-of-threat theory argues that states are actually more sensitive to *threats*, which are a function of several different components. The first is *aggregate power*: other things being equal, the greater a state's total resources (such as population, industrial and military capability, raw material endowment, etc.), the greater the threat it can pose to others. The level of threat is also affected by *perceptions of intent*: if a state is believed to be unusually aggressive, potential victims will be more willing to use force to reduce its power, to moderate its aggressive aims, or to eliminate it entirely. Finally, the level of threat is also affected by the *offense-defense balance*: states will be less secure when it is easy for them to harm one another and when the means for doing so are easy to acquire. Furthermore, incentives to use force increase when the offense has the advantage, because the expected cost to the attacker will decline and the expected benefits of aggression will increase. Offensive power is usually defined in terms of specific military capabilities (that is, whether the present state of military technology favors attacking or defending), but political factors can be equally important. In particular, the ability to undermine a foreign government through propaganda or subversion can be an especially potent form of offensive power, because it allows one state to "conquer" others at little or no cost to itself. In general, the greater a state's offensive power is, the greater the threat it will pose to others and the greater their incentive to try to contain or reduce the danger.[2]

By incorporating the other factors that will shape a state's estimates of its level of security, balance-of-threat theory provides a more complete and accurate account of the forces that influence state behavior.[3] The question, therefore, is whether revolutions affect the balance of threats in ways that increase the intensity of international conflict and raise the danger of war. To begin to answer that question, let us consider the nature of the revolutionary process in a bit more detail.

The Revolutionary Process

The main object of revolutionary struggle is control of the state.[4] A revolutionary *situation* exists when control of the government becomes "the object of effective, competing, mutually exclusive claims on the part of two or more distinct polities." A revolutionary *outcome* occurs when the challengers are able to defeat the old regime and erect a new and fundamentally different political order.[5]

The specific process by which a revolution occurs will vary, but nearly all revolutions exhibit certain common features. First, revolutions become possible when the administrative and coercive capacities of the state have been weakened by a combination of internal and external challenges.[6] Second, revolutions feature an explosion of political activity. In a mass revolution, this activity is conducted by individuals who were marginalized or excluded under the old regime. In an elite revolution, the movement is led by dissident members of the old regime (usually military bureaucrats) who become convinced that a revolution is necessary to protect the nation from foreign domination and whose positions grant them access to capabilities (such as the armed forces) that are needed to challenge the old regime.[7] In either type, this explosion of participation takes the form of illegal methods and activities, because the institutions and principles of the old regime offer no legitimate outlet for them.[8] Third, revolutions alter the language of political discourse and foster the development of new symbols and social customs.[9] Fourth, revolutions also alter the principles by which leaders are chosen. In most cases, the new rulers will be drawn from groups that were formerly barred from power while excluding prominent members of the old regime. Thus, revolutions inevitably involve a redefinition of the political community.

Finally, revolutions are usually characterized by violence. Force is often needed in order to oust the old regime, and even when it collapses without a fight, there are likely to be violent struggles among competing revolutionary factions.[10] The issues at stake are enormous, because the process of redefining a political community places everyone at risk. Until a new order is in place, no one is safe from exclusion, and the temptation to use force to enhance one's position is difficult to resist. The possibility that winners will take all and losers will lose everything heightens the level of suspicion and insecurity. Fears of plots and conspiracies abound. Disagreements over specific policies can become life-or-death struggles, if they are seen as reflecting an inadequate commitment to the revolutionary cause.

In sum, revolutions are deadly serious contests for extremely high stakes. The collapse of the old regime places all members of society on shaky ground. Conflicts can be resolved only by tests of strength, and no one's interests or safety are assured. As a result, revolutions are usually violent and destructive, especially when they involve the replacement of the existing elite by previously excluded members of society.[11]

Capabilities

Owing to the features just described, revolution usually reduces a state's capabilities in the short term. The demise of the old regime hinders any efforts to mobilize resources for war (at least until the new regime acquires the institutional capacity to tax and allocate resources), and the armed forces will be severely disrupted if they have not collapsed completely. In the absence of a viable central authority, previously suppressed groups may assert new claims, and certain regions or groups may try to gain their independence, thereby adding to the new regime's burdens and reducing its overall capabilities.

In addition, many revolutionary elites will be poorly prepared for running a government or managing its diplomacy, and key members of the old regime are likely to flee the country or to be purged by the new regime.[12] Thus, the new regime may lack experienced diplomats, trained commanders, and disciplined armies, unless it has also fought a civil war and therefore controls a military establishment of its own. In the latter case, however, its strength will be sapped by the destruction caused by the civil war. Uncertainty about the future cripples economic activity and encourages the flight of capital and expertise, reducing the capabilities of the new state even more.

The damage produced by a revolution is often temporary, and its magnitude is difficult to estimate in any case. By definition, successful revolutionary organizations are good at mobilizing social power and directing it toward specific political ends. Although a revolution harms a state's power in the short term, therefore, it is likely to improve it in the long run.[13] Measuring the precise impact of a revolution on the balance of power will be especially difficult, however, if the new order is based on a radically different model of social and political organization. Thus, while a revolution may appear to create an inviting window of opportunity, at the time it is unclear how large the window is and how long it is going to remain open.

Revolutionary Ideologies, State Preferences, and Elite Perceptions

In a revolution, the old ruling elite is replaced by individuals committed to different goals and infused with a radically different worldview. When a revolutionary movement takes power, therefore, its ideology shapes both the preferences of the new regime and its perceptions of the external environment. Unfortunately, most revolutionary ideologies contain ideas and themes that can create (or exacerbate) conflicts of interest and magnify perceptions of threat.

Successful revolutions are rare, because even weak and corrupt states usually control far greater resources than their internal opponents. States have better access to the means of violence and can use these tools to monitor, suppress, or co-opt potential challengers.[14] It is not surprising, therefore, that most revolutionary movements are rapidly extinguished, and would-be revolutionaries often end up in prison, in exile, or dead. Indeed, it is perhaps more surprising that revolutions ever succeed.

The inherent difficulty of overthrowing an existing state is compounded by the familiar problems of collective action.[15] Because some of the benefits from a revolution are indivisible (once provided, they are available to all), individual citizens can profit from a revolution even if they do nothing to help bring it about. Moreover, each individual's contribution is too small to determine the outcome, so a rational actor would inevitably choose a "free ride" rather than incur the risks and costs of joining a revolutionary movement. Indeed, if people were motivated solely by self-interest and guided by an accurate assessment of costs and benefits, then the lack of willing participants would make revolutions impossible.[16]

A number of scholars have suggested that revolutionary movements can overcome the free-rider problem by offering positive inducements or threatening negative sanctions.[17] Yet this explanation is only partly satisfying. Although specific incentives such as food or protection may help convince uncommitted individuals to support a revolutionary movement, they do not explain either why individuals will risk their lives to expand the movement or how an organization gets started in the first place, before it was able to provide these benefits. Given the high probability of failure and the risks that revolutionaries face, the payoffs would have to be enormous for joining a revolutionary movement to be a rational choice.[18] And testimony from several revolutionary leaders suggests that they did not expect to be rewarded at all.[19] According to Che Guevara, who lost his life trying to foment revolution in Bolivia, "Each guerrilla must be prepared to die, not to defend an ideal, but to transform it into reality."[20] So the puzzle remains: how do revolutionary movements convince potential members to bear the costs and risks of this activity, and how do revolutionaries sustain their commitment through prolonged, difficult, and uncertain struggles?[21]

Part of the answer lies in the possibility that participation in a revolution is motivated as much by moral commitments as by narrow self-interest. For those who believe that abolishing the present order is a moral imperative, individual benefits are secondary or irrelevant.[22] More fundamentally, perceptions of costs and benefits ultimately rest on subjective beliefs about the consequences of different choices. If individuals believe that a revolution is possible and will bring them great benefits—irrespective of the actual possibilities—they will be more likely to support it, particularly if they are also convinced that success requires their participation.[23] Revolutionary movements therefore try to convince potential members, first, that seeking to overthrow the existing order is the morally correct position; second, that doing so will bring significant benefits; and third, that the probability of success is high *if* they act.

Persuading uncommitted individuals of these "facts" is one of the principal functions of a revolutionary ideology, either as a means of gaining the strength needed to challenge the old regime and overcome rival contenders for power or as an instrument for sustaining popular support and legitimizing their subsequent right to rule.[24] Let us examine some of the forms that this all-important ideology can take.

An ideology is a normative theory of action. Ideologies "explain" prevailing social conditions and provide individuals with guidelines for how to react to them. In nonrevolutionary societies, for example, the dominant ideology discourages disobedience and free-riding by persuading citizens "to conceive of justice as coextensive with the existing rules, and accordingly, to obey them out of sense of morality," in the words of Douglass North. By contrast, "the objective of a successful counterideology is to convince people not only that the observed injustices are an inherent part of the system but also that a just system can come about only by active participation of individuals in the system."[25] Revolutionary ideologies present a critique of the current system (as Marx's analysis of capitalism did), together with a strategy for replacing it.[26] In addition, North writes, a revolutionary ideology serves to "energize groups to behave contrary to a simple, hedonistic, individual calculus of costs and benefits. . . . Neither maintenance of the existing order nor its overthrow is possible without such behavior."[27] To nourish this altruistic behavior, revolutionary ideologies tend to emphasize three key themes.

First, revolutionary groups usually portray opponents as intrinsically evil and incapable of meaningful reform.[28] This theme enhances the moral basis for revolutionary participation: if the current system is unjust and cannot be improved, then efforts at compromise are doomed, and revolution is the only acceptable alternative. It was this issue that ultimately separated Lenin and the Bolsheviks from the "Economists" in Russia and from social democrats such as Karl Kautsky; where the latter believed that tsarism and capitalism could be reformed, the Bolsheviks denied that compromise was possible and remained committed to overthrowing both.[29] Portraying enemies as irredeemably hostile can also strengthen the solidarity of the revolutionary movement and enhance its discipline by making any ideological variations appear treasonous. Indeed, the tendency to view the world in Manichean terms can leave a revolutionary organization prone to fratricidal quarrels in which dissenters are castigated as traitors and blamed for any setbacks that occur.[30]

This element of revolutionary ideologies is similar to the popular propaganda that emerges within nation-states during wartime, and for many of the same reasons. Revolutions and wars are violent and dangerous; in order to justify the costs that are inherent in both activities, leaders try to portray opponents as evil or subhuman.[31] After all, if one's enemies are truly wicked, then compromising with them would be both risky and immoral, and eliminating them forever may be worth a great sacrifice. In each case, compromise will give way to more radical solutions.

The second theme is that victory is inevitable. A revolutionary movement will not get very far unless potential supporters believe their sacrifices will eventually bear fruit. Thus, revolutionary ideologies are inherently optimistic: they portray victory as inevitable despite what may appear to be overwhelming odds. To reinforce this belief, the ideology may invoke irresistible or divine forces to justify faith in victory. For Marxists, for example, the "laws" of history led inexorably toward proletarian revolutions and the establishment of socialism.[32] For Islamic fundamentalists, optimism rests on faith in God. Revolutionaries may also cite the successes of earlier movements to sustain confidence in their own efforts; thus, the Sandinistas saw Castro's victory in Cuba as evidence that their own efforts in Nicaragua could succeed.[33]

Optimism can also be encouraged by dismissing an opponent's apparent superiority as illusory. Mao Tse-tung argued that "reactionaries" were "paper tigers," and Lenin described imperialism as containing both the power to dominate the globe *and* the seeds of its inevitable destruction at the hands of the proletariat.[34] Depicting opponents in this way is an obvious method for sustaining commitment within the movement: no matter how hopeless a situation appears to be, success is assured if the revolutionary forces simply persevere.

At the same time, the real difficulties of the struggle demand that revolutionary movements temper their optimism with elements of caution. Even if victory is inevitable, for instance, it may require heroic efforts and repeated sacrifices. Such beliefs address the free-rider problem directly: if potential members are convinced that victory is inevitable regardless of whether they joined or not, then the temptation to let others bear the burdens of the struggle would be too strong. Thus, Mao warned his followers to "despise the enemy strategically while taking full account of him tactically": overcoming the enemy would require careful preparation and repeated sacrifices, but victory was assured because the enemy was vulnerable.[35] In the same way, Lenin warned his followers that faith in victory should neither lead to overconfidence nor preclude setbacks and tactical retreats along the path to power.[36]

The worldview of most revolutionary movements will thus exhibit a strong tension between optimism and prudence. Two important questions, therefore, are which of these tendencies will exert the greatest influence on the perceptions and behavior of the new state, and how its external situation and the responses of other powers will affect the relative weight given to these competing imperatives.

The third key theme is an insistence that the revolution has universal meaning. Specifically, revolutionary movements often believe that the principles of the revolution are relevant for other societies and should not be confined within the boundaries of a single state. In extreme cases, the ideology may go so far as to reject the nation-state as a legitimate political unit and call for the eventual elimination of the state system itself.

That revolutionary ideologies contain universalist elements should not surprise us. If the failures of an old regime are the result of external forces such as the "tyranny of kings," "capitalist exploitation," or "Western interference," then action beyond the state's own borders may be necessary to eliminate these evils once and for all. Such views promise adherents an additional reward for their sacrifices: the revolution will not only be good for one's own society but will ultimately benefit others as well. Moreover, in order to attract popular support, revolutionary ideologists tend to portray their new political ideas as self-evident truths—creating a strong bias toward universalism. After all, how can a self-evident political principle be valid for one group but not others? Could the Jacobins argue that the "Rights of Man" applied only to the French? Could Marx's disciples claim that his inexorable "laws of history" were valid in Russia alone? Could the Iranian revolutionaries think that an Islamic republic was essential for Persians but not for other Muslims?

A few caveats are in order here. These ideological themes are neither necessary nor sufficient conditions for revolutionary success. One or more may be missing in some cases. Nor do revolutions automatically occur whenever some group adopts these ideological formulas. The likelihood of a revolution is also affected by a number of other conditions and by the old regime's ability to respond to the challenge.[37] But it is striking that, as we shall see, the ideological programs of revolutionary movements as varied as those of the American Founding Fathers, the Russian and Chinese Communists, and the Iranian fundamentalists all incorporated variations on these three principles. Moreover, even when the social and organizational prerequisites are present, it is hard to imagine a mass revolution succeeding without some kind of ideological program that justifies revolt and also gives participants a reason to believe they will win.[38] In short, although the inherent difficulty of revolution and the logic of the free-rider problem do not require that revolutionary movements adopt these ideological formulas, such tenets are likely to give them an advantage over rivals who lack a similar set of ideas.

Revolutionary ideologies should not be seen as wholly different from other forms of political belief. Indeed, often they are simply more extreme versions of the patriotic ideals that established regimes use to encourage individual sacrifice. Just as states in war portray their enemies as evil, victory as certain, and their own goals as pure and idealistic ("to make the world safe for democracy," "to promote a new world order," etc.), revolutionary movements encourage similar sacrifices through the three ideological themes described above. Because the risks are great and the odds of success low, however, revolutionary movements will try to indoctrinate members even more enthusiastically than other states. And whereas states ordinarily abandon wartime propaganda when the conflict is over, revolutionary movements that face continued internal opposition may continue using the ideology as a mobilizational device even after the struggle for power has been won.

The elements of revolutionary ideology identified here will be most common in mass revolutions. Because elite revolutions originate within elements of the existing state bureaucracy and are usually less violent, they face less severe collective-action problems than other revolutionary movements. And because such revolutions ordinarily arise in response to the threat of foreign domination, elite leaders can rely primarily on nationalism to mobilize their followers and legitimize the seizure of power. As a result, elite revolutions present less fertile ground for the Manichean worldview and universalistic ambitions that mass revolutions often foster.

By definition, revolutions are conducted by movements that oppose the policies of the old regime. If they succeed in taking power, they invariably attempt to implement policies designed to correct the objectionable features of the old order. Thus, all revolutions entail the emergence of a new state whose preferences differ in important ways from those of the old regime. The new government is virtually certain to adopt new domestic and foreign policies, even at the risk of provoking both internal and external opposition.

The revolutionary process will shape the perceptions of the new ruling elite as well. The ideologies of many revolutionary movements describe opponents as incorrigibly evil and destined for the dustbin of history. As we shall see, this trait encourages them to assume the worst about their enemies and intensifies each side's perceptions of threat. This is most true of mass revolutions, but elements of these ideas appear in elite revolutions as well.

Uncertainty and Misinformation

In the wake of revolutions, uncertainty about the balance of power grows, and so does the danger of war via miscalculation. Estimating intentions is harder, and prior commitments and understandings are called into question as soon as the new leaders take power.

Other states are equally uncertain about the new regime's true aims and its willingness to bear costs and run risks; the old regime's reputation for credibility, restraint, prudence, and so on is of little or no use. Thus, other states have to start from scratch in gauging how the new regime is likely to behave. The same is also true in reverse: the new regime cannot know exactly how others will respond, although it can use their past behavior as a rough guide to their future conduct. These conditions magnify the importance of ideology. Lacking direct experience, the revolutionary regime will rely on its ideology to predict how others will behave, while the other powers will use the same ideology as a guide to the likely conduct of the new regime.

The problem of uncertainty is not confined to relations between the revolutionary state and other powers. In addition, states observing a revolution cannot know how other actors in the system will respond to it. Revolutions thus exert direct and indirect effects on the foreign policies of other states, which must respond both to the new regime and to the uncertain reactions of the entire international community.

Third, revolutions exert unpredictable effects on other societies. As discussed at greater length below, a central issue in the aftermath of a revolution is the likelihood of its spreading to other states. The question of whether (or how easily) it will spread is of tremendous importance to both sides, yet neither side can form a reliable answer. This problem stems partly from sheer ignorance about political conditions in other countries but even more importantly from the fundamental incalculability of a revolutionary upheaval. As Timur Kuran has shown, an individual's willingness to rebel is a form of private information that cannot be reliably estimated in advance, especially when there is a threat of repression, giving the potential revolutionaries a strong incentive to misrepresent their true preferences.[39] As a result, neither the new revolutionary regime nor its potential adversaries can obtain an accurate assessment of the odds that the revolution will move beyond its original borders, a situation creating additional room for miscalculation. And because an individual's true level of support (or opposition) to the new regime cannot be directly observed, neither the new regime nor its foreign counterparts can estimate either its own popularity or the likelihood of counterrevolution.

Unfortunately, the available evidence on these issues is virtually certain to be ambiguous. A mass revolution will always attract some adherents in other countries—thereby supporting the new regime's hopes and its neighbors' worries—but neither side will know if these sympathizers are merely isolated extremists or the tip of a subversive iceberg. Similarly, there will almost always be some evidence of internal resistance after a revolution, yet neither the new regime nor its adversaries will know how strong or widespread such sentiments are. Because these appraisals are central to each side's decisions and yet unreliable at best, the danger of miscalculation is especially severe.

To make matters even worse, the information that both sides receive is likely to be biased by the transnational migration of exiles and revolutionary sympathizers. Revolutions invariably produce a large population of exiles who flee abroad to escape its consequences.[40] Many of them are members of the old regime, and therefore hostile to the revolutionary government and eager to return to power. They tend to settle in countries that are sympathetic to their plight, where they may try to obtain foreign assistance for their counterrevolutionary efforts. To do so, they will portray the new regime as a grave threat to other states and will stress its potential vulnerability to counterrevolutionary action. Moreover, despite their obvious biases, exiles are often seen as experts on conditions in their home country at a time when other sources of information are scarce, so their testimony is overvalued.[41] In much the same way, revolutionary sympathizers flock to the new capital after the revolution, eager to learn from its experiences, lend support to its efforts, or seek assistance for their own struggles.[42] Such groups portray their home countries as both hostile and ripe for revolution, in order to obtain external support for their efforts. In the revolutionary state, these newcomers are regarded as having special knowledge about conditions back home, despite their obvious interest in providing a distorted picture. The two-way, parallel migration of exiles and sympathizers is a feature of most revolutions, and it increases the danger that each side's perceptions and policies will be based on biased evidence.

Finally, revolutions damage the normal channels of communication between states at precisely the time when the need for accurate information is greatest, hindering even more the ability of both sides to understand the information they do have. Diplomatic representatives are often withdrawn or replaced and intelligence networks disrupted, making it more difficult for each side to determine what the other is doing and why. A shortage of adequate facilities and trained personnel can also impair the new regime's ability to evaluate others' conduct and to communicate its intentions. These various sources of uncertainty enhance the probability of miscalculation, as we shall see.

In sum, the process of revolution exerts a profound influence on the state that emerges from it, as well as its peers. Revolutions reduce a state's capabilities in the short term (although they often produce dramatic increases over time). Revolutionary movements are often based on optimistic and universalistic ideologies that portray opponents as irredeemably hostile, and they come to power in circumstances where accurate information about capabilities, intentions, and future prospects is difficult or impossible to obtain. These characteristics help explain how revolutions encourage international conflict.

Why Revolutions Cause Conflict and War

The Balance of Power and Windows of Opportunity

By altering the balance of power, revolutions intensify the security competition between states in at least two ways. First, other states may see the revolutionary state's weakness as an opportunity to improve their relative positions—either by seizing valuable territory or by seeking important diplomatic concessions—or as a chance to attack a state that was previously protected by the old regime. In either case, the revolution creates a window of opportunity for others to exploit.

Second, revolutions can exacerbate security competition *among* other states. If a foreign power becomes concerned that one of its rivals will take advantage of the revolution in order to improve its own position, the foreign power may be forced to take action either to obtain spoils for itself or to prevent its rival from doing the same thing. Thus, the window of opportunity created by the revolution may inspire conflict among third parties so that they intervene, even if they have no particular quarrel with the new regime.[43]

Ideology, Intentions, and Spirals of Suspicion

The movements that revolutions bring to power are by definition opposed to most (if not all) of the policies of the old regime. States with close ties to the old regime will naturally view the revolution as potentially dangerous and its new initiatives as a threat to their own interests. For purely rational reasons, therefore, revolutionary states and foreign powers are likely to experience sharp conflicts of interest and to regard each other's intentions with suspicion.

In addition, actions that one state takes to increase its security—such as strengthening its military forces—will tend to reduce the security of other states.[44] The other states may consequently exaggerate the hostility or aggressiveness of their adversary, thereby inflating the level of threat even more. The resulting spiral of suspicion raises the odds of war, as compromise appears infeasible and both sides begin to search for some way to eliminate the threat entirely.[45]

Revolutionary states are prone to spirals of suspicion for several reasons. First, as noted above, a revolutionary regime will be unsure about other states' intentions, simply because it has little or no direct experience in dealing with them. Lacking direct evidence, it will fall back on ideology, which in most revolutionary situations tends to portray opponents as incorrigibly hostile.[46] Thus, even a mild diplomatic dispute is likely to escalate. Concessions may be viewed with skepticism, because conflict is seen as inevitable and compromise as naive or even dangerous.

Second, revolutionary regimes may harbor suspicions based on historical experience. If the revolutionary leaders are eager to redress past wrongs (as is generally the case), they will be especially wary of the foreign powers they hold responsible for earlier transgressions. Thus, Mao Tse-tung's suspicions of the United States were based in part on past Western interference in China, and revolutionary forces in Mexico, Nicaragua, and Iran preoccupied themselves with the possibility of U.S. intervention for similar reasons.[47]

Under these conditions, revolutionary regimes, assuming the worst about other states, will interpret ambiguous or inconsistent policies in a negative light. Threats and signs of opposition simply confirm the impression of hostility, while concessions and signs of approval are regarded as insincere gestures masking the opponent's true intentions.[48] Unfortunately, the other states' policies are almost sure to be ambiguous, if only because it takes time for them to decide how to respond to the new situation. This problem is compounded by the difficulty of trying to understand the new political order, by the states' ignorance of the background and beliefs of the new regime, and by the obstacles to obtaining reliable information. Even when foreign powers are not especially hostile, therefore, some of their actions and statements will probably reinforce the suspicions of the revolutionary regime.

Third, a spiral of suspicion will be more likely if the elite (or a faction within it) exaggerates a foreign threat in order to improve its internal position, exploiting it either to rally nationalist support for the new leaders or to justify harsh measures against their internal opponents. Such exaggerations will be especially effective when there is some truth to the accusations: for example, if foreign powers that had been allied with the old regime now seem to be suspicious of the new government. This tactic can be dangerous if it magnifies a conflict that might otherwise have been avoided or mini-mized, but the risk can be reduced if the revolutionary elite continues to base its policy decisions on its true assessment of others' intentions rather than the myth it has manufactured. Maintaining such fine control is tricky, however. Even if the revolutionary leadership knows the myths to be myths, the campaign may be so convincing that it becomes the basis for pol-icy. Moreover, efforts to enhance domestic support by exaggerating exter-nal threats can be self-fulfilling: if foreign powers do not recognize the real motive behind such a campaign, they will take the revolutionary state's ac-cusations at face value and conduct themselves accordingly. If they react de-fensively—as one would expect—it will merely confirm the bellicose image that they have been given.

Other states contribute to the spiral of hostility. To begin with, they may fail to understand that the revolutionary state's version of history probably differs from their own. Revolutionary states ordinarily emphasize past in-justices, including what they regard as illegitimate foreign interference. But because all states view their own history in a favorable light, foreign powers will not understand why the new regime sees them as objects of hatred and suspicion and will consider the new state's defensive responses to be evi-dence of its aggressive character.[49] Thus, U.S. policy makers saw Chinese intervention in the Korean War as evidence of the expansionist tendencies of international Communism, in part because politicians such as Secretary of State Dean Acheson, who believed that U.S. policy in the Far East was in China's best interest, failed to appreciate that Western actions in the Far East had actually left a far more negative impression on the minds of China's new leaders.[50] Similar problems afflicted U.S. relations with Fidel Castro: because U.S. leaders such as President Dwight D. Eisenhower be-lieved that U.S. policy had been largely beneficial for Cuba, they saw Cas-tro's hostility as unjustified aggression rather than as an understandable (if excessive) reaction to past U.S. behavior.[51] Even where tangible grounds for conflict exist (as they did in both these cases), ignorance of the historical basis for suspicion will cause the foreign powers to misinterpret the revolu-tionary state's bellicosity.

Foreign powers may also start a negative spiral if the new regime's do-mestic programs affect their interests adversely. Such a situation is a legiti-mate basis for conflict, of course, but the threat will be magnified if actions taken for internal reasons are also viewed as evidence of aggressive intent. Groups whose interests are harmed (such as foreign corporations whose assets have been seized) may try to convince their home governments that the new regime is a threat to security, in the hope of obtaining diplomatic or military support. Thus, Castro's land reform program exacerbated the spiral of hostility between the United States and Cuba, and Arbenz's land reforms in Guatemala moved the United Fruit Company to organize a public relations campaign that formed the backdrop for the U.S.-led coup that overthrew him.[52]

To make matters worse, revolutions alter international relations in ways that exacerbate perceptions of hostility. First, each side is likely to underestimate the other's sense of vulnerability, leading it to discount the role of defensive motivations in explaining the other side's conduct. In addition to the burdens of organizing a government and rebuilding a damaged society, revolutionary states usually face continued domestic opposition. Fearful of having only a precarious hold on power, they are more likely to overreact to threats.[53] Yet revolutionary states also try to portray themselves as firmly in control, in order to discourage counterrevolution at home and to attract recognition abroad. If this public relations effort is successful, however, other states will underestimate the extent to which the revolutionary state's actions are driven by insecurity, interpreting its defensive actions as a sign of aggressive intent rather than as a reaction to legitimate fears. Furthermore, the other states may not recognize, first, that a new regime must build a reputation for defending its interests in order to deter future challenges and, second, that this will motivate it to respond vigorously when conflicts of interest arise.

The same tendency can occur in reverse as well. Fully aware of its own weaknesses, a revolutionary state may find it hard to understand why it is considered dangerous. If so, it may view the opposition of other states as evidence of their intrinsic hostility rather than as a response to its own actions. Foreign powers will be concerned with building a reputation as well, in order to teach the new regime that they cannot be exploited. Thus, both sides will be prone to see even purely defensive policies as signs of aggressive intent, especially when real conflicts of interest are also present.

A second exacerbating factor is the pernicious influence of exiles and revolutionary sympathizers. As suggested above, exiles from the revolutionary state have an incentive to portray the new regime as especially hostile, in order to convince other states to support their counterrevolutionary ambitions. Similarly, revolutionary sympathizers from other countries are likely to reinforce the new regime's own suspicions by portraying foreign governments as deeply hostile. The more vocal and visible these groups are, the greater the tendency for both sides to conclude that the host country supports their aims. A large and vocal population of exiles will be seen as a sign that the host country is hostile to the revolution, just as a large and vocal group of foreign sympathizers will be taken as evidence that the new regime is actively seeking to spread its ideals elsewhere. Taken together, the parallel migration of exiles and sympathizers and the testimony they provide to their hosts will strongly reinforce each side's beliefs that the other is inherently dangerous.

A third factor inflating the perception of hostility is the loss of expertise that accompanies a revolution, particularly when revolutionary governments purge people with ties to perceived or potential enemies. The Iranian revolutionaries removed officials with close links to the United States, and Communist China persecuted its own "America Hands" in the 1950s. Ironically, as the treatment of the State Department's "China Hands" suggests, the same process may occur within the nonrevolutionary states as well.[54] By removing experienced individuals, each side further reduces its capacity to understand the other. Thus, the personnel changes set in motion by a revolution will exacerbate the prevailing uncertainty and reinforce mutual suspicion.

Because revolutions unleash a variety of forces that make it more difficult for the revolutionary state and its neighbors to assess each other's intentions accurately, each is likely to view the other as more hostile than it really is. Such a conclusion hampers their ability to reach a satisfactory modus vivendi and strengthens the position of those who favor direct action to eliminate the threat.

Each side's tendency to exaggerate the other's hostility helps explain why security competition increases after a revolution, but it does not explain why *war* occurs. After all, the United States and the Soviet Union were extremely hostile for much of the Cold War, but neither saw actual war as an attractive option for dealing with the situation. Thus, the next question is why war is often seen as a reasonable response.

Revolution, the Offense-Defense Balance, and War

All else being equal, war is more likely when national leaders believe that offense is easier than defense. When offense is easy, states are less secure yet simultaneously have greater incentives to try to improve their relative positions. At the same time, using force promises greater benefits because it will be simpler to gain a decisive victory over the opponents. Thus, offense dominance both raises the perceived level of threat and suggests that it will be easy to reduce. The result is more international competition and a higher risk of war.[55]

Revolutions are a powerful source of this danger. In addition to creating distorted perceptions of hostility, revolutions also encourage both sides to exaggerate their own vulnerability and also the vulnerability of their opponents. This tendency is partly due to the inherent difficulty of estimating the balance of power after a revolution, which makes it more likely that each will exaggerate its military prospects. In addition, the belief that the revolution will either spread to other countries or readily succumb to counterrevolutionary pressure magnifies this sense of vulnerability. Unable to estimate with high confidence the likelihood of either possibility, all sides will tend to assume the worst. For both military and political reasons, therefore, a revolution heightens each side's sense of threats and opportunities.

Taken together, these factors encourage both parties to believe that the other presents a grave threat, yet they also encourage the belief that the threat can be eliminated fairly easily. Furthermore, these perceptions may encourage third parties to intervene either to eliminate a potential revolutionary threat or to prevent other powers from gaining an advantage by doing it themselves. Once again, we can best understand these dynamics by examining revolutionary states and foreign powers separately.

Why are revolutionary states simultaneously insecure and overconfident?

To begin with, the inherent optimism of most revolutionary ideologies encourages the new leaders to overstate the odds of victory, so they become more willing to contemplate the use of force. Arguments of this sort are difficult to counter without appearing disloyal; if victory is inevitable and opponents are destined for the dustbin of history, then expressing doubts about the certainty of victory betrays a lack of confidence in the revolution and could easily undermine one's political position at home.

Second, the optimism of revolutionary states rests on the belief that opponents will be undermined by the irresistible spread of revolutionary ideas. This hope reflects the universalism common to many revolutionary ideologies and the assumption that their opponents will be unable to fight effectively owing to lack of popular support. Mao's claim that "a single spark can ignite a prairie fire" nicely conveys this faith in the catalytic effects of revolutionary action, as does the so-called *foco* theory of guerrilla warfare developed by Che Guevara.[56] This view is also fueled by the tendency for rebellious collective action to occur in distinct waves or cycles. Although most dissident social movements do not lead to a revolution, the leaders of a revolutionary state are likely to interpret signs of turbulence in other societies as evidence that their own victory is merely the first of many.[57]

Revolutionary states can be further misled if they give too much credence to the testimony of foreign sympathizers, whose desire for external support inspires them to exaggerate the prospects for revolution back home. Such testimony will encourage active efforts to export the revolution (which will exacerbate tensions with other states) and fortify the new regime's confidence when it contemplates war. Moreover, their own success in gaining power against seemingly impossible odds may convince the revolutionary leaders that they can triumph over more powerful international opponents (this tendency will be compounded if other societies show signs of a similar level of discontent, even if rebellious action elsewhere does not lead to a full-fledged revolution). Furthermore, divisions within the revolutionary elite may encourage overly ambitious objectives, particularly if a willingness to export the revolution becomes a litmus test of revolutionary convictions.[58]

Finally, and somewhat paradoxically, a revolutionary state's own vulnerability may cause its interest in expansion to grow, at least in ideological terms. Fearing that their hold on power is fragile, revolutionary leaders are likely to view domestic opponents as potential fifth columns for their external foes. Exporting the revolution becomes the only way to preserve their positions at home: unless opposing states are swiftly overthrown, the argument runs, they will eventually join forces with domestic counterrevolutionaries in order to crush the revolutionary state. To avoid this fate, the revolutionaries may conclude their only hope is to strike first.

Meanwhile, foreign powers are also both insecure and overconfident after a revolution. Why them as well?

Other states fear the spread of revolutionary ideas, especially when the ideas challenge their own form of government directly. But they also think this threat an easy problem to solve. Because of the disorder that accompanies a revolution, other states view the new regime as weak and vulnerable, especially because of the inherent difficulty of estimating a new state's ability to fight. (By definition, revolutionary states rest on novel forms of social organization; revolutionary movements succeed because they exploit new ways to mobilize previously untapped sources of social power. Unfortunately, the novelty of these institutions renders any meaningful evaluation of their impact on national capabilities nearly impossible.) Ideological biases may amplify this tendency, because states based on different political principles have trouble acknowledging that a revolutionary government could be popular or effective. (This problem affected U.S. perceptions of revolutionary states such as China, Cuba, and Nicaragua, for instance; because U.S. leaders believed that Communism was illegitimate and immoral, they had difficulty recognizing these regimes as independent states commanding substantial popular support.[59]) And if they believe that a revolutionary state is inherently unpopular, the other states will exaggerate their own ability to confront it successfully.

The uncertainty surrounding a revolution contributes to the problem; as discussed above, foreign powers will exaggerate the threat of subversion. Having witnessed an unexpected revolutionary upheaval, mindful of the confident proclamations of the revolutionary forces, and aware that some members of their own society might harbor similar ideas (especially when there are clear signs of unrest), other states are likely to see contagion as more likely than it really is. The universalism of most revolutionary ideologies compounds these worries, because the other states fear that an alliance of like-minded revolutionary powers could leave them adrift in a hostile ideological sea.

Even in the absence of clear evidence of the revolution spreading, other states cannot be completely confident that subversive movements do not lurk beneath the surface. European fears of a Jacobin conspiracy and the U.S. "Red scares" of the 1920s and the 1950s illustrate the tendency for foreign powers to misread the ideological appeal (and therefore the offensive power) of revolutionary states. Because the threat these states pose is not simply a function of material capabilities, revolutions will seem even more dangerous than they are. And a similar logic applies to counterrevolutions: the inevitable signs of internal discord will encourage other states to try to reverse the revolution, even when it is impossible to determine the chances of success.

Once again, the perception of the threat from a revolutionary state and its susceptibility to outside pressure will be exacerbated by testimony from self-interested exiles and revolutionary sympathizers. The former portrays the revolutionary state as both a dangerous adversary and a disorganized, unpopular, and vulnerable target, while the latter depicts foreign powers as both hostile and ripe for revolution. And if their respective hosts do not discount this testimony accordingly, they are more likely to fall into a precarious web of fear and overconfidence.

Thus, in addition to altering the balance of power, revolutions also shape perceptions of intent and estimates of the offense-defense balance in especially dangerous ways. Both the revolutionary regime and the leaders of outside states view the other's existence as a serious challenge, yet neither can estimate the danger accurately. Lacking reliable information about the magnitude of the threat or their ability to overcome it, both will rely on ideology to fill in the gaps in their understanding, and will be susceptible to self-interested testimony from émigrés or itinerant revolutionaries, particularly when this advice confirms preexisting beliefs. Therefore, although each side fears the other, it is also likely to conclude that the threat can be eliminated at relatively low cost. In short, the beliefs that opponents are hostile, dangerous, *and* vulnerable readily combine to support preventive and preemptive wars.

When a revolution topples an apparently viable regime, it is not surprising that other states fear that they might be next. Similarly, if the revolutionary state has suffered extensive damage and faces continued internal opposition, its leaders have reason to worry that their success will be short lived. . . . However, both sides are usually wrong.

Revolutions are a relatively poor export commodity, and although counterrevolutionary efforts face somewhat better prospects, reversing a revolution from outside usually proves more difficult than its advocates expect.[60] If each side's hopes and fears were accurate, the struggle between them would be a swift and decisive triumph for one side or the other. But instead of a wave of revolutionary upheavals or the swift collapse of the new regime, the normal result is either a brief, inconclusive clash (such as the Allied intervention in Russia or the Bay of Pigs invasion) or a protracted, bloody struggle (such as the Iran-Iraq war or the *contra* war in Nicaragua). The final irony, therefore, is that each side's perceptions of threats and vulnerabilities are usually mistaken.

Why are revolutions hard to export, and why do foreign interventions fail? First, the universalist ideological rhetoric notwithstanding, a revolution is, above all, a national phenomenon. A campaign to export a revolution to other countries will immediately bring it into conflict with the national loyalties of the intended recipients. And the principle that people who conceive of themselves as a nation are entitled to their own independent state has proven to be a far more powerful social force in modern history than any notion of universal revolutionary solidarity.[61] Foreign populations are likely to view efforts to export the revolution as unwarranted acts of aggression, in turn making it easier for the ruling elites to resist the revolutionary forces. Even if conditions in other countries resemble those that produced one revolution in a general way, the special circumstances that enabled that one revolution to succeed are unlikely to exist elsewhere. Even if social unrest does transcend national boundaries and the success of one movement does inspire like-minded individuals abroad, actually causing a revolution to occur in a foreign country is another matter altogether.

Second, until a revolution actually occurs, other states may not have taken the possibility seriously, but once the danger is demonstrated, potential victims will take steps to avoid a similar fate (for example, through defensive alliances, internal reforms, or more extensive repression). Thus, the Cuban Revolution inspired the U.S. "Alliance for Progress" in Latin America (intended to forestall additional "Cubas" by promoting economic and political development) and encouraged Latin American oligarchies to suppress their domestic opponents more vigorously. Again, the point is not that revolutions pose no danger, but rather that other states can usually take a number of steps to contain the threat.

Efforts to support a counterrevolution fail for somewhat different reasons. Revolutionary leaders are usually dedicated, highly motivated individuals who have been successful precisely because they are good at organizing support in the face of impressive obstacles. They are likely to be formidable adversaries, because the same skills will aid their efforts to mobilize the nation for war.[62] Foreign interventions also fail, because they provide the domestic legitimacy that a revolutionary regime needs: the same nationalist convictions that prevent a revolution from adapting smoothly to other states will also complicate foreign intervention against a revolutionary regime. And there is an inherent paradox in trying to use exiles as the core of the counterrevolutionary movement: if these groups require extensive foreign assistance in order to challenge the new regime, their ability to command indigenous support is probably limited and their prospects for success comparatively low.

To summarize: the pressure for war produced by a revolution results from two parallel myths: the belief that the revolution will spread rapidly if it is not "strangled in its crib," and the belief that such a reversal will be easy to accomplish. Among other things, this argument implies that war would be most likely when the revolutionary state espouses a universalist ideology, because such ideologies can easily be regarded as a potent (though unmeasurable) source of threat by other states. Contrary to these expectations, however, the normal result is neither a swift tide of revolutionary contagion nor the quick and easy ouster of the new regime. Instead, the more frequent result is a prolonged struggle between the unexpectedly resilient revolutionary regime and its surprisingly impervious opponents.

The explanation outlined in this chapter may also provide a more complete explanation of why revolutionary states tend to alter their behavior over time. Many of the problems caused by a revolution arise from misjudging the balance of power, the intentions of others, and the probability of contagion or counterrevolution. From this perspective, "socialization" is simply the process by which both sides acquire greater information about each of these factors. As evidence accumulates, the uncertainty that permits exaggerated perceptions of threat to flourish declines proportionately. Even if the new regime does not abandon its ultimate objectives, it is likely to modify its short-term behavior in accordance with this new information. Relations between the revolutionary states and the rest of the system will become increasingly "normal," assuming, of course, that each side is capable of evaluating and revising its policies in light of experience.[63]

Two caveats should be noted at this point. First, because elite revolutions feature less extreme ideological visions and exert less dramatic internal effects than mass revolutions, they will have less effect on the balance of threats, and so the risk of war will be lower than it is after a mass revolution. Second, the level of conflict will be greatest when the revolution creates a new state whose characteristics and ideological foundations depart sharply from the domestic orders of the other great powers. By contrast, if a revolution brings a state into conformity with prevailing sociopolitical forms, then the new regime will be seen as less hostile and the danger of contagion may be slim to nonexistent. One cannot understand the international impact of a revolution by looking solely at the revolutionary state; one must also consider the external environment in which the revolution occurred.

NOTES

1. See my *Origins of Alliances* (Ithaca: Cornell University Press, 1987), and "Testing Theories of Alliance Formation: The Case of Southwest Asia," *International Organization* 42, no. 2 (1988), and "Alliances, Threats, and U.S. Grand Strategy: A Reply to Kaufman and Labs," *Security Studies* 1, no. 3 (1992).

2. See George Quester, *Offense and Defense in the International System* (New York: Wiley, 1977); Robert Jervis, "Cooperation under the Security Dilemma," *World Politics* 30, no. 2 (1978); Stephen Van Evera, *Causes of War*, vol. 1: *The Structure of Power and the Roots of War* (Ithaca: Cornell University Press, forthcoming).

3. In earlier presentations of balance-of-threat theory, I included geographic proximity as another element of threat. Because a state's geographic location is not affected by a revolution, I have omitted it from this discussion, although I would expect states to be more sensitive to revolutions near their own borders than to ones at a distance.

4. Lenin once remarked, "The key question of every revolution is undoubtedly the question of state power. Which class holds power decides everything." *Selected Works* (Moscow: Progress Publishers, 1970–71), 2:276.

5. See Charles Tilly, *From Mobilization to Revolution* (New York: Random House, 1978), esp. 191; and Peter Amann, "Revolution: A Redefinition," in *Why Revolution? Theories and Analyses,* ed. Clifford Paynton and Robert Blackey (Cambridge, Mass.: Schenkman, 1971), 58–59.

6. Thus, Theda Skocpol refers to prerevolutionary governments as "old regime states in crisis." *States and Social Revolutions: A Comparative Analysis of France, Russia and China* (Cambridge: Cambridge University Press, 1979). State power may decline for a variety of reasons. The demand for resources may exceed the ability of existing institutions to provide them (as in France), the coercive apparatus may dissolve after a military defeat (as in Russia), or the legitimacy of the existing order may be challenged on moral grounds (as in Iran).

7. See Samuel P. Huntington, *Political Order in Changing Societies* (New Haven: Yale University Press, 1968), 266; and Ellen Kay Trimberger, *Revolution from Above: Military Bureaucrats and Development in Japan, Turkey, Egypt, and Peru* (New Brunswick, N.J.: Transaction Books, 1978).

8. A. S. Cohan writes that "in a revolution, one system of legality is substituted for another." *Theories of Revolution: An Introduction* (New York: Wiley, 1975), 25; see also Lyford P. Edwards, *The Natural History of Revolution* (Chicago: University of Chicago Press, 1970), 107–12.

9. Thus, revolutionary states ordinarily adopt new names, flags, anthems, and social practices, such as the French revolutionary calendar or the reimposition of the women's *chador* in Iran.

10. The estimated death tolls confirm the ubiquity of violence in modern revolutions: France, at least 35,000 dead; Russia, 500,000; China, 1 million; Cuba, 5,000; Iran, 17,000; Mexico, 250,000; Nicaragua, between 30,000 and 50,000. These estimates are based on Melvin Small and J. David Singer, *Resort to Arms: International and Civil Wars, 1816–1980* (Beverly Hills, Calif.: Sage, 1986); and Donald Greer, *The Incidence of the Terror in the French Revolution* (Cambridge: Harvard University Press, 1935).

11. . . . . These characteristics are most apparent in mass revolutions. The level of violence is usually lower in an elite revolution, because the revolutionaries typically seek less radical goals, the old regime usually collapses more rapidly, and the new leaders

already control elements of a new state apparatus and can establish their authority more easily. See Ellen Kay Trimberger, "A Theory of Elite Revolutions," *Studies in Comparative International Development* 7, no. 3 (1972); and Erik Allardt, "Revolutionary Ideologies as Agents of Structural and Cultural Change," in *Social Science and the New Societies,* ed. Nancy Hammond (East Lansing: Social Science Research Bureau, Michigan State University, 1973), 154.

12. As Lenin once admitted, the Bolsheviks "really did not know how to rule." Quoted in John Dunn, *Modern Revolutions: An Introduction to the Analysis of a Political Phenomenon* (Cambridge: Cambridge University Press, 1972), 18–19, 47; see also William Henry Chamberlin, *The Russian Revolution 1917–1921* (1935; reprint, Princeton: Princeton University Press, 1987) 1: 351.

13. See Theda Skocpol, "Social Revolutions and Mass Military Mobilization," *World Politics* 40, no. 2 (1988), and Ted Robert Gurr, "War, Revolution, and the Growth of the Coercive State," *Comparative Political Studies* 21, no. 1 (1988).

14. Indeed, some writers assert that revolution is impossible so long as the armed forces retain their loyalty and cohesion. See Katherine C. Chorley, *Armies and the Art of Revolution* (London: Faber and Faber, 1943); Jonathan R. Adelman, *Revolution, Armies, and War: A Political History* (Boulder, Colo.: Lynne Rienner, 1985); Anthony James Joes, *From the Barrel of a Gun: Armies and Revolutions* (Washington, D.C.: Pergamon-Brassey's, 1986); and John Ellis, *Armies in Revolution* (New York: Oxford University Press, 1974).

15. See Mancur Olson, *The Logic of Collective Action: Public Goods and the Theory of Groups* (Cambridge: Harvard University Press, 1971); and Russell Hardin, *Collective Action* (Washington, D.C.: Johns Hopkins University Press/Resources for the Future, 1982).

16. Applications of collective-goods theory to the problem of revolution include Gordon Tullock, "The Paradox of Revolution," *Public Choice* 11 (fall 1971); Philip G. Roeder, "Rational Revolution: Extensions of the `By-Product' Model of Revolutionary Involvement," *Western Political Quarterly* 35, no. 1 (1982); Morris Silver, "Political Revolution and Repression: An Economic Approach," *Public Choice* 17 (spring 1974); Samuel L. Popkin, *The Rational Peasant: The Political Economy of Revolution in Vietnam* (Berkeley: University of California Press, 1979); Michael Taylor, "Rationality and Revolutionary Collective Action," in *Rationality and Revolution,* ed. Michael Taylor (Cambridge: Cambridge University Press, 1988); James DeNardo, *Power in Numbers: The Political Strategy of Protest and Rebellion* (Princeton: Princeton University Press, 1985); Edward N. Muller and Karl-Dieter Opp, "Rational Choice and Rebellious Collective Action," *American Political Science Review* 80, no. 2 (1986); and Mark I. Lichbach, *The Rebel's Dilemma* (Ann Arbor: University of Michigan Press, 1995).

17. See Jeffrey Race, "Toward an Exchange Theory of Revolution," in *Peasant Rebellion and Communist Revolution in Asia,* ed. John Wilson Lewis (Stanford: Stanford University Press, 1974); Joel S. Migdal, *Peasants, Politics, and Revolution: Pressures toward Political and Social Change in the Third World* (Princeton: Princeton University Press, 1974); and the references in n. 16 above.

18. As Charles Tilly notes, "why and how . . . the group committed from the start to fundamental transformation of the structure of power . . . forms remains one of the mysteries of our time." *From Mobilization to Revolution,* 203.

19. That revolutionaries are often surprised to gain power suggests that they were not motivated by prospects of future gain. Lenin told a socialist youth group in January 1917, "We of the older generation may not live to see the decisive battles of this coming revolution," and the Sandinista leader Daniel Ortega admitted that as late as July 1979, he did not expect to see the revolution succeed in Nicaragua. Ayatollah Khomeini was reportedly surprised by the speed with which the shah's regime collapsed as well. Chamberlin, *Russian Revolution,* 1:131, 323; Robert Pastor, *Condemned to Repetition: The United States and Nicaragua* (Princeton: Princeton University Press, 1987), xiv; and Marvin Zonis, "A Theory of Revolution from Accounts of the Revolution," *World Politics* 35, no. 4 (1983), 602.

20. Quoted in Robert Blackey, *Revolutions and Revolutionists: A Comprehensive Guide to the Literature* (Santa Barbara, Calif.: ABC-Clio, 1982), 405.

21. "How do we account for . . . the willingness of people to engage in immense sacrifice with no evident possible gain (the endless parade of individuals and groups who have incurred prison or death for abstract causes)?" Douglass C. North, *Structure and Change in Economic History* (New York: W.W. Norton, 1981), 10–11.

22. Chamberlin describes Lenin's "intense faith" in Marxism in *Russian Revolution,* 1:135, 140. For a general discussion, see James B. Rule, *Theories of Civil Violence* (Berkeley: University of California Press, 1988), 35–39.

23. Recent sociological research suggests that political organizations encourage collective action by promoting beliefs about the seriousness of the problem, the locus of causality or blame, the image of the opposition, and the efficacy of collective response. See David A. Snow, E. Burke Rochford, Jr., Steven K. Worden, and Robert D. Benford, "Frame Alignment Processes, Micromobilization, and Movement Participation," *American Sociological Review* 51, no. 4 (1986); David A. Snow and Robert Benford, "Ideology, Frame Resonance, and Participant Mobilization," in *From Structure to Action: Comparing Social Movement Research across Cultures,* ed. Bert Klandermans, Hanspeter Kriesi, and Sidney Tarrow (Greenwich, Conn.: JAI Press, 1988); and Jeffrey Berejikian, "Revolutionary Collective Action and the Agent-Structure Problem," *American Political Science Review* 86, no. 3 (1992), 652–55.

24. Thus, Sandinista leader Humberto Ortega admitted having exaggerated the feasibility of revolution: "Trying to tell the masses that the cost was very high and that they should seek another way would have meant the defeat of the revolutionary movement." Quoted in Tomas Borge et al., *Sandinistas Speak* (New York: Pathfinder, 1982), 70–71.

25. North, *Structure and Change,* 53–54.

26. According to Mark Hagopian, "There are three structural aspects of revolutionary ideology: *critique,* which lays bare the shortcomings of the old regime; *affirmation,* which suggests or even spells out in detail that a better society is not only desirable but

possible; and in recent times, *strategic guidance,* which tells the best way to make a revolution." *The Phenomenon of Revolution* (New York: Dodd, Mead, 1974), 258.

27. North, *Structure and Change,* 53–54. According to Ted Robert Gurr, "one of the most potent and enduring effects of 'revolutionary appeals' is to persuade men that political violence can provide value gains commensurate to or greater than its cost in risk and guilt." *Why Men Rebel* (Princeton: Princeton University Press, 1970), 215–16.

28. Jack A. Goldstone, "The Comparative and Historical Study of Revolutions," *Annual Review of Sociology* 8 (1982), 203.

29. Edward Hallett Carr, *The Bolshevik Revolution, 1917–1923* (New York: Macmillan, 1950–53), 1:11.

30. Lewis A. Coser, *Greedy Institutions: Patterns of Undivided Commitment* (New York: Free Press, 1974), 110.

31. For examples of this tendency, see John Dower, *War without Mercy: Race and Power in the Pacific War* (New York: Pantheon, 1986); and John MacArthur, *Second Front: Censorship and Propaganda in the Gulf War* (New York: Hill and Wang, 1992).

32. Thus, the inaugural issue of *The American Socialist,* published by an obscure Trotskyite splinter group, proclaimed, "We are part of the stream of history. We are confident of our future because we believe we have the correct understanding and tactic[s] and . . . the grit and tenacity to carry on. Do not anybody despair because of our small numbers. . . . We are like the American abolitionists of a hundred years ago. We are like Garrison and Wendell Phillips and Frederick Douglass and John Brown." Quoted in Coser, *Greedy Institutions,* 111–12.

33. See the testimony in Dennis Gilbert, *Sandinistas: The Party and the Revolution* (London: Basil Blackwell, 1988), 5, 56.

34. Lenin, "Imperialism: The Highest Stage of Capitalism," in his *Selected Works,* 1:667–768.

35. Peter Van Ness, *Revolution and Chinese Foreign Policy: Peking's Support for Wars of National Liberation* (Berkeley: University of California Press, 1970), 40–41. Mao also told his followers that imperialism was "rotten and had no future" and "we have reason to despise them." Yet he cautioned, "We should never take the enemy lightly . . . and concentrate all our strength for battle in order to win victory." Mao Tse-tung, *Selected Works* (Beijing: Foreign Languages Press, 1965), 4:181; and Tang Tsou and Morton Halperin, "Mao Tse-tung's Revolutionary Strategy and Peking's International Behavior," *American Political Science Review* 59, no. 3 (1965), 89.

36. In 1919, Lenin warned, "We may suffer grave and sometimes even decisive defeats. . . . If, however, we use all the methods of struggle, victory will be certain." *Selected Works,* 3:410–11.

37. For macro theories of revolution, see Skocpol, *States and Social Revolutions;* and Jack A. Goldstone, *Revolution and Rebellion in the Early Modern World* (Berkeley: University of California Press, 1991). On the importance of political opportunities, social networks, and mass communication in facilitating (revolutionary) collective action, see

Tilly, *From Mobilization to Revolution,* chaps. 3–4; Doug McAdam, "Micromobilization Contexts and Recruitment to Activism," in Klandermans, Kriesi, and Tarrow, *From Structure to Action;* and Sidney Tarrow, *Power in Movement: Social Movements, Collective Action, and Politics* (Cambridge: Cambridge University Press, 1994). Susanne Lohmann has recently analyzed the problem of collective action as a signaling game in which decisions to rebel are based on an individual's personal "threshold for action" and the information he or she receives about the likelihood that others will act as well. Information indicating that the old regime has weakened will lower the expected costs of protest and allow potential dissidents to send "costly" (i.e., credible) signals of their own willingness to act. Under certain conditions, seemingly isolated acts of protest can produce a "cascade" of such information and trigger a sudden outburst of revolutionary activity. See her article "Dynamics of Informational Cascades: The Monday Demonstrations in Leipzig, East Germany, 1989–91," *World Politics* 47, no. 1 (1994); as well as the related works by DeNardo, *Power in Numbers;* Dennis Chong, *Collective Action and the Civil Rights Movement* (Chicago: University of Chicago Press, 1991); Mark Granovetter, "Threshold Models of Collective Behavior," *American Journal of Sociology* 83, no. 6 (1978); and Timur Kuran, "Sparks and Prairie Fires: A Theory of Unanticipated Revolution," *Public Choice* 61, no. 1 (1989). These perspectives complement the focus on ideology I have adopted here. In my account, revolutionary ideologies seek to lower the individual threshold for rebellion by portraying the existing regime as evil and doomed to defeat. In other words, revolutionary ideologies try to create conditions in which an "informational cascade" is more likely to occur.

38. According to Franz Borkenau, "if violence is the father of every great upheaval, its mother is illusion. The belief which is always reborn in every great and decisive historical struggle is that this is the last fight, that after this struggle all poverty, all suffering, all oppression will be a thing of the past." "State and Revolution," 74–75.

39. See Timur Kuran, "Sparks and Prairie Fires," and "Now Out of Never: The Element of Surprise in the Revolutions of 1989," *World Politics* 44, no. 3 (1991); but see also Nikki Keddie, "Can Revolutions Be Predicted; Can Their Causes Be Understood?" *Contention* 1, no. 2 (1992); and Jack A. Goldstone, "Predicting Revolutions: Why We Could (and Should) Have Foreseen the Revolutions of 1989–91 in the USSR and Eastern Europe," *Contention* 2, no. 2 (1993).

40. Yossi Shain, *The Frontier of Loyalty: Political Exiles in the Age of the Nation-State* (Middletown, Conn.: Wesleyan University Press, 1989).

41. This is not a new phenomenon. As Machiavelli observed: "How vain the faith and promises of men are who are exiles from their own country. . . . Whenever they can return to their country by other means than your assistance, they will abandon you and look to the other means, regardless of their promises to you. . . . Such is their extreme desire to return to their homes that they naturally believe many things that are not true, and add many others on purpose; so that, with what they really believe and what they say they believe, they will fill you with hopes to that degree that if you attempt to act upon them, you will incur a fruitless expense, or engage in an undertaking that will

involve you in ruin." *The Prince and the Discourses* (New York: Modern Library, 1950), 388–89.

42. Examples are ubiquitous: the American Thomas Paine traveled to France in the 1790s, along with would-be revolutionaries from the rest of Europe, and socialists such as John Reed, Louise Bryant, and Emma Goldman journeyed to Russia after the Bolshevik seizure of power in 1917. Havana, Tehran, and Managua have been minor meccas for foreign revolutionaries as well.

43. Jennifer Bailey, "Revolution in the International System," in *Superpowers and Revolution,* ed. Jonathan Adelman (New York: Praeger, 1986), 19.

44. This is the familiar security dilemma identified by John Herz in "Idealist Internationalism and the Security Dilemma," *World Politics* 2, no. 2 (1950). See also Jervis, "Cooperation under the Security Dilemma."

45. Robert Jervis, *Perception and Misperception in International Politics* (Princeton: Princeton University Press, 1976), chap. 3. For important refinements to Jervis's presentation, see Charles L. Glaser, "The Political Consequences of Military Strategy: Expanding the Spiral and Deterrence Models," *World Politics* 44, no. 4 (1992).

46. Thus, at the end of World War I, Lenin predicted that "world capital will now start an offensive against us." Quoted in Chamberlin, *Russian Revolution,* 2:155–56. He also told the Third Comintern Congress in June 1921 that "the international bourgeoisie . . . is waiting, always on the lookout for the moment when conditions will permit the renewal of this war" with Soviet Russia. Quoted in Leites, *Study of Bolshevism,* 405.

47. See Mao Tse-tung, *Selected Works,* 4:447–50; Gilbert, *Sandinistas,* 153–75; and James A. Bill, *The Eagle and the Lion: The Tragedy of American-Iranian Relations* (New Haven: Yale University Press, 1988), 96–97.

48. On the tendency to fit ambiguous information into existing beliefs, see Jervis, *Perception and Misperception,* 143–54.

49. Stephen Van Evera, *Causes of War,* vol. 2: *National Misperceptions and the Roots of War* (Ithaca: Cornell University Press, forthcoming), chap. 11; and E. H. Dance, *History the Betrayer: A Study in Bias* (London: Hutchinson, 1960).

50. Richard Ned Lebow, *Between Peace and War: The Nature of International Crisis* (Baltimore: Johns Hopkins University Press, 1981), 205–16; and Jervis, *Perception and Misperception,* 70–72.

51. Richard Welch, *Response to Revolution: The United States and the Cuban Revolution, 1959–1961* (Chapel Hill: University of North Carolina Press, 1985), 41.

52. On Cuba, see Richard Moss, "The Limits of Policy: An Investigation of the Spiral Model, The Deterrence Model, and Miscalculations in U.S.-Third World Relations" (Ph.D. diss., Princeton University, 1987), 160–64, 193–94. On Guatemala, see Richard H. Immerman, *The CIA in Guatemala: The Foreign Policy of Intervention* (Austin: University of Texas Press, 1982); and Stephen Schlesinger and Stephen Kinzer, *Bitter Fruit: The Untold Story of the American Coup in Guatemala* (Garden City, N.Y.: Anchor Books, 1983).

53. According to George Pettee, "revolutionists enter the limelight not like men on horseback, as victorious conspirators appearing in the forum, but like fearful children,

exploring an empty house, not sure that it is empty." *The Process of Revolution* (New York: Harper Brothers, 1938), 100–101.

54. The "China Hands" were a group of China experts accused of disloyalty and purged from the State Department during the McCarthy era. See E. J. Kahn, *The China Hands: America's Foreign Service Officers and What Befell Them* (New York: Viking, 1975).

55. See the references in n. 2 above.

56. On the basis of his experience in the Cuban revolution, Guevara argued that acts of violence by a small revolutionary band (the *foco*) could spark a successful revolution even if strong indigenous support were lacking. The strategy was a dismal failure, and Guevara was killed trying to implement it in Bolivia. See Che Guevara, *Guerrilla Warfare* (New York: Monthly Review Press, 1961); and also Regis Debray, "Revolution in the Revolution? Armed Struggle and Political Struggle in Latin America," *Monthly Review* 19, no. 3 (1967).

57. Sidney Tarrow, *Struggle, Politics, and Reform: Collective Action, Social Movements, and Cycles of Protest,* Occasional Paper 21, Western Studies Program (Ithaca: Center for International Studies, Cornell University, 1989).

58. . . . When a revolutionary movement is deeply divided, extremists may advocate an aggressive foreign policy as a means of undermining the revolutionary credentials of their more moderate opponents.

59. Thus, Assistant Secretary of State Dean Rusk claimed that the Communist regime in China was "a colonial Russian government . . . it is not Chinese." Quoted in Michael J. Schaller, *The United States and China in the Twentieth Century* (New York: Oxford University Press, 1979), 125.

60. Examples of successful counterrevolutions include the Austro-Prussian intervention in Belgium in 1790, the Russian and Austrian interventions in Italy and Greece in the 1830s, the U.S.-backed coups in Iran, Guatemala, and Chile, the U.S. invasion of Grenada in 1983, and the Vietnamese overthrow of the Khmer Rouge in Cambodia in 1979. With the exception of Cambodia, however, none of these regimes came to power through a prolonged revolutionary struggle, and none attempted (let alone accomplished) a thorough social transformation. Moreover, these are all cases where the intervening powers were overwhelmingly larger and stronger than the governments they overthrew.

61. See Ernest Gellner, *Nations and Nationalism* (Ithaca: Cornell University Press, 1983), 1–7; and Eric J. Hobsbawm, *Nations and Nationalism since 1780: Programme, Myth, Reality* (Cambridge: Cambridge University Press, 1990), 9–12.

62. Skocpol, "Revolutions and Mass Military Mobilization."

63. David Armstrong, *Revolution and World Order: The Revolutionary State in International Society* (Oxford: Clarendon Press, 1993), esp. 302–304. For a useful survey of the literature on how states learn, see Jack Levy, "Learning and Foreign Policy: Sweeping a Conceptual Minefield," *International Organization* 48, no. 2 (1994).

3

War and Revolution

Fred Halliday

Fred Halliday's voluminous research on revolution runs the gamut from narrow case studies, such as Revolution and Foreign Policy: The Case of South Yemen, 1967–1987 *(1990), to broad theoretical analyses, such as* Revolution and World Politics: The Rise and Fall of the Sixth Great Power *(1999). The following selection is drawn from the latter.*

Whereas Walt analyzes how revolution can lead to war between revolutionary and status quo powers, Halliday argues here that interstate war can lead to revolution. War distracts or weakens the states engaged in it, thus limiting their ability to suppress revolution in other countries or even at home. World War I directly contributed to the Russian Revolution of 1917 as well as to revolutionary upheavals in many other countries. Similarly, World War II contributed to the rise of Marxist revolutionary movements in several countries, including Yugoslavia, Albania, China, North Vietnam, and others.

Like Walt, Halliday allows for the possibility of revolution leading to war. Unlike Walt, though, Halliday suggests that when war between status quo and revolutionary powers occurs, it is usually because the former are attempting to suppress the latter. Halliday sees the status quo powers as principally to blame for these conflicts.

Overall, Halliday sees revolution and war as interrelated phenomena rather than as each other's cause or effect.

Critical Questions

1. How does Halliday envision interstate war leading to revolution within individual states?

2. When revolution leads to war, why does Halliday lay the "blame" for such wars primarily on the status quo powers?

3. To what extent are Halliday's and Walt's theories about the relationship between revolution and war contradictory? To what extent are they complementary?

. . . The history of revolutions is repeatedly combined with that of war. This was never more so than in the twentieth century. It was the upheavals accompanying two world wars that provided the context for revolutionary triumph and counter-revolutionary reversal alike. A survey of the relationships between war and revolution can therefore serve to . . . examine more closely some of the ways in which this phenomenon, political as well as military, relates to revolution. Revolutions, in addition to precipitating wars, guerrilla or conventional, are themselves often caused by wars. Perhaps most importantly, wars in many ways *resemble* revolutions, and are indeed, in some approaches, assimilated to them. That they are interrelated, but distinguishable, is one starting point for an overall assessment of how these two formative processes interact.

It is in part this resemblance between war and revolution which explains the contradictory attitude of revolutionaries to war. On the one hand, revolutionary thinking, and in particular the internationalism of post-1789 radicalism, has been associated with opposition to war, with pacifism in the broad sense of being in favour of peace. One of the central promises of revolution has been that it, and only it, can abolish war. This was the claim of the French and Russian revolutions, just as Mao Tse-tung in 1938 envisaged, in visionary terms, a coming epoch in which, after the defeat of fascism and capitalism, there would be no more war.[1] On the other hand, revolutionary leaders have been drawn to war, fascinated by its mobilisatory potential and by its moral challenge, and, both before and after coming to power, shaped by it. Trotsky argued that war was "the locomotive of history," Che Guevara that "There is no deeper experience for a revolutionary than the act of war." It is worth noting, however, that while most revolutionary leaders have talked and written of war, and some, such as Trotsky, Mao and Tito have commanded wide-ranging military campaigns, only Fidel Castro is known to have had direct battlefield exposure, dodging bullets in a sugar-cane field as Batista's forces tried to eliminate the guerrilla force that had recently landed on the eastern coast of Cuba.[2]

For revolutionaries, the most immediate relationship between war and revolution is that of war as the *instrument* for the revolutionary attainment of power. It was guerrilla war—that form of irregular revolutionary warfare—which was so central to revolutionary movements in the latter part of the twentieth century. However, . . . guerrilla war . . . is far from being a sufficient approach to the subject. Guerrilla war is by no means an exclusive instrument of revolutionary movements: it can equally be the instrument of those opposed to revolutionary regimes, as indeed it was in its original form, as a method of resistance to the Napoleonic occupation of Spain.[3] Moreover, guerrilla war is not the only means by which revolutions use violence in pursuit of their ends. Revolutionary states use war, i.e. their conventional armies, for foreign policy purposes, particularly to extend the influence of revolution to other states. . . .

Similarities, Distinctions

The similarities between war and revolution are significant for both. In the first place, war and revolution share the characteristic of being resorts to violence in the context of breakdowns of hitherto prevailing patterns of political interaction, be they of political life within a state or of diplomatic and other interaction between states. Both war and revolution involve this use, or threat, of violence as the means for defeating the opponent and imposing acceptance of the victor's will when other forms of policy have broken down: hence Lenin's fascination with von Clausewitz's *political* understanding of war. Secondly, both involve the application of intention, of conscious political purposes, towards the attainment of a goal, even as any such application takes place within objective constraints, a structure, that limits the effect of these intentions and may well confound them. War and revolution are also unpredictable, involving a high degree of chance and uncertainty, within which factors that might otherwise be of minor importance—the personality of a leader, accidents of politics, chance coincidences—come to play an important and possibly decisive part. For all that structural and objective factors do limit outcomes, in wars as in revolutions there is a heightened element of contingency; von Clausewitz wrote of the "free play of the spirit" in war,[4] and this has been noted in revolutions as well, not least by Lenin. In broader historical terms, wars and revolutions involve certain analogous processes and consequences. In both, large numbers of people are mobilised in collective projects which, whatever their outcome, have longer-run effects on the societies in question. In both, too, subsequent patterns of political and social power, and the very boundaries of states, are shaped by the particular outcomes of these two variants of collective struggle. Both are, in this sense, *formative* processes.

It is not therefore surprising that some theorists have seen war and revolution as similar processes, be it in behaviouralist conceptions of revolution as "internal war," or Marxist theories of "class war." The Bolsheviks and their successors, up to 1956, asserted that war between their revolutionary state and the West was inevitable, that while distinct the two phenomena were historically conjoined. Yet the distinctions between them, theoretically and analytically, are significant. In the first place, wars involve a symmetry, a conflict between two constituted states, each with its own territory and delimited population. Revolutions, by contrast, are based on the asymmetrical conflict between a political movement and a state, each contesting the same territory and population. Secondly, while ideological differences may and do enter into war, the justifications for war may be other—disputes over territory, or economic issues. In revolutions, the two sides differ above all because of the varied and contrasting ideological programmes they offer, combined with the different social interests embodied in them. Revolutions are, initially, conflicts over the bases of power and legitimacy *within* states; wars about power between them. Neither in theory nor in their historical impact are these two processes assimilable.[5] What we are left with are two major historical and political phenomena, similar and overlapping in some respects but conceptually and historically distinct. The task is to specify how they interrelate.

Four forms of interconnection suggest themselves. In the first place, wars can be seen as the *precipitant* or *cause* of revolutions. The weakening of states in inter-state conflict, through outright defeat or over-extension short of defeat, may so affect the state-society relationship that forces opposed to the state are able successfully to challenge it. Secondly, revolution precipitates armed conflict. Most obviously war may be seen as the *result* of revolutions. . . . Successful revolutions frequently lead to war with status quo powers, the dynamic in the direction of war being evident in both camps. However, war may be seen in a different, indeed contrary, way to be a *product of particular state-society contradictions,* of domestic crises in which ruling groups resort to war to manage internal political conflicts. The most obvious argument here would be that such wars are launched to prevent revolutionary challenges, but the relationship may be different. As Arno Mayer has suggested, the onset of wars may reflect not the deflection of a pre-revolutionary situation, but the confidence of an elite that revolution has been contained and that it is possible to resolve domestic questions without running the risk of a social explosion.[6] Finally, war may be seen as the *instrument* of revolution. This is exemplified in conceptions of war as a means of attaining power, as in theories of armed insurrection and guerrilla war, or of the revolutionary offensive war.

Wars as Precipitant

Wars have acted as precipitants of revolutions most evidently by weakening the power of states. The forms of this weakening have been mentioned in several contexts above: wars weaken the coercive powers of states, by reducing the strengths of armies; they delegitimate states by denying them the supreme claim to loyalty, that of defenders of the security of the nation; they weaken the ability of the state to provide goods required by citizens; they weaken the cohesion of society by sharpening social conflicts. In all three of the major general crises of the international system—the seventeenth century, the Atlantic revolution, the twentieth century—it can plausibly be argued that revolutions were encouraged by, and not merely chronologically followed from, the incidence of inter-state war. War so altered the political and ideological situation within countries and exacerbated state-society conflict that social upheaval ensued.

The third wave of international revolution, that of the twentieth century, provides striking illustration of this connection. After the First World War and the Second World War the general "world" war was followed by an almost equally widespread incidence of political upheaval, within states hitherto involved in the conflict. The First World War led, whilst still being fought, to the Bolshevik revolution in Russia. In the aftermath of the armistice of November 1918 political upheaval engulfed many of the former combatant states: Germany, Italy, Hungary and Austria in Europe; Mongolia, China and Korea in the Far East; Egypt, Iraq and Iran in the Middle East. Each of these had their specific national roots, but their occurrence was more than just a coincidence, a product not only of the spread of particular ideas of socialist and nationalist insurgency but also of the international political situation, the weakening or destruction of hegemonies, provoked by the First World War. On an even greater scale, a "world" revolutionary upheaval was to follow the Second World War, which, in most of the victor states as in the defeated, was to promote a crisis of hegemony at both the ideological and coercive levels. Thus the defeat of the Axis powers in 1945 was followed by the triumph of revolutionary guerrilla movements in Yugoslavia and Albania, widespread social unrest in France and Italy, and, most strikingly, the emergence of revolutionary communist regimes in the Far East—in Korea, Vietnam and China. The Second World War was thus a conflict that developed on several levels—that of inter-state conflict on the one hand, that of exacerbated social, nationalist and political conflict within states on the other.[7] It led, after a brief pause, to its aftermath, forty years of Cold War, a global political conflict, regulated by nuclear weapons and the arms race.

This connection between war and revolution applies not only to situations of actual combat, but also to the effects of long-term strategic competition between states, the result of which is to place greater strain on the state-society relationship in the countries concerned. An earlier example of this . . . was that of the Seven Years War on both Britain and France: the strain on state finances, leading to increased taxation, was a precipitant of, respectively, the American and French revolutions a later example was that of the effect of the Cold War and the attendant arms race upon the USSR. Most discussion of this military competition was in terms of the necessities and dynamics of the arms race itself. The main public justification within both camps was that the accompanying expenditures were necessary to counter the policies of the other side; the main political argument was that military competition and the maintenance of some concept of "balance" were inescapable parts of the global competition for influence and power between the blocs. But there was a third dimension to this, namely the Western belief that the arms race itself, by placing unsustainable burdens on the Soviet Union would precipitate a crisis within it. This could never be said to be the sole or dominant consideration in Western strategy; the main *political* goal of the Western arms buildup was to reduce Soviet influence in crisis situations. But the belief that such forms of rivalry would weaken the USSR was on occasion articulated, as Kissinger was subsequently to indicate:

> Arms control had become an abstruse subject involving esoteric fine points that, even with the best intentions, would take years to resolve. But what the Soviet Union needed was immediate relief, not simply

from tensions but from economic pressures, especially from the arms race . . . . In this manner, arms control negotiations were becoming a device for applying pressure on the rickety Soviet system—all the more effective because they had not been designed for that purpose.[8]

Near the end of the Cold War, this approach was to receive belated comparative confirmation in the work of Paul Kennedy, which located the decline of hegemonic systems in overextension, i.e. in situations where military expenditure and dominion were expanded to protect economic and political interests, but in so doing went beyond the capabilities of the state.[9]

None were more cognisant of this relationship, of war as a stimulant to revolution, than Lenin and Trotsky who, after August 1914, saw in the outbreak of the "inter-imperialist" war the opportunity for a revolutionary breakthrough in Russia. This, not the analysis of north–south relations, was the central message of Lenin's 1916 work *Imperialism* as it was of Trotsky's *The War and the International* published in 1914.[10] In many cases of war between states opponents of one or other have hoped that this will provide the opportunity for them to take power. Thus during the First World War it was not only the Bolsheviks but also the Irish nationalists of *Sinn Fein* who took what they saw as the insurrectionary option. The 1916 Easter Rising in Dublin failed because, in contrast to the situation prevailing in St. Petersburg in October 1917, the old regime, in this case the British state, *could* go on ruling in the old way. During the Second World War, a range of nationalist movements in the Middle East and in Asia saw in the beleaguered condition of the imperial powers—British, French, Dutch—an opportunity for asserting their programmes. One of the most striking instances of this dialectic occurred in the context of the Iran–Iraq conflict of 1980–88, the longest inter-state war of the post-1945 period. While opponents of the Iranian regime sought aid from the government in Baghdad for military and political actions against the Islamic Republic, Iran provided substantial assistance to the Kurdish and Shi'ite Muslim oppositions operating within Iraq.

However, such support had drawbacks which, beyond their implications for this particular kind of political alliance, point to limits in establishing any simple relation between wars and revolution. The great danger run by those who seek such alliances in the midst of inter-state war is that they discredit themselves in the eyes of their own population: the charge of "treason" is easily levied. This indicates that for states involved in such wars, conflict with another state can be two-sided, weakening it in some respects but providing it with legitimation for more effectively mobilising the population and containing opposition. States may initiate wars precisely in order to preempt opposition within: here war serves not to weaken but to enhance the powers of states. Equally, once involved in war, states will find it easier to control and suppress opposition. Such was the experience of, for example, the British state in the 1790s and 1800s, when the outbreak of war with France was used to control domestic sympathy for the French revolution, or of the Polish state in 1920 when, faced with an "internationalist" military intervention by the Bolsheviks, it mobilised nationalist sentiment against a threat seen in national, i.e. anti-Russian, terms. Hence it cannot be argued that, in any universal sense, wars serve to weaken the state and so facilitate the work of its opponents: the impact of wars is contradictory, a product of the more general interplay of political and social factors with the ever uncertain fortunes of war itself.

Success and Failure: War as Consequence

The incidence of revolution as a precipitant of war is as common as that of war as a prelude to revolution. Indeed, while avoiding suggestions of any *laws* of history, it is an almost universal generalisation that revolutions lead to wars between the revolutionary state and other states, involving some combination of the use of war by the revolutionary state and contrary counter-revolutionary war by status quo powers. . . .

The historic sequence of revolution and war is striking. In the sixteenth and seventeenth centuries, the revolutions of Holland and Britain led to inter-state conflict, the former involving the Habsburg empire and its opponents, the latter pitting Cromwellian England against Holland and Spain. The American revolution, a conflict between the insurgents and the English crown, was followed by the Anglo-American war of 1812–13 in which counter-revolutionary Loyalists who had fled to Canada returned to combat their American opponents. The French revolution was followed by over twenty years of war between France on the one side, and a changing alliance of opponents on the other. In the twentieth century the link has endured: . . . the outbreak of the First World War was preceded by a range of revolutionary upheavals, expressions of the growing social and political tensions accumulating during the late nineteenth century. The Bolshevik revolution was followed immediately by the war of intervention, which lasted from

1918 to 1921, and by armed interventions in Poland, Iran, and Mongolia. In a less direct but none the less definable way, 1917 was a major precipitant of the Second World War. In the post-1945 epoch the pattern has continued: the triumph of the Chinese revolution in October 1949 was followed by the outbreak of the Korean War in June 1950; the Cuban revolution of 1959 led to the attempted armed invasion of April 1961 and the missile crisis of October 1962; the Iranian revolution of February 1979 was followed by the Iraqi invasion of September 1980 and an eight-year war; that of Nicaragua in July 1979 was followed by a decade of conflict in Central America, involving not only the already present civil war in El Salvador, but also the creation of a new opposition force, the Nicaraguan *contra*. One partial exception to this pattern might appear to be the Mexican revolution of 1910–20. Largely contained within Mexico, and marginal to world politics after the outbreak of the First World War in 1914, this nevertheless led to significant international military action, with Pancho Villa's forays into Texas and the despatch of US expeditionary forces to occupy areas of Mexico.[12]

The relationship suggested here is that revolution serves as a cause of war because of the impact it has on the international system, through changes in the policy of the revolutionary state and through the response of status quo powers. One example given has been that of the period prior to the First World War, one of widespread social and political crisis in much of the world. The period from the 1890s onwards was indubitably one of "general crisis," involving a move towards war on the one hand, and social and political upheaval in many states on the other. It can plausibly be argued that the rising tide of revolution contributed to the general crisis and so to the outbreak of war. Yet there is another explanation of this period which stresses not *revolution as a cause of war* but of *counter-revolution as a cause of war*. This is the theory of counter-revolution developed by Arno Mayer. . . . Mayer has argued that war is a response by elites to strengthen their position when faced with challenges from below that they feel they can contain, and with divisions within the ruling bloc:

> Not pre-revolutionary pressures but cleavages in the hegemonic bloc and unsettlement or stalemate of government are the womb of crisis and of crisis-generated war. This is not to say that these political distempers have no deep socioeconomic roots and that pressures from below are of no consequence. But the impact of these pressures is not a function of their high intensity and their imminent explosion into revolutionary unrest. If anything, the opposite holds true: the insufficiency and

decline of social rebellion favors divisions in the hegemonic bloc which, in turn, foment war.[13]

The "general crisis" of the early twentieth century was "a crisis of *over*-reaction, whose main expression was the politics of unreason and domination at home and the diplomacy of confrontation and war abroad."[14] Such crises, and the wars they lead to, do not necessarily lead to revolution: indeed they only do so if defeat so weakens the incumbent regimes that they are challenged or overthrown by revolutionary oppositions. The conclusion would be that wars may well lead to revolutions, but that these wars are not caused by revolutions so much as by the attempts of elites to enhance their positions against oppositions domestic and international, and that revolutions ensue only when these elites fail in such an endeavour. It is this which marks out the contrast between the Russian and German elites after the First World War. The former faced such a crisis of society that they succumbed to a revolutionary movement; the latter, despite insurgent challenges, survived, only to launch an even more ferocious war two decades later. In neither country were revolutionary forces on the brink of taking power in 1914. It was the war which provided the opportunity for the Russian opposition to seize power; no comparable opportunity of a disintegrating state was offered to the numerically and politically much more influential German socialist movement. . . .

A Contingent Relationship

The relationship between war and revolution is not, therefore, one of cause and effect, so much as of two contrasted and combined forms of mobilisation and conflict, two intertwined expressions of a broader social context. Both are political processes, the organisation and character of which have changed substantially over the past two centuries. Both take on their meaning within a broader context of "general crisis." Insofar as any individual revolution, and the international response to it, has to be seen as part of a wider, internationalised pattern of social and political conflict then the revolution can be seen not so much as initiating conflict as exacerbating an already present set of tensions within states. The reason why revolutions lead to war is not therefore that revolutionary states are wilfully belligerent, dissatisfied or revisionist, or that their opponents are militaristic and expansionist. Rather, by dint of the very tensions that led to revolution occurring, other states and societies are affected by them. Thus war is a means by which both groups of states, the revolutionary and the counter-revolutionary, respond to changes in domestic and international politics.

Both groups of states are caught in the difficulty posed by all attempts to link internal political organisation with inter-state relations, namely that of relating but also separating the two dimensions of security. In each case there is an evident relationship between domestic or "vertical" security, that of the state, and international or "horizontal" security, peace between states. It is a relationship that allows of no easy resolution. A policy of fully accepting the relationship would mean that any consistent pursuit of international peace would entail regular interference in the internal affairs of other countries. A policy of denying any connection would entail ignoring the international consequences of revolutions and other upheavals. Both revolutionary and counter-revolutionary states are therefore caught in a process that leads to war, but which at the same time is constrained by the political character of states and of relations between them. For both, . . . a set of recurrent dilemmas are evident. Firstly there is that of calculating the benefits of war, in terms of mobilisation and furthering of foreign policy goals, against the costs, in terms of domestic resistance. In both revolutionary and counter-revolutionary states, involvement in external conflict, especially where the ideological rationale seems greater than the national interest, can lead to a loss of support at home. Secondly, both forms of war run the risk of mobilising resistance in the target state on a nationalist basis. The export of revolution, as much as that of counter-revolution, provokes resistance to it. Thirdly, both forms of war violate the principle on which much inter-state relations rest, and which revolutionaries and counter-revolutionaries invoke to legitimise their own cause, namely sovereignty.

The resolution of this problem has, in practice, involved a set of limited commitments, to the export of revolution by revolutionary states, and to the promotion of counter-revolution by status quo powers. If the Soviet Union, China and other revolutionary states of the twentieth century found it difficult to provide support for fellow insurgents in other states, the status quo powers have found comparable difficulties in extending their campaigns. Nowhere was this more striking than in the war in Vietnam, when the USA was constrained from taking the step that could have decisively weakened the insurgent movement in the south, namely the launch of a ground offensive against North Vietnam. Yet such violations of the conventions of sovereignty recur. They are a result of the very internationalised character of revolutions themselves. While over time such violations abate on both sides, and while both forms of external policy have been remarkably ineffective, they recur as long as revolutionary states themselves remain committed to distinct paths of domestic development.

NOTES

1. "A War for Eternal Peace," in Stuart Schram, *The Political Thought of Mao Tse-tung* (London: Praeger, 1964) pp. 267–9.

2. Tad Szulc, *Fidel. A Critical Portrait* (London: Hutchinson, 1986) pp. 7–8.

3. According to *The Oxford English Dictionary* the term entered English in 1809 as a result of the Peninsular War (1808–14). It referred first to a combatant engaged in such a war, then to the war itself. For general histories, see Gerard Chaliard (ed.), *Stratégie de la Guerrilla* (Paris: Mazarine, 1979); Walter Laqueur, *Guerrilla: A Historical and Critical Study* (London: Weidenfeld & Nicholson, 1977).

4. von Clausewitz, *On War*; Raymond Aron, *Clausewitz* (London: Routledge & Kegan Paul, 1985), chapter 5, "The Moral and the Physical."

5. It is worth noting that those within the social sciences who wish to dissolve the distinction tend to be those who deny the importance of revolutions, while those who do so within political rhetoric tend to downplay the costs of war.

6. Arno Mayer, "Internal Crisis and War Since 1870," [in Charles Bertrand, ed., *Revolutionary Situations in Europe, 1917–1922* (Montreal: ICES, 1977)].

7. Ernest Mandel, *The Meaning of the Second World War* (London: Verso, 1986) p. 45, distinguishes *five* different conflicts within the overall process of the Second World War.

8. Henry Kissinger, *Diplomacy* [(London: Simon & Schuster, 1994)], p. 790.

9. Paul Kennedy, *The Rise and Fall of the Great Powers* (London: Unwin Hyman, 1988). For later, supportive, use of this argument, see Henry Kissinger, *Diplomacy*.

10. On Trotsky, [Issac Deutscher,] *The Prophet Armed* [(Oxford: Oxford University Press, 1954)], pp. 214–15; on Lenin, George Lukacs, *Lenin, The Unity of His Theory* (London: Verso, 1970) chapter 4, "Imperialism: World War and Civil War."

. . . .

12. Friedrich Katz, *The Secret War in Mexico. Europe, the United States, and the Mexican Revolution* (Chicago: Chicago University Press, 1981).

13. Mayer, "Internal Crisis and War Since 1870," pp. 230–1.

14. Ibid., p. 201.

4

The U.S. and Third World Revolutionary States: Understanding the Breakdown in Relations

Robert S. Snyder

In the following selection, Robert S. Snyder inquires as to why U.S. relations with revolutionary regimes in the developing world usually break down. One common explanation, he notes, is that the U.S. government is hostile toward these regimes. Another explanation is Stephen Walt's theory that the breakdown in relations occurs through a spiral of mounting misconceptions and suspicions on both sides. Snyder believes that both of these explanations are incorrect. He argues, instead, that revolutionary regimes in the developing world have been responsible for the breakdown in their relations with the United States.

As Jack Goldstone also observed in his selection, the revolutionary coalition usually breaks down once the old regime has been overthrown. A struggle for power then ensues between the "moderates" and the "extremists." The moderates, Snyder notes, usually have ties with the United States and want to develop good relations with it. Fearing that the moderates and the United States will act together against them, the extremists have a powerful incentive to exacerbate relations between their country and Washington. By doing so, the extremists can exploit deteriorating relations with the United States to rally nationalist sentiment to their side and to discredit the moderates who call for improved relations with "the enemy" at a time of crisis. Hostile relations with the United States, then, may allow the extremists to win their internal power struggle with the moderates.

Robert S. Snyder, "The U.S. and Third World Revolutionary States: Understanding the Breakdown in Relations," *International Studies Quarterly* 43, no. 2 (June 1999): 265–290. Copyright © 1999 International Studies Association. Reprinted with permission of Blackwell Publishers.

Author's note: I have benefited from the comments of Timothy White, Douglas Macdonald, John Leffler, Michael Ryan, Eric Selbin, Elaine Spencer, and anonymous reviewers on earlier drafts of this article.

Critical Questions

1. Why, according to Snyder, is the United States not responsible for the breakdown in its relations with revolutionary regimes in the developing world?

2. Why, according to Snyder, do revolutionary regimes usually prefer hostile relations with the United States to friendly ones?

3. Why was the government of Robert Mugabe in Zimbabwe—a revolutionary regime that established friendly ties with the United States—an exception to this pattern?

4. Do you agree with Snyder's theory? Why or why not?

Although scholars focused on Soviet–American relations during the Cold War, the greatest number of conflicts for the U.S. occurred in the Third World, and most of these were with revolutionary states.[1] From the Chinese Revolution in 1949 to the Nicaraguan Revolution in 1979, Washington became embroiled in many different conflicts. Many scholars and non-scholars alike maintain that U.S. foreign policies toward the new revolutionary states could have prevented their hostility, and indeed Washington had cordial ties with some revolutionary states for several months. Could American policies toward these new regimes have prevented the almost universal collapse in relations between the U.S. and Third World revolutionary states? If not, why not?

The breakdown in ties between the U.S. and these revolutionary states can best be conceptualized as a conflict-generating shift in alliances. Although it is not easily operationalized, the breakdown occurred after the first state publicly declared the other to be its enemy, consistently took steps to prepare for conflict with the second state or its ally, and resisted diplomacy to solve the problems between the two states; and it was complete when the second state reciprocated the actions of the first state. This topic is analytically interesting because of the two distinctly different types of states and because of the complicated interactive processes involving both domestic and international politics.

Two general explanations for this breakdown have been American hostility toward revolutionary change in the Third World, given the U.S.' economic or ideological goals, and the spiral model, which emphasizes the mutual suspicions and misperceptions of the two states. I argue that both explanations give inadequate attention to domestic politics in the revolutionary states, and I demonstrate for certain types of revolutionary states that their domestic politics was the critical factor in the breakdown in relations between them and the U.S.

I challenge the first theory, which is perhaps the biggest myth about American foreign policy, that the U.S. could not tolerate radical change within Third World revolutionary states and, therefore, rapidly confronted them. This explanation incorrectly maintains that internal factors determined U.S. foreign policy but external factors, namely, American aggression, determined the foreign policy of revolutionary states. On the contrary, domestic politics in the revolutionary states was often the most important factor in the making of their foreign polices, and the external alignment of revolutionary states was almost always the paramount consideration in the making of American foreign policy.

Moreover, the spiral model, or Stephen Walt's (1992, 1996) variant of it,[2] has problems explaining dyads involving *Third World* revolutionary states. Emphasizing external security threats and misperceptions in determining the foreign policies of both states, the spiral model, or Walt's variant, may explain the cases in which both states were internally unified and there was not an ideological clash between them. Nevertheless, they fail to explain cases involving revolutionary states in which some groups had strong transnational ties to the U.S. or other Western countries and the revolutionary ideologies were anti-Western.

Using recent sources about some of these individual cases that challenge these two explanations, I develop an alternative theory to explain these cases and to test across other ones. I base what I call this theory of externalization on Charles Tilly's (1975, 1978) and Theda Skocpol's (1988) ideas that revolutions are fundamentally about state-building, and that state-building is often best promoted through international conflict. As Tilly (1975:42) says, radical internal changes are often best achieved by engaging in external hostilities. I argue that the radicals in these revolutionary states initiated hostilities with the U.S. in order to externalize their domestic conflicts with the liberal bourgeoisie, who were previously part of the revolutionary coalitions. Since the bourgeoisie had strong transnational ties with the U.S., the radicals believed they had to defeat these moderates in order to establish completely new orders. Although the U.S. at first did not respond to the antagonism of these revolutionary states, Washington in time reciprocated their hostility after they befriended the Soviet Union (or communist ally) or maintained their extreme antagonism. The U.S. then escalated the conflict. I conclude by looking at a different type of revolutionary state, demonstrating with this critical case the general importance of revolutionary states' domestic politics and ideological goals in understanding the collapse in relations between them and the U.S.

The next section, which discusses the research methodology, is followed by a presentation of the three explanations for the breakdown. I then examine the cases and conclude by discussing some implications.

Research Methodology

Since the circumstances of many cases involving the U.S. and Third World revolutionary states were complicated and open to interpretation, and since the number of cases is fairly small,[3] this article employs the comparative case approach and uses the critical case method.[4] To illustrate the complexity of these cases: the universe of cases reveals with few exceptions that revolutionary states that became hostile to the U.S. had revolutionary elites who had expressed anti-Western views before they came to power, yet this correlation does not prove that ideology, as opposed to Walt's theory emphasizing security, explains the breakdown until individual cases are carefully examined. Likewise, the evidence indicates with few exceptions that the U.S. became hostile to these states after they befriended the Soviet Union, yet this does not necessarily disprove the hypothesis of American aggression toward revolutionary change because the foreign and domestic policies of these states were related.

Selecting a cluster of similar cases (similar types of revolutions and similar historical relationships with the U.S.) as the basis for theory-building, this article examines the collapse in ties between the U.S. and Cuba, Iran, and Nicaragua following their respective revolutions. All three were multiclass rebellions against neopatrimonial rulers tied to the U.S. in semi-urban countries.[5] They were distinctly revolutions as opposed to also being anti-colonial movements or civil wars. The revolutionary coalitions in these three upheavals consisted of the liberal bourgeoisie, who were important to the success of these revolutions yet had strong transnational links with the U.S. Moreover, each of the three revolutions eventually led to a major crisis for American foreign policymakers.

I choose these cases because they are "hard cases" in challenging the hypothesis that Washington could not tolerate revolutionary change in the Third World, for the U.S. had greater incentives to initiate hostilities with Cuba, Iran, and Nicaragua than with other revolutionary states given its greater economic interests in and historical ties to these three states. I also select these cases because the U.S. had cordial relations with these three revolutionary states for several months, thus allowing for greater interaction between the two.[6] Therefore, they should be "easy cases" for Walt's variant of the spiral model given the initial positive relations, security concerns of the revolutionary states, and the lengthy strategic interactions that led to the breakdown in relations.

Since the U.S. had dominated Cuba, Iran, and Nicaragua for decades, what is puzzling about their hostility toward America? There is nothing inevitable about a former dominated country becoming overtly hostile to its former imperialist power. Paradoxically, American dominance of these countries entailed less direct political control and use of repression than most colonial powers exercised over their colonies, yet the U.S. encountered far greater wrath from these countries than most colonizers faced from their newly freed colonies (e.g., Great Britain and India, France and several West African states). The rabid anti-Americanism of the Iranian Revolution stands in stark contrast to the minimal hostility of the Eastern European countries shown the Soviet Union following their liberal revolutions in 1989. In short, the past imperialist relationship may be a necessary condition but is not a sufficient one for understanding these states' foreign policies; as with many other types of conflict, the goals of the political elites and the *process* in the collapse of relations were crucial.

In only focusing on the critical period when the two states moved from cordial to hostile relations, I use the process-tracing method, which demonstrates path dependency and multiple causation (George and McKeown, 1985). I rely primarily on secondary works of the individual cases, many of which utilize non-American sources. Although these cases have been somewhat controversial, the pattern I observe across them and the theory I use to explain this pattern add weight to the growing number of works that interpret the cases as I present them.

Although these cases can only be suggestive of other ones, in order to generalize I vary the dependent variable and examine Zimbabwe as a critical case. Zimbabwe was one of only two illiberal revolutionary states (along with Bolivia) during the Cold War with which the U.S. did not see a collapse in relations. I show that the break in relations did not occur because the conditions for externalization in the previous cases were absent in Zimbabwe.

American Hostility to Revolutionary Change

Many believe that the U.S. could not and cannot tolerate Third World revolutions. Most fall into one of two camps. For Marxists, the U.S. could not accept Third World revolutions because nearly all challenged capitalism (Williams, 1972; LaFeber, 1984; Kolko, 1988). Following in the tradition of Louis Hartz (1955), others believe, however, that the U.S. could not respect social revolutions in the Third World because the U.S. had never experienced a social revolution (Feinberg and Oye, 1983; Hunt, 1987). Thus, Washington through its antagonistic actions—economic sanctions, public pronouncements, military threats, covert aid, political pressures and gestures—pushed new revolutionary regimes to unwanted and defensive positions of hostility toward the U.S. Arguing that antagonism to social revolutions even formed the core of America's national identity, Michael Hunt writes:

> Our inability even in the face of failure to modify our rigid, reflexive attitudes toward revolutions has tended to make a bad situation worse. This inflexibility has made Washington unresponsive to overtures from new revolutionary regimes eager to neutralize American hostility and thereby avoid a prolonged and costly confrontation. Confirmed in their suspicions of implacable American hostility, revolutionary leaders have turned to cultivate friends in the anti-American camp. (1987:175)

A major consequence of the U.S.' alleged "rigid, reflexive" hostility was that it drove many Third World revolutionary states to the Soviets. Many leftist revolutionary states presumably would not have chosen to align themselves with the Soviet Union but had little choice when "pushed into the Kremlin's arms by American bellicosity" (Van Evera, 1990:73).

Thus,

H_{1a} The U.S. became hostile to the revolutionary states as soon as the new regimes were established or after these states promoted nationalizations or other internal changes that adversely affected American economic interests.

H_{1b} The U.S. became hostile after seeing the moderates lose their grip on power.

The Spiral Model

A popular model for understanding many conflicts, the spiral model has been put forth as an explanation for the breakdown in relations between the U.S. and Third World revolutionary states.[7] Given the anarchic structure of the international system, a state that takes steps to enhance its security unintentionally threatens the security of another. The result may be a "spiral of insecurity," in which each actor, in misperceiving the other's defensive intentions, builds up in response to the other (Jervis, 1978). In developing a variant of the spiral model, Walt maintains that the anarchic structure is a necessary but not a sufficient condition for conflict between revolutionary states and status quo states; instead, revolutions for a variety of reasons lead to mutual "suspicions" on the part of both actors.[8] Walt (1996:33–37) asserts that a "spiral of suspicion" as opposed to a "legitimate clash of interest" explains the conflict. Following Walt's theory, we would expect the revolutionary states to have been reactive toward the U.S. and to have become hostile for reasons of security. This contrasts with the theory of externalization, which argues that the revolutionary states were proactive and became antagonistic for ideological and domestic reasons. Thus,

H_2 Preferring to cooperate, the revolutionary states took defensive steps after the U.S. initiated an action that they perceived as potentially threatening or in anticipation of U.S. aggression in the near future.

Revolutionary Goals, Externalization, and the Defense of the Revolution

The theory of externalization that I develop comes from some of Tilly's and Skocpol's ideas about revolutions. Tilly's writings on revolutions, however, are part of his larger focus on state-building. For Tilly (1975, 1978), state-building in Europe involved two distinct features: violence and a close interaction between internal and external factors. One of the greatest internal changes came with revolutions, which entailed both a radical transformation of the domestic orders and drastic realignments of political coalitions. Revolutions accomplished these internal transformations, however, often through engaging in external conflict or under the threat of international violence, thus leading one to deduce that international conflict may be necessary or highly desirable for revolutionaries who seek large-scale domestic changes. In Skocpol's (1988) definitive work on the relation between revolutionary states and international politics, she argues that the perpetuation of revolutionary mobilization became for revolutionaries an end in itself; the biggest consequence of social revolutions, therefore, was mass military mobilization.

Since most states in the Third World were established by the Western powers and remained highly penetrated by them as well, revolutionary rulers in these states who sought radical changes had particularly strong incentives to promote anti-Western foreign policies. Moreover, since most revolutionaries wanted absolute power and totally new political coalitions, they needed to defeat those groups, usually the bourgeoisie, who had close ties with the Western powers and resisted their efforts to concentrate power.

Thus, the theory of externalization has two parts, which are usually related. First, Third World revolutionary states projected external threats in order to withdraw to make drastic changes in policy and to perpetuate revolutionary mobilization. Second, and more specifically, revolutionaries in these states fomented tensions with the U.S. in order to weaken or defeat other groups in the polities that (allegedly) had vulnerable links to it.[9] The group that initiated the international conflict in order to weaken the internal target group had an intermediate level of strength.[10] If the initiating group had been weak, it would have risked domestic defeat as a consequence of international conflict; if the initiating group had total control that could not have been challenged, however, it would not have needed to provoke international conflict for internal reasons.

This theory of externalization is different from the classic diversionary theory, which has been regarded as the most important domestic-based explanation of international conflict.[11] It states that elites use international conflict to alleviate domestic problems in having citizens "rally around the flag." It has three assumptions: the international target of conflict is usually irrelevant; groups within the state that use international conflict to divert attention are discrete and separate from foreign actors; and international conflict is a result of domestic tensions, yet the domestic consequence of this international conflict is, ironically, to make domestic politics irrelevant. The theory of externalization has three different assumptions from the diversionary theory: the target of international conflict matters; groups within the state that initiates conflict have transnational connections; and, most important, international conflict does not, as the diversionary theory suggests, minimize, remove, or freeze domestic politics; it changes domestic politics. As the cases highlight, the bourgeoisie were removed from the revolutionary coalitions.

With respect to the Cuban, Iranian, and Nicaraguan revolutions, how can we know that the radicals sought to externalize their conflicts with the moderates? More generally, how can we know the motivations of the revolutionaries? Indeed the radicals probably had no preexisting plan to externalize their domestic conflicts with the moderates, rather this developed as the radicals confronted the moderates in attempting *both* to gain power for themselves and to promote their ideological objectives. We can ascertain the motivations of the revolutionaries through their actions, particularly the sequence or stages of their actions, and through their goals, which are best revealed in the absence of political constraints. Consequently, the radicals most revealed their goals through their writings and statements during the prerevolutionary period before their coalition with the moderates and with their policies after they consolidated power and faced lesser opposition. Given the difficulties of determining the goals of elites, however, we can assert but not conclusively prove that the radicals had the following preferences:

Their principal goal after coming to power was to establish dictatorships and repress opposing groups even though they had presented themselves as social democrats during the period that toppled the old rulers.[12] They wanted to initiate social revolutions that would eliminate the institutions of the old regimes and to create their own, cut their countries' old international links, and extract considerable capital from within. The radicals sought to promote anti-American foreign policies and to play large roles on the world stage.[13] These foreign policy goals may have been as important as any domestic objectives, but they could only be accomplished if the bourgeoisie were defeated.

The many bourgeoisie were the greatest immediate impediment to the radicals and their goals, for they wanted a more liberal order and to maintain their friendly ties with the U.S.[14] Their participation in the rebellions to remove the old regimes was essential to the success of the revolutions. Although they rebelled for several reasons, they especially detested the neopatrimonial nature of the ancien regimes.[15] Consequently, since all three were revolts of societies against the states, engaging in class warfare would have been difficult. Moreover, the revolutionary ideologies used to oust the old rulers had emphasized nationalism, social unity, and pluralism, making it difficult for the radicals to attack the moderates head-on.

Although they probably had no conscious plan, the radicals discovered big opportunities in exploiting conflict with Washington. The U.S. had been a neocolonial power toward these countries, for it had had a large hand in the creation of the ancien regimes, supported the old rulers, and contributed to the numerous distortions that made the revolutions possible. The key fact, however, is that the liberal bourgeoisie had strong transnational ties to the U.S. Thus, in waging conflict with the U.S., the radicals delegitimized the bourgeoisie's revolutionary and nationalist credentials, and they argued that drastic actions needed to be taken against the moderates to safeguard the revolutions. Hostility toward the U.S. militarized the revolutions and mobilized the anomic masses, who formed the social base of each against the now potentially traitorous bourgeoisie.

Conflict with the U.S., however, could only work under certain international conditions. The radicals (except in Iran) needed to align their countries with the Soviet Union both to antagonize the U.S. and to contain potential American hostility. They turned to the Soviet Union in the knowledge that such a move would elicit a negative reaction from the U.S., regardless of administrations.[16] Nevertheless, they befriended Moscow not merely for strategic reasons but also for ideological reasons (Domínguez, 1989; Kagan, 1996), for siding with the Soviet Union expressed their goal of worldwide revolution.

Given its imperialist past, however, the U.S. was a potential threat to the revolutions, and the radicals were obsessed with Washington's responses toward the new regimes. Thus, one might claim that the radicals made preemptive moves in striking at the bourgeoisie in order to hinder the U.S. from using the moderates to overturn the revolutions. Associated conceptually with the spiral model, a preemptive strike involves one side attacking first in the belief that the other is poised to attack (Reiter, 1995:6–7). Since the U.S. was not prepared to strike at the time, this concept and the spiral model would not appear to be applicable. The radicals, however, may have *perceived* that the U.S. was prepared to strike given its imperialist past and given their paranoia; perhaps no conclusive proof exists to refute this assertion, but the considerable evidence to the contrary and the opportunistic actions of the radicals cast doubt that this was indeed their perception. Nevertheless, the radicals probably made *preventive* strikes, seeking decisive breaks with Washington and quick victories over the moderates before the two could consolidate their opposition to the revolutions, which the radicals saw as inevitable. The fact that the Cuban and Iranian Revolutions maintained their radical policies after they became more secure from the U.S. years later suggests that domestic factors drove the early revolutions more than "internalization" or American aggression or anticipated aggression through manipulation of the moderates.[17] The U.S. did not control the moderates early on. Indeed, moderate leaders like H. Matos (Cuba), M. Bazargan (Iran), and V. Chamorro (Nicaragua) were hardly U.S. stooges. The alliance and aggressive policies that the U.S. and bourgeoisie jointly pursued in opposition to the radicals (e.g., the contras in Nicaragua) occurred *after* the breakdown in relations between the two states.

The U.S. did not at first respond to the revolutionary states' hostility, for it wanted to maintain the cordial relations it had with the new regimes. It was rational for the U.S. to give the new regimes the benefit of the doubt, and it was cheaper to use positive inducements as opposed to negative instruments of statecraft. Although American policymakers have been criticized for having pushed Third World states toward the Soviet Union, the evidence indicates that this was of utmost concern to them (Macdonald, 1992:11–28). Following realist principles, however, Washington reciprocated the revolutionary states' hostility after they moved to befriend the Soviet Union or a communist ally, or in the case of Iran, took the U.S. Embassy. After the U.S. engaged the revolutionary states, the conflicts deepened. The U.S. reacted so aggressively after the breakdown because it believed that it had exhausted positive inducements, and because it did not want to be embarrassed during the Cold War by its inability to influence weak powers. Washington was also quick to reciprocate their hostility in part for its own domestic reasons; administrations did not want to be criticized by the opposite party for being a sucker in following conciliatory policies too long.

Thus,

H_{3a} The revolutionary states externalized their domestic conflicts with the U.S. following the radicals' efforts to defeat the moderates.

H_{3b} The U.S. became hostile to the revolutionary states after they befriended the Soviet Union (or communist ally) or maintained their extreme antagonism.

With all three hypotheses, much of the evidence involves the sequence of events and the motivations of elites as revealed by former participants, government documents, and their actions at the time. Although it is difficult to ascertain the motives of elites as demonstrated by the different interpretations of the cases over the years, I base my interpretations primarily on recent works that rely extensively on primary sources. I use the process-tracing method in examining the movement from cordial relations to hostile ones. Although the presentation of the cases simplifies complex interactions, each of the three cases followed the same four stages. In Stage One domestic conflicts developed between the radicals and moderates in the revolutionary states. In Stage Two the radicals became hostile to the U.S. In Stage Three Washington resisted responding to the revolutionary states' hostility. In Stage Four the U.S. reciprocated the revolutionary states' antagonism for fear of Soviet gains, and the radicals then moved to defeat the bourgeoisie. Stage Four differs in the Iran case, for the U.S. reacted to the taking of the U.S. Embassy as opposed to the fear that Tehran was becoming too close to the Soviet Union.

The Cases

Cuba

The U.S. established a protectorate over Cuba following the island's independence from Spain at the turn of the twentieth century,[18] but Washington renounced direct interference in Cuba's affairs when it rescinded the Platt Amendment in the 1930s. Fidel Castro's guerrilla revolt from the mountains brought the Batista government down in late 1958. The upheaval depended on the support of the urban middle classes who were attracted to Castro's social democratic message (Draper, 1962:5–11), and the U.S. also played a critical role in Batista's downfall when it imposed an arms embargo (Domínguez, 1989:13).

To demonstrate this theory of externalization requires that other interpretations about the breakdown in relations be refuted. Using Soviet archives, Fursenko and Naftali (1997:5–19), in their path-breaking book, reject the hypotheses that the Soviets controlled Castro in the early days of the revolution or that Fidel had cast his lot with the communists before coming to power. A third perspective maintains that, given the U.S.' efforts to prevent Castro from acquiring power, Washington initiated hostile relations (Morley, 1987). In examining American government documents, Morley (1987) shows that U.S. leaders disliked Castro well before the formal break in relations. Nevertheless, the Eisenhower administration decided to accept the new revolutionary government in spite of its efforts in late 1958 to find a third alternative to Batista and Castro, and in spite of its reservations about Castro. Indeed, Smith writes that "relations between the U.S. and Cuba were rather good during the first half of 1959" (1987:43). Ambassador Bonsal and other top officials in the State Department believed that the U.S. should recognize Castro as a Cuban nationalist and not as a communist and should support social reform (Thomas, 1971:1061; Welch, 1985:29; Smith, 1987:47). A level of mistrust persisted, however, as Castro periodically denounced the U.S., and some in Congress and the American media criticized the Cuban leader for his actions (Welch, 1985:36). Castro accepted an invitation in the spring of 1959 to visit the U.S. Top American officials offered him financial support, with Cuba's Central Bank president later saying that they were "more than willing, anxious, avid, desperate" to give aid (quoted in Domínguez, 1989:18). Fidel refused to accept the assistance.

The first major event to test the friendship between the two states occurred with the Cuban government's land reform in May, for it took property from American nationals. The U.S. government sent a note in support of reform but requested its citizens be justly compensated. Although some suggest that the U.S. note demonstrated Washington's hostility to change and Castro's revolution H_1, Smith, a harsh critic of U.S. foreign policy, nevertheless writes: "If examined objectively, the famous U.S. note on agrarian reform could hardly be construed as a rejection; rather, it emphasized U.S. acceptance of Cuba's right to impose such reform" (1987:47). On the idea that Castro *perceived* U.S. antagonism, he adds: "If this was Castro's preconceived conviction, it was held against considerable evidence to the contrary" (1987:49). In fact, the two states maintained their cordial relations for a few more months.

Stage One (Domestic Conflict).   By the late spring of 1959, Castro was facing domestic opposition. Before leaving for Washington, he called off elections. The cancellation of elections and land reform galvanized many in the bourgeoisie to oppose the course of the revolution. After criticizing Fidel for moving too close to the communists, President Urrutia and most in the cabinet were dismissed during the summer. Castro resented the charge that the communists were playing an increasing role in the revolution, yet by the fall he became more dependent on their support.

The fall marked a turning point in the revolution. Castro arrested many who opposed him and took control of key organizations, putting known leftists such as Che Guevara in charge of the national treasury and his brother, Raúl, in charge of all security forces. The arrest and trial of Húbert Matos on the charge of disloyalty became a pivotal event in demonstrating the lack of tolerance for those who criticized Castro (Thomas, 1971:1244–47; Szulc, 1986:506). Through intimidation, Fidel gained control of the labor organizations, the University of Havana, and the press by early 1960. In order to protect the revolution, he formed revolutionary militias that numbered 100,000 persons by the spring (Thomas, 1971:1260–62).

Stage Two (Externalization). Castro largely justified his seizure of dictatorial control by claiming that the U.S. threatened the revolution. According to several scholars, the event that led Cuba to end its positive ties with the U.S. occurred when Castro charged that the U.S. had attacked Cuba following the Díaz Lanz raid in October 1959.[19] Díaz Lanz, a former head of the Cuban air force, had flown an airplane originating from Florida over Havana, dropping leaflets that denounced the regime. Within the course of a day, Castro was rallying the Cuban nation "against the U.S. government, an enemy it did not know it had" (Domínguez, 1989:20).

Cuba began to re-orient its foreign policy between the superpowers. Fursenko and Naftali (1997:20–34) demonstrate that the Soviets and the leftist revolutionaries explored ways to forge an alliance as early as the fall of 1959. Castro in the late fall of 1959 "passed word to the Soviets that if done `very carefully' a dramatic shift in Cuban foreign policy could be carried off" (Fursenko and Naftali, 1997:36). Since these talks originated before the Díaz Lanz raid, Domínguez (1989:20–23) argues that this evidence proves that the U.S. did not push Castro toward the Soviets, thus rebuking the spiral model H_2. Nevertheless, a loose interpretation of the spiral model maintains that, in recalling Washington's intervention in Guatemala in 1954, Castro became hostile to the U.S. in anticipation of American antagonism following his efforts to defeat the moderates. Using the Soviet archives, Naftali (1998) challenges this popular but unproven interpretation when he says that "Castro did not start to complain to Moscow about U.S. threats to his regime before March 1960" even though "as of November 1959 discussions between the Cuban government and the Soviets were quite advanced." Moreover, he adds that other leftist leaders at this time told the Soviets that Castro did not sufficiently fear the U.S. The Cubans made this growing shift in foreign policy known, however, when Castro ceremoniously welcomed and dined Deputy Prime Minister Mikoyan for two weeks in February 1960. The two governments signed trade agreements.

The event that triggered the U.S.' hostile response came in March. Recalling the sinking of the *Maine,* Castro, without evidence, blamed Washington for the explosion of the French ship *Coubre* in Havana.[20] Following Mikoyan's visit, "Castro was mentally prepared to confront the Colossus of the North" (Fursenko and Naftali, 1997:41). Fursenko and Naftali add:

> For two years the Cubans had wanted Eastern bloc assistance to come covertly so as to deceive the U.S. regarding the extent of the revolution's anti-Americanism. Now Castro wanted Moscow to consider overt assistance to deter an American intervention. (1997:42)

In anticipating Washington's angry reaction to his incendiary accusations, "Castro was prescient" (Fursenko and Naftali, 1997:43). Now with the U.S. prepared to combat the revolution, Castro "unleashed his security forces against all manifestations of the counterrevolution in Cuba" (Fursenko and Naftali, 1997:41).

Stage Three (U.S. Hesitation).   U.S. government documents indicate that top officials had suspicions of Castro dating back to the period before he came to power (Paterson, 1994), although the CIA insisted for a long time that Castro was not a communist and had no knowledge of his contacts with the Soviets in the fall of 1959. Nevertheless, Morley (1987:83–87) and Benjamin (1989:152–54) maintain that, based on government documents, top U.S. officials rejected the Castro regime during the fall of 1959, demonstrating that the U.S. could not accept the *internal* changes of the Cuban Revolution H_{1b} and, disproving H_{3b}, that Cuba's alignment with Moscow caused U.S. anger. Benjamin presents as evidence a memo from Secretary of State Herter to Eisenhower suggesting that the U.S. "encourage opposition by suitable elements presently outside of the Castro regime with a view towards a step-by-step development of coherent opposition" (1989:153). But, as Benjamin (1989:153) admits, the Herter memo was in response to Castro's accusations *against the U.S.,* and Morley even says that "Castro's decision to pursue an independent foreign policy was, however, singled out for attention" (1987:85). More important, as Luxenberg (1988:50) says, Eisenhower still "sought a rapprochement with the Havana regime" in spite of

Herter's memo and the administration's doubts about the ascendancy of the radicals. Thus, Washington reacted primarily to Cuba's foreign policy yet still tried to keep the positive relationship.

Indeed, Washington vigorously denied the charges that it was behind the Díaz Lanz raid and conducted an investigation. Although many in Congress and the American media denounced the radical turn of the revolution, the administration refrained from criticizing domestic events in Cuba. Following Castro's tirades against the U.S. and efforts to beef up Cuban security in preparation for an alleged U.S. attack, Ambassador Bonsal returned to Washington for consultations in January 1960. The administration considered sanctions against Cuba but instead chose to keep its conciliatory policy. Shortly thereafter Eisenhower made a public statement reiterating that the U.S. would not interfere in Cuban affairs, respected Cuba's desire for reform, and would work to stop Cuban exiles from using Florida as a base to harass the island (Welch, 1985:43–44; Smith, 1987:55). The Argentine government offered to mediate the disputes, telling the Cuban government that Washington sought to correct misunderstandings. Castro rejected the mission (Welch, 1985:44; Domínguez, 1989:23). For over a year the U.S. skeptically accepted the revolution, offered financial assistance, supported land reform, sought to correct misunderstandings, and encouraged third party mediation. These positive actions were lessened, however, by the criticisms of some in Congress and by the failure to bring anti-Castro activities by some exiles to a halt, if this was possible.

Stage Four (U.S. Hostility).   The U.S. changed its policy of forbearance in March 1960 following Mikoyan's visit and Castro's accusations after the *Coubre* incident (Welch, 1985:46–47; Szulc, 1986:515; Smith, 1987:56; Domínguez, 1989:24). As Welch says: "Neither Eisenhower's ethnocentric bias nor limited knowledge of Cuban history was the most decisive factor for these actions; it was Castro's overtures to the Soviet Union" (1985:60). Eisenhower authorized the CIA to work with anti-Castro exiles. The hostility escalated when the U.S. government asked American refineries in Cuba not to refine Soviet oil in May 1960. When the companies complied, Castro nationalized them. Washington responded by refusing to purchase the remainder of Cuba's sugar quota. The Cuban government then nationalized 600 American firms and expropriated all American sugar mills. Following the Soviets' statement that they would purchase the remainder of the sugar, and following Khrushchev's speech which said that the Soviets would defend Cuba in a "figurative sense," the administration escalated its hostile actions. Eisenhower imposed an embargo in October. In January 1961, the administration broke diplomatic relations.

Before the U.S. responded to Cuba's hostility, Castro had used alleged American provocations to remove political rivals, to take control of organizations within Cuban society, and to enlarge the security forces. But faced with American aggression, Fidel began his all-out assault on the Cuban bourgeoisie on the grounds that they were a threat to the revolution. He said: "For each economic aggression, adopt a revolutionary law" (quoted in Domínguez, 1989:24). Thus, in addition to nationalizing U.S. property, the government seized the property of its own citizens as well. Responding to the U.S. embargo, Castro nationalized 382 large Cuban firms. Cuba's social revolution against the bourgeoisie can only be understood in terms of its conflict with the U.S. Contrary to the Marxist version of H_1, however, the U.S.' negative reactions to the nationalizations occurred as a consequence of this Cold War struggle and was not the cause of its hostility.

In sum, contrary to the spiral model H_2, the U.S. did not begin its hostile actions in March 1960 because of misperceptions about the revolution; instead, following months of anti-American diatribes, Washington found Cuba's turn to the Soviet Union to be unacceptable. Given its past interference in Cuba's affairs, Castro had strong reasons to be suspicious of, if not obsessed with, the U.S. Instead of making a preemptive strike as suggested by the spiral model, however, Castro made a preventive strike against the U.S. before it and the Cuban bourgeoisie could consolidate their opposition to the revolution (Smith, 1987:50). Externalization entails using international conflict for domestic purposes, but perhaps, as Smith (1987:49–50) and Domínguez (1989) argue, Castro's principal goal in wanting to eliminate the bourgeoisie was to remove the domestic obstacles to launching and leading a larger Latin American or Third World revolt against the imperialist U.S. In this way he would be perpetuating the revolution, and he needed the Soviet Union to protect him and to infuriate Washington.

Iran

The U.S. and Iran had little interaction before the Second World War, but following the war Iran became a pivotal state in the Cold War.[21] Fearing that the chaos in Iran would make it vulnerable to the communists, the Eisenhower administration supported a coup in 1953 that removed the nationalist Mossadegh in favor of the Shah.[22] Inspired in part by Carter's policy of human rights (Chehabi, 1990:224–30), the Iranian Revolution of 1978–79 brought together different classes and represented a rebellion of society against the state. Ayatollah Khomeini and other revolutionary elites around him promised to establish a just Islamic order, but they remained vague about the specifics. The Carter administration was slow to react to the evolving revolution in the fall of 1978; its advice to the Shah provided no clear direction as to how he should respond.[23] After Khomeini returned from exile in February 1979, the American ambassador left Iran, and the U.S. suspended arms shipments.

Relations between the U.S. and the new revolutionary regime were cool but not hostile. The new rulers promised to repay Iran's debt, and the government came to the defense of the U.S. Embassy after it was attacked in February. Although Khomeini denounced the U.S. periodically, Prime Minister "Bazargan and his associates were quite willing to maintain normal diplomatic relations with the U.S." (Bill, 1988:265). Contrary to H_1, "US policy . . . was premised on the assumption that the emerging Islamic Republic was an established fact," and "the Department of State was prepared to establish correct formal relations with the new regime" (Cottam, 1988:207). Following a September meeting between Secretary of State Vance and Foreign Minister Yazdi at the United Nations, National Security Advisor Brzezinski met with Bazargan in October in Algiers, and the two agreed that the U.S. would resume arms shipments to Iran (Sick, 1985:221–22).

Stage One (Domestic Conflict).   For the first few months of the revolution, Iranians focused on punishing officials from the Shah's regime. Nevertheless, a power struggle was developing between the moderate Bazargan government, which had been appointed by Khomeini, and Islamic radicals, best represented by the Revolutionary Council.[24] Bazargan wanted a liberal democracy guided by Islamic principles, but the Islamic radicals sought to destroy the secular institutions established over half a century by the Pahlavi dynasty and to create Islamic ones. By the summer the Revolutionary Council was gaining an edge, for only it and not the government could control the ad hoc committees *(komitehs)* that were developing throughout the country, and the creation of the Revolutionary Guards and Islamic Republican party strengthened the radicals' cause. A major clash arose between the liberals and leftists on the one side and the Islamic radicals on the other with the writing of the new constitution. The Islamic radicals wanted to give the clerics through the institutions of the *velayat-e faqih* and the Assembly of Experts final authority over the policies of the government, but the liberals and leftists wanted to maintain the secular order.

Stage Two (Externalization).   Iran crossed the threshold of hostility with the U.S. when Islamic radicals stormed the U.S. Embassy in November following the admittance of the Shah into the U.S. for medical treatment. The radicals demanded that the Shah be returned to Iran in exchange for the release of the hostages and embassy. Furthermore, they claimed they wanted to prevent the U.S. from launching a coup against the revolution (Milani, 1989:165). Even recognizing Iranian memories of the 1953 coup, one cannot plausibly claim that the Shah's arrival in the U.S. foreshadowed Washington's intervention H_2. The U.S. had not intervened to support the Shah during the revolution, and the Carter administration accepted the new regime. Moreover, the monarch's arrival in the U.S. received little attention in Iran for days (Sick, 1985:239), and the radicals had planned to attack the embassy anyway (Zabih, 1982:46–47; Hiro, 1985:136; Milani, 1989:166). More damaging to H_2 is the fact that Khomeini, who supported the takeover, privately expressed his confidence in the revolution and the view that the U.S. was a declining power not to be feared (Cottam, 1988:211–12). Moreover, according to Cottam, Khomeini "understood very well that Jimmy Carter could not extradite the Shah to Iran . . . and this was not a real condition for the release of the hostages" (1988:211–12). Given that the embassy seizure expressed the flexing of Iran's power, this event was intended less to "prevent" future U.S. intervention than to prevent the moderates from increasing ties to the U.S. More accurately, it began the "second revolution" to eliminate the moderates and U.S. influence.

Stage Three (U.S. Hesitation).   Although he froze Iranian assets in U.S. banks before Tehran could withdraw them, and asked the Security Council for an embargo against Iran, Carter generally followed a conciliatory approach and sought a peaceful solution to the crisis in its first few months.[25] Wanting to give Tehran a chance to get its government in place, Carter believed that a tough American response would only hurt the moderates and help the radicals. In early December Carter declared the lives of the hostages to be his first priority. The Soviet invasion of Afghanistan that same month reaffirmed his view that the U.S. and Iran were natural allies, and that he should not take actions that would further damage the relationship.

Stage Four (U.S. Hostility).   Carter changed his policy in the early spring of 1980 after the Iranians failed to comply with various agreements with third party mediators, and after the newly elected President Banisadr proved unable or unwilling to gain the release of the hostages. A half-year into the crisis the U.S. broke diplomatic relations with Iran. In late April it launched the ill-fated rescue operation. Following the release of the hostages in January 1981, however, the incoming "Reagan administration perceived little threat to American objectives in the Middle East from Iran" (Cottam, 1988:238). Because of Iran's anti-Soviet foreign policy, the Reagan administration attempted to befriend Tehran for years in spite of the hostility it demonstrated toward the U.S.

The hostage crisis led to what Arjomand calls the "clerical coup d'etat" (1988:137). Indeed, the success of the clerics in creating a theocratic state can only be understood in the context of Iran's clash with the U.S. After months of trying to gain control of events in Iran, Bazargan and Yazdi resigned following the seizure of the embassy. Thus, the radicals achieved their immediate objective with the takeover. Of greater long-term significance, however, the clerics won the popular vote one month after the seizure for the constitution that gave them virtual dictatorial power. They presented the issue in stark terms: the liberals and leftists who opposed the constitution were lackeys of the West; only revolutionary Islam could humiliate the "Great Satan" and defend the nation. In December and January, the radicals launched their attack on the moderate, but influential, clerics who opposed the constitution, using as they would do many times later "documents" from the U.S. Embassy that allegedly implicated their foes as "American spies" (Hiro, 1985:139–44). Emphasizing their anti-imperialist credentials, the radicals took this banner from the leftists.

Throughout the crisis the radicals moved to extirpate well-established institutions and to create their own. The secular judiciary was put in the hands of the clerics. The bureaucracy was purged and women were forced to wear "proper Islamic dress." Leftists were attacked and removed from the universities. The liberal press was muzzled. A new parliament dominated by the clerics was created. The military was purged and the security forces loyal to the Islamic Republican party were strengthened. It is little wonder, therefore, that when Iran decided to release the hostages after over a year in captivity its chief negotiator described Iran's new position this way: "The hostages are like a fruit from which all the juice has been squeezed out" (quoted in Bakhash, 1984:149).

In sum, the radicals used Iran's conflict with the U.S. to attack the moderates on the grounds that they were too pro-Western and not sufficiently

Islamic. In building its institutions and political coalition, the Iranian Revolution largely defined its Islamic identity in opposition to the West.

Nicaragua

Wanting to remove its troops from Nicaragua, the U.S. helped to establish the Somoza regime in the 1930s when it assisted in the creation of the National Guard.[26] The Nicaraguan Revolution of 1979 was a multiclass rebellion. The leftist Sandinistas (FSLN) took the lead in ousting the Somoza regime, but the bourgeoisie's withdrawal of support for it paved the way for the revolution's victory. The Carter administration had tried for months to get Somoza to leave in the hope that the liberal bourgeoisie would assume power; it failed, however, in spite of having ended its financial and military support.[27]

Wary of each other, the U.S. and the new regime nevertheless established cordial ties. Carter believed that the U.S. should support the new regime for several reasons: it deserved the benefit of the doubt; Washington's assistance could perhaps influence the revolution in a positive direction; and the U.S. owed the Nicaraguan people its help in reconstructing their devastated country following decades of Washington's support of the corrupt Somoza family (Pastor, 1987:191–97). Desperately in need of capital, and wanting to maintain its friendship at the time with the U.S., the new regime accepted American assistance. From 1979 until its end in 1981, Washington provided $118 million in direct aid, making it Nicaragua's largest donor and providing an amount far greater than it had provided the Somoza regime during any similar time period. As a condition for continuation of the aid, Washington insisted that Managua not support the hardline Marxist rebels (FMLN) in El Salvador, who had strong links with Cuba (Pastor, 1987:208–12; Kagan, 1996:134–47). The Sandinistas accepted the condition but believed that it infringed upon Nicaragua's sovereignty and natural propensity to want to support another revolutionary movement. For Washington, the condition was not unreasonable, given its level of support, and given the Sandinistas' ties to Cuba and the Soviet bloc.

Stage One (Domestic Conflict). Like most revolutions, the revolutionary coalition experienced a honeymoon following its victory. Since the Sandinistas had led the revolt against Somoza and controlled the guns, they were the dominant group. The Sandinistas' National Directorate became the power behind the government, which was headed by a five-member Junta consisting of two prominent members (Alfonso Robelo and Violeta Chamorro) from the bourgeoisie.[28] Although party documents indicate that the FSLN regarded their alliance with the bourgeoisie as only temporary, they said upon coming to power that they were committed to free elections, a pluralist society, and a mixed economy (Gilbert, 1988:36–40).

The rupture between the two groups came in the spring of 1980 when the Sandinistas proposed expanding the parliament to a number that would assure Sandinista control (Christian, 1985:147–60). Robelo and Chamorro resigned from the Junta in protest. In August the Sandinistas declared that elections would be postponed for five years. Dismayed by the turn of events, some in the bourgeoisie contemplated violence while others began open protests.

Stage Two (Externalization).   Just as the clash between the Sandinistas and the bourgeoisie was becoming full-blown, the FSLN began arming and assisting the Salvadoran rebels in the fall of 1980. The Carter administration accused Managua in September of sending small amounts of arms to the insurgents and threatened to cut off its aid; the Sandinistas responded for a brief period by suspending its support (Pastor, 1987:227–28). By November, however, Nicaragua began shipping numerous weapons. Aware of Managua's actions, Carter terminated aid shortly before he left office in January 1981.

Why did the Sandinistas send these arms to the Salvadoran rebels? Their motivations are debatable and not entirely clear (Pastor, 1987:224–25). One interpretation is the spiral model: the Sandinistas supported the guerrillas because they feared President-elect Reagan, whose Republican platform in the summer of 1980 called for an end of U.S. support for the "Marxist government" in Managua. Basing his mammoth study of U.S.–Sandinista relations on interviews of elites from both countries, Kagan disputes this. He claims that the FSLN was going to send arms to the rebels regardless of the U.S. election results but delayed the timing in order to help Carter's campaign:

> The Sandinistas, however, had established their plans for resuming arms shipments at least two weeks before the American election, at a time when the contest was judged too close to call. . . . Their decision to resume shipping the weapons was unrelated to the American election results. (1996:162)

Certainly the Sandinistas supported the rebels for ideological reasons, and some immediate factors included the guerrillas' planned offensive for later that year, the pressures from communist states to deliver the weapons, and the FSLN's desire to gain a regional ally (Kagan, 1996:160–62). Nevertheless, this action marked the biggest turning point of the revolution, for the Sandinistas knowingly brought Nicaragua into conflict with the U.S. and escalated their struggle with the bourgeoisie. The Sandinistas immediately and boldly increased their aggression against the moderates, claiming that their ties to the U.S. threatened the revolution. In summarizing the FSLN's domestic actions in just the first couple of weeks of arming the rebels, Pastor says:

> The FSLN strengthened its armed forces and stepped up its harassment of internal moderate groups. The police arrested Robelo on November 9, 1980, and censored press coverage of his political party's upcoming rally at Nandaime. Salazar was killed one week later, and the government began to harass and restrict the access to the radio by the church and especially Archbishop Obando y Bravo. (1987:223)

The suspicious murder of Jorge Salazar, who represented many farmers, ended the challenge of the Sandinistas' most populist and threatening foe (Christian, 1985:170–85).

Stage Three (U.S. Hesitation).   Carter's decision to end the assistance in January 1981 brought relations between the two states into conflict. Managua and the new Reagan administration had a chance, although a poor one, to repair the relations. Contrary to what many believe, "U.S. policy," says Pastor, was not "so neatly divided between the Carter and Reagan administrations" (1987:191). Neither Carter nor Reagan in 1981 wanted a break in ties (Kagan, 1996:173–74). And contrary to H_{1b} that the U.S. became hostile when the radicals ousted the moderates in the spring of 1980, U.S. Ambassador Pezzullo even encouraged the bourgeoisie not to take a confrontational stance toward the Sandinistas (Kagan, 1996:138–39; Pastor, 1997:211–12). Moreover, during the fall of 1980 when the bourgeoisie became more aggressive, Pastor (1987:221–23) says that Washington did not intervene to support them.

Stage Four (U.S. Hostility).   The new Reagan administration in 1981 made a weak effort to mend the damaged relations between the two states. Reagan authorized the CIA to work with exiles in March; the administration cut off aid in April in spite of evidence that the Sandinistas had curtailed their support of the rebels; and the U.S. began military exercises with Honduras in October during negotiations with Managua. Nevertheless, the

Sandinistas might have seized an opportunity to repair the relations in the fall if they were so inclined. Supporting H_{3b}, Reagan officials worried almost exclusively about the Sandinistas' support of the Salvadoran guerrillas (Kagan, 1996:167–77). Believing that it had few options, the administration skeptically sought a diplomatic solution with Nicaragua. Assistant Secretary of State Enders traveled to Managua in August and proposed that the U.S. restore its aid to Nicaragua and pledge not to intervene in or threaten to use force against Nicaragua in exchange for Managua's end of support of the rebels (Kagan, 1996:191). The exchanges were heated, and the Sandinistas resented Enders's imperious manner (Gutman, 1988:77), yet they considered the proposal for over two months in spite of some doubts about the sincerity of Washington. In late October they responded to the proposal by calling it "sterile" (Miranda and Ratliff, 1993:156). The administration decided not to pursue the negotiations any further in spite of some indications that the Sandinistas were still willing to talk.[29] In blaming both sides for the failures of the negotiations, Pastor writes:

> The Sandinistas thus failed to respond specifically to the proposal from Washington and the Reagan administration was unable to return to Managua to explore the nature and the depth of the Sandinistas' concerns. (1987:235)

If in mistrusting the Reagan administration, however, the Sandinistas chose not to cooperate for reasons of security, this would be evidence in support of the spiral model H_2. Miranda and Ratliff instead maintain that ideology and not security determined Managua's foreign policy, claiming that during this time "the Sandinista revolution was in a blooming stage, self-confident and unbending in its rejection of the U.S. and support for both Cuba and the Salvadoran guerrillas" (1991:157). Kagan maintains that the FSLN believed the international "correlation of forces" favored socialism and not the U.S. In rejecting H_2, he says:

> the Sandinistas' actions in the fall of 1981 showed their enormous confidence in the future. It was not fear of the U.S. that prompted the Sandinistas to take a hard line in their foreign and domestic policies, but rather their lack of fear. (1996:197)

Although it might have pursued the diplomatic course more vigorously, the Reagan administration believed that it was running out of options in influencing the Sandinistas to desist from supporting the guerrillas. In December Reagan authorized American support to Nicaragua's anti-Sandinista rebels, the contras, in Honduras, hoping to gain bargaining leverage to counter Managua's support of the Salvadoran rebels (Kagan, 1996:200–203). Following the successful Salvadoran elections in March 1982, the administration made Nicaragua a major target in its anti-communist crusade.

Just as the Sandinistas significantly increased their repression of the bourgeoisie after arming the insurgents in November 1980, they likewise escalated tensions with the moderates during and after the negotiations with Enders. Kagan writes:

> The link between foreign and domestic policies was never clearer than during the three months after Enders's last visit to Managua. As the Sandinistas chose the course of confrontation with the U.S., they also took further steps against their bourgeois opponents. One week after Enders left Managua, the Sandinistas closed *La Prensa* for three days. At the beginning of September the government announced a state of "economic and social emergency" that was to last for one year. (1996:197)

In sum, although the Sandinistas supported the Salvadoran guerrillas for ideological reasons, this policy knowingly and most consequentially entailed bringing Nicaragua into conflict with the U.S. and radicalizing the revolution against the bourgeoisie. The Sandinistas' aggressive foreign policy of aiding the Salvadoran rebels and confronting the U.S. made it much easier to justify internal repression of the bourgeoisie, to strengthen their dictatorship, and to perpetuate revolutionary mobilization. The unwillingness or inability of the Sandinistas to "Mexicanize" their foreign policy attests to the essential role that conflict with the U.S. played for the revolutionary regime.

The Critical Case of Zimbabwe

Zimbabwe is a strong critical case, for Zimbabwe was one of only two revolutionary states during the Cold War with which the U.S. did not see a break in relations.[30] Unlike the other cases, Zimbabwe had a small bourgeoisie and weak historical ties to the U.S. Moreover, the revolutionary government came to power when the U.S. had its most virulent anti-communists in office in the Reagan administration, and Zimbabwe's revolutionary leader, Robert Mugabe, was an avowed Marxist (unlike other revolutionary leaders who concealed their radicalism). Thus, if the U.S. found it difficult to accept revolutionary states, or if there was a case in which there would develop a spiral of hostility for reasons of mutual suspicions, this should be an excellent case to demonstrate it. Instead, not only did the U.S. and Zimbabwe maintain cordial relations, but they did so for reasons related to the goals of the revolutionary elites and the inapplicability of the theory of externalization.

The revolutionaries took control in April 1980 following a long struggle that ended the white-dominated state of Rhodesia and replaced it with the black-majority state of Zimbabwe.[31] Although the whites under the leadership of Ian Smith had declared independence from Great Britain in 1963, Rhodesia was not recognized by the international community because of its failure to accept majority rule. The white-dominated government faced an internal guerrilla rebellion and an external embargo. Squeezed from both directions, the whites in the late 1970s accepted the Lancaster House Agreement and dissolved the old political order (Davidow, 1984). The new revolutionary government was headed by ZANU (Zimbabwe African National Union) and its leader Mugabe.

Zimbabwe was unique as a revolutionary state in that the ancien regime had been cut off from the international community. Thus, while other revolutions in the Third World sought to sever their countries' previously strong ties with the imperialist powers and to portray the U.S. as hostile in order to initiate radical change, the new revolutionary regime in Zimbabwe instead sought to increase ties with the West. Since the white bourgeoisie were not part of the revolutionary coalition, the revolution in Zimbabwe did not follow the stages, particularly the first stage in which there is a clash between the radicals and moderates, that developed in the previous cases. The revolutionary government, however, faced a serious political challenge from Joshua Nkomo's ZAPU, but it was unlikely that conflict with the U.S. would have strengthened the government against ZAPU given Nkomo's lack of ties to the U.S. Mugabe moved to make Zimbabwe a one-party state and to promote social reforms.[32] Nevertheless, the government refrained from large-scale nationalizations for fear of alienating the whites. Unlike in the previous cases, Mugabe sought to keep the bourgeoisie content in order to utilize their economic skills. Since the revolutionary government wanted to keep the whites from fleeing in fear, it had few reasons to externalize its domestic problems with the bourgeoisie. Moreover, Harare sought to gain considerable capital from abroad, in part because of its unwillingness to extract capital from its own bourgeoisie. Consequently, it did not need to portray the U.S. as hostile for domestic reasons, and it did not want to antagonize Washington and hurt its chances for international capital by be-friending Moscow.

Zimbabwe declared itself to be nonaligned and pledged its support for socialism and the anti-imperialist struggle, but it refused arms from Moscow and a request for a Soviet military base. Instead, Harare primarily relied on Great Britain for its arms and security ties. The U.S. and Zimbabwe maintained friendly relations throughout most of the first part of the 1980s (Davidow, 1982–83). From 1981 to 1986 Zimbabwe became the largest recipient of American aid in sub-Saharan Africa, receiving $350 million. Reagan invited Mugabe to the White House in 1982. There stood shoulder-to-shoulder the guerrilla leader who had proclaimed socialism's inevitable triumph and America's most hardline president toward the Left in Cold War history. One might argue that the administration did not behave aggressively because it did not care about Africa, but it did oppose the Marxist regime in Ethiopia, which had previously cut ties with the U.S. and aligned itself with the Soviet Union.[33] Demonstrating that alignment and not ideology motivated its foreign policy, Washington supported Jonas Savimbi's UNITA, a Marxist group, in Angola against the Marxist government, which had aligned itself with Moscow. One might also argue that the U.S. did not act in a hostile way because Zimbabwe was not that radical in its domestic policies. But Mugabe was a Marxist, sought to create a one-party state, and implemented some socialist measures (Shaw, 1986). In fact, the U.S. did not react so much to increasing radicalism in Zimbabwe's domestic realm as it responded to hostile changes in Harare's foreign policy (Herbst, 1990:232–33). Thus, after Zimbabwe had co-sponsored the United Nation's resolution that condemned the American invasion of Grenada,[34] but refused to vote for the resolution condemning the Soviet downing of South Korean Airliner 007, Washington reduced Zimbabwe's foreign aid (Nichol, 1983:600).

Some Generalizations and Implications

How generalizable is this theory to other cases involving the breakdown in relations between the U.S. and Third World revolutionary states? It might appear that this explanation would not be applicable to some other cases, for the Cuban, Iranian, and Nicaraguan revolutions were urban-based and multiclass, yet many revolutions in the Third World occurred in primarily agrarian countries with a smaller bourgeoisie. Moreover, many of these revolutionary movements had become consolidated before they gained power (Dix, 1983). Thus, perhaps there was not the need to externalize an internal power struggle.

Externalization, however, was a, if not the, critical factor in the foreign policy of nearly all other revolutionary states. The U.S. had fewer possibilities of establishing friendly links with consolidated revolutions (e.g., Algeria, Mozambique) given their initial pro-Soviet ties, yet these revolutions tended to be anti-colonial ones that had become consolidated as a consequence of having engaged in conflicts with their colonial powers. After years of colonial rule and looking outward to the imperialist powers, the revolutionary elites wanted to turn inward and eliminate the distortions from colonial rule, defeat or destroy the old groups that had cooperated with the colonial powers, and gain capital to reconstruct new societies (Young, 1994). In order to make these radical changes, the revolutionaries projected or continued to project the West as its enemy; the U.S., representing the West and status quo, became a target for their wrath. With agrarian revolutions, the revolutionaries faced fewer domestic challenges from other rivals for control of the revolutions than from the old groups tied to colonialism. International tensions were primarily used to weaken the "old interests . . . in the destruction of the existing state" (Conge, 1996:28).

Recent scholarship on the early relations between the Chinese Revolution and the U.S. supports this theory. This case was of great importance for U.S. foreign policy and international politics. It is important in testing the strength of this theory, for, unlike the three original cases, China had a relatively small bourgeoisie and the U.S. did not have a strong imperialist legacy, and the U.S. had incentives to initiate hostilities with China given that the revolution was communist. For decades many have believed that "alleged" American aggression and policy mistakes toward the revolution in the late 1940s prevented what was dubbed a "lost chance" to establish friendly ties. Although controversial foreign policy issues are rarely resolved, leading scholars in a recent symposium in the journal *Diplomatic History* (Chen, 1997; Cohen, 1997; Garver, 1997; Sheng, 1997; Westad, 1997) all reject the "lost chance" argument as a myth. It is also dismissed by Christensen (1996:139–42) and Sheng (1998) in their path-breaking books. These scholars support this theory of externalization in arguing that Mao's ideological goals in transforming Chinese society in general and his political goal of eliminating groups with international links in particular required that he treat the U.S. as an enemy. Chen says that "the Chinese Communist Party's confrontation with the U.S. originated in the party's need to enhance the inner dynamics of the Chinese Revolution" (1997:77). Westad adds that Mao "realized that the Chinese bourgeoisie and the intellectuals, including quite a number of party activists . . . wanted China to keep a door open to the U.S.," and he "worried that without closing the door to the Chinese Revolution could lose its momentum" (1997:115). With respect to the Chinese Revolution and the Cold War, Garver writes:

> China's leaders in 1949 understood that they had the option of accommodation with the U.S.—that the Truman administration sought such an outcome. They deliberately rejected that path and decided instead to bring the PRC into a close and comprehensive alliance with the USSR. (1997:92)

Contrary to the allegations of Hunt and others who maintain that U.S. foreign policy was "rigid" and "reflexive" in its antagonism to revolutionary states, Washington was instead "rigid" and "reflexive" toward Third World states, revolutionary or not, that befriended the Soviet Union. But there were only three illiberal revolutionary states—Zimbabwe, Iran, and Bolivia in the 1950s—during the Cold War that did not establish warm ties with the Soviet Union. The Bolivian Revolution is particularly salient in supporting the hypothesis that U.S. foreign policy was motivated by Cold War/realist considerations instead of the alternative Marxist hypothesis emphasizing economic interests; for in spite of the fact that the revolution involved nationalizations that adversely affected American economic interests, the U.S. maintained good ties because La Paz kept its distance from Moscow. Likewise, and contrary to the Marxist hypothesis, for many years before the Cold War the U.S. had uneasy relations with the Mexican Revolution, yet Washington established warmer ties in the 1930s just when Mexico nationalized the oil industry. In fact, the U.S. had few economic interests in most revolutionary states, and there is little evidence that American political elites thought in economic terms about them. Iran was the one revolutionary state that had bad relations with the U.S. and also had poor relations with the Soviet Union. Yet the Reagan administration, ironically, was willing to befriend the extremely hostile Iranians in selling them arms at the expense of the less hostile Nicaraguans, largely because Iran was also antagonistic to the Soviet Union and Nicaragua was an ally of Moscow. The

U.S.' support for Titoism, or national communism, and its alliance with Communist China after its break with Moscow, demonstrate that alignment and not ideology determined U.S. foreign policy.

This research not only challenges Walt's spiral model with respect to this dyad, but casts doubts on his theoretical understanding of revolutionary states, particularly Third World ones, as well. The transnational linkages associated with Third World revolutionary states call into question the spiral model's assumption that these states can be treated as unitary actors. Using a structural realist framework, moreover, Walt assumes that anarchy compels all states to seek security as its overriding goal (Waltz, 1979:93–97). Thus, he does not differentiate between status quo states and revolutionary states in this regard. But revolutionary states are different from status quo states, for they often value power and their ideological interests over security (once a minimal level is achieved). Indeed, these cases demonstrate how the radicals risked their states' security in seeking absolute domestic power and international clout in challenging the U.S.; they, however, enhanced their own political security. Walt dismisses ideology as the basis for the foreign policy of revolutionary states as being too vague (Walt, 1992:325–27), yet Third World revolutionary states, given their imperialist legacies, had ideologies that specifically targeted the West for their anger. If the Cuban, Iranian, and Nicaraguan revolutionaries had sought security above all else, they could have achieved this given the ample opportunities they could have pursued with Washington during the early days of their regimes; but doing so would have required that they abort their revolutions' anti-American core. Ironically, Walt's study of revolutionary states attempts to overlay a structural realist framework on a topic traditionally studied by classical realists. Whereas structural realists emphasize anarchy and the defensive goals of states, classical realists (Organski, 1968; Kissinger, 1973; Schweller, 1994; Rose, 1998; Zakaria, 1998) stress power and interests, specifically, with respect to revolutionary states, the dramatic remaking of power and interests often for offensive purposes. In showing the limits of Walt's theory, this article demonstrates the need to bring back to the study of international politics what Schweller (1994) calls the "revisionist state." However, the revisionist state need not be a major power seeking hegemony but may even be a weak state capable of manipulating the international environment.

This article contributes to revolutionary theory in demonstrating how important international conflict was to the consolidation of revolutions. But the starting point in understanding this international conflict should be the domestic conflicts in the revolutionary states. Being fundamentally different from other states, revolutionary states crave a status quo enemy. Moreover, one of the more vexing problems has been why there have not been more successful revolutions given the high number of rebellions throughout the Third World (Dix, 1984). These cases suggest the tenuous relation between the bourgeoisie and their support for revolution. When the bourgeoisie supported the revolutions, the potential for conflict between them and the radicals after the fall of the ancien regimes was high. It is tempting to attribute the hostility of Cuba, Iran, and Nicaragua following their upheavals to previous American imperialism toward them before their revolutions, but the ideological goals of the radicals and the sharp clash between the radicals and bourgeoisie in these three revolutions greatly contributed to their strong hostility toward the U.S.

In spite of its minimal attention, this theory of externalization should be applicable in the future even if it does not involve a revolutionary state. As globalization and transnationalism increase, polities may become divided between groups that have international connections and those that do not. Domestic conflict may lead one group to use international conflict to weaken another group. For example, one can imagine in Russia anti-Western groups provoking conflict with the U.S. and Europe in order to weaken other pro-Western groups, given the divergent views that different groups have historically held about the West, and given the social rifts and problems that have been occurring as the country has tried to integrate itself into the world economy. Moreover, many think that ethnic conflict will become more prevalent in the future, and externalization can occur between two states with overlapping ethnic groups. A different ethnic group in one of the states might instigate hostilities with the other state in order to justify repression of the other ethnic group within its own country (Saideman, 1997).

Conclusion

The breakdown in relations between the U.S. and these Third World revolutionary states was caused primarily by the revolutionary states. The choices that they made were largely determined by their revolutionary goals and constrained by their domestic politics. Given the ties that the bourgeoisie in the revolutionary states had with the U.S., the radicals were able to externalize their struggles with the bourgeoisie in provoking hostility with Washington. This article refutes the commonly held view that the U.S., antagonistic to revolutionary change, pushed the revolutionary states to an unwanted position of hostility. This view mistakenly believes that Washington provoked the conflicts, for it had been an imperialist power with regard to the three countries, became antagonistic to the revolutionary regimes at some point, and was the more powerful of the two states. I also demonstrate the limits of Walt's theory with respect to Third World revolutionary states.

This study also strikes a blow at the dominant school of thought about the Cold War—post-revisionism (Gaddis, 1972, 1983), which believes that while U.S. policies in Europe were appropriately reactive, American policies in the Third World were mistakenly aggressive. The post-revisionists accept "U.S. European policy while separating it sharply from U.S. Third World policies" (Macdonald, 1995–96:155). This research shows with respect to this critical dyad, however, that although the U.S. overreacted after the breakdown in relations, its policies were initially reactive. Post-revisionism criticizes Washington for its failure during the Cold War to distinguish between "nationalists" and "communists," yet both types, in seeking to varying degrees to re-order society and withdraw from the international system, became hostile to the U.S.[35] The post-revisionists, moreover, ridicule the idea of "monolithic communism," yet with few exceptions Third World revolutionary states were natural allies of the Soviet Union (although not "controlled" but led) in their hostility toward the U.S. In short, the failures of U.S. policies in the Third World were less a result of misperceptions and misunderstandings, and more the consequence of genuine differences between the two. One of the biggest of these, given the legacy of imperialism, was the lack of stability in some Third World states.

NOTES

1. On the U.S. relations with Third World revolutionary states see Pastor, 1987, 1991; Feinberg and Oye, 1983; Macdonald, 1992; Peceny, 1995; Lake, 1985; LaFeber, 1984; Blasier, 1976; Kolko, 1988; Adelman, 1986; and Blachman, LeoGrande, and Sharpe, 1986.

2. Although Walt examines the more general relations of revolutionary states and status quo powers as opposed to the U.S. and Third World revolutionary states, and although his dependent variable is limited to war as opposed to other kinds of hostility short of it, his ideas are applicable to the dyad examined in this article. In fact, Walt

(1996:2) asserts that his research is motivated by the problems that the U.S. has had with revolutionary states.

3. This article considers only illiberal revolutions during the Cold War. They involved the violent overthrow of the old regimes by mass-based social movements, and they also entailed the creation of new political, social, and economic orders with an emphasis on promoting social equality and the centralization of political power. I exclude liberal revolutions from the population set, for these revolutions, which emphasize liberty and the decentralization of the political order, were not common in the Third World during the Cold War. I consider the following to have been illiberal revolutions during the Cold War: Afghanistan 1978, Algeria 1962, Angola 1975, Benin 1972, Bolivia 1952, Burma 1962, Cambodia 1975, China 1949, Cuba 1959, Egypt 1952, Ethiopia 1974, Grenada 1979, Guinea-Bissau 1974, Iran 1979, Iraq 1958, Laos 1975, Libya 1969, Madagascar 1975, Mozambique 1975, Nicaragua 1979, North Korea 1948, South Yemen 1967, Vietnam 1945, and Zimbabwe 1980. There is no universally accepted population set of revolutions, but for a good typology of revolutions see Dix, 1983; and Shugart, 1989. On social revolutions see Skocpol, 1979, 1994.

4. On the case study approach see Eckstein, 1976; Lijphart, 1971; George, 1979; and King, Keohane, and Verba, 1994.

5. On the similarities of these revolutions in spite of striking ideological differences see Dix, 1983; Farhi, 1990; and Shugart, 1989.

6. The assumption is that the U.S. at least theoretically had a chance to establish positive relations with these revolutionary states. Because of its involvement in the war in Indochina, however, the U.S. had little chance to establish cordial ties with Vietnam following its successful revolution in 1975. Nevertheless, Vietnam was the exception to the U.S. policy of not supporting the colonial powers (France) against anti-colonial movements.

7. On the spiral model see Jervis, 1976, 1978; and Glaser, 1992. On its applications or a variant of it to this dyad see Walt, 1996.

8. These suspicions usually occur because of the revolutionaries' hostile ideology, different interpretation of their historical relationship, and difficult domestic concerns; the status quo states contribute to the suspicions because of their difficulty in perceiving the revolutionaries' intentions, their reliance on hostile exiles, and in the loss of diplomatic expertise. See Walt, 1996:33–37.

9. The idea that the foreign policy of Third World states is often motivated more by internal threats as opposed to external ones has been well established (David, 1991; Ayoob, 1995).

10. This point that externalization is likely to occur when the radicals are at moderate strength is supported in the literature. See Levy, 1989:273.

11. For a discussion of this externalization theory and the relevant literature see Levy, 1988, 1989; Stein, 1976; and Stohl, 1980. On the classic diversionary theory see Mayer, 1967; Bueno de Mesquita and Lalman, 1990; and Fisher, 1967.

12. Szulc, 1986; Arjomand, 1988; and Miranda and Ratliff, 1993 in particular emphasize these goals in guiding the revolutions.

13. Domínguez, 1989: Ramazani, 1988:9–31; and Kagan, 1996 in particular stress the early anti-American objectives of the radicals.

14. They were liberal in the sense that they wanted democracy and pluralism, but their commitment to social reform and change varied substantially.

15. On the weakness of neopatrimonial regimes see Goodwin and Skocpol, 1989.

16. The revolutionary elites knew that aligning their state with the Soviet Union would provoke a hostile U.S. response. This was a universally understood principle.

17. Internalization would involve the U.S. use of the moderates as stooges in its struggles with the radicals, but the radicals in the early period probably worried more about the moderates using their ties to the U.S. to strengthen their position.

18. On early Cuban–American relations see Thomas, 1971; Benjamin, 1990; Domínguez, 1978; Paterson, 1994; and Morley, 1987.

19. For compelling claims that Castro manipulated this event for domestic purposes and lied about the facts see in particular Domínguez, 1989:19–20; Draper, 1965:122–24; Smith, 1987:52; and Bonsal, 1971:100–109.

20. The cause of the explosion has never been determined, but Cuban dock workers believed that it was an accident. See Thomas, 1971:1269–71.

21. On American–Iranian relations see Cottam, 1988; Gasiorowski, 1991; Bill, 1988; and Rubin, 1980.

22. On U.S. motivations for the coup see Gasiorowski, 1987.

23. On the U.S.' advice to the Shah see Sick, 1985:chs. 4–7.

24. On the clash between the moderates and radicals see Bakhash, 1986:ch. 3; Milani, 1989:ch. 9; Arjomand, 1988:ch. 7; Hiro, 1985:ch. 4; and Chehabi, 1990:ch. 7.

25. On Carter's diplomatic approach see Sick, 1985:255–93.

26. On early American–Nicaraguan relations see Millett, 1977; Walker, 1991; and Berman, 1986.

27. On the Carter administration's reaction to the revolution see Lake, 1989; Pastor, 1987; and Morley, 1994.

28. On Nicaragua's bourgeoisie see Gorman, 1981; and Everingham, 1996.

29. Gutman (1988) maintains that the administration's efforts were largely a sham, while Kagan (1996:190–99) asserts that the Sandinistas failed to accept serious proposals from Washington.

30. On Zimbabwe as a revolutionary state see Scarritt, 1991.

31. On the transition from Rhodesia to Zimbabwe see Wiseman and Taylor, 1981; Martin and Johnson, 1981; and Gann and Henriksen, 1981.

32. On internal policies see Herbst, 1990.

33. On the Ethiopian Revolution's foreign policy and its hostility toward the U.S. see Tekle, 1989.

34. On the breakdown in relations between the U.S. and revolutionary Grenada see Pastor, 1986; Pastor supports the argument made in this article.

35. This research highlights the difficulty of distinguishing between "nationalists" and "communists": Castro claimed early on to be a non-Marxist nationalist, yet later became a staunch communist; Mugabe claimed to be a Marxist but did not engage in extensive nationalizations and did not side with the Soviet Union; and the Sandinistas fused nationalism with Marxism–Leninism.

REFERENCES

Adelman, J., ed. (1986) *Superpowers and Revolution*. New York: Praeger.

Arjomand, A. (1988) *The Turban for the Crown: The Islamic Revolution in Iran*. New York: Oxford University Press.

Ayoob, M. (1995) *The Third World Security Predicament: State Making, Regional Conflict and the International System*. Boulder, CO: Lynne Rienner.

Bakhash, S. (1986) *The Reign of the Ayatollahs*. New York: Basic Books.

Benjamin, J. (1989) Interpreting the U.S. Reaction to the Cuban Revolution, 1959–1960. *Cuban Studies* 19:145–165.

Benjamin, J. (1990) *The U.S. and the Origins of the Cuban Revolution*. Princeton, NJ: Princeton University Press.

Berman, K. (1986) *Under the Big Stick: Nicaragua and the U.S. Since 1848*. Boston: South End Press.

Bill, J. (1988) *The Eagle and the Lion: The Tragedy of American-Iranian Relations*. New Haven, CT: Yale University Press.

Blachman, M., W. LeoGrande, and K. Sharpe, eds. (1986) *Confronting Revolution: Security through Diplomacy in Central America*. New York: Pantheon.

Blasier, C. (1976) *The Hovering Giant: U.S. Responses to Revolutionary Change in Latin America*. Pittsburgh, PA: University of Pittsburgh Press.

Bonsal, P. (1971) *Cuba, Castro, and the U.S.* Pittsburgh, PA: University of Pittsburgh Press.

Bueno de Mesquita, B., and D. Lalman (1990) Domestic Opposition and Foreign War. *American Political Science Review* 84:747–765.

Chehabi, H. E. (1990) *Iranian Politics and Religious Modernism: The Liberation Movement of Iran Under the Shah and Khomeini*. Ithaca, NY: Cornell University Press.

Chen, J. (1997) The Myth of America's "Lost Chance" in China: A Chinese Perspective in Light of New Evidence. *Diplomatic History* 21:77–86.

Christensen, T. (1996) *Useful Adversaries: Grand Strategy, Domestic Mobilization and Sino-American Conflict, 1947–1958*. Princeton, NJ: Princeton University Press.

Christian, S. (1985) *Nicaragua: Revolution in the Family*. New York: Random House.

Cohen, W. (1997) Symposium: Rethinking the Lost Chance in China. *Diplomatic History* 21:71–75.

Conge, P. (1996) *From Revolution to War*. Ann Arbor: University of Michigan Press.

Cottam, R. (1988) *Iran and the U.S.: A Cold War Case Study*. Pittsburgh, PA: University of Pittsburgh Press.

David, S. (1991) Explaining Third World Alignment. *World Politics* 43:233–256.

Davidow, J. (1982–83) Zimbabwe Is a Success Story. *Foreign Policy* 49:93–106.

Davidow, J. (1984) *A Peace in Southern Africa: The Lancaster House Agreement*. Boulder, CO: Westview Press.

Dix, R. (1983) Varieties of Revolution. *Comparative Politics* 15:281–299.

Dix, R. (1984) Why Revolutions Succeed and Fail. *Polity* 16:423–446.

Domínguez, J. (1978) *Cuba: Order and Revolution*. Cambridge, MA: Harvard University Press.

Domínguez, J. (1989) *To Make A World Safe for Revolution*. Cambridge, MA: Harvard University Press.

Draper, T. (1965) *Castro's Revolution: Myths and Realities*. New York: Praeger.

Eckstein, H. (1976) "Case Study and Theory in Political Science." In *Handbook of Political Science Strategies of Inquiry*, edited by N. Polsby and F. Greenstein. Reading, MA: Addison-Wesley.

Everingham, M. (1996) *Revolution and Multiclass Coalition in Nicaragua*. Pittsburgh, PA: University of Pittsburgh Press.

Farhi, F. (1990) *States and Urban-Based Revolutions: Iran and Nicaragua*. Urbana–Champaign: University of Illinois Press.

Feinberg, R., and K. Oye (1983) After the Fall: U.S. Policy Toward Radical Regimes. *World Policy Journal* 1:201–215.

Fisher, F. (1967) *Germany's Aims in the First World War*. New York: W. W. Norton.

Fursenko, A., and T. Naftali (1997) *"One Hell of a Gamble": Khrushchev, Castro, and Kennedy, 1958–1964*. New York: W. W. Norton.

Gaddis, J. (1972) *The U.S. and the Origins of the Cold War*. New York: Columbia University Press.

Gaddis, J. (1983) The Emerging Post-Revisionist Synthesis on the Origins of the Cold War. *Diplomatic History* 7:171–190.

Gann, L., and T. Henriksen (1981) *The Struggle for Zimbabwe: Battle in the Bush*. New York: Praeger.

Garver, J. (1997) Little Chance. *Diplomatic History* 21:87–94.

Gasiorowski, M. (1987) The 1953 Coup d'Etat in Iran. *International Journal of Middle East Studies* 19:661–686.

Gasiorowski, M. (1991) *U.S. Foreign Policy and the Shah: Building a Client State in Iran*. Ithaca, NY: Cornell University Press.

George, A. (1979) "Case Studies and Theory Development: The Method of Structured, Focused Comparison." In *Diplomacy: New Approaches in History, Theory and Policy*, edited by P. G. Lauren. New York: Free Press.

George, A., and T. McKeown (1985) "Case Studies and Theories of Organizational Decisionmaking." In *Advances in Information Processing in Organizations*, edited by R. Coulam and R. Smith. Greenwich, CT: JAI Press.

Gilbert, D. (1988) *The Sandinistas: The Party and the Revolution*. New York: Basil Blackwell.

Glaser, C. (1992) Political Consequences of Military Strategy: Expanding and Refining the Spiral and Deterrence Models. *World Politics* 44:497–538.

Goodwin, J., and T. Skocpol (1989) Explaining Revolutions in the Contemporary Third World. *Politics and Society* 17:489–507.

Gorman, S. (1981) Power and Consolidation in the Nicaraguan Revolution. *Journal of Latin American Studies* 13:133–149.

Gutman, R. (1988) *Banana Diplomacy: The Making of American Policy in Nicaragua.* New York: Simon and Schuster.

Hartz, L. (1955) *The Liberal Tradition in America: An Interpretation of American Political Thought Since the Revolution.* New York: Harcourt, Brace.

Herbst, J. (1990) *State Politics in Zimbabwe.* Berkeley: University of California Press.

Hiro, D. (1985) *Iran Under the Ayatollahs.* New York: Routledge.

Hunt, M. (1987) *Ideology and U.S. Foreign Policy.* New Haven, CT: Yale University Press.

Jervis, R. (1976) *Perception and Misperception in International Politics.* Princeton, NJ: Princeton University Press.

Jervis, R. (1978) Cooperation Under the Security Dilemma. *World Politics* 30:167–214.

Kagan, R. (1996) *A Twilight Struggle: American Power and Nicaragua, 1977–1990.* New York: Free Press.

King, G., R. Keohane, and S. Verba (1994) *Designing Social Inquiry: Scientific Inference in Qualitative Research.* Princeton, NJ: Princeton University Press.

Kissinger, H. (1973) *A World Restored.* Boston: Houghton Mifflin.

Kolko, G. (1988) *Confronting the Third World: U.S. Foreign Policy, 1945–1980.* New York: Pantheon.

LaFeber, W. (1984) *Inevitable Revolutions: The U.S. in Central America.* New York: W. W. Norton.

Lake, W. A. (1985) "Wrestling with Third World Radical Regimes: Theory and Practice." In *U.S. Foreign Policy and the Third World: Agenda 1985–86,* edited by J. Sewell, R. Feinberg, and V. Kallab. New Brunswick, NJ: Transaction Books.

Lake, A. (1989) *Somoza Falling.* Boston: Houghton Mifflin.

Levy, J. (1988) Domestic Politics and War. *Journal of Interdisciplinary History* 18:653–673.

Levy, J. (1989) "The Diversionary Theory of War: A Critique." In *Handbook of War Studies,* edited by M. Midlarsky. Boston: Unwin Hyman.

Lijphart, A. (1971) Comparative Politics and the Comparative Method. *American Political Science Review* 65:682–694.

Luxenberg, A. (1988) Did Eisenhower Push Castro into the Arms of the Soviets? *Journal of Interamerican Studies and World Affairs* 3:37–67.

Macdonald, D. (1992) *Adventures in Chaos: American Intervention for Reform in the Third World.* Cambridge, MA: Harvard University Press.

Macdonald, D. (1995–96) Communist Bloc Expansion in the Early Cold War. *International Security* 20:152–188.

Martin, D., and P. Johnson (1981) *The Struggle for Zimbabwe: The Chimurenga War.* London: Faber and Faber.

Mayer, A. (1967) "Domestic Causes and Purposes of War in Europe, 1870–1956." In *The Responsibility of Power*, edited by L. Krieger and F. Stern. New York: Doubleday.

Milani, M. (1989) *The Making of Iran's Islamic Revolution*. Boulder, CO: Westview Press.

Millett, R. (1977) *The Guardians of the Dynasty: A History of the U.S.-Created National de Nicaragua and the Somoza Family*. Maryknoll, NY: Orbis Books.

Miranda, R., and W. Ratliff (1993) *The Civil War in Nicaragua: Inside the Sandinistas*. New Brunswick, NJ: Transaction.

Morley, M. (1987) *Imperial State and Revolution: The U.S. and Cuba*. Cambridge: Cambridge University Press.

Morley, M. (1994) *Washington, Somoza, and the Sandinistas: State and Regime in U.S. Policy Toward Nicaragua, 1969–1981*. New York: Cambridge University Press.

Naftali, T. (1998) "REPLY: Cuba and the U.S." in H-DIPLO, <H-DIPLO at H-NET.MSU.EDU>, 07 August 1998.

Nichol, D. (1983) U.S. Foreign Policy in Southern Africa: Third World Perspectives. *Journal of Modern African Studies* 21:587–603.

Organski, A. F. K. (1968) *World Politics*. New York: Knopf.

Pastor, R. (1986) Does the U.S. Push Revolutions to Cuba?" The Case of Grenada. *Journal of Interamerican Studies and World Affairs*, 1–33.

Pastor, R. (1987) *Condemned to Repetition: The U.S. and Nicaragua*. Princeton, NJ: Princeton University Press.

Pastor, R. (1991) Preempting Revolutions: The Boundaries of U.S. Influence. *International Security* 15:54–86.

Paterson, T. (1994) *Contesting Castro: The U.S. and the Triumph of the Cuban Revolution*. New York: Oxford University Press.

Peceny, M. (1995) Two Paths to the Promotion of Democracy During U.S. Military Interventions. *International Studies Quarterly* 39:371–402.

Ramazani, R. K. (1988) *Revolutionary Iran: Challenge and Response in the Middle East*. Baltimore, MD: Johns Hopkins University Press.

Reiter, D. (1995) Exploding the Powder Keg Myth: Preemptive Wars Almost Never Happen. *International Security* 20:5–34.

Rose, G. (1998) Neoclassical Realism and Theories of Foreign Policy. *World Politics* 51:144–172.

Rubin, B. (1980) *Paved with Good Intentions: The American Experience and Iran*. New York: Oxford University Press.

Saideman, S. (1997) Vulnerability versus Ethnic Ties in Secessionist Conflicts. *International Organization* 51:721–754.

Scarritt, J. (1991) "Zimbabwe: Revolutionary Violence Resulting in Reform." In *Revolutions of the Late Twentieth Century*, edited by J. A. Goldstone, T. R. Gurr, and F. Moshiri. Boulder, CO: Westview Press.

Schweller, R. (1994) Bandwagoning for Profit: Bringing the Revisionist State Back In. *International Security* 19:72–107.

Shaw, W. (1986) Towards a One-Party State in Zimbabwe: A Study of African Political Thought. *Journal of Modern African Studies* 24:373–394.

Sheng, M. (1997) The Triumph of Internationalism: CCP-Moscow Relations before 1949. *Diplomatic History* 21:95–104.

Sheng, M. (1998) *Battling Western Imperialism: Mao, Stalin, and the U.S.* Princeton, NJ: Princeton University Press.

Shugart, M. (1989) Patterns of Revolution. *Theory and Society* 18:249–271.

Sick, G. (1985) *All Fall Down: America's Tragic Encounter with Iran.* New York: Penguin Books.

Skocpol, T. (1979) *States and Social Revolutions.* Cambridge: Cambridge University Press.

Skocpol, T. (1988) Social Revolutions and Mass Military Mobilization. *World Politics* 40:147–167.

Skocpol, T. (1994) *Social Revolutions in the Modern World.* New York: Cambridge University Press.

Smith, W. (1987) *The Closest of Enemies.* New York: W. W. Norton.

Stein, A. (1976) Conflict and Cohesion. *Journal of Conflict Resolution* 20:143–172.

Stohl, M. (1980) "The Nexus of Civil and International Conflict." In *Handbook of Political Conflict,* edited by T. R. Gurr. New York: Free Press.

Szulc, T. (1986) *Fidel.* New York: Morrow.

Tekle, A. (1989) The Determinants of the Foreign Policy of Revolutionary Ethiopia. *Journal of Modern African Studies* 27:479–502.

Thomas, H. (1971) *Cuba: The Pursuit of Freedom.* New York: Harper and Row.

Tilly, C., ed. (1975) *The Formation of National States in Western Europe.* Princeton, NJ: Princeton University Press.

Tilly, C. (1978) *From Mobilization to Revolution.* New York: Random House.

Van Evera, S. (1990) The Case Against Intervention. *Atlantic Monthly,* pp. 65–75.

Walker, T. (1991) *Nicaragua: The Land of Sandino.* Boulder, CO: Westview Press.

Walt, S. (1992) Revolution and War. *World Politics* 44:321–368.

Walt, S. (1996) *Revolution and War.* Ithaca, NY: Cornell University Press.

Waltz, K. (1979) *Theory of International Politics.* Reading, MA: Addison-Wesley.

Welch, R., Jr. (1985) *Response to Revolution: The U.S. and the Cuban Revolution, 1959–1961.* Chapel Hill: University of North Carolina Press.

Westad, O. A. (1997) Losses, Chances, and Myths: The U.S. and the Creation of the Sino-Soviet Alliance, 1945–1950. *Diplomatic History* 21:105–115.

Williams, W. (1972) *The Tragedy of American Diplomacy.* New York: Delta.

Wiseman, H., and A. M. Taylor (1981) *From Rhodesia to Zimbabwe: The Politics of Transition.* New York: Pergamon Press.

Young, C. (1994) *The African Colonial State in Comparative Perspective.* New Haven, CT: Yale University Press.

Zabih, S. (1982) *Iran Since the Revolution.* Baltimore, MD: Johns Hopkins University Press.

Zakaria, F. (1998) *From Wealth to Power: The Unusual Origins of America's World Role.* Princeton, NJ: Princeton University Press.

II

Counterinsurgency and Revolution

As the selections in Part I showed, status quo powers fear successful revolutions. It is not surprising, then, that they seek to prevent the occurrence of revolution, often through military means. Some revolutions, however, occur too quickly for external status quo powers to suppress them. Successful revolutions can occur suddenly through insurrection (a mass uprising that quickly topples the regime it is aimed at) or a coup d'état (a much smaller uprising on the part of the regime's own armed forces that accomplishes the same thing). In either event, the status quo powers find that they face not a revolutionary movement, but a revolutionary regime—and all the possible complications in dealing with it that were analyzed in Part I.

If the target regime, however, cannot be overthrown quickly, then a revolutionary movement often attempts to weaken it steadily through a long-term military campaign known as an insurgency. Indeed, one prominent scholar of this type of conflict, Timothy Lomperis, defined insurgency as "a revolution 'on the slow burn'" (1996, 33). When revolutionary movements attempt to seize power via insurgency, both the besieged government and other status quo powers have the opportunity to stop the revolution— through an operation known as counterinsurgency.

Even militarily powerful states, however, can fail miserably at counterinsurgency, as the United States demonstrated in Vietnam (1964–1973) and the Soviet Union did in Afghanistan (1979–1989). On the other hand, some counterinsurgency efforts have succeeded despite their long duration, such as the British experience in Malaya (1948–1960), which is now part of Malaysia, and Oman (1965–1975), which neighbors oil-rich Saudi Arabia and the United Arab Emirates on the Arabian Peninsula.

Status quo powers prefer to undertake counterinsurgency by "indirect" means—that is to say, through providing arms, training, advisers, or any other form of assistance short of sending their own armed forces to under-take the main burden of militarily defeating the insurgents. For this method to succeed, however, the recipient government must be capable of using the indirect assistance effectively against its revolutionary opponents. Where recipient governments have been unable to do so, external status quo powers have sometimes launched "direct" counterinsurgency efforts in which large numbers of their own troops have borne the main burden of attempting to defeat the revolutionaries.

The two selections reprinted here examine the conditions under which each type of counterinsurgency effort, indirect and direct, can succeed or fail. Timothy P. Wickham-Crowley analyzes the effectiveness of indirect American military involvement in six different Latin American insurgen-cies, and John A. Nagl compares the failure of direct American military in-tervention in Vietnam with the success of direct British military intervention in Malaya.

REFERENCE

Lomperis, Timothy J. 1996. *From People's War to People's Rule: Insurgency, Intervention, and the Lessons of Vietnam.* Chapel Hill: University of North Carolina Press.

5

The Role of Military Power

Timothy P. Wickham-Crowley

Timothy P. Wickham-Crowley examines the validity of the widely held viewpoint that American military assistance was responsible for the defeat of several Latin American guerrilla movements during the 1960s, following the rise to power in Cuba of Fidel Castro. The cases he examines are Bolivia, Colombia, Cuba, Guatemala, Peru, and Venezuela.

The United States did not send its own forces to participate directly in any of these conflicts but did provide arms, training, and other indirect assistance to government forces to aid in their counterinsurgency efforts. Wickham-Crowley argues that this assistance was not the decisive factor in determining the outcome of most of these conflicts. Instead, the loyalty of each country's armed forces to the regime was the most important variable affecting their outcome. Only in Guatemala, according to him, can the United States be said to have played a decisive role in defeating the insurgents.

Although Wickham-Crowley examines only Latin American cases in which the United States was the principal external actor supporting government counterinsurgency efforts, his method of analysis can be applied to other external actors supporting counterinsurgency elsewhere.

Critical Questions

1. Under what circumstances will a country's armed forces become disloyal to the regime they are supposed to serve?

2. How can U.S.-supplied arms and military training intended to bolster a government have the opposite effect?

3. What conditions present in Guatemala made indirect U.S. military involvement decisive to the outcome there?

4. *Although Wickham-Crowley draws his cases from the 1950s and 1960s, to what extent can his analysis be applied to contemporary cases? What has changed, and what has remained the same?*

The governing assumption of this chapter is that the success or failure of guerrilla movements versus government armed forces depends in part on three variables: the internal "financing" of their respective armed forces; their internal solidarity as fighting forces supporting or opposing a political system; and the support each army enjoys from actors outside the nation-state. These three variables, measured for both the government and the opposition guerrilla forces, will jointly determine the relative military strength of the guerrillas and their chances of bringing their irregular war to a successful military conclusion.

We must first confront, though, a curious dichotomy of thought in the literature on guerrilla warfare. In these writings, the success of guerrilla movements is often attributed solely to the national animus of "the people," while the suppression of such movements is often traced directly to U.S. imperialism (i.e., military assistance to Latin American governments).[1] Fidel Castro, in his Second Declaration of Havana, wrote that "Revolutions are not exported; revolutions are the work of the people." Richard Kiessler retorted that guerrilla movements cannot act autonomously but are rather subsystems, with special roles deriving from their location in "global systems of the international revolutionary movement."[2] Few debates concerning the import of U.S. or Cuban "intervention" in Latin America have risen above the level of polemics, and neither polar solution offered above is satisfactory.

I will rather adopt an agnostic view, one that insists upon evidence for either position. From such a perspective, the concept of rendering external "support" for or against guerrilla movements must be better defined than it has been to date in the literature, where support can mean anything from good wishes to shipments of tanks, Kalashnikovs, or napalm.

Governments: Internal Military Resources

Whether or not such external aid is decisive in the outcomes of guerrilla struggles is dependent not only on military assistance itself, but also on the respective military capabilities of governments and guerrillas.[3] This observation is of fundamental importance, for the military capabilities of Latin American armed forces vary enormously. Let us examine such variations more closely.

The simplest way of comparing the military capabilities of the government armed forces is through the study of military budgets, and the work of Joseph Loftus on defense expenditures is particularly helpful here.[4] Elsewhere I have converted the budgets for our six countries [Bolivia, Colombia, Cuba, Guatemala, Peru, and Venezuela] into 1960 U.S. dollars in order to make revealing comparisons about the resources governments were able to commit to counterinsurgency.[5] Venezuela devoted far greater annual resources ($150–250 million) to the military in its guerrilla period than did any of the other five nations. Guatemala ($10–30 million) and Bolivia ($5–12 million) spent far less than the remaining three countries (ca. $50–110 million). Such variation remains even if we compare data for the peak years of guerrilla activity in each country. Each government was typically faced by a group of a few hundred guerrillas, yet their capacities to confront such a challenge—at least as measured by military budgets—exhibited qualitative differences, a point driven home by the data in table 5-1. The ratio of the highest to lowest figures in table 5-1 is more than 25 to 1; even the ratio of the highest to the mean is more than 2.5 to 1.

If one looks closely at Loftus's or my own data, they show that there is no *systematic* tendency for military budgets to increase as guerrilla activity appears or increases. Guatemala, from 1902 to 1966, shows the most pronounced increase in spending, followed by Venezuela (1962–1966), and Cuba (1955–1958). Colombia (1964–1967) exhibits a mixed pattern, and Peru (1965) and Bolivia (1967) show decreases from the previous year. Perhaps more importantly, neither do military shares of government spending show systematic increases in this period. To summarize: "repressive capacity" in our six nations varies greatly, and there is no systematic pattern of increases in military spending—whether in real dollars or in budget shares—in response to guerrilla threats.[6]

If we move instead to *relative* measures of military strength—relative to population, expenditure per soldier, and the like—we still arrive at broadly similar conclusions. If we look at military expenditures per inhabitant, Venezuela again leads the way, followed by Peru, Cuba, and Colombia, with Guatemala and Bolivia again at the bottom, with but a small fraction of the expenditure per person typical of Venezuela.[7] If we consider military

Table 5-1.   Military Expenditures in Years
of Peak Guerrilla Activity (Millions of 1960 U.S. $)

Country/Year	Military Spending	% of Government Spending
Cuba, 1958	$58–64 mil.	13%
Venezuela, 1964	190.2	10
Guatemala, 1966	14.4	11
Colombia, 1965	94.0	26
Peru, 1965	71.0	17
Bolivia, 1967	7.9	16

Sources: Loftus, *Defense Expenditures*, tables 1 and 5; Wickham-Crowley, "A Sociological Analysis of Latin American Guerrilla Movements," chap. 5; see note 4.

expenditure per member of the armed forces, Venezuela leads with $2,809, again followed by Colombia, Peru, and Cuba, all between $1,300 and $1,600 spent per soldier, with Guatemala ($1,115) and Bolivia ($687) spending substantially less than the leaders.[8]

Finally, if we look at the absolute size of the armed forces, and the number of armed-forces personnel per thousand inhabitants, Venezuela is no longer the leader. At the peak of the guerrilla struggles, the Peruvian armed-forces numbered about 70,000, the Venezuelan, Cuban, and Colombian forces numbered about 40,000, the Guatemalans 15,000, and the Bolivians 8,000. Peru and Cuba had the greatest number of soldiers per inhabitant with about six per thousand, followed by Venezuela and Bolivia (four per thousand), and Guatemala and Colombia (two per thousand).[9]

What patterns, then, have we found overall in our quantitative indicators of military strength? First, Venezuela consistently ranked first in any measure of military expenditure, followed rather consistently by Peru, Cuba, and Colombia, and trailed by Guatemala and then Bolivia. That is, richer countries spent more than poorer ones. Second, if we measure repressive power by the relative size of the armed forces, then Peru and Cuba were the leading nations, and Guatemala and Colombia had the lowest numbers of soldiers relative to population. If we conceptualize guerrilla war as a labor-intensive activity, clearly the Guatemalan and Colombian militaries were least prepared for such a conflict, and the Cubans and Peruvians most ready. If we view the ability to equip and train one's soldiery as decisive, then Venezuelan capabilities were superior to those of Peru, Cuba, and

Colombia, which in turn outstripped those of Guatemala and Bolivia. I wish to stress that the ranking of countries on military expenditures parallels their ranking on more conventional measures of economic power, such as GNP per capita—Venezuela leads the group of six, and the poorest countries, Guatemala and Bolivia, trail far behind. Both of these ways of considering military capabilities are illuminating yet incomplete, as we shall see.

Yet *qualitative* aspects of domestic military resources should also be examined. How prepared were Latin American militaries to fight a *guerrilla* war, quite apart from U.S. training programs? The answer is straightforward. Only the Colombian armed forces had any appreciable wartime experience, having fought against *La Violencia* for fifteen years (as well as in the Korean War) and thus possessing exceptional anti-guerrilla experience. In contrast to the Colombians, army and national guard patrols in the five other countries were routinely routed in their early engagements with guerrillas. Latin American soldiers simply were untrained to fight guerrilla wars until the United States began training their officers in counterinsurgency strategy and tactics in Panama and elsewhere.

The theory of anti-guerrilla warfare was also generally underdeveloped in the military journals issued by the various armed forces. Colombia's *Revista de las Fuerzas Armadas* clearly stood out for its high quality in this field, and showed considerable foreign influence in the articles published therein. The theory of guerrilla war was also relatively well developed in the *Revista Militar del Peru* and in journals published by the Peruvian Escuela Superior de Guerra (Army War College) and by the Centro de Instrucción Militar (Military Instruction Center). In one instance, officer-students in 1966 were given as a classroom exercise the suppression of a guerrilla movement, the outlines of which are clearly that of the previous year's guerrilla struggle![10] Venezuela's military journals, in contrast to these two, gave considerably less coverage to the problem of guerrillas, and military-theoretical treatment of guerrilla warfare was simply nonexistent in Guatemala and Bolivia.

What of Cuba, the locale where it all began? While there were thirty-nine articles and editorials from 1953 to 1958 in Cuba's *Boletín del Ejército* (Army Bulletin) on the subjects of guerrilla warfare, irregular war, civil war, subversive war, and terrorism, their theoretical foundations were uniformly weak, especially in contrast to similar articles in Peru and Colombia. Two issues in 1958 featured pictures of men on horseback, of all things (including one on the cover), and an article on guerrillas in the Cuban war for independence defined guerrillas as Spanish troops! The sense of unreality is capped by the fact that the *Boletín del Ejército* never acknowledged that the army was engaged in a guerrilla war. The other armed forces committed many errors, but only the Cuban military went so far as to deny the very existence of its opponent (although it was common practice to label the guerrillas bandits).

Governments: Military Solidarity

The preceding emphasis on the purely quantitative strength of armed forces is somewhat misplaced. War is *not* simply a competition between the size of purses or the number of warm bodies that can be fielded, as the United States government discovered in Indochina. It is also a contest of wills, of commitment to the struggle. The control over the instruments of violence is crucial in war, and such control entails the commitment to the cause by those who wield those instruments. Most importantly, soldiers' commitment to the *patria* or to the military as an institution need not be in the service of causes widely held to be "good" or "noble," for the morale and combative spirit of German troops during World War II were exceptionally high.[11] Morale depends on other things.

Loyalty to the government is the most critical qualitative characteristic of armed forces, for the outcomes of rebellions and revolutionary wars hinge on that loyalty. Sociological analysis, especially in its Marxist variants, tends to deemphasize such military forces in favor of attention to long-term social trends and social causes leading to revolutionary success. Contrariwise, Barrington Moore, a longtime student of revolutions, argues that such an over-emphasis is misplaced, and that the importance of control over the means of violence—i.e., the loyalty of the armed forces—is better understood by Marxist revolutionaries than by Marxist historians.[12]

In a rigorous analysis of the correlates of modern revolutions, Diana Russell found that high disloyalty of the armed forces toward incumbent governments was well correlated with rebel success, and strong loyalty with failed revolts.[13] In Latin America, significantly, both successful guerrilla movements to date have occurred in countries where the army was perceived to be, and in fact was, the tool of a personalistic dictator, rather than an arm of the federal bureaucracy, with the president merely as titular and temporary commander-in-chief. In Cuba and Nicaragua in the 1930s, the old armies were effectively destroyed, and the new armed forces—in

Nicaragua, the National Guard—were rebuilt virtually as the personal armies of Fulgencio Batista (Cuba) and Anastasio Somoza García (Nicaragua). Promotion in these armies was based on loyalty to the national *caudillo* (personal political leader or warlord), who frowned on any independent shows of skill or initiative.[14] The first Cuban military academy did not appear until the 1940s, and those officers with professional military training in the United States were consistently passed over for promotion in favor of Batista's personal favorites. This led to deep political cleavages in the Cuban officer corps. The military's personal loyalty to the younger Somoza was far stronger in Nicaragua (1977–1979) than it was to Batista in Cuba (1956–1958), yet the distinctiveness of these two military histories is striking. That two armies dissolved under the attack of guerrilla units strongly suggests that personalistic military leadership is not conducive to maintaining commitment to battle and the loyalty of the rank and file. . . .

In contrast to these two cases, in those instances where the military can cultivate among the ranks loyalty to the military as an institution and can successfully identify the military as the representative of nationhood (the *patria),* the loyalty of the troops will be far more steadfast. The military, as a total institution, is more capable of generating institutional commitment than any other political organization, to elicit what one author has nicely termed "independent morale." Attempts to understand military behavior through "class analysis" fail utterly to grasp this peculiar capacity of total institutions to suppress class-based differentials.[16] To put it in axiomatic form: The less permeable an organization is to influences stemming from civil society, the more likely that the behavior of the membership will respond to organization-oriented rather than to class-oriented impulses.

In Peru and Colombia, the development of intra-military solidarity appears to have been strong. The military's self-definition of its goals and its stances on key issues in Peru were elaborated in the Centro de Altos Estudios Militares (CAEM—Center of High Military Studies), the rough equivalent of the U.S. Army War College or the military academies. Allemann terms the Peruvian military one of the most "self-defined" armed forces in the region. In the Colombian case, military solidarity was less predicated upon the common organizational experience of the officer corps than on the common combat experiences of the soldiery in the battle against *La Violencia* in the 1950s and 1960s. This campaign against bandits (real and alleged) resulted in a great deal of experience in guerrilla warfare and enhanced troop morale. Soldiers came to see themselves as the last barrier between civilization and complete barbaric anarchy.[17] As the 1960s progressed, however, the Colombian military increasingly found itself defending, as one analyst noted, not civilization, but a particular social order and a particular minority-backed government, creating chinks in that solid morale. Yet the morale of the special elite troops (similar to the U.S. Green Berets), who carried on the bulk of the anti-guerrilla fighting, remained extremely high, supported by special elite perquisites, higher pay, and better training and equipment.[18] Such elite troops appeared elsewhere in Latin America as well and were generally composed of those who had received U.S.-sponsored anti-guerrilla training in Panama.[19]

We have seen that the Cuban army showed very weak internal solidarity when confronted with the guerrillas, while the Peruvian and Colombian armed forces, in contrast, maintained strong institutional coherence. Our other cases lie in the gray area in between. The Bolivian army was composed in its bulk of peasant conscripts who received no pay, but only room, board, and uniforms.[20] Little information exists on Bolivian military solidarity in 1967, save for a few fragmentary items. First, Bolivians have been an extremely nationalistic people—at least since the 1952 revolution. This has implications for soldiers' behavior in a battle against guerrilla forces led by Cubans. Second, the military high command initially resisted, not welcomed, U.S. aid in the suppression of the guerrilla movement.[21] Third, President René Barrientos was an army officer whose major social support stemmed from the Quechua-speaking Bolivian peasantry, who formed the bulk of the armed forces. Fourth, there is no evidence of officer desertions to the guerrillas despite Guevara's highly charitable treatment of captives. All these facts suggest a moderately high degree of solidarity within the Bolivian armed forces in 1967.[22]

There remain the cases of Venezuela and Guatemala, which are distinctive in that military officers contributed either a substantial number of (Venezuela) or virtually all (Guatemala) the early guerrilla leadership. The desertions of junior officers to join a guerrilla movement provide prima facie evidence that military solidarity was considerably less than airtight in these cases (with desertions common in Cuba as well).

In Venezuela, the armed forces had been discredited by the simultaneously inefficient and repressive performance of military governments from 1948 to 1958, including that of Pérez Jiménez. His 1958 overthrow (with military support) had apparently spread social reformist, if not revolutionary, ideas among the junior officers, who could not be immune to the revolutionary currents then coursing through Venezuelan society.

The first three years of the Betancourt presidency (1959–1964) saw his governing AD party trying to accommodate both leftists and right-wing military *golpistas* (coup-makers), the latter staging several coup attempts in that period. The alliance of left-wing junior officers with parties of the radical left—the Communists (PCV) and the Fidelista MIR—grew stronger as Venezuelan society became more polarized up to 1962. The results in 1962 were two military revolts—with some civilian support—at the port cities of Carupano (May) and Puerto Cabello (June). Both were suppressed by loyalist forces, the latter with very heavy bloodshed. Participating officers who escaped the ensuing cleanup joined the nascent FALN guerrillas in the mountainous areas of the interior. . . . The decisive suppression of these revolts apparently broke the back of the radical left within the military, which thereafter showed relatively high degrees of solidarity in its anti-guerrilla campaigns, especially in the years 1964 to 1966.

The internal influence of officers-turned-guerrillas on FALN policy was appreciable. In their early days, the guerrillas tried to avoid at all cost the killing of soldiers, trying to limit their opponents' firefight casualties to policemen and members of DIGEPOL (the national police force). In conjunction with this policy, their pamphlets called upon soldiers to desert or to turn their guns back upon their commanding officers. President Betancourt, although apparently under considerable pressure, did not untie the hands of the army and air force until after the guerrillas killed four members of the national guard in an attack on an excursion train in September, 1963. Massive roundups followed, several radical congressmen lost parliamentary immunity and were put under house arrest, and the armed forces were given a somewhat freer hand to pursue the guerrillas. At the time, a MIR leader charged that in fact a shadow coup had taken place, with the military in real control of the government, a charge that Betancourt vehemently denied. Once the FALN had killed the guardsmen—in what was widely characterized as a cowardly attack—attempts by the FALN to distinguish between police and soldiers could no longer be effective. The *cazadores* (hunters or rangers), the elite trained by the United States at Fort Gulick in Panama, apparently were exceptionally strong in their anti-guerrilla feelings.[23] Various guerrilla memoirs indicate the immunity of this group to the guerrillas' "subversive" appeals during the military campaigns of 1964–1966.

Finally, in Guatemala, the fact that the guerrilla movement began as an abortive military coup had great consequences for the nature of the anti-guerrilla campaigns of the 1962–1965 period. Given that Guatemalan Indian peasant recruits were more or less pressed into service in virtual village roundups,[24] a pattern common in Central America, one would not expect high solidarity with the nationalist and institutional appeals of their *Ladino* officers. When one adds the military revolt of 13 November 1960—in which the latter-day guerrilla chiefs had participated—which was nationalist and anti–United States in its origins, one can see that the guerrillas had strong claims on the very symbols that military organizations try to employ, while the military had few solidary foundations. In addition, guerrilla leaders Turcios Lima and Yon Sosa maintained close contacts with their old junior-officer cohorts, and both are rumored to have appeared at officers' parties in the capital during the insurgent period. As a result of these conditions, the anti-guerrilla campaign (until 1966) has been described as "insouciant," and another observer said that the guerrillas were treated "with great indulgence" until the latter period.[25] Yet another source of cleavage in the Guatemalan armed forces was an internal split between the old-line officers (e.g., Carlos Arana Osorio, who directed the brutal 1965–1967 anti-guerrilla campaign) and the graduates of the Escuela Politécnica, among whose ranks was numbered former president Jacobo Arbenz.[26]

This "indulgent" situation changed drastically in the mid-1960s. The campaign of 1966–1967 was apparently guided by U.S. Green Beret advisors who found in Colonel Arana a man who would take their advice, as one observer put it. Army intelligence was gathered by working over revolutionaries, from guerrilla deserters, and from retired NCOs and former soldiers living in the target villages. Indulgence was replaced by very nearly its opposite, which suggests that guerrilla sympathizers had been purged from the army, or that the command structure of the army was transforming otherwise-reluctant soldiers into effective anti-guerrilla fighters. The army became a profoundly conservative organization, perhaps partly in response to the latest of recent attempts by the revolutionary left to arm the peasantry to create a counterforce to oppose the army. (The previous attempt to do so, in 1954, may well have been the prime reason the military leadership stood aside when the Arbenz government was faced with the U.S.-organized Castillo Armas invasion.)[27]

We may summarize our analysis of military solidarity in table 5-2, where I indicate (roughly) the state and trend of solidarity in the armed forces in

Table 5-2. Trends in Military Solidarity
in Response to Guerrilla Conflicts

Country	Changes in Solidarity
Cuba	Moderately low to low
Venezuela	Moderately low to moderately high
Guatemala	Moderately low to moderately high
Colombia	High to moderate
Peru	High to moderately high
Bolivia	Moderate/High (?) to Moderate

Source: See text.

each nation. The first measure of solidarity is taken prior to the guerrilla struggle, and the second indicates the direction in which solidarity moved in response to the struggle.

Finally, one should not underestimate the impact of the Cuban revolution itself on "closing the ranks" of the armed forces in the other five nations. No military institution will stand aside and watch the government create an independent counterforce, such as Arbenz may have attempted to do in Guatemala in importing arms. The fact that Castro had, upon achieving power, destroyed the old armed forces was imprinted strongly in the minds of the officer corps in Latin America. Especially memorable may have been Castro's killing of 600 senior officers of Batista's army. Hence, senior officers in Latin America routinely stressed that the guerrillas' plans involved "elimination of the Armed Forces . . . as happened in Cuba."[28]

Governments: External U.S. Military Assistance

The literature abounds with (mostly scattered) references to this or that item of the role of the United States in the anti-guerrilla struggle, whether to a yearly purchase of helicopters, the use of napalm, Panamanian anti-guerrilla training, or government-to-government pressure. Rather than survey this largely impressionistic material, I will systematically analyze four forms in which U.S. military aid may have affected the outcomes of Latin American guerrilla struggles: through grants and sales of goods and services, through military training and intelligence, through informal pressures, and through the commitment of troops.

Money and Weaponry: Grants

The United States has provided military assistance to Latin American and other nations in the form of credits and loans for military purchases, surplus stock grants, and military training. It is necessary to put this assistance to Latin America in comparative perspective, as is rarely done in the literature. From 1950 to 1973, the United States' Military Assistance Program (MAP) totaled some $35.9 billion, of which only $0.8 billion went to Latin America. During this same period, the U.S. government and private companies sold and delivered some $13.4 billion worth of war matériel throughout the world as Foreign Military Sales (FMS), about $0.5 billion going to Latin America.[29] Latin American nations were thus recipients of about 2 percent of all U.S. military assistance and about 4 percent of all U.S. military sales. The region received a far lower share of military assistance and sales, in fact, than it did of U.S. trade, investment, or economic aid.[30] The widely held notion that Latin America was a *special* focus of United States' quantitative military largesse is mistaken.

These broadly sketched figures do not indicate, however, in what way these relatively modest expenditures affected the repressive power of Latin American armed forces. If the United States were funding half of the military budget of Cuba during a guerrilla war, this would have greater consequences than if it were to fund one-hundredth of the Venezuelan military budget in peacetime. We have evidence that some U.S. MAP aid is factored into the budget-making process of Latin American militaries.[31] How important was such aid in funding military activity in our six select nations?

In table 5-3 I have displayed data on U.S. military assistance to our six countries, as a percentage of each nation's military expenditures. All raw data have been transformed into 1960 U.S. dollars as I did earlier. Only in Bolivia during the 1960s and (with large swings) in Peru throughout the entire two decades, does U.S. military assistance consistently exceed 10 percent of a nation's military budget. The idea that the United States "poured in" aid to support Cuba's Batista is shown to be highly misleading from our comparative perspective. In contrast, that the Guatemalan military received substantial U.S. aid in its anti-guerrilla struggle is borne out by the data, as seen in the jumps in aid in the early 1960s. Looking at the guerrilla years, we

Table 5-3. U.S. Military Assistance as a Percentage of Latin American
Military Expenditures, 1953–1970 (Millions of 1960 U.S. $)

Column A: U.S. Military Assistance
Column B: Military Expenditures of Country
Column C: A as a percentage of B

	Cuba			Venezuela			Guatemala		
	(A)	(B)	(C)	(A)	(B)	(C)	(A)	(B)	(C)
1953	0.5	(50)	1%	—	67.9	0%	—	6.2	0%
1954	1.3	(53)	2	—	65.9	0	—	5.8	0
1955	1.8	(51)	4	—	105.3	0	—	7.2	0
1956	1.9	(53)	5	—	131.6	0	0.4	8.2	4.9
1957	2.1	(56)	4	—	106.7	0	0.3	8.6	3.5
1958	3.1	58–64	5	—	174.2	0	0.1	9.2	1.1
1959	0.4			13.5	191.7	7.0	*	9.6	*
1960	0.2			8.3	174.6	4.8	0.2	9.6	2.1
1961	0.1			9.5	147.6	6.4	0.4	9.3	4.3
1962				10.0	156.5	6.4	1.3	9.0	14.4
1963				7.4	183.0	4.0	2.5	9.3	26.9
1964				9.4	190.2	4.9	1.3	10.9	11.9
1965				6.1	221.5	2.8	1.4	14.1	9.9
1966				10.7	233.4	4.6	1.3	14.4	9.0
1967				0.8	266.9	0.3	1.0	16.0	6.3
1968				0.8	264.2	0.3	0.9	15.1	6.0
1969				0.6	249.3	0.2	1.9	14.7	12.9
1970				0.6	253.7	0.2	1.1	26.3	4.2

see that U.S. aid to Peru (1965) actually dropped 25 percent from the previous year, while that to Bolivia (1967) increased by a similar percentage. Aid
to Peru and Colombia was very erratic, while annual aid to Venezuela hov-
ered around 5 to 6 percent in the mid-1960s, dropping to less than 1 percent
after the guerrilla struggle begins to decline.

It is difficult to believe that military aid amounting to 5 percent or 10
percent of the budget can substantially increase the fighting ability of the
military in these countries. Yet an inside look at the data reveals a more
important role for U.S. aid than might be inferred from these figures. Unlike the United States military, which may be seen as a "capital-intensive"

Table 5-3. (cont.)

	Colombia			Peru			Bolivia		
	(A)	(B)	(C)	(A)	(B)	(C)	(A)	(B)	(C)
1953	4.0	55.0	7.3%	2.6	36.6	7.1%	—	4.2	0%
1954	2.9	62.7	4.6	4.0	33.7	11.9	—	?	0
1955	4.2	63.8	6.6	4.1	35.9	11.4	—	?	0
1956	2.6	62.8	4.1	9.9	59.1	16.8	—	2.4	0
1957	2.4	53.6	4.5	10.7	53.8	19.9	—	2.5	0
1958	2.7	48.9	5.5	7.7	61.0	12.6	0.1	2.1	4.8
1959	2.5	42.2	5.9	4.2	52.3	8.0	0.3	2.8	10.7
1960	2.7	47.3	5.7	3.5	50.1	7.0	*	4.0	*
1961	16.8	54.6	30.8	22.6	51.9	43.5	0.4	4.6	8.7
1962	5.8	90.7	6.4	14.2	51.9	27.4	2.1	4.7	44.7
1963	8.1	90.3	9.0	7.8	80.7	9.7	2.3	6.0	38.3
1964	6.2	85.7	7.2	9.9	78.7	12.8	3.0	4.9	61.2
1965	5.3	94.0	5.6	7.6	71.0	10.7	1.8	9.0	20.0
1966	12.3	94.6	13.0	9.1	70.7	12.9	2.6	8.4	31.0
1967	8.3	97.2	8.5	4.5	89.7	5.0	3.2	7.9	40.5
1968	4.1	127.7	3.2	1.2	89.8	1.3	2.0	7.5	26.7
1969	3.2	73.8	4.3	0.4	?	?	1.6	7.4	21.6
1970	5.6	90.1	6.2	0.5	?	?	1.1	9.7	11.3

Sources: For Column A—U.S. Agency for International Development (AID), Statistics and Reports Division, *U.S. Foreign Assistance and Assistance from International Organizations, July 1, 1945–June 30, 1962* (Revised), pp. 28–50; and *U.S. Overseas Loans and Grants and Assistance from International Organizations: Obligations and Authorizations, July 1, 1945–June 30, 1966,* pp. 25–52; and (same title), *July 1, 1945–June 30, 1975,* pp. 33–61. Column B—Same as for table 5-1.

( ) denotes estimate.

* less than $50,000.

industry, the armed forces of Latin America are labor-intensive organizations. That is, relatively few of their expenditures are for arming the rank and file or for equipment in general. Various sources indicate that 70 to 90 percent of military budgets in the region were for personnel costs in the 1960s, even in a relatively well equipped army such as Colombia's.[32] Only about 10 percent of the budgets are for arms costs, according to one estimate. In such a situation, military assistance equaling 10 percent of the overall budget may, in Edwin Lieuwen's estimation, increase the *arms* budget of the military by 50 to 90 percent, the latter in some of the smaller countries. (This figure was challenged by one congressional witness, who put the increases at closer to 10 percent.)[33]

Not all MAP aid is in the form of weapons grants, but we can estimate the impact of U.S. military assistance on equipment from the sources used in the previous table. We will assume (generously) that 15 percent of Latin American military budgets are for arms procurement and compare the resulting dollar values to the weapons portion of U.S. MAP aid (i.e., not aid in the form of training, etc.) for the mid-1960s, and the late 1950s for Cuba.

In table 5-4, MAP weapons data are derived from the same source as for table 5-3. After trying to exclude non-weapons aid in the data, the resulting estimates of weapons aid are surely still generous as estimates of arms shipments, for Edwin Lieuwen's report to Congress shows other grant expenses which are included in MAP, such as conferences, seminars, and civic-action programs.[34]

Keeping in mind that the estimates of arms spending in the military budgets are generous, and that the estimates of weapons aid are high as well, table 5-4 exhibits a sharp contrast with the overall data of table 5-3. All countries save Venezuela apparently received substantial portions of their weaponry through outright grants. Bolivia's procurement grew an estimated 150 percent through U.S. grants, while the estimated Peruvian, Guatemalan, and Colombian weapons budgets grew by half in response to yearly aid. Cuba's arms capabilities were increased by about one-fourth. If these data are even roughly accurate, U.S. military-assistance programs had a substantial effect on the military capabilities of five of these six countries.

Certain data should be highlighted. Batista's Cuba did not receive especially large amounts of weapons aid from the United States. Since weapons aid from the United States was such a small percentage of the Venezuelan budget, no argument tracing the suppression of the guerrillas to U.S. weapons grants can be sustained. The remaining nations all apparently received substantial boosts in weapons capacity from the grants, even though none of the weaponry sent to Latin America during this period was of the latest design, and much of it came from "excess stocks." Bolivia's army is said to have been virtually rebuilt through United States aid since 1952, and the 1960s budget figures support such a picture. Thus, if we see weaponry in general as crucial to waging counterguerrilla war, then Bolivia was helped the most by such aid, followed by Guatemala, Colombia, and Peru, then by Cuba, and last, receiving little or no weapons grants, Venezuela.

Table 5-4. U.S. Weapons Assistance to Latin America
as a Percentage of Estimated Arms Budgets

Column A: Estimated weapons aid in millions of 1960 $
Column B: Column A as % of estimated military weapons budget, which is estimated at
15% of military spending

	Cuba		Venezuela		Guatemala		Colombia		Peru		Bolivia	
	(A)	(B)	(A)	(B)	(A)	(B)	(A)	(B)	(A)	(B)	(A)	(B)
1956	1.7	21%										
1957	1.8	21										
1958	2.7	28–31										
1959	0.3	?										
. . .												
1962			0.2	4%	1.0	71%	5.2	38%	4.0	52%	1.4	200%
1963			0.3	5	1.9	136	7.4	55	4.4	36	1.6	178
1964			0.3	5	1.0	63	5.4	42	8.3	70	2.0	286
1965			0.3	5	1.1	52	4.9	35	6.7	63	1.2	86
1966			0.04	0	0.8	36	9.6	68	6.8	64	1.6	123
1967			0.04	0	1.4	58	7.3	50	3.6	27	2.0	167
1968			—	0	0.6	26	3.4	18	1.1	8	1.1	100
Totals	6.5	25	1.2	5	7.8	58	43.2	42	34.9	44	10.9	149

Sources: Military spending from table 5-1; weapons share of military spending is estimated at 15% of the total—see text; weapons share of MAP grants: for grants themselves, see US-AID sources for table 5-3; for estimate of weapons share thereof, see text.

We would expect, since these are the nations that experienced major bouts of guerrilla warfare, that they would stand out as targets of military assistance during their guerrilla struggles. In table 5-5 we can examine this hypothesis by comparing military aid in our six countries to the overall Latin American figures for the period 1953–1970.

Aid to this select group of countries, even when taken over this longer period, was 40 percent higher than in the area overall. The other countries in the region received even less aid than the $5.29-per-capita figure would indicate, since our target countries pull up the average. Are these figures "high" or "low?" That is a difficult matter to assess. To put these numbers in one perspective, for example, Soviet military aid to Cuba from 1960 to 1969 was $1.5 billion, just under $200 per capita, $20 per capita per annum. Both

Table 5-5. U.S. Military Assistance Per Capita
in Latin America, 1953–1970 Totals

Country	Military Assistance (millions 1960 $)	Population, 1960 (thousands)	Aid per Capita (1960 $)
Bolivia	$20.5	3,696	$5.55
Colombia	99.7	15,468	6.47
Cuba*	11.4	6,153 (1955)	3.70*
Guatemala	14.1	3,765	3.75
Peru	124.5	10,199	12.21
Venezuela	76.7	7,394	10.37
6-Nation Average	346.9	47,319†	7.33
Latin America	1,097.9	207,379	5.29

Sources: Military assistance—as for table 5-3; population—from J. Mayone Stycos and Jorge Arias, *Population Dilemma in Latin America* (Washington, D.C.: Potomac Books, 1966), p. 2. Cuban population in 1955 is interpolated between the 1950 and 1960 figures. "Latin America" includes the twenty nations listed in table 5-[9].

* Since Cuba received aid for only half of this period, the per capita figure is doubled to match the time periods of the other five nations.
† Uses Cuba's 1960 population: 6,797,000.

figures were about forty times the average value of contemporary U.S. aid to the Latin American nations.[35]

We can focus our attention even more closely by measuring aid in *annual* dollars of military assistance per capita for the area and for our six nations for the entire period, as well as focusing on the period of guerrilla activity proper. The results of these calculations appear in table 5-6.

The data in this table seem clearer. Per capita military assistance to the entire region grew only slightly in the sixties—supposedly the decade of the U.S. counterinsurgency push in Latin America—but was appreciably higher than average in four of our six countries during their periods of guerrilla activity. Bolivia and Cuba show the highest increases in per capita aid over the norm, while Peru and Colombia show only slight, region-wide increases (these two countries, despite internal violence in the latter, were politically more stable than the other nations during their guerrilla periods). Guatemala and Venezuela show increases larger than the last two countries but smaller than the first pair.

Table 5-6. Annual U.S. Military Assistance to Latin America
(in 1960 U.S. Dollars per Capita)

	1953–1970	Guerrilla Period
Latin America	$.30	$.32
Bolivia	.31	.63
Colombia	.36	.37
Cuba	.21	.38
Guatemala	.21	.30
Peru	.68	.72
Venezuela	.58	.74

Source: Tables 5-4 and 5-5; the 1953–1970 column is the last column of table 5-5 divided by 18, except for the Cuban figure, divided by 9. Guerrilla periods are defined as follows: Latin America 1961–70; Bolivia, 1967–68; Colombia, 1964–70; Cuba, 1956–58; Guatemala, 1962–67; Peru, 1965–66; and Venezuela, 1962–68. Population in 1965 is used to calculate per capita figures for the guerrilla period for all countries save Cuba, for which 1955 figures are used. See table 5-5 sources for population data.

What may we conclude? Although our analysis of overall military aid and military budgets shows that U.S. military grants have no appreciable influence in maintaining overall regional military strength, closer examination shows that such aid may be decisive in the crucial area of weaponry. Table 5-7 summarizes our findings by ranking nations according to the degree that they were helped by U.S. assistance. Interestingly enough, we find a pattern opposite to that of domestic military capabilities. The reader may recall that Venezuela consistently ranked first in financial measures of fighting ability, and Bolivia and Guatemala last. This pattern is reversed for military assistance from the United States. Perhaps unsurprisingly, despite all the care and effort involved in the preceding analyses, U.S. military aid went mostly to those countries least financially able to support their own forces and least to those that could, which is precisely the intent of military aid. Sometimes sociology does confirm the obvious, after all.

*Money and Weaponry: Sales**

*Ed. note: This section has been omitted.

Table 5-7. Ranks of Six Nations on the Impact of U.S. Military Assistance
on Anti-Guerrilla Fighting Capacity

Column A: Overall Levels of Military Aid
Column B: Impact on Weaponry
Column C: Degree of Response to Guerrilla Conflict

Country	Rank A	Rank B	Rank C	Final Rank and Average
Bolivia	1	1	1	1
Guatemala	3	2	3	2.7
Peru	2	3.5	5	3.5
Cuba	6	5	2	4.3
Colombia	4	3.5	6	4.5
Venezuela	5	6	4	5

Sources: Column A is from table 5-3; column B is from table 5-4; column C is from table 5-6.

Military Training and Intelligence

In the postwar period through 5 September 1973, Michael Klare reports that the U.S. Army had trained 33,147 Latin American soldiers in the Army School of the Americas in the Panama Canal Zone. In another table, however, he reports 28,621 trained in both the United States and in the Canal Zone in the 1950-to-1975 period, with an additional 43,030 trained in "other areas" (presumably right at home).[39]

Why is the training of soldiers so relevant? Primarily because guerrilla war is a labor-intensive form of war, in which only limited kinds of weaponry (e.g., helicopters, patrol boats, small arms) are effective. As one Peruvian colonel aptly noted, "Guerrilla war is the place where machines are least able to supplant man." Robert Lamberg, perhaps the closest student of the Latin American guerrillas, argued that the most important element of U.S. military aid was training, not money—and that, overall, U.S. aid was "relatively restricted" but "highly effective."[40]

U.S. training at Fort Gulick in the Panama Canal Zone was oriented both to civic action and to the purely military aspects of counterinsurgency. In the Internal Security Department officers were trained in guerrilla, counterinsurgency, and intelligence operations, while in the Technical Department the school had (by 1965) graduated 11,000 officers in "various areas of technical and logistical support," including auto repair, general mechanics, construction engineering, radio repair, medical care, and other areas.[41] Exceptional students were sent for further training to Fort Bragg, Georgia. Among the alumni of the two schools were Marco Yon Sosa and Luis Turcios Lima, later to become Guatemalan guerrilla leaders. (Of the former, one U.S. spokesman noted ruefully, "You can bet he won't be getting any more scholarships from us.")

From the qualitative point of view, the efficacy of such counterguerrilla training is certainly subject to dispute. One alumnus-turned-guerrilla was "scornful" of the value of such training, calling it "mechanical" in that it merely tries to separate the "fish" from the "water" in its inversion of Mao's dictum. A critic of U.S. military-aid programs claims that such training only serves to produce strident anticommunism, further politicizing the armed forces rather than making them professional.[42] Despite these criticisms, and given the rather impressive performance of the Guatemalan guerrillas for half a decade, it seems unwise simply to write off U.S. training as worthless, for the military backgrounds of the guerrilla leadership were clearly helpful in increasing the longevity and fighting experience of the Guatemalan insurgents.

Was U.S. training of Latin American officers of great importance throughout the region, or was it only important in certain countries, perhaps those that actually experienced insurgency? I attempted to judge the focus of U.S. training programs by comparing the number of officers trained in Panama and elsewhere with the armed forces manpower in 1965. The reader is reminded that it is far from clear that all the Panama graduates received counterinsurgency combat training, as can be seen by the distribution of courses in the School of the Americas.

The patterns of table 5-9 are clear, and have little or nothing to do with guerrillas or with patterns of social and political unrest: yet again, small countries close to the United States receive a disproportionate share of U.S. military "attention." This finding holds true whether or not there is a great deal of unrest in each particular nation (compare Costa Rica and Guatemala). Areas that experienced large-scale guerrilla warfare do not stand out in this table, nor do those such as Brazil, Panama, Nicaragua, and the Dominican Republic, which experienced other forms of social unrest at various times. Very little aid went to Cuba, reflecting the fact that training for counterinsurgency began in earnest only after the success of the Cuban revolution. The U.S. Army trained more Bolivians (600) in Bolivia in four

Table 5-9. U.S. Counterinsurgency Training of Latin American Officers
Compared to Armed Forces Manpower (1950–1975)

	A	B	C	D	E
	No. of Officers Trained		Armed Forces		
	U.S./Panama	Total	Manpower, 1965	A/C	B/C
Latin America	28,621	71,651	734,500	.04	.10
Panama	60	4,130	3,500	.02	1.18
Nicaragua	808	4,897	5,000	.16	.98
Honduras	388	2,641	4,000	.10	.66
Costa Rica	33	529	1,200	.03	.44
Guatemala	729	3,030	8,000	.09	.38
Bolivia	502	3,956	15,000	.03	.26
El Salvador	239	1,682	6,600	.04	.25
Ecuador	1,601	4,556	18,000	.09	.25
Dominican Republic	782	3,705	19,300	.04	.19
Uruguay	1,120	2,537	14,000	.08	.18
Colombia	2,527	6,200	40,000	.06	.16
Venezuela	1,675	5,341	35,000	.05	.15
Chile	2,811	6,328	46,000	.06	.14
Paraguay	402	1,435	11,000	.04	.13
Peru	3,385	6,734	70,000	.05	.10
Haiti (to 1963)	475	567	5,900	.08	.10
Brazil	7,544	8,448	200,000	.04	.04
Argentina	2,766	3,676	132,000	.02	.03
Cuba (to 1960)	307	521	40,000 (1958)	.01	.01
Mexico	467	738	60,000	.01	.01

Sources: Columns A and B—Klare and Stein, Armas y poder, pp. 159–60; column C—Loftus, Defense Expenditures, p. 87. Cuban armed forces data are for 1958, based on estimates in the literature on armed forces at their peak under Batista.

months than it trained Cubans anywhere in a decade. Overall the pattern is, once again, for small, low-GNP countries to receive relatively large amounts of counterinsurgency training, while larger, high-GNP nations receive relatively little. Countries close to the United States (geographically speaking) are also clustered near the top, with the major exception of Mexico.

However, if we step back from the numbers for a moment, evidence of the importance of U.S. training programs becomes somewhat more persuasive. The clearest case is that of Bolivia, 1967. In that country, a Mobile Training Team headed by Major Ralph "Pappy" Shelton was dispatched in April with some twenty Green Berets to begin a crash anti-guerrilla training course for six hundred Bolivian soldiers.[43] In late August the "graduates" went into the field against Ché's guerrillas, and he noted in his diary the improvement in the fighting quality of the opposition. One month later the *foco* had been shattered. Given the evidence of the internal decay of the guerrillas, it is still not clear, however, that the training course was instrumental in Ché's demise.

A second important qualification of the numbers in table 5-9 is that those officers and soldiers trained in Panama and elsewhere by the United States tended to be in the forefront of the fighting wherever the guerrillas appeared. Therefore, their importance in the fighting part of the guerrilla war far over-shadowed their relatively modest numbers in the armed forces overall. Judgments of the qualitative impact of such training are quite varied. We have already seen that some alumni of the programs did not think they were worth much. In contrast, two former Panama trainees (one later a guerrilla) allegedly were taught to torture prisoners using a combination of brutal and gentle measures and were even told to do away with prisoners when they could not be taken along.[44] These are serious allegations, indeed, but the evidence for them is somewhat thin—unless we consider similar, validated reports from Indochina, in which case they are more plausible.

Finally, the United States military was an important source of intelligence on guerrilla movements in several countries. U.S. military advisors and CIA agents in Bolivia began examining the guerrilla movement there as early as March 1967, reporting back to Washington on the situation in Santa Cruz. The Guatemalan armed forces, lacking an intelligence section, are said to have relied completely on U.S. intelligence sources during 1966. One might have suspected that two such poor countries might lean heavily on the United States for such help, since it is a relatively refined area of military expertise. Yet in oil-rich Venezuela as well, the United States reportedly "completely" controlled the military cartography section.[45]

To summarize our discussion of the impact of military training on the outcomes of guerrilla war: The quantitative comparative evidence does not support the idea that U.S. counterinsurgency training was critical in defeating the guerrillas, nor was it focused in areas affected by insurgency. However, the qualitative evidence, although only sketchy, suggests greater importance for the content of training, especially in supplying an elite core of manpower that could be directed into counterinsurgency operations, and also for "rounding out" those areas in which Latin American armed forces had limited capabilities.

Informal Pressures*

Military Personnel/Combat Troops

Colonel George S. Blanchard has listed four graduated steps in levels of military assistance for counterinsurgency. First come Military Assistance Advisory Groups (MAAGs), which were present in forty-five countries in 1964. They operate as "efficiency experts," evaluating a nation's counterguerrilla performance and abilities, making recommendations, perhaps even supervising actions carried out by domestic agencies. Second in line are Special Action Forces, groups combining talents in medicine, civic action, engineering, intelligence, and psychological warfare. These units go where local requirements go beyond already-existing levels of U.S. support. Within these SAFs, the Mobile Training Teams (MTTs)—such as the one sent to Bolivia in 1967—are a common form due to their "unique counterinsurgency capabilities," and may number from one to fifty persons. In 1965 alone, fifty-two such special missions went to Latin America. Blanchard's third line is only fuzzily outlined: "the Army is prepared to dispatch other types of support forces to the area," as in Vietnam in 1964.

The fourth and final line is the dispatch of conventional combat troops to a region.[54] This obviously occurred in Vietnam, but there is a (less well known) good chance that Green Berets fought in Guatemala, as well as (less well founded) charges that they fought against domestic guerrillas elsewhere in the region, perhaps in Venezuela and Bolivia. In Peru and Colombia—with one exception—charges by the insurgents referred only to "assistance" and "direction," and not to actual combat.[55] To my knowledge, not even these more modest charges were tendered during the Cuban guerrilla war.

For Venezuela and Bolivia, the sources alleging U.S. combat troops' participation in counterinsurgency are from unreliable guerrilla sources of information.[56] In the absence of any other confirmatory evidence, these

*Ed. note: This section has been omitted.

reports should be discounted. In contrast, the variety and number of sources suggesting Green Beret combat roles in Guatemala—in the 1966–1967 campaign—is rather more impressive. They include a Catholic priest, a U.S. reporter, various chroniclers of the guerrilla movement, and, of course, the guerrillas themselves.[57] The number of such combatants, however, probably numbered considerably less than the "thousand(s)" mentioned by the insurgents. If certain reports are accurate, the U.S. advisors exercised virtual control over the *fighting* part of the Guatemalan army—through the cooperation of then-Colonel Arana Osorio—as well as over the intelligence services and the secret police. The guerrillas even believed that there was an unspoken policy of "showing" the Green Berets to peasants and insurgents, to intimidate the guerrillas into believing their cause a lost one.[58]

Summary of United States' Influence

While there is no mathematically simple way of calculating the tipping points beyond which U.S. assistance was decisive in defeating the guerrillas, we can make some rough commonsense distinctions. U.S. military aid *cannot* have been decisive where such aid (1) was a small share of the military budget, especially for weapons; (2) did not result in great advances in counterinsurgency training; (3) was not associated with a great deal of influence or control over the armed forces; or (4) did not appreciably improve domestic military strength or solidarity. In addition, the weaker and the more fragmented were the guerrillas, the less importance we must attach to the U.S. for their defeat.

Judging by these criteria, Guatemala and Venezuela lie at opposite ends of our spectrum of influence. Venezuela had domestic military strength greatly superior to Guatemala's; it had much smaller shares of U.S. military aid in its military budget, virtually no weapons aid, and bought its weaponry from a more diverse group of vendors; retained far more domestic control over its military apparatus; and improved its military solidarity after 1962 quite independently of U.S. assistance. It seems absurd to judge U.S. aid of decisive importance in the defeat of the guerrillas, especially given the fact that the governing AD party clearly had more backing from the nation's peasantry than did the insurgents.

Guatemala provides a striking contrast. The United States held a hegemonic position there in military aid, military sales, aid to the police, and other economic assistance; the U.S. military exercised far more influence through training and clout in the armed forces; U.S. military aid increased noticeably as guerrilla activity grew in the mid-1960s; the performance of the Guatemalan armed forces improved markedly during 1966–1967, the period of perhaps greatest U.S. influence; and U.S. combat troops may well have participated in that campaign. Politically, the governing party had little or no popular backing, the 1966 elections had resulted in virtual usurpation of power by the military, and the guerrillas were among the best-prepared and most popularly supported in the region. Given those features, if U.S. support was decisive anywhere, that place was Guatemala in the 1960s. . . .

A superficially strong argument can be made for a similar role in Bolivia. U.S. influence on the Bolivian military and its reconstruction had been at least as large as in Guatemala, and the Bolivian army was as ill prepared for war as its Guatemalan counterpart. However, in strong contrast to Guatemala was the strong peasant support for President René Barrientos, whatever his electoral bona fides for holding that office. Also in contrast is the tragicomedy of errors that constituted the military history of Ché's *foco,* for the group had no popular support and lost several persons in attrition for reasons unrelated to combat or desertion. Ill fed, ill informed, tired, and sick, there was quite simply no way they could have defeated the Bolivian army, sorry as the latter may have been. The peasantry who informed on them throughout the campaign would eventually have brought them to defeat if the army could not have done so alone.

For the remaining cases, U.S. military support could only have been decisive if we view it as the result of *long-term* military training and aid, and not as short-term responses to domestic upsurges. No significant, short-term aid responses to Peru or Colombia can even be remotely viewed as decisive in the defeat of the insurgents (short-term is what those defeats were in Colombia, however). In both cases, as elsewhere, U.S.-trained soldiers were at the forefront of counterinsurgency. Despite this, the guerrillas were too fragmented and disorganized in both countries to mount a serious military or political threat to incumbent governments. In Peru, the guerrillas counted on simultaneous, spontaneous strikes and uprisings nationwide to force the military to disperse its forces. Instead, the military picked off the *foco* sites one by one. The dispatch with which the Peruvian armed forces disposed of the insurgents can only be laid at the doorstep of the United States with arguments strained exceedingly thin.

Table 5-10. Military Conditions Favoring Government (+)
or Insurgents (–) in Outcomes of Guerrilla Warfare

	U.S. Training	U.S. Military Aid	Domestic Military Strength	Guerrilla Vulnerability
Bolivia	++	++	–	++
Colombia	+	+	++	–
Cuba	0	+	–	–
Guatemala	+(+)	++	–	– –
Peru	+	+	+	+(+)
Venezuela	+	0	+(+)	–

Sources: See text and preceding chapter tables.

Colombia's military, in contrast, faced several well-armed, popularly supported, experienced guerrilla groups. Here U.S. assistance might have been
critical. Yet it was in Colombia that the key element of such assistance—
counterinsurgency training—was least required, for the Colombian armed
forces had acquired far more experience in fighting guerrillas, in fifteen
years of guerrilla-style civil war, than they could possibly gain in a course in
Panama. The United States' military in turn pointed to the Colombians as
the exemplary Latin American model for counterinsurgency technique.
Colombia's soldiery, or at least the elite troops, were sufficiently well
trained to head off any hopes of fragmented guerrillas seizing power in the
Cuban style.

Let us summarize our discussion, giving a plus (+) to any conditions that
aided the suppression of the insurgents, a minus (–) to those that favored
the guerrillas, and a zero (0) for a neutral role. Double signs (++, – –) indicate particularly strong conditions. The results appear in table 5-10.

We might say, roughly, that U.S. influence could have been decisive when
a strong U.S. presence (pluses in the first two columns) was paired with relatively weak domestic armed forces and a strong guerrilla movement (mi-
nuses in the second pair of columns). We can now better understand the
distinctiveness of the Guatemalan guerrilla war in its international context:
strong U.S. aid and training were paired with a weak domestic military and
a strong guerrilla movement. The result may well have been the insurgents'
defeat.

Guerrillas: Finances, Solidarity, and External Aid

There exists no a priori reason not to extend the preceding analysis to the *guerrillas'* armed forces. Both analyses would then partake of similar "hydraulic" models; the investigator makes a reasoned judgment as to how much "pressure" each contender can exert on the other, and finds out how that balance changes when the variable of outside assistance to one or both contenders changes the scenario.[59] We have seen that U.S. assistance appreciably increased the fighting strength of some militaries, and this is true for outside support to guerrilla forces as well—some of them benefited more than did others. Our subsequent analyses, however, must be far more qualitative, given the paucity of systematic information available on "underground" aid to insurgent forces.

Yet there are those who oft'times object: outside assistance can *never* be crucial to the success of insurgent movements, whose success derives solely from the popular support they secure. That is, winning the hearts and minds of the people always yields eventual victory to the insurgents. This objection contains more ideology than analysis, for it is not, in fact, true that guerrillas have been successful irrespective of secure lines of outside support. Leites and Wolf argue that rebellions can never be successfully repressed *unless* external aid is somehow denied the rebels. Walter Laqueur argues a similar case in his world-historical survey of guerrillas, citing specific cases, such as the Greek Communist resistance of post–World War II.[60] Notwithstanding its great importance, popular support is not the be-all and end-all of a guerrilla failure or triumph, and it cannot be the sole focus of our analysis.

When we read of "outside" assistance to guerrillas in Latin America, the writer above all usually intends us to think of Cuban aid. How did such aid—paralleling our previous analysis—improve the training, finances, and armaments of the 1960s guerrilla movements? To answer, here is a summary of our following discussion: Outside assistance to guerrillas seems to have been most effective in training new insurgents, but where money was important the Cuban guerrillas of the 1950s, and *not* their 1960s imitators, benefited most. . . .

How many Latin Americans did the Cubans train? Estimates of such numbers vary widely and sometimes wildly. (Here we must take care not to equate a mere trip to Cuba [e.g., the Venceremos Brigade, etc.] with a visit made to secure training in the strategy and tactics of insurgency.) In early

1963, the CIA estimated before Congress that 1,000 to 1,500 Latin Americans had been so trained up to that time. Two years later, a U.S. Army colonel gave a figure of 1,500 for 1962 alone, but his figures included those receiving "ideological indoctrination" as well. By 1966, [Norman] Gall estimated 1,200 trainees to date; by 1967, another observer placed the cumulative total at 2,500; and by the late 1970s an estimate for the period to 1967 totalled 3,000.[62]

We suspect that by that latter year the peak period of training guerrillas had passed—although it clearly continued well into the 1970s, if not beyond—and that 2,000 to 3,000 trainees for the entire period does not seem like an overestimate. This might seem to pale beside U.S. efforts in training tens of thousands of soldiers. Yet the generally accepted ratio of conventional soldiers needed to confront guerrillas successfully is 10 soldiers for each guerrilla; therefore, the training efforts of the United States and Cuba in Latin America may not have been all that disproportionate.

Estimates of Cuban efforts in each target nation vary widely as well. Whatever the actual numbers, it does appear that the ratio of overall Cuban trainees to the maximum number of guerrillas at any one time was very high, perhaps surpassing one-half (note that this does not mean that one of every two guerrillas was trained there; there were, after all, deaths, desertions, and turnover as well). One source estimates 300 Venezuelan trainees through 1967, under 200 for Guatemala in the same period, and 2,500 overall in Latin America. A Peruvian military source estimated that 1,200 Peruvians were trained in various communist nations by 1965, far more than the 150 or so who participated in the 1965 *focos*. Peru's Haya de la Torre, by 1965 a staunch anticommunist, even estimated the figure at 1,055 for 1964 alone. These last two estimates almost surely conflate guerrilla trainees with left-wing tourists to communist countries, if we are to give them any credence at all. Discrepant figures exist for Colombia as well, where *Time* counted 700 ongoing Cuban trainees in 1965, while another source more modestly counted 200 overall through 1967. Finally, for Bolivia, the U.S. ambassador in 1967 estimated that 250 to 400 Bolivian nationals trained in Cuba from about 1962 to 1967.[63]

Which countries sent the most pupils to Cuba for military training? Here again our numbers are unreliable, but perhaps very roughly indicative. Writing in 1965, Gall thought that the majority were from Colombia and Venezuela, and he is a most reliable source in guerrilla matters. [Robert] Lamberg, also a reliable source, thought the list of major contributors was larger: Venezuela, Ecuador, Peru, Bolivia, Argentina, and Central

America.[64] Despite the disagreement on Colombia, we do see a rough Cuban pattern that mirrors the efforts of the United States in the region: Cuban "military training," like that of its rival to the north, concentrated in the *Caribbean* region, with relatively little attention to most of South America. That Colombia and Venezuela were its "most-favored" targets seems consistent with references in the literature on those two nations, which indicate the routine nature of the "Cuban training course," as well as other routine contacts.

The Cuban revolution of course provides us with a special case, since no "Cuban model" for insurgent assistance then existed. Nonetheless, our analytical tools can help us here as well. In this case, however, money rather than training was of greatest importance to the guerrillas. Castro was well financed by fund-raising campaigns among Batista exiles and American sympathizers in the United States. Indeed, [Ramón] Barquín suggests that Castro's funding amounted to hundreds of thousands of dollars. A single gift from the interim revolutionary government of Venezuela (in 1958) came to $50,000. Near the end of the guerrilla war, in fact, the M-26 apparently had a steady monthly income in excess of $10,000.[65]

The Cuban guerrillas were also quite well supplied with weaponry in their struggle, better than their 1960s imitators, but not so well equipped as some of the later guerrillas. In guerrilla wars where no secure border provides an easy channel for arms shipments, weapons usually come from dead or captured enemy soldiers. In Cuba, however, extensive gunrunning from the U.S. mainland became a major source of arms for Castro's M-26. In 1957, the U.S. government intercepted some $250,000 worth of such shipments yet estimated that more than that had gotten through. Ex-president Carlos Prío Socorras was among those charged with felonies in the U.S. for such activity. For example, the weaponry used in the Granma landing, as well as the boat itself, was mostly of American manufacture. Dickey Chapelle estimated that about 15 percent of Castro's weaponry was so obtained.[66] At one point in the war, a Costa Rican plane carrying arms to the rebels employed one of the rough Sierra Maestra landing strips to deliver the hardware. Relative to the 1960s guerrillas, then, the Cubans enjoyed fairly long-term and sustained financial and arms assistance from abroad.

Venezuela was the venue of the most publicized evidence of Cuban support to the 1960s guerrilla movements—apart from Ché's Bolivian *foco*. A U.S. congressional report in 1967 concluded that Venezuela was one of four Latin American nations—along with Guatemala, Puerto Rico, and the

Dominican Republic—in which Cubans were supporting guerrillas. From 1964 to 1967 the Cubans, for their part, candidly acknowledged their role in training and otherwise assisting the Venezuelan insurgents. Indeed, training was by all indicators a commonplace there, for an internal PCV memo of 1965 suggested training in Cuba for *all* guerrilla cadres who were not from the state in which their guerrilla *foco* was sited.[67]

It is impossible to estimate precisely how much money the Venezuelan insurgents received from abroad, but fragmentary evidence may suggest the magnitude of the operations. In April 1965, three Italian Communists were arrested and charged with attempting to smuggle in $330,000 to the FALN. In that same year, police estimated that the largest single sum delivered to the guerrillas was $300,000, sent from Peking (Beijing). In the period after 1966, Douglas Bravo's Falcón guerrillas were the main recipients of foreign largesse. While submitting requests to Cuba for money in 1967, Bravo received $50,000 from China, and then complained that Castro was spending his money on automobiles instead of supporting "people in the mountains."[68] After a lengthy period of disengagement from support of Bravo's guerrillas, Cuba in 1970 even ended hortatory revolutionary radio broadcasts aimed at Venezuela. Since Cuba was widely cited as the major supporter of the Venezuelan guerrillas, its aid must have been substantial indeed to surpass the sums from China and Italy suggested here. The guerrillas themselves evidently entertained no illusions that "popular support" alone was sufficient to fuel their movement, since their newspaper *Revolución* described aid from the "world revolutionary camp" as something that was "as indispensable to us as the wind is to the sail."[69]

If Venezuela stood out as a focus of external financial support for insurgency, it also was outlined (briefly) as a focus of weapons aid. In November 1963 a farmer found a three-ton weapons cache buried on a beach on the Paraguana peninsula in Falcón State. At first, the Venezuelan government believed the 4,230 cubic feet of weapons to have been taken from Venezuelan troops and hidden there for future use. Close examination instead revealed them to be of Belgian origin, coming from a Belgian shipment to Cuba some time before. Despite the notoriety of this particular find, Allemann is probably correct in his evaluation of the Venezuelan guerrillas' armaments supplies: they were vastly inferior in weaponry to their governmental opponents, whose weapons purchases were backed by taxing vast oil revenues. Internal documents of the MIR indicated that neither the internal arms market, nor weapons captured from government troops, nor supplies from friendly lands—individually or collectively—ever adequately supplied the guerrillas with a fighting power capable of confronting their opponents. This contrasts markedly with Fidel Castro's situation in Cuba by 1958.[70]

Venezuela is also, again apart from the obvious case of Bolivia, the one country in the hemisphere for which certain evidence of Cuban combat guerrillas is documented. Some Cubans by birth who fought in the FALN were pre-1958 emigrants to Venezuela. They should not be confused with the Cuban assistance corps that landed on the Venezuelan coast in mid-1966; or with a commando raid in May 1967, in which Venezuelan authorities captured three guerrillas identified as Cuban army officers; or with the Cuban guerrilla volunteer whose diary the Venezuelan authorities seized and later published. (In an earlier period, the Communist PCV had rejected Castro's offer to have Ché Guevara come fight in Venezuela. Times had obviously changed.) Still, as with the case of weapons, there is no evidence of sustained, large-scale reinforcements to the Venezuelan guerrillas.[71] Overall, there is little doubt that Venezuela stands out as a major focus of Cuban training, financial and military supply, and combat troop support in the hemisphere during the 1960s. Perhaps indicative of the closeness of the social ties between guerrillas and their foreign benefactor is the Venezuelan FALN, which was officially represented in Havana, complete with its own office and stationery headed República de Venezuela—Fuerzas Armadas de Liberación.

Three of the four proven Cuban interventions in Latin America took place in Venezuela. The fourth, in Guatemala, occurred in 1966 through a Cuban-based group working out of Mexico.[72] However, there is little evidence of more extensive Cuban aid to Guatemala's insurgents. Guerrilla leaders Luis Turcios Lima and Marco Yon Sosa visited Cuba more than once, and many Guatemalans trained there, but little else. Castro reportedly offered both arms and men to Turcios, who declined the offers. Eighty percent of the rebels' weaponry reportedly was taken from the Guatemalan army, both from defeated soldiers and through outright purchases from army stocks through the guerrillas' old-boy networks in the military.[73] Cuban involvement in Guatemala was substantially less, therefore, than in Venezuela.

In Colombia, Cuban aid had some impact in the early 1960s. The peasant republic of Marquetalia received some initial organizing help from Cuban and Chinese instructors. Later on the ELN, usually described as Fidelista in its politics, began with the training of an entire cohort of its leaders in Cuba before returning to Colombia for its first military activity. The Colombian government claimed only that the ELN guerrillas received Cuban money and advice, not arms or military leadership. ELN leader Fabio Vasquez was never satisfied with the level of Cuban aid—in money or weapons—even though an ex-member reported that Vasquez began to base the ELN's strategy on such external aid in late 1967. This may explain the vehemence of Vasquez's break with Castro in 1970, when he termed the Cuban leader a "traitor to the guerrilla cause," while breaking off financial, military, and ideological relations. The text of a government interrogation of a left-wing Mexican journalist, who had just visited the ELN's camp in 1966, also suggests that the guerrillas largely obtained their weapons from Colombian soldiers, and not from Cuban shipments.[74] The level of Cuban aid in Colombia, then, seems more like the Guatemalan than the Venezuelan example.

The Peruvian case also resembles the preceding two instances, differing mainly in the extreme numbers that the authorities claimed had secured training in Cuba (and elsewhere).[75] Evidence suggests that the Cubans arranged some arms shipments through Bolivia, filtered through Czech agents in La Paz. As in the case of the Colombian ELN, a Peruvian cohort of proto-guerrillas trained in Cuba and then returned to begin the revolution: Javier Héraud's ill-fated group of 1963, who entered southeastern Peru near Puerto Maldonado and were quickly wiped out. The extent of the government's claims, including a list of fourteen Peruvians allegedly trained in China, suggests that the training of Peruvians in various communist countries may indeed have been more extensive than in the cases of Guatemala and Colombia, at least up through 1965.[76]

Bolivia, of course, stands out as the sui generis case of Cuban support for guerrilla movements. The *foco* there was led, financed, and armed in such a manner that the Bolivians' participation was more peripheral then central to the movement—more like liaisons than cadres. Guevara had argued that Bolivia was to be but the first stone to fall in a broader continental revolution—but one star in the revolutionary cosmos—and if necessary was to be sacrificed in order to achieve that larger goal. The Bolivian adventure is less notable for its scope—militarily it was the least impressive of the six cases under review—than for the notoriety engendered by Ché's presence. The foreign sponsorship of the Bolivian *foco* was also accompanied by a series of striking Cuban denials (concerning the Cubans' presence) and absurd counterassertions (concerning the scope of American military involvement).[77]

Conclusions

Cuban aid to the Latin American guerrilla movements of the 1960s was variable, but generally quite limited, therefore having little effect on the outcomes of the region's guerrilla wars. Putting aside the Bolivian case—a virtual Cuban "export" to that nation—Cuba gave its greatest support to the Venezuelan insurgents. After Venezuela, there is little to differentiate the degree of Cuban aid to Guatemala, Colombia, and Peru. In all four of those cases, Cuban guerrilla training must be adjudged of prime importance, if the life courses of the insurgencies were indeed extended for external reasons. Money and weapons assistance was extremely limited, even to Venezuela. Indeed, despite the enormous brouhaha over *1960s* Cuban aid to revolutionaries in the region, there may be better evidence of large-scale aid to the *later* guerrillas, those of the 1970s and 1980s. Indeed, the scale of many of those later insurgencies was substantially greater: the numbers of insurgents, the numbers of dead, the violence of the confrontation (especially the numbing levels of government terror against the peasantry), and the degree of aid supplied by both the United States and Cuba to some of the principals.

Returning to the earlier period, and most interestingly, there is good reason to believe that the greatest degree of external support to a guerrilla movement went to the Cuban insurgents of 1956–1958. The Cuban guerrillas' supplies of both money and weaponry seem to have been both larger and more secure than those of their 1960s imitators. Surprisingly, then, it was a "pre-Cuba" yet Cuban guerrilla movement that was able to elicit the most extensive external support for its cause, and not those later movements whose leaders had most been led to expect regular and massive aid from the "world revolutionary camp" (i.e., wind for their sails), simply because of their Fidelista bona fides.

Finally, in contrast to Cuban assistance, military aid from the United States may have had a decisive impact on the outcome of one revolutionary movement of the 1960s—the Guatemalan—in the lending of critical assistance to a weak, weak-willed, and weakly supported military establishment. However, it is only for Guatemala that such a scenario is even plausible, for even in Bolivia one cannot make a strong case that, absent such U.S. aid, the guerrillas would have prevailed, or even gotten a longer lease on life. This conclusion applies *a fortiori* to Colombia, Peru, and most especially to Venezuela. . . .

NOTES

1. Representative of this "school" are [Richard] Gott, *Rural Guerrillas [in Latin America* (Harmondsworth, Eng.: Penguin, 1973)], and [James] Petras, "Revolution and Guerrilla Movements [in Latin America: Venezuela, Colombia, Guatemala, and Peru," in *Latin America: Reform or Revolution?,* ed. James Petras and Maurice Zeitlin (Greenwich, Conn.: Fawcett, 1968): 329–69].

2. Richard Kiessler, *Guerilla und Revolution: Parteikommunismus und Parti-sanenstrategie in Lateinamerika* (Bonn-Bad Godesberg: Verlag Neue Gesellschaft GmbH., 1975), pp. 1, 353.

3. For a general discussion of the relative importance in sociological analysis of "intrusive elements" and the social systems they affect, see Ralph H. Turner, "The Quest for Universals in Sociological Research" in *Research Methods: Issues and Insights,* ed. Billy J. Franklin and Harold W. Osborne (Belmont, Calif.: Wadsworth, 1971), p. 35.

4. Joseph Loftus, *Latin American Defense Expenditures, 1938–1965,* Rand Research Memorandum, No. RM-5310-PR/ISA (Santa Monica, Calif.: Rand Corporation, 1968). I have extended his figures, corrected a few of them, and adjusted them for inflation in my thesis; cf. "A Sociological Analysis of Latin American Guerrilla Movements, 1956–1970." Ph.D. diss., Cornell University, 1981, chap. 5. My own data are presented here.

5. In addition to Loftus's and my own estimates, see (for data after 1965) United Nations, *Statistical Yearbook,* various editions, always using the latest available data for each given year. Exchange rates per U.S. 1960 $ are as follows: Cuba, 1.02 pesos; Venezuela, 3.35 bolivares; Guatemala, 1.00 quetzales; Peru, 26.76 soles; and Bolivia, 11.885 pesos. For the Cuban data, all years are fiscal years, not calendar years.

6. Loftus, *Defense Expenditures,* pp. vii–viii, comes to similar conclusions after comparing military spending to the levels of internal and external violence; only Venezuela, in his view, seems to provide an exception.

7. See the data in *Statistical Abstract of Latin America* 18 (Los Angeles: UCLA Latin American Center, 1977), pp. 160–61, table 1-1; for Latin American national population figures, see United Nations, Statistical Yearbook 18 (1966): 80–81.

8. United Nations, *Statistical Yearbook* 18 (1966): 80–81. All data are in 1960 U.S. dollars. . . .

9. See Loftus, *Defense Expenditures,* p. 87, for armed-forces personnel, and the same U.N. source for population. In this paragraph, all national data are for 1965, save for Cuba, where 1958 or 1960 data are employed.

10. Segunda Sección Académica de la ESG, "El destacamiento aerotrasportado en un asalto para destruir un base de apoyo de guerrilleros" *Revista de la Escuela Superior de Guerra* (Peru) 13 (April–June 1966): 63–79.

11. D. E. H. Russell, *Rebellion, Revolution, and Armed Force* (New York: Academic, 1974), develops the thesis that the (dis)loyalty of the armed forces lies at the crux of revolutionary success or failure. On German soldiers' morale in World War II, see Morris Janowitz, *Military Conflict* (Beverly Hills, Calif.: Sage, 1975), pp. 177–220.

12. [Barrington] Moore [Jr.], *Injustice[: The Social Bases of Obedience and Revolt* (White Plains, N.Y.: M.E. Sharpe, 1978),] pp. 82–83.

13. Russell, *Rebellion, Revolution, and Armed Force,* passim; also see the capsule summary in [Charles] Tilly, *From Mobilization to Revolution* [(Reading, Mass.: Addison-Wesley, 1978),] pp. 214–16.

14. Writing as a former Cuban officer, Ramón Barquín, *Luchas guerrilleras,* expresses particular personal bitterness over Batista's unwillingness to professionalize the armed forces.

. . .

16. Erving Goffman notes this in his original essay on total institutions; cf. *Asylums* [(Garden City, N.Y.: Anchor, 1961)], pp. 119–21.

17. The image of the army as the final bulwark against a descent into barbarism is clear in Evelio Buitrago Salazar, *Zarpazo the Bandit: Memoirs of an Undercover Agent of the Colombian Army* (Tuscaloosa: University of Alabama Press, 1977).

18. Richard L. Maullin, *Soldiers, Guerrillas, and Politics in Colombia* (Toronto: Lexington, 1973), pp. 113–16; [Fritz René] Allemann, *Macht und Ohnmacht [der Guerilla* (Munich: R. Piper, 1974)], p. 274.

19. There is an interesting postscript to Bolivia, 1967: a radical critic asserted that the officers supporting Hugo Banzer's conservative military coup of the early 1970s were drawn largely from those trained by U.S. advisors during the 1967 insurgency.

20. Norman Gall, "The Legacy of Che Guevara," *Commentary* 44 (December 1967): 32.

21. [Luis J.] Gonzalez and [Gustavo A.] Sanchez [Salazar], *The Great Rebel[: Che Guevara in Bolivia* (New York: Grove Press, 1969),] pp. 103–4.

22. In the period since 1967, however, the military has been plagued by left- and right-wing conflicts, factionalism, and drug-based corruption.

23. On the *cazadores'* response to encountering some captured guerrilla suspects see [Angel Raúl] Guevara, *Los cachorros del Pentagono* [Caracas: Salvador de la Plaza, 1973)], pp. 53–54.

24. [Donn] Munson, *Zacapa* [Canoga, Calif.: Challenge, 1967)], p. 21.

25. Malcolm Deas, "Guerrillas in Latin America: A Perspective," *World Today* 24 (February 1968): 78.

26. Richard N. Adams, *Crucifixion by Power* (Austin: University of Texas Press, 1970), p. 249.

27. [Jean] Lartéguy, *The Guerrillas* [(New York: The World Press, 1970)], pp. 88–89, and Adams, *Crucifixion,* pp. 266–67, 468–69. Two suggestive experiments demonstrated that situations of authority, command structures, and even simple role assignments may be effective in eliciting compliance in the performance of supposedly unthinkable actions: the Milgram shock experiments and the Zimbardo prison experiment, in which a "guard" self-described as a pacifist prior to the experiment tormented and even force-fed inmate(s); cf. Stanley Milgram, *Obedience to Authority* (New York: Harper and Row, 1974) and Moore's comments on this study in *Injustice,* pp. 94–100; Philip G. Zimbardo, "The Mind is a Pirandellian Prison," *New York Times Magazine,* 8 April 1973, 38–40+.

28. Edwin Lieuwen, "Militarism in Latin America: A Threat to the Alliance for Progress," *World Today* 19 (May 1963): 198; *El Nacional* (Caracas), 4 May 1962.

29. United States Department of Defense, Security Assistance Agency, *Foreign Military Sales and Military Assistance Facts* (April 1974): 12, 16–19.

30. In 1970, the U.S. had some $75.5 billion in direct investments in foreign countries, of which $11.1 billion, or about 15 percent, was in Latin America. U.S. trade with Latin America in 1965 amounted to about 15 percent of all U.S. foreign trade. Net economic assistance to Latin America from 1948 to 1978 totalled $7.2 billion, or about 10 percent of the global assistance total of $70.2 billion. See U.S. Department of Commerce, *Statistical Abstract of the United States 1979* (Washington, D.C.: U.S. Govt. Printing Office), tables 1497, 1511, 1504, respectively.

31. Maullin, *Soldiers, Guerrillas, and Politics*, p. 103; U.S. Senate, Committee on Foreign Relations, *United States Military Policies and Programs in Latin America* (Washington, D.C.: U.S. Govt. Printing Office, 1969), pp. 44–45.

32. Maullin, *Soldiers, Guerrillas, and Politics*, p. 94; U.S. Senate, *U.S. Military Policies*, p. 64.

33. U.S. Senate, *U.S. Military Policies*, pp. 73–74.

34. See U.S. Department of Defense, *Foreign Military Sales and Military Assistance Facts* (December 1977): 19–20, 23–24, 28–30 for data sources. . . .

35. [Jorge I.] Domínguez, *Cuba: Order and Revolution* [(Cambridge, Mass.: Belknap Press of Harvard, 1978)], p. 151.

   . . .

39. [Michael T.] Klare and [Nancy] Stein, *Armas y poder [in América Latina* (México, D.F.: Serie Popular Era, 1978)], pp. 120, 159–60.

40. Lt. Colonel Milton Delfin Cataldi, "Las guerrillas," *Revista Militar del Peru* 17 (March–April 1962): 74; [Robert F.] Lamberg, *Die castristiche Guerilla [in Lateinamerika: Theorie und Praxis eines revolutionären Modells* (Hannover, Germany: Verlag für Literatur und Zeitgeschehen, 1971)], p. 44, and idem, "Consideraciones concluyentes [en torno a las guerrillas castristas en Latinoamérica," *Aportes* 25 (July 1972)], 116–17.

41. "Armies Can Be Builders," *Army Information Digest* 20 (February 1965): 16–19.

42. Eduardo Galeano, "With the Guerrillas in Guatemala," in Petras and Zeitlin, eds., *Latin America*, p. 373; Klare and Stein, *Armas y poder*, pp. 94–95.

43. This followed the confirmation of guerrilla activity there; see Gott, *Rural Guerrillas*, pp. 526–27 for details.

44. Guevara, *Los cachorros del Pentagono*, p. 46; Galeano, "With the Guerrillas," 371; [Rogger] Mercado, *Las Guerrillas [del Peru* (Lima: Fondo de Cultura Popular, 1967)], pp. 221–22.

45. Gott, *Rural guerrillas*, p. 526; Georgie Anne Geyer, "The Blood of Guatemala," *Nation* 207 (8 July 1968): 10.

   . . .

54. Colonel George S. Blanchard, "Special Warfare—NOW!" *Army Information Digest* 19 (January 1964): 20–26. On the 1965 MTT missions, see Gott, *Rural Guerrillas*, pp. 568–70.

55. For typical Peruvian allegations, see [Sara Beatriz] Guardia, *Proceso a campesinos [de la Guerrilla "Túpac Amaru"* (Lima: impresiones y Publicidad, 1972)], p. 15; Mercado, *Las*

guerrillas, p. 179; Américo Pumaruna, "Peru: Revolución, insurrección, guerrillas," *Pensamiento Crítico* (February 1967): 95; and *La Prensa,* 12 September 1965. For the Colombian exception, see Munson, *Zacapa,* pp. 62–63.

56. The source for Venezuela is Douglas Bravo, who even lied to his Cuban allies; cf. [François] Maspero, *Avec Douglas Bravo [dans les maquis vénézuéliens* (Paris: François Maspero, 1968)], p. 36; while assertions by Bravo and other guerrillas may be treated with less skepticism on other matters, on these issues one approaches all claims with special caution. The source for Bolivia is Albert-Paul Lentin, "Des Experts de Punta del Este aux `Berets Verts' de Santa Cruz," *Partisans* (Paris) 37 (April–June 1967): 126, where he claims that "entire units" of Green Berets engaged Ché's guerrillas in Bolivia. Guevara's diaries support no such allegations. A much more selective role for U.S. combat personnel is implied by Allemann, *Macht und Ohnmacht,* p. 404, where he says that occasionally U.S. officers were "present in the ranks" at the close of the Bolivian campaign. The charge that Guevara was "executed by the CIA" is not even supported by the article bearing that title; cf. Michèle Ray, "The Execution of Che by the CIA," *Ramparts* 6 (March 1968): 21–37. Compare Gott, *Rural Guerrillas,* pp. 553–54, for a different view of events by another left-wing critic of U.S. policy. See the information supplied by Colonel John D. Waghelstein, "Che's Bolivian Adventure," *Military Review* 59 (August 1979): 44, who argues that Barrientos gave the order to execute Ché against advice from the United States.

57. See *Nation* 206 (4 March 1968): 291; Munson, *Zacapa,* pp. 52, 58–59, 201–2; and Allemann, *Macht und Ohnmacht,* p. 187 for a few examples.

58. [Camilo] Castaño, "Avec les guérillas du Guatemala," [*Partisans* (Paris) 38 (July–September 1967):] 151, 154; Lartéguy, *The Guerrillas,* p. 111; Orlando Fernandez, "Situación y perspectivo del movimiento revolucionario guatemalteco," *Pensamiento Crítico* 15 (1968): 9.

59. This analysis bears some resemblance to some systems analyses, e.g., [Nathan] Leites and [Charles] Wolf's *Rebellion and Authority[: An Analytic Essay on Insurgent Conflicts* (Chicago: Markham, 1970)] . . . .

60. Leites and Wolf, *Rebellion and Authority,* pp. 21–25; [Walter] Laqueur, *Guerrilla[: A Historical and Critical Study* (Boston: Little, Brown, and Co., 1976)], pp. 263, 313.

. . .

62. Octavio Arizmendi Posada, "Latinoamérica: Guerra de guerrillas," *Istmo* 27 (July–August 1963): 56; Lt. Colonel Harold R. Aaron, "The Export of Revolution to Latin America," *Army* 15 (June 1965): 96–97; [Barry] Lando, "Latin-American Guerrillas," [*Atlantic Monthly* (December 1967),] 26; William Ratliff, *Castroism and Communism in Latin America, 1959–1976* (Washington, D.C. and Stanford, Calif.: American Enterprise Institute for Public Policy Research and Hoover Institution on War, Revolution, and Peace, 1976), p. 42.

63. Lando, "Latin-American Guerrillas," 26; [Norman] Gall, "Revolution without Revolutionaries," [*The Nation* 203 (22 August 1966),] 149; *New York Times,* 8 September 1965; *Time,* 22 January 1965, 30; Daniel James, "Latin America: How Many Vietnams?" *National Review* 19 (5 September 1967): 950.

64. Norman Gall, "The Continental Revolution," *The New Leader*, 12 April 1965: 4; [Robert F.] Lamberg, "Kubas Einfluss auf Lateinamerika," *[Der Ostblock und die Entwicklungsländer (VJB-FFES)* 20 (June 1965),] 147.

65. Barquín, *Luchas guerrilleras* 1: 220; [Hugh] Thomas, *Cuba[: The Pursuit of Freedom* (New York: Harper and Row, 1971)], p. 986.

66. Hispanic American Report 11 (September 1958): 496; *Newsweek*, 24 February 1958, 54; Barquín, *Luchas guerrilleras* 1: 231; James E. Bond, *The Rules of Riot: Internal Conflict and the Laws of War* (Princeton, N.J.: Princeton University Press, 1974), p. 85.

67. *Daily Journal* (Caracas), 3 July 1967; *El Nacional* (Caracas), 22 April 1965; *New York Times*, 14 December 1964; 19 May 1967, 11; Allemann, *Macht und Ohnmacht*, pp. 145–46.

68. To put these figures in perspective, our numbers on military aid to Venezuela from the U.S. were $6.1 million in 1965 and about $800,000 in 1967. See table 5-3.

69. On the sums of money involved, see *Daily Journal*, 11 April 1965; *New York Times*, 17 October 1965; Allemann, *Macht und Ohnmacht*, p. 156; on Bravo's reliance on Cuban aid in general, see [Norman] Gall, "Teodoro Petkoff[: The Crisis of the Professional Revolutionary—Part] II[: A New Party," *American Universities Field Staff Reports—East Coast South America Series* 17, no. 9 (August 1973)], 20; [Luigi] Valsalice, *Guerriglia e Politica[: L'esempio del Venezuela, 1962–1969* (Florence, Italy: Valmartina Editore, 1973)], p. 117; for the quote, see *New York Times*, 6 November 1964.

70. *Daily Journal*, 4 November 1963; Kenneth O. Gilmore, "Cuba's Brazen Blueprint for Subversion," *Readers' Digest* 87 (August 1965): 67–75; Allemann, *Macht und Ohnmacht*, pp. 142–43.

71. *Daily Journal*, 18 and 19 November 1964; 13 and 19 May 1967; Allemann, *Macht und Ohnmacht*, pp. 154–55; [Angela] Zago, *Aquí no ha pasado nada* [(Caracas: El Sobre, 1972)], p. 17; Gall, "Teodoro Petkoff II," 3; Valsalice, *Guerriglia a Politica*, p. 189. For some of the contents of the Cuban volunteer's diary, see Allemann, pp. 155–56.

72. Gott, *Rural Guerrillas*, pp. 53–54.

73. Alan Howard, "With the Guerrillas in Guatemala," *New York Times Magazine* (26 June 1966): 16, 18, 20; Allemann, *Macht und Ohnmacht*, pp. 172–73.

74. Lartéguy, *The Guerrillas*, p. 160; Maullin, *Soldiers, Guerrillas, and Politics*, pp. 23–24; Allemann, *Macht und Ohnmacht*, p. 261; Lamberg, *Die castristiche Guerilla*, p. 103; [Jaime] Arenas, *La guerrilla por dentro* [(Bogota: Tercer Mundo, 1970)], pp. 155, 195.

75. See the numerical estimates discussed at the beginning of this section.

76. Peru, Ministerio de Guerra, *Las guerrillas en el Peru [y su represión* (Lima: Ministerio de Guerra, 1966)], p. 30; [General Armando] Artola [Azcarate], *¡Subversión!* [(Lima: Editorial Jurídica, 1976)], pp. 28–31, 85. Artola outlines the "typical" program.

77. See Martin D. Gensler, "Cuba's Second Vietnam: Bolivia," *Yale Review* 60 (Spring 1971): 345–46. Radio Havana reported 3,800 Green Berets in Bolivia (up from its earlier report of 100) and denied Cuban ties to the Bolivian guerrillas, describing the movement as a "purely Bolivian explosion."

6

Learning to Eat Soup with a Knife:[1]
British and American Army Counterinsurgency
Learning during the Malayan Emergency
and the Vietnam War

John A. Nagl

America's failure in Vietnam has given rise to a rich literature in which scholars and others debate what the "lessons" of the war are. John A. Nagl, a U.S. Army officer and professor at the U.S. Military Academy at West Point, has contributed to the literature the following selection, which compares the failed U.S. military intervention in Vietnam with the successful British intervention in Malaya (which later became part of Malaysia).

According to Nagl, the factor that best explains the difference in American and British performance in these two cases is whether or not counterinsurgency is the primary mission for which the military organization prepares and at which it has experience. Nagl argues that the primary mission of the U.S. Army has been to prepare for conventional warfare—such as a potential war in Europe or the 1991 Gulf war—and that its leadership has shown little interest in counterinsurgency. The British Army, by contrast, has had vast experience in counterinsurgency, and its leadership is comfortable with this mission.

There are, of course, many other factors that affect the outcome of counterinsurgency efforts against revolutionary movements. However, if Nagl is correct, then whether or not intervening forces know how to conduct counterinsurgency warfare will be a key determinant of their success.

John A. Nagl, "Learning to Eat Soup with a Knife: British and American Army Counterinsurgency Learning during the Malayan Emergency and the Vietnam War." *World Affairs* 161 (spring 1999): 193–199. Copyright American Peace Society. Reprinted with permission.

Critical Questions

1. *Would the outcome in Vietnam have been different, as Nagl suggests, if the U.S. Marine Corps had been solely responsible for the counterinsurgency effort there and the U.S. Army had not been involved?*

2. *Could the British Army have won the war in Vietnam, as Nagl suggests?*

3. *What other factors may have explained the failure of the U.S. counterinsurgency effort in Vietnam?*

4. *Would the United States now be willing and able to fight an extended counterinsurgency campaign? Would Britain or any other Western state be willing and able to?*

5. *Several non–Western states have been engaged in extended counterinsurgency campaigns, such as Russia in Chechnya, India in Kashmir, and China in Xinjiang. Have these efforts been successful? Why or why not?*

From 1948 through 1960, the British army fought a counterinsurgency campaign in what was then called Malaya. Although its initial efforts were not particularly successful, the British army adapted over time, changing both its counterinsurgency doctrine and practice. In contrast, the American army was unable to change its counterinsurgency doctrine or practice during twenty-five years of fighting in Southeast Asia, from 1950 through 1975. I have argued elsewhere that it was the organizational culture of the British army that allowed it to learn counterinsurgency principles effectively during the Malayan emergency, whereas the organizational culture of the U.S. Army blocked organizational learning during—and after—the Vietnam War. In this article, I attempt to place these conclusions in the wider context of international relations as a discipline, evaluating the current literature on military innovation, examining the effectiveness of organizational learning theory as a tool with which to analyze organizational change, and discussing the impact of varying organizational cultures on the learning abilities of different organizations.[2] I will then . . . conclude with a theoretical examination of how to make military forces adaptable in the light of changes in warfare. I will also look at the question of how to overcome institutional culture when necessary in building learning institutions.

Ideas and International Relations

This article is a look inside the "black boxes" that represent "realism" and "game theory" models of state behavior to examine a factor that affects the ability of states to achieve their goals and preserve their positions in the state system. It also affects those states on which they exercise their power.[3] The organizational culture of military forces is a decisive determinant in the decisions of *whether to apply* and of *how to apply* force in international politics, but it is a factor that to date has not been adequately examined.

The ability of military organizations to adapt to change—whether that change occurs in military technology, in the structure of the international system, or in the nature of war itself (or of our understanding of the nature of war)—is not an unimportant component of a state's ability to guarantee its own security and that of its allies. In short, military institutions that are "learning institutions" add to the influence of their states in the international system, as was the case for the United Kingdom in the wake of the Malayan emergency. Military organizations that are unable to learn can substantially damage the ability of their states to influence the international system, as was the case for the United States during and after the Vietnam War. *Understanding* the organizational culture of military institutions, and the effects of that culture on their ability to learn, increases our ability to understand how states act and react in the international system.

Evaluating the Literature on Military Innovation

Current literature on military innovation focuses on the question of whether forces *internal* to armed services can modify military doctrine to deal with changes in their external environment,[4] or whether civilian leadership *external* to the military must exert pressure to force innovation.[5] Some authors have found that civilian reformers and members of the military combine to create changes in doctrine, an *integrative* model of military innovation.[6] Most of that research has been done on military innovation in peacetime rather than while military forces are engaged in conflict. It is an acknowledged fact, however, that the processes of innovation and the necessity to innovate are markedly different in wartime. Rosen notes that military forces

> exist in order to fight a foreign enemy, and do not execute this function every day. Most of the time, the countries they serve are at peace. . . . In-

stead of being routinely "in business" and learning from ongoing experience, they must anticipate wars that may or may not occur.[7]

There have been few studies on military innovation under the pressures of fighting in a war. One of the few is Timothy T. Lupfer's *The Dynamics of Doctrine: The Changes in German Tactical Doctrine During the First World War.*[8] Although it examines only tactical level innovations, the study is nonetheless significant for its description identifying intervening steps, or cause-and-effect links, between them.[9]

Another examination of the civilian-military interface as an explanatory variable for military innovation in wartime is Deborah Avant's *Political Institutions and Military Change: Lessons from Peripheral Wars.*[10] Avant presents an integrative model of military innovation in her comparison of British army innovation during the Boer War and the Malayan emergency with American army innovation in Vietnam. Rather than focusing on the differences between the armies as the variable explaining the different patterns of innovation, Avant believes that the different political systems of the United States and Britain led the two nations' politicians to create different militaries:

> The roots of the variations lie in the way civilian leaders chose to set up and oversee the armies. . . . [C]ivilian leaders chose to oversee military organizations in a way that enhanced their ability to maintain domestic power. The difference in electoral rules between the two countries, then, was an important issue in the development of different military biases.[11]

Avant concludes her examination of British and American army innovation:

> [C]ivilian leaders in Britain, who had institutional incentives to act as a unit, had an easier time agreeing on both policy goals and oversight options to ensure that the Army followed these goals. Under these conditions, the British army reacted more flexibly to changes in civilian leaders' goals. Conversely, civilian leaders in the United States, who had institutional incentives to act separately, found it harder to agree on policy goals and often chose more complex oversight mechanisms, which did not always induce the U.S. Army to respond easily to change.[12]

According to this view, British army officers responded directly to their political masters in the Cabinet, creating a more flexible military than the American model, in which the military had the ability to "trade off" demands made by the Congress against the president, or vice versa. There are wider implications: "Differences in institutional structures that affect ensuing differences in the growth of parties, the issue-focus of voters, the interpretation of the international system, and the terms of delegation will lead to differences in the preferences of military organizations and civilian leaders. These variations explain the deviations in policy."[13]

This study comes to different conclusions, arguing along with Barry Watts and Williamson Murray that "[a]s a corollary to the importance of bureaucratic acceptance among senior military leaders, the dynamics evident in the case studies suggest that the potential for civilian or outside leadership to *impose* a new vision of future war on a reluctant military service whose heart remains committed to existing ways of fighting is, at best, limited."[14] The critical independent variable is not the nature of national government, which in most cases has little impact on which policies the military chooses to adopt; it is instead the organizational culture of the military institution that determines whether innovation succeeds or fails.

Evaluating the Effectiveness of Learning Theory as a Tool for Analyzing Military Innovation

Given the lack of a consensus in the literature on causes of military innovation, I have attempted elsewhere to explain why one military force successfully adapted to change and another failed to do so by tracing the *process* of organizational learning through case studies of the British army in the Malayan emergency and the American army in the Vietnam War. Using a theory of organizational learning first developed from observations of business management, the study focused on the process through which change developed or failed to develop. I found that the *organizational culture*—the "persistent, patterned way of thinking about the central tasks of, and the human relationships within, an organization"[15]—played a key role in allowing an organization to create a consensus either in favor of or in opposition to proposals for change. Changes that conflict with the ideas of the dominant group in the organization about the best roles and missions for the organization—the *essence of the organization*—will not be adopted; leaders of the organization, conditioned by the culture that they have absorbed through years of service in it will prevent changes in the core mission and roles. The key variable explaining when militaries will adapt to changes in warfare is the creation of a consensus among the organization leaders that such innovation is in the long-term interests of the organization itself.[16] This study thus supports Richard Downie's conclusion, developed after examining peacetime changes in U.S. Army Low-Intensity Conflict Doctrine, that

> doctrine is not likely to change, despite the presence of external pressures, until the military institution is able to identify and achieve consensus on both the problems that made its past performance unsuccessful, and appropriate solutions to those problems, or the new ones. Conversely, case study findings highlight that doctrine will change when the military institution's level of learning permits an appropriate organizational response to these external influences.[17]

Unfortunately, organizational learning theory is not a succinct explanation for why some military forces innovate while others do not. Because it uses the technique of process tracing, learning theory demands in-depth study of individual cases of innovation or failure to innovate, often requiring internal organization decision papers that may remain classified or unavailable to the researcher for years. Its emphasis on organizational culture and protection of the "essence of the organization" by elite decision makers within the organization similarly demands a high degree of familiarity with the organization under examination, as neither the identities of the dominant members of an organization nor their views on its core roles and missions are always immediately apparent. If "a remembered past has always more or less constricted both action in the present and thinking about the future,"[18] then understanding that past—and understanding *how it is remembered* by those who direct an organization's present and future—is essential to understanding how the organization will adapt to changes in its environment. U.S. Army Lieutenant Colonel Jay Parker concurs:

> In brief, information is processed from the top down based on preconceived theories structured to organize and explain the world rather than the harsh realities of new data. In the face of barriers change is slow and incremental at best. Individuals may go so far as to shut down the evaluation process and come to premature mental "closure" rather than contend with complex decisions.[19]

To understand how and why an organization will change, examine its past successes and failure—and those of the individuals who control the institution.[20]

The Impact of Organizational Culture
on Organizational Learning

The organizational culture of the British army, developed over many years of service in colonial wars—and just as important, in *preventing* colonial wars through sound administration in conjunction with British police forces and colonial administrators—reflected experiences in more than merely conventional conflict on the continent of Europe. The leadership of the British army shared a common conception that the essence of the organization included colonial policing and administration. When conventional tactics and strategy failed in Malaya, the British army had few problems creating an internal consensus that change was needed, and that political rather than purely military solutions were well within its purview. An innovative and varied past created a culture amenable to the changes required to defeat a complex opponent in a new kind of war.

The organizational culture of the American army, conversely, allowed no doubt in that army's leadership about the essence of the organization; its core competence was defeating conventional enemy armies in frontal combat. The organization never developed a consensus that change in its procedures—and in fact, in its definition of its responsibilities—was required by the nature of the revolutionary war it confronted in Vietnam. An unshakable belief in the essence of the organization precluded organizational learning and has continued to preclude consensus on the "lessons of Vietnam" and on required changes in the organization through the present day. Words recently applied to the Soviet system also describe the U.S. army of the time: "The person at the head of the hierarchical system was given great power—but he was given that power only so long as he did not use it in a way which threatened the continuation of the system."[21]

Even under the pressures for change presented by ongoing military conflict, a strong organizational culture can prohibit learning the lessons of the present and can even prevent the organization from acknowledging that current policies are not completely successful:

> Most people so restrict their frame of reference, or context, for the problem they are facing that little change can occur. They get into such a routine with their work that they view virtually all problems in a similar way—back to all problems looking like nails when all you have is a hammer. Consequently, when asked to change matters, they tend to operate

in a confined "single loop" of learning on which they can only do "more of" or "less of" the same thing because of the given context.[22]

The "get a bigger hammer" approach to making organizations more effective has implications not only when armies are engaged in a conflict but when that conflict is over if the lessons of the past war have not been noted and internalized. As Carl H. Builder noted:

> How the services perceive the next major war they must fight is an important determinant of the types of forces they try to acquire, the doctrine they develop, and the training they follow for the use of those forces in combat.[23]

How the services perceive themselves, their roles, and missions—their *essence*—helps to determine not only how they will prepare for the next war, but how flexible they will be in responding to unexpected situations when that war occurs. Chief of the British army's General Staff, General Sir Charles Guthrie, recently paraphrased Michael Howard to the effect that "in structuring and preparing an Army for war you can be clear that you will not get it precisely right, but the important thing to ensure is that it is not too far wrong, so that you can put it right quickly."[24] The culture of the British army encourages such an attitude and such responses to changed situations; the culture of the American army does not, unless the changed situation falls within the parameters of the kind of war it has defined as its primary mission.

The demands of conventional and unconventional warfare differ so greatly that an organization optimized to succeed in one will have great difficulty in fighting the other and in adapting itself to meet changing requirements in the course of the conflict. In fact, the very organizational culture that makes an institution effective in one area may blind it to the possibility that its strengths in that field are crippling deficiencies in a different situation—the more debilitating for being so deeply rooted in the culture that they are never even recognized, much less questioned.

The implications are dramatic. If it is in fact impossible for the same organization to perform effectively two very disparate tasks because the organizational culture that makes it effective in achieving one is counterproductive in accomplishing the other,[25] then organizations should focus on achieving only one critical mission. Those that attempt to perform a mission for which they are unprepared and unsuitable by organization, training, doctrine, leadership style, organizational infrastructure, and equipment—all of which both contribute to and flow from organizational culture—will face grave difficulties in adapting to the new challenges they face. The U.S. Army in Vietnam is a classic example, but fairness demands that the very evident weaknesses of the British and French armies in meeting the demands of high-technology combined arms conventional conflict in the Persian Gulf War of 1990–91 also be noted.[26]

Arguably, then, the United States Army should devote itself exclusively to preparing for mid-intensity combined arms warfare, giving the low-intensity conflict mission to the United States Marine Corps, which has an organizational culture better suited to meeting the demands of unconventional war and which has seen the need for its more recent organizational *raison d'etre,* amphibious assault, diminishing since the Korean War.[27] A former U.S. marine made the argument to Field Marshal Sir Gerald Templer in 1968:

> The sad part of this whole Viet Nam business, pacification and all, is that the States, namely my old Corps, the Marines, has had ample experience and historical background in handling matters of this nature. In Haiti, Santo Domingo and in Nicaragua the Corps ran the whole show—if not officially in control, exercising actual *de facto* control, of both the government and military forces. The pattern being that selected officers and NCOs of the Marines would actually be seconded to and commissioned in the country's army/constabulary type of force and would command units directly as well as the districts occupied by these units.[28]

Surprisingly, one of the primary architects of the U.S. Army's strategy in Vietnam agrees. General William DePuy noted in retrospect, "I have always felt that regular US Army troop units are peculiarly ill suited for the purpose of 'securing' operations where they must be in close contact with the people. They can, of course, conduct 'clearing' operations, and are perfectly suited for 'Search and Destroy.' The closer one moves toward the political and psychological end of the spectrum, the more inappropriate is the use of foreign troops who don't speak the language, and who may well have a negative effect on pacification efforts."[29]

The British army, with its tradition of colonial policing, arguably should focus itself on the peacekeeping and other types of low-intensity conflict for which its history and strategic and organizational culture render it far more capable.[30] . . .

Building Learning Institutions:
Making Military Forces Adaptable in Light
of Evolving Changes in Warfare

"Building learning organizations entails profound cultural shifts."[33] The British army's organizational culture, developed over many years of colonial policing, not only encouraged but actively expected innovation. For years, informally developed "doctrine" was disseminated by word of mouth and through the unofficial writing of participants in the campaigns; the fact that it is now official and prescribed from the new Doctrine and Training Directorate in Wiltshire may be the first step toward discouraging innovation in the British army. Organizational culture is hard to change, however; General Sir Frank Kitson's belief that "No one would read it if they did write it down"[34] may yet preserve the institutional flexibility that played such an important role in defeating the communist insurgency in Malaya. As the assistant under secretary (programmes) recently said to the Defence Committee in the House of Commons, "We have structured our forces precisely to deal with the unexpected."[35]

Is it possible for the U.S. Army to develop such a culture? Williamson Murray suggests that some improvements can be made, given efforts to "push cultural changes to encourage rather than discourage the process of innovation." Chief among these is a new "approach to military education that encourages changes in cultural values and fosters intellectual curiousity" in order to "foster a military culture where those promoted to the highest ranks possess the imagination and intellectual framework to support innovation."[36]

In the rapidly changing world of the post–cold war era, such flexibility is critical to the ability of military forces to meet the security demands that their governments will place on them. The Persian Gulf War of 1990–91 may well have been an aberration, the last of the conventional industrial age conflicts; it was certainly a lesson to the states and nonstate actors of the developing world not to confront the West in conventional combat. There are many other ways to use force to achieve political goals: terrorism, subversion, insurgency. The much-heralded revolution in military affairs[37] will not alter this fact:

> Just as nuclear weapons did not render conventional power obsolete, this revolution will not render guerrilla tactics, terrorism, or weapons of mass

destruction obsolete. Indeed, the reverse may be true: where unconventional bypasses to conventional military power exist, any country confronting the United States will seek them out.[38]

The vast majority of armed conflict today occurs inside states rather than between them. "For many countries in the world simmering internal war is a permanent condition."[39] Martin van Creveld predicts that "[a]s war between states exits through one side of history's revolving door, low-intensity conflicts among different organizations will enter through the other."[40] Sharing this view, one American army officer recently demanded, "To meet future challenges, America's Army must turn from the warm and well-deserved glow of its Persian Gulf victory and embrace, once more, the real business of regulars, the stinking gray shadow world of `savage wars of peace,' as Rudyard Kipling called them."[41]

In this new climate of dirty, difficult wars, in which political and military tasks intertwine and the objective is more often "nation-building" than the destruction of an enemy army, the ability to learn quickly during operations, to create an organizational consensus on new ways of waging war (or of waging peace), and then to implement those changes may be of more importance for modern military institutions than ever before. It then behooves military institutions to accept as an integral part of their organizational culture the need to function in this new conflict environment at all times as "learning institutions."

NOTES

1. "To make war upon rebellion is messy and slow, like eating soup with a knife." T. E. Lawrence, *Seven Pillars of Wisdom: A Triumph* (London: Penguin Books, 1971), 132.

2. See Theo Farrell, "Figuring Out Fighting Organisations: The New Organisational Analysis in Strategic Studies," *Journal of Strategic Studies* 19 (March 1996): 122–35.

3. See Charles Powell, James Dyson, and Helen Purkitt, "Opening the 'Black Box': Cognitive Processing and Optimal Choice in Foreign Policy Decision Making," in *New Directions in the Study of Foreign Policy.* Charles Herman, Charles Kegley, and James Rosenau, eds. (Boston: Allen & Unwin, 1987), 203–20.

4. See Stephen P. Rosen, *Winning the Next War: Innovation and the Modern Military* (Ithaca, NY: Cornell University Press, 1991).

5. See Barry R. Posen, *The Sources of Military Doctrine: France, Britain, and Germany Between the World Wars* (Ithaca, NY: Cornell University Press, 1984).

6. Kimberly Martin Zisk, *Engaging the Enemy: Organization Theory and Soviet Military Innovation, 1955–1991* (Princeton, NJ: Princeton University Press, 1993).

7. Rosen, *Winning the Next War,* 8. Rosen discusses wartime innovation on 22–24.

8. (Fort Leavenworth: Combat Studies Institute, 1981).

9. Alexander George, "Case Studies and Theory Development: The Method of Structured, Focused Comparison," in *Diplomacy: New Approaches in History, Theory, and Policy,* Paul Gordon Lauren, ed. (New York: MacMillan, 1979), 40.

10. (Ithaca, NY: Cornell University Press, 1994).

11. Avant, *Political Institutions and Military Change,* 21.

12. Ibid., 130–31.

13. Ibid., 139.

14. Barry Watts and Williamson Murray, "Innovation in Peacetime," in *Military Innovation in the Interwar Period,* Murray and Alan R. Millett, eds. (Cambridge: Cambridge University Press, 1996), 410.

15. James Q. Wilson, *Bureaucracy* (New York: Basic Books, 1989), 91.

16. "I'm not going to destroy the traditions and doctrine of the United States Army just to win this lousy war." An anonymous army officer quoted in Brian M. Jenkins, *The Unchangeable War* (Santa Monica, CA: RAND, 1972), 3; in Guenter Lewy, *America in Vietnam* (New York: Oxford University Press, 1978), 138.

17. Richard Downie, "Military Doctrine and the Learning Institution: Case Studies in LI," Ph.D. dissertation, University of Southern California, 1995, 354.

18. John Shy, "The American Military Experience: History and Learning," *Journal of Interdisciplinary History* I (Winter 1971): 210.

19. Jay M. Parker, "Change and the Operational Commander," *Joint Forces Quarterly* (Winter 1995/96): 92.

20. These results parallel those of Richard E. Neustadt and Earnest R. May in *Thinking in Time: The Uses of History for Decisionmakers* (New York: The Free Press, 1986), especially Chapter 9, "Placing Strangers," and Chapter 12, "Placing Organizations." For more insight into how early experiences condition cognition in decision makers, see Yuen Foong Khong, *Analogies at War: Korea, Munich, Dien Bien Phu, and the Vietnam Decisions of 1965* (Princeton, NJ: Princeton University Press, 1992).

21. Professor Archie Brown, on Mikhail Gorbachev, Oxford, 28 October 1996.

22. Bob Garratt, *The Learning Organization* (London: Harper Collins, 1994), 42–43.

23. Carl H. Builder, *The Masks of War: American Military Styles in Strategy and Analysis* (Baltimore: Johns Hopkins University Press, 1989), 128.

24. General Sir Charles Guthrie, "The British Army at the Turn of the Century," *RUSI Journal* 141 (June 1996): 6. The original citation is Michael Howard, "Military Science in the Age of Peace," *RUSI Journal* (March 1974): 34.

25. The "conventionalization" of U.S. Army Special Forces throughout their history by the much more pervasive organizational culture of the conventional army shows this process at work; see Thomas Adams, "Military Doctrine and the Organization Culture of the United States Army," Ph.D. thesis, Syracuse University, 1990.

26. Among the generally mutually and self-congratulatory literature on the war, see Rick Atkinson, *Crusade* (New York: Random House, 1992) for references to the training,

planning, and especially logistical problems of these two armies in the war. Reports that a banner proclaiming "We only do deserts" appeared on the Pentagon the day of the cease-fire recognize the fact that the Gulf War was exactly the war the United States would have chosen to fight if it could have scripted the scenario: mid-intensity combined arms warfare on a battlefield generally free of civilians.

27. For proposals on restructuring U.S. ground forces, see Douglas A. Macgregor, *Breaking the Phalanx: A New Design for Landpower in the 21st Century* (Westport, CT: Praeger/CSIS, 1997).

28. Letter from Edward C. Noden, HQ KMAG (DCSPER), to Field Marshal Templer, 6 April 1968. *Templer Papers*, Box 30.

29. General William E. DePuy, in Romie L. Brownlee and William J. Mullen III, *Changing an Army: an Oral History of General William DePuy, U.S. Army Retired* (Washington, DC: U.S. Government Printing Office, 1988), 133.

30. John Hillen, "Rethinking the Bosnia Bargain," *Backgrounder No. 1096* (Washington, DC: The Heritage Foundation, 15 October 1996).

. . .

33. Peter M. Senge, *The Fifth Discipline: The Art and Practice of the Learning Organization* (New York: Doubleday, 1990), xv.

34. General Sir Frank Kitson, interview in Devon, 12 December 1995.

35. Session 1991–92, Third Report, question 1190, 16, quoted in Eric Grove, *The Army and British Security After the Cold War: Defence Planning for a New Era* (London: Strategic and Combat Studies Institute/HMSO, 1996), 10.

36. Murray, "Past and Future," in *Military Innovation in the Interwar Period*, 326–27.

37. The so-called "revolution in military affairs" results from the application of digitized information to warfighting theory and weaponry. For a good summary of the current state of thinking on the "RMA," see "The Future of Warfare," *The Economist*, 8 March 1997, 23–26.

38. Eliot Cohen, "A Revolution in Warfare," *Foreign Affairs* 75 (March/April 1996): 51.

39. Steven Metz, "Insurgency After the Cold War," *Small Wars and Insurgencies* 5 (Spring 1994): 63.

40. Martin van Creveld, *The Transformation of War* (New York: The Free Press, 1991), 224.

41. Daniel P. Bolger, "The Ghosts of Omdurman," *Parameters* (Autumn 1991): 31–32. The U.S. Army is resisting this call, as this study of its organizational culture would predict; there are proportionally more armored and mechanized divisions in the U.S. Army today (as compared to light infantry formations, more suitable for low-intensity conflicts) than there were during the cold war.

III

Democratization and Revolution

The selections in Part I discussed revolution's negative international effects on status quo powers. The selections in Part II examined how status quo powers often attempt to prevent these negative effects from occurring through the forceful suppression of revolution and how such efforts often prove to be costly failures. There is, however, an alternative means of attempting to forestall revolution: democratization.

The opportunity to forestall revolution through democratization arises when a democratic status quo power (such as the United States) is concerned about the possibility of revolution against an authoritarian regime allied to it. As the selection by Jeff Goodwin in Part V observes, no revolution "has ever overthrown a consolidated democratic" government. The only governments that revolutions have succeeded in overthrowing are authoritarian ones—though not all authoritarian regimes succumb to revolution.

While it is debatable whether democratic states are invulnerable to revolution, they do appear to be much less vulnerable to it than authoritarian states. Encouraging the democratization of their authoritarian allies, then, is a possible strategy for Western status quo powers seeking to forestall revolutions and their negative international consequences, including the likely termination of the revolutionary state's alliances with Western powers.

Like counterinsurgency, democratizing an authoritarian regime battling against a strong revolutionary opposition is no easy task. Indeed, both the authoritarian regimes and the Western states they are allied to have often opposed or abandoned democratization efforts for fear that the revolutionary opposition would "take advantage" of free elections to come to power and then destroy democracy afterward. That was the reason cited by the Algerian government for canceling the final round of the 1992 parliamentary elections, which Islamist forces appeared poised to win. Fighting between the authoritarian government and the revolutionary opposition has continued ever since then. Sometimes, though, the replacement of an authoritarian ruler by a popularly elected one can serve to fatally undercut even a powerful revolutionary movement, as occurred in the Philippines in 1986.

In this section, two scholars examine the factors affecting the success or failure of two very different methods of attempting to forestall revolution through democratization. Robert Pastor analyzes several U.S.-sponsored democratization efforts that have sought to exclude the revolutionary opposition. By contrast, Matthew Shugart discusses several democratization efforts that have sought to include it.

All the cases that these two authors examine are authoritarian *status quo* regimes. Of course, the democratization of authoritarian *revolutionary* regimes is also a possibility, as the election in the Islamic Republic of Iran of a reformist president in 1997 and a reformist parliament in 2000 have shown. However, democratization of an authoritarian revolutionary regime usually occurs only after the authoritarian regime has gone through the initial phase of extreme hostility toward the status quo powers, as did the Islamic Republic of Iran. The possibility of democratizing authoritarian revolutionary regimes is one of the themes that will be explored in Part IV.

7

Preempting Revolutions:
The Boundaries of U.S. Influence

Robert A. Pastor

Robert A. Pastor served on the National Security Council during the administration of Jimmy Carter (1977–1981), a period that witnessed the Iranian and Nicaraguan Revolutions, among other tumultuous events. He later wrote an influential analysis of the U.S. role in Nicaragua en-titled, Condemned to Repetition: The United States and Nicaragua *(1987).*

In the following selection, Pastor examines why some U.S. attempts to forestall revolution through promoting the democratization of hith-erto authoritarian regimes have succeeded while others have failed. He analyzes seven cases in which the United States played an important role: Cuba in the late 1950s; the Dominican Republic and Haiti in the early 1960s; Iran and Nicaragua in the late 1970s; and the Philippines, Haiti (again), and Chile in the 1980s.

Although the United States pursued similar policies in all of these cases, their outcomes varied considerably. Anti-American revolutionary regimes came to power in Cuba, Iran, and Nicaragua, whereas democratic transitions occurred in Chile and the Philippines. Revolution was forestalled in the Dominican Republic and Haiti, but the democratization process in them was more problematic. The key to understanding these cases, Pastor argues, is an "interactive perspective" that "seeks to understand how local and external actors interact to produce a particular outcome."

Robert A. Pastor, "Preempting Revolutions: The Boundaries of U.S. Influence," *International Security* 15:4 (spring 1991): 54–79, 85–86. © 1991 by the President and Fellows of Harvard College and the Massachusetts Institute of Technology. Reprinted with permission.

I would like to express my gratitude to Joseph S. Nye, Jr., Robert Lieber, and Thomas Remington for their comments on earlier drafts. The article is the better for their efforts.

Critical Questions

1. What are the four stages that Pastor identifies as being common to each of the country cases he analyzes?

2. If, as Pastor argues, the United States pursued basically the same foreign policy in all of these cases, then what accounts for their varying outcomes?

3. Might any of these cases have turned out differently if the United States had attempted to include the revolutionaries in the democratization process instead of excluding them?

One of the most frustrating and difficult challenges faced by the United States in the postwar period has been coping with revolutionary regimes in Cuba, Iran, and Nicaragua that replaced others that were friendly to the United States. Critics have asked: "Who lost these countries?" and "Could U.S. policy-makers have anticipated and preempted the revolutions?"

Protracted dictatorships have not always given way to hostile revolutionary regimes: the assassination of Dominican dictator Rafael Trujillo in 1961 led to a period of instability but eventually to democracy; the threat of Marxist revolution in the Philippines was reduced and democracy's prospects enhanced after the flight of Ferdinand Marcos in 1986; and the military filled the vacuum left by the departure of Haitian leader Jean-Claude Duvalier in February 1986. But why were some dictators replaced by belligerent revolutionary regimes while others were not? Did U.S. foreign policy make the difference?

The focus of this article is on succession crises, in which a declining dictator, who had been friendly to the United States but ruthless to his own people, faces or could soon face a broadly-based national movement to unseat him. The element that transforms this issue into a national security problem for the United States is the existence or the possible emergence of a revolutionary group that views the United States as its enemy. The essence of the challenge for the United States, however, is not how to deal with the revolutionaries, but rather how to persuade or coerce the declining dictator to yield power in such a way that the successor is least likely to be anti-American and most likely to be democratic.

This article will begin by distinguishing succession crises from other U.S. foreign policy challenges such as revolutions. It then analyzes eight cases with different outcomes, and seeks explanations for why a revolution occurs or is preempted, why U.S. policies have tended to look similar in apparently different circumstances, and what lessons can be drawn for dealing with similar crises in the future.

In analyzing the seven succession crises, a surprising aspect is the similarity of U.S. policies over a span of thirty years. Presidents as different as Eisenhower and Carter, Kennedy and Reagan expended considerable time and political capital to cope with these crises, but the responses of each did not differ greatly from those of the others. An effective formula eluded all of them. George Shultz, Reagan's secretary of state, wondered, "how do you go about the move from an authoritarian governmental structure to one that is more open and democratic? The more you study that, the more you see that it is hard."[1]

If U.S. policy is similar in each of these cases, then what accounts for the different outcomes? A few theoretical studies have addressed issues related to declining dictators, and there have been many excellent case studies, but there has not been a systematic comparative analysis of the process by which long-standing dictators have fallen. . . . The case studies have tended to approach their subject from one of two directions. One group finds the answer to the question of why revolutionaries overthrow dictators in U.S. policy, but these answers sometimes differ. For example, on the Nicaraguan case, Jeane Kirkpatrick argued that Jimmy Carter "brought down the Somoza regime" and helped the Sandinistas take power.[3] William LeoGrande also blames Carter's policy, but for the opposite reason: he thinks Carter failed because he did *not* try to overthrow Somoza.[4]

A second group locates explanations inside the country undergoing the crisis, although again, there are differences in the emphasis on social, economic, or political factors. If the first group of analysts fails to take into account local actors, the problem with this second approach is the opposite: it fails to take into account the effect of powerful international actors on smaller, more vulnerable states. Obviously, the external and internal approaches are not incompatible, but most scholars have stressed one or the other, and few have tried to integrate these two approaches. This article will argue that internal factors were more important in explaining the evolution and outcome of these succession crises, but a complete explanation requires an "interactive perspective," one that seeks to understand how local and external actors interact to produce a particular outcome.[5]

Defining the Problem

A recurring problem that the United States has confronted in the third world is how to preclude the emergence of hostile regimes that would invite powerful rivals to defend them or would otherwise advance their interests at the expense of those of the United States. That problem is frequently defined by asking whether the United States can live with revolutions. Echos of this kind of question—"who lost Cuba?"—can be heard throughout the literature of U.S. relations with the Third World.[6] The answer has proven elusive partly because the question blurs two distinct challenges for U.S. policy-makers: (a) affecting the succession crisis of a declining dictator; and (b) dealing with a revolutionary regime. This article is concerned with the first challenge, which is serious precisely because revolutionary regimes have proven so problematic for the United States. U.S. policy-makers have therefore believed that U.S. influence is greater, and the risks to world peace fewer, if the United States acts to avert a hostile group from taking power than if it tries to prevent an anti-U.S. government from asking help from the Soviet Union or Cuba.

All three great Latin American revolutions—in Mexico, Cuba, and Nicaragua—began as crises of political succession. When there are no legitimate procedures for transferring power in a country, political violence is the only option. Most often, the violent change is quick—a *coup d'état* in which one ruling faction ousts another. But a succession crisis occurs when the transition is prolonged or uncertain. There are many varieties, but each involves the awkward period before and after the exit of long-standing dictators. This article will examine a sample of those succession crises which (a) exhibit similar patterns; (b) involve a substantial American role; and (c) have different outcomes. My purpose is to identify the key variables that explain the different outcomes. The article will review seven cases: Cuba (1958–59), the Dominican Republic (1960–61), Haiti (two phases: 1961–63, and 1985–86), Iran (1978–79), Nicaragua (1978–79), the Philippines (1983–86), and Chile (1988–89).

Each crisis began with a key event that shook the dictator, and each ended with his death or departure. A shared characteristic of these succession crises is the contemporary and historical involvement of the United States in the internal affairs of each of these seven countries. Only Chile had not at some time been occupied by U.S. troops. Indeed, the constitutions of Cuba, Nicaragua, the Dominican Republic, and Haiti had each once included clauses that granted rights to the United States to intervene in their internal affairs. Even after the United States repudiated these rights and withdrew its troops, the psychological residue of this period of U.S. control continued to affect local politics.

When dictators took power in each of these countries, they generally supported U.S. foreign policies and tried to make it appear as if the United States supported them. Their purpose was to try to isolate their opposition. The United States sometimes rejected this identification; other times, it acquiesced; and sometimes, it embraced the dictator. Unfortunately, most of the people in these countries tended to recall—even exaggerate—only the last relationship of identification. One of the consequences was that the dictator's enemies viewed the United States as their enemy as well. Thus, the United States sometimes found itself entangled in succession crises that became violent struggles between illegitimate dictators and anti-American revolutionaries.

U.S. objectives in each of these crises exhibited a similar pattern. They were crisply defined by President John F. Kennedy as he surveyed the Dominican Republic after the assassination of Rafael Trujillo in 1961: "There are three possibilities in descending order of preference: a decent democratic regime, a continuation of the Trujillo regime, or a 'Castro' regime. We ought to aim at the first, but we really can't renounce the second until we are sure that we can avoid the third."[7] From the U.S. perspective, the worst outcomes occurred in Cuba, Iran, and Nicaragua, where anti-American revolutionary regimes took power.[8] The best outcomes were where democratic transitions occurred in the Philippines and Chile. Ambiguous outcomes occurred in the Dominican Republic because democracy eventually took hold, but only after years of instability and a major U.S. intervention, and in Haiti, where military officers retained effective power.

Each of these succession crises passed through four stages that are defined by the changes in the relations among the various actors. These stages will serve as signposts for narrating the cases. The first stage was the *identification* of the dictator with the United States in the country's collective mind. Sometimes that has been an accurate reflection of U.S. policy, and sometimes it has been due to misperception.

As middle-class disenchantment and rebel violence against the dictator increases, or a traumatic event causes local and international actors to fear a revolutionary outcome, U.S. policy moves to the second stage, of *distance and dissociation* from the dictator.

The third stage occurs as the dictator's position weakens and the possibility of a successful insurgency increases; at this time, moderate groups seeking a peaceful, political change either *ally with and legitimize the left* or they remain independent. Moderate neighboring governments often exert important influences on the decisions of these groups. If such an alliance is forged, then the United States moves rapidly toward the fourth stage: *encouraging the military to reject the dictator and support a "third force,"* that is, a moderate alternative to the insurgents and the dictator. The emergence of a third force or the defection of important military figures from the dictator's camp can preempt the revolution. But if this fails, then the United States must decide whether to intervene or to allow the insurgents to take power.

U.S. policy was strikingly similar in each of the cases examined below: the United States first identified with the dictator, then distanced and dissociated from him, and when the moderates legitimized the left, it tried to locate and support a moderate third force.

The following variables were crucial in explaining why some revolutions were preempted and some were not: (a) the existence of a guerrilla insurgency; (b) whether the middle sectors allied with the left or with some part of the military; (c) the nature of the military response; and (d) the conduct of genuinely free elections. (See Table 1).

The pattern of outcomes suggests the following hypotheses:

(1) If the moderate sectors ally with friendly regional governments and with the guerilla insurgency, and if the military remain united until the dictator flees, and if elections are openly fraudulent or not held, then the prospects for anti-U.S. revolution are the highest.

(2) If there is no guerrilla movement, and if the military divides and some or all defect from the dictator, then a military takeover is most likely.

(3) If there is a guerrilla insurgency, if the middle sector supports elections, and if the military divides but does not collapse, then the prospects are best for democracy.

Table 1. Pre-empting Revolutions: Factors and Outcomes

Countries and revolutions	Dictatorship	Outcome	Does U.S. policy follow pattern?[1]	Was there a guerrilla movement?	Role of middle sector and regional actors	Military defection from dictator/collapse?	Characteristics of elections
1. Cuba (1958–59)	Batista, 26 years (direct and indirect rule) (1933–59)	Anti-U.S. revolution	Yes	Yes	Allied with guerrillas	No/Yes	Fraud/Abstention (1958)
2. Nicaragua (1978–79)	Somoza family, 43 years (1936–79)	Anti-U.S. revolution	Yes	Yes	Allied with guerrillas	No/Yes	Fraud/Abstention (1972); None in 1979
3. Iran (1978–79)	Shah, 37 years (1941–79)	Anti-U.S. revolution	Ambiguous	Yes	Alienation	No/Yes	None
4. Dominican Republic (1960–61)	Trujillo, 31 years (1930–61)	Military takeover	Yes	No	Disassociation from dictator	Yes/No	None
5. Haiti a. (1961–63); b. (1985–86)	Duvalier family, 29 years (1957–86)	No change (1963); Military takeover (1986)	Yes; Yes	No; No	Disassociation from dictator	No/No; Yes/No	None
6. Philippines (1983–86)	Ferdinand Marcos, 21 years (1965–86)	Democracy	Yes	Yes	Autonomous opposition	Yes/No	Free, but attempted theft
7. Chile (1988–89)	Augusto Pinochet, 17 years (1973–90)	Democracy	Yes	Yes, but weak	Support for election	Yes/No	Free

Notes: 1. "Yes" indicates that in this case, U.S. policy followed the pattern of (1) identification, followed by (2) distance/dissociation, and then, in reaction to moderates' alliance with and legitimation of the left, by (3) encouraging the military to reject the dictator, and (4) seeking a moderate "third force" to support.

The Cases

Cuba, 1958–59

Most of the time from August 1933 until he fled the country on New Year's Day 1959, Fulgencio Batista ruled Cuba either directly or through surrogates. In 1952, he ran for president. When the polls showed he might lose, he seized power. This led to widespread protests, some violent, including an attack against one of his barracks led by young Fidel Castro on July 26, 1953. The opposition did not prevent Batista from consolidating policy, nor did it inhibit the praise he received from U.S. Ambassador Arthur Gardner (1953–57). This was the period of "identification," and Vice President Richard Nixon's visit at this time reinforced the view that the United States stood firmly behind the dictator because he shared its views of the Communist threat.

By 1957, however, the protests against Batista had become increasingly violent, and the moderate sectors began to lend their support to the young rebels. Castro, who had been exiled, sailed to Cuba from Mexico with a small cadre in December 1956. He sought to place himself at the center of the opposition by issuing moderate, idealistic manifestos calling for free elections, a constitutional government, and agrarian reform.

On March 1, 1958, Cuban bishops called for an investigation of the regime's brutality and asked Batista to step down in favor of a government of national unity. The new U.S. ambassador, Earl Smith, also began to criticize the repression, but the clearest sign of a new policy of distancing and dissociation from the regime was the U.S. arms embargo against Batista announced by Secretary of State John Foster Dulles on April 8, 1958.

The next day, Castro called a general strike, and on July 20, 1958, representatives of all the opposition groups met in Caracas to sign a pact that named an opposition government led by a moderate judge as president and Castro as commander-in-chief. This legitimization of the leftist guerrillas represented the third stage of the succession crisis. The Venezuelan site was important symbolically because it heralded a new alignment of Latin American democratic forces behind Castro. Costa Rican President José Figueres was already giving Castro covert military support, having sent a planeload of arms on March 30, 1958, and Carlos Andres Pérez, a leader of the Venezuelan Social Democratic party, also sent arms to Castro. Figueres later explained that he "helped Fidel Castro as much as I could because . . .

we were completely willing to help overthrow all military dictatorships. We didn't know, and I think nobody knows, what were Fidel Castro's ideas regarding Communism at the time."[9]

The fourth stage—the desperate United States search for a third force—occurred after the opposition decided not to participate in what turned out to be a fraudulent election in November 1958. Senior officials in the Eisenhower administration asked William Pawley, an American businessman with experience in Latin America, to undertake a secret mission. As Pawley later described his goal, it was to "get Batista to capitulate to a caretaker government, unfriendly to him but satisfactory to us, whom we would immediately recognize and give military assistance to in order that Fidel Castro should not come to power."[10] Pawley proposed to Batista that he transfer power to Colonel Ramón Barquín, who had tried unsuccessfully to overthrow Batista in 1956. Without authority, Pawley offered Batista the chance to live in Florida. Batista refused the proposal and the offer.[11]

In December, the Eisenhower administration desperately sought to locate and support a third force. The Central Intelligence Agency (CIA) tried to get Barquín released from prison and to have him ally with Justo Carillo and other moderate civilians. Castro was wary of these plots, concerned that if Batista were replaced by someone credible and independent like Barquín, the revolution could come to a premature halt. But Batista unwittingly saved Castro when he transferred power to one of his staff, General Cantillo, and then flew to Miami.

Cantillo, however, decided it was futile to try to hold the army together, and he handed over power to Barquín, who was released from prison. Barquín then surprised everyone by telephoning Castro and surrendering the army, giving up, according to historian Hugh Thomas, "what chance there was of a government of the center."[12] The Cuban military disintegrated in a matter of days, and Castro's lieutenants took control of the remaining army units while Castro gathered political support on his journey to Havana.

Dominican Republic, 1960–61

Both the Eisenhower and the Kennedy administrations drew the conclusion that "Castro's road to power was paved by the excesses of Batista," and that similar conditions existed in the Dominican Republic under a brutal dictator, General Rafael Trujillo, who had ruled since 1930.[13] Even before Castro took power, the United States had begun to distance itself from Trujillo because of his notorious repression. Ambassador Joseph Farland adopted a cool approach to the dictator and opened the U.S. embassy to Dominican dissidents.[14]

Such efforts were accelerated after Castro's victory. In April 1960, President Eisenhower approved a contingency plan which provided that if the situation deteriorated, "the United States would immediately take political action to remove Trujillo from the Dominican Republic as soon as suitable successor regime can be induced to take over with the assurance of U.S. political, economic, and—if necessary—military support."[15] He then sent Pawley to talk to Trujillo, who said prophetically: "I'll never go out of here unless I go on a stretcher."[16]

While the April 1960 plan to remove Trujillo was not implemented, the Kennedy administration continued Eisenhower's policy of encouraging the overthrow of Trujillo by Dominican dissidents. But after the embarrassment caused by the failure of the Bay of Pigs invasion on April 17, 1961, Kennedy did not want to make another mistake in the Dominican Republic. He was worried that the assassination of Trujillo would create a power vacuum that could be exploited by Castroite radicals. Kennedy administration officials instructed the CIA to tell its station to "turn off" the coup. The rebels replied that the coup was their affair.[17]

At a National Security Council meeting on May 5, 1961, President Kennedy decided "that the United States should not initiate the overthrow of Trujillo before we knew what government would succeed him, and that any action against Trujillo should be multilateral."[18] Upon learning of this decision, Henry Dearborn, the U.S. embassy contact with the dissidents, reminded the State Department that the embassy had been supporting efforts to overthrow Trujillo for a year. Dearborn cabled that it was simply "too late to consider whether United States will initiate overthrow of Trujillo."[19]

As the rebels were about to strike, Kennedy was apparently torn by contrary concerns. He feared being too directly linked to a coup that might fail. If the coup resulted in serious instability in the Dominican Republic, he would be blamed.[20] On the other hand, it would be desirable to be identified with the rebels if they succeeded. The White House therefore sent a cable, approved by President Kennedy, to Dearborn on May 29, 1961, affirming that U.S. policy was "not [to] run [the] risk of U.S. association with political assassination, since [the] U.S. as a matter of general policy cannot condone assassination." At the same time, the cable communicated the approval of the administration should the dissidents succeed. In short, U.S.

objectives were deliberately contradictory: to encourage the rebels to think they had U.S. support if they succeeded, but to dissociate from them if they failed. The next day, May 30, 1961, Trujillo was shot.[21]

The new problem was how to maintain order, facilitate a transition to constitutional democracy, and keep Trujillo's sons from power. Kennedy sent a flotilla of nearly forty ships to the Dominican coast as a warning to the Trujillo family, but he was also very concerned with the immaturity and divisiveness of the Dominican opposition. "The key in all these countries," said Kennedy, "is the emergence of a leader. . . . The great danger . . . is a take-over by the army, which could lead straight to [another] Castro."[22]

In December 1962, Juan Bosch, a Social Democrat, was elected president in a fair election. Although he enjoyed Washington's support, the military overthrew him within a year. When one part of the military tried to restore Bosch to power in 1965, the country fell into civil war, and President Johnson dispatched 22,000 Marines to restore order and prevent any radicals from taking power. Presidential elections were held within a year and have been repeated at four-year intervals since then. In 1978, the first peaceful transfer of power from one political party to another occurred; the second occurred in 1986.

Haiti, Two Phases

The same concern that led the United States to take preemptive action in the Dominican Republic led it to focus on Haiti, where another brutal dictator, François "Papa Doc" Duvalier, had ruled since 1957. However, the experience in the Dominican Republic made the Kennedy administration even more cautious in its approach to Haiti.

Initially, the State Department considered a plan proposed by Undersecretary of State Chester Bowles to assemble a donors' consortium and offer Duvalier substantial aid if he accepted democratic and financial reforms. If Duvalier rejected the plan, the United States would impose an embargo against Haiti. According to Edwin Martin, who was assistant secretary of state for inter-American affairs at the time, the plan was not approved because of the administration's "reluctance to offer so much as Bowles proposed to such a government and the conviction of Haitian experts that Duvalier would accept neither proposal."[23]

After the Cuban missile crisis, President Kennedy personally initiated a review of policy toward Haiti. At the conclusion of that review, in January

1963, Kennedy decided that the "replacement of Duvalier was a prerequisite to the achievement of U.S. interests in Haiti." However, Kennedy insisted on three conditions before he would approve a plan to implement that objective: (1) the plan would have to have a high probability of success; (2) assurances were necessary that the new regime would be better than the existing one; and (3) the plan would have to be implemented by Haitians or by a third country. These conditions proved too stringent to permit action.[24]

The Kennedy administration's sense of urgency was based on fear that the longer Duvalier stayed in power, the more likely it was that he would be replaced by a Castroite revolution. The premise proved to be flawed; "Papa Doc" and his son, Jean-Claude "Baby Doc" Duvalier, who inherited the presidency after his father's death in 1971, continued to rule for twenty-three years after Kennedy's death.

1985–86. During the younger Duvalier's tenure, U.S. policy remained relatively consistent in a broad sense. The United States did not cultivate a warm relationship; it either ignored Haiti, or used a mix of carrots and sticks—promises of aid and threats of withdrawal—to encourage Duvalier to respect human rights, open the political system, end corruption, and cooperate on controlling illegal emigration (which went mostly to the United States). Within these broad parameters, the Carter administration tended to make more human rights demands on the Haitian government and give less aid, whereas the Reagan administration tended to make fewer demands and deliver more aid. During Reagan's term, Congress added stiff human rights conditions to the aid, which nonetheless grew from about $30 million in 1981 to about $50 million in 1984. Other donors and international development banks also increased their aid commitments as Duvalier pledged to improve administration of the aid program and to open the political system.

Duvalier permitted elections for a legislative assembly in 1984, although he then manipulated them to ensure victory for his candidates. When aid donors expressed disappointment, Duvalier announced anti-corruption and judicial reforms, and relaxed press censorship. He then held a referendum in July 1985, and he was confirmed as president-for-life with more than 99 percent of the vote. Soon after, violence erupted in numerous towns, culminating in November with riots in Gonaives, which many date as the beginning of the end of the regime.[25]

On January 29, 1986, after riots spread over the island and Duvalier invoked martial law, the middle class distanced itself from Duvalier, as did

Secretary of State George Shultz in announcing that new aid commitments to Haiti would be delayed. The pressure on Duvalier to resign increased from all sectors, including the military, and on February 6, 1986, Duvalier asked the U.S. embassy to provide a plane for him to depart.

When he was asked about the role of the United States in the last week of the regime and whether the U.S. ambassador gave Duvalier "any strong advice to leave," President Ronald Reagan responded that the United States never gave any such advice and Duvalier had "never asked us for any." The only role played by the United States, according to President Reagan, was "providing an airplane to fly him to France."[26]

A military-civilian junta led by General Henri Namphy took power, and the United States restored aid after Namphy promised free elections. On election day, November 29, 1987, gunmen who were either allied with or directed by the military killed 34 voters and confiscated ballots. Namphy then called off the election and dissolved the electoral commission. After Washington suspended aid, Namphy called another election in January 1988, but almost all of the candidates and the vast majority of eligible voters refused to participate. Leslie Manigat, a scholar who had been in exile for most of the Duvalier regime, was elected, but when he tried to exercise some independence five months later, he was toppled by the military. The army continued to govern either directly or through a provisional government, but free elections were finally permitted on December 16, 1990, in the presence of large numbers of observers from the United Nations, the Organization of American States, and the Council of Freely-Elected Heads of Government chaired by former U.S. President Jimmy Carter. A democratic government took power on the fifth anniversary of Duvalier's departure, but in an uncertain climate, shadowed by a strong and wary military.

Nicaragua, 1978–79

In the Nicaraguan drama, virtually all of the key actors in the United States, Nicaragua, and neighboring countries were determined to avoid the Cuban scenario and outcome, but all repeated the same actions in Nicaragua that they or their counterparts had taken in Cuba.

Anastasio Somoza Garcia was appointed commander of the National Guard in 1933 by his uncle, Juan Sacasa, whom he deposed as president three years later. Somoza followed by his two sons ruled Nicaragua as their personal fiefdom until the Sandinistas overthrew his youngest son, Anastasio Somoza Debayle, on July 17, 1979. The Somoza dynasty cultivated a public image of partnership with the United States, although the United States had tried to persuade one Somoza or another to step down or not seek re-election on four different occasions (1945, 1947–49, 1963, 1975–79).[27] Nonetheless, the perception of identification, partly the result of two obsequious U.S. ambassadors, remained more influential than the reality of a complicated relationship.[28]

In 1975, the Ford administration distanced itself from Somoza because of increasing concern with his corruption and repression, and it opened contacts with the opposition. This trend was accelerated when Carter took office in 1977. The decisive event triggering the Nicaraguan insurrection occurred in January 1978 with the assassination of Pedro Joaquín Chamorro, the editor of *La Prensa* and leader of the moderate opposition. This transformed the moderate sectors from passive opponents to new militants who were prepared to consider alliances with their former enemies to get rid of Somoza.

The Sandinista National Liberation Front (FSLN), which had been founded in 1961 as a Marxist, Castro-oriented guerrilla group, had decided in the mid-1970s to broaden its membership, expand its relationship within Nicaragua and internationally, and moderate its Marxist rhetoric. Its initial success was apparent in the popular enthusiasm that greeted the Sandinista raid on the National Palace in August 1978.

That event and the arrest by Somoza of hundreds of moderate leaders during a September insurrection mobilized the U.S. government to take the lead in forming a multilateral mediation process under the auspices of the Organization of American States (OAS) to facilitate a democratic transition. The Carter administration warned Somoza that if he did not accept reasonable standards for a fair plebiscite, then the United States would impose economic and diplomatic sanctions. In February 1979, after Somoza rejected the terms, the United States imposed sanctions.

Between February and June 1979, the moderate opposition and the democratic Latin American governments gradually moved toward an alliance with the Sandinistas. Alfonso Robelo, a Nicaraguan businessman, later said that he joined the Sandinista coalition at that time "because the support of [Panama's General] Torrijos, [Venezuelan President] Carlos Andres Pérez, and [Costa Rican President] Rodrigo Carazo gave me confidence that it was the right thing to do."[29] The Costa Rican and Venezuelan governments provided open political support and covert military aid to the Sandinistas, as they had to Castro. These governments and Panama also helped cover Cuban aid and advice to the FSLN. Until the Sandinistas launched their "final offensive" in mid-June 1979, the U.S. government was unaware of the nature and depth of their strength. Then, the United States desperately sought to fashion an "Executive Committee," a non-Somocista third force, to negotiate with the Sandinista-led junta. Unfortunately, most of the moderate leadership had already associated with the Sandinistas, and the few who considered becoming the third force wanted unequivocal assurances from the United States that were not forthcoming.

The U.S. government also tried to locate post-Somoza leadership for the National Guard, but these efforts failed because Somoza effectively shielded the Guard from any outside contacts, lest some ambitious officer decide to remove him. Therefore, he blocked the appointment of General Gutiérrez, favored by the United States, as commander (just as Batista had blocked Colonel Barquín). Carter was unwilling to offer assurances of aid to new Guard leaders without support from Latin American democratic leaders. In the end, a transitional agreement involving Somoza's successor Francisco Urcuyo, the Guard, and the Sandinistas was disregarded by both the Sandinistas and Somoza after Somoza's flight on July 17, 1979.[30] Two days later, the Sandinistas marched into Managua.

Iran, 1978–79

The period of the Nicaraguan succession crisis overlapped with that of Iran, and the parallels were so numerous that U.S. policy-makers kept track of some of the actors in one country by referring to their counterparts in the other.[31] However, Carter and his senior advisers were much more directly engaged in the succession crisis in Iran than in Nicaragua because of the direct impact that events in Iran could—and did—have on the U.S. economy (doubling of oil prices, inflation) and on U.S.–Soviet strategic relations. Carter judged that "our nation would not be threatened by the Sandinistas as it would be by the fall of the Shah."[32] In his memoirs, Zbigniew Brzezinski merely mentions Nicaragua in a sentence, while devoting more than a chapter to the Shah's fall, calling the latter episode the "administration's greatest setback" and "disastrous strategically."[33]

The Shah of Iran had been on the Peacock Throne since 1941, and because of his anti-communism and his nation's long border with the Soviet Union, he forged a particularly close relationship with the United States. In

1953, the CIA orchestrated a series of events in Tehran that helped him secure the resignation of Mohammed Mossadegh, who was then Prime Minister. That event reinforced the myth of the Shah as "a pliant creature of the United States." That perception remained "a vivid political reality" in Iran twenty-five years later, although by then the U.S. government viewed the uncooperative Shah more as a "testy and imperious monarch."[34]

The Shah pursued economic without political modernization, and in doing so he alienated both the religious fundamentalists and the modernist intellectuals. Despite this, the U.S. relationship became even closer in 1972 when President Richard Nixon decided to make the Shah the principal guardian of western interests in the Persian Gulf in exchange for providing whatever military equipment and technology the Shah wanted. This unprecedented agreement contributed to a role reversal, with the Shah dictating the terms of the relationship.[35] Carter accepted the bi-national agreement, although he tried to persuade the Shah to scale down his military purchases and curb his secret police. Despite his advice, Carter admitted in his memoirs that "it soon became obvious that my expression of concern would not change the policies of the Shah in meeting a threat which, I am sure, seemed very real to him."[36]

The political situation worsened until, on January 9, 1978, the Shah's police opened fire on a religious demonstration. The Iranian revolution had begun.[37] The response by President Carter to the succession crisis in Iran was different from his response to the crisis in Nicaragua. Whereas he urged Somoza to accept a vote on his tenure, Carter's message to the Shah was:

> that whatever action he took, including setting up a military government, I would support him. We did not want him to abdicate. [The Shah was] a staunch and dependable ally ... [who] remained the leader around whom we hoped to see a stable and reformed government. ... We knew little about the forces contending against him, but their anti-American slogans and statements were enough in themselves to strengthen our resolve to support the Shah.[38]

By November 1978 however, the State Department and particularly the U.S. ambassador to Tehran, William Sullivan, wanted to encourage the Shah to abdicate, and had begun to work closely with the Ayatollah Khomeini in the hopes of moderating his anti-Americanism. Similarly, and for the same reasons, seven months later the State Department recommended a more positive approach to the Sandinistas. In the case of Nicaragua, Carter gradually accepted the State Department position, but with regard to Iran, he reprimanded State and reaffirmed support for the Shah.

At the end of December 1978, the Shah tried to regain control of events by appointing Shahpour Bakhtiar as his prime minister. Bakhtiar, however, decided to establish his independence by calling for the secret police to be disbanded and the Shah to leave Iran. Carter did not waver from his unconditional support for the Shah even though Carter recognized that "the Shah would have to leave the country before order could be restored."[39] After the Shah's departure on January 16, 1979, Bakhtiar was soon overwhelmed by a religious movement deeper and more powerful than anything the West had seen since the Crusades. On February 1, the Ayatollah Khomeini flew to Tehran from France and was met by hundreds of thousands of devoted followers. Khomeini quickly took control of the government, and by February 11, the military surrendered to his followers.

The Philippines, 1983–86

Having been colonized by both Spain and the United States, the Philippines shares a number of characteristics with the nations of the Caribbean Basin. Unlike the Caribbean, however, the Philippines had maintained a democratic tradition from independence in 1946 until Ferdinand Marcos declared martial law in 1972 to suppress a Communist guerrilla insurgency. Marcos had been a popular leader who won election as president in 1965 and 1969, but during the 1970s, he grew increasingly corrupt and repressive.

The Catholic Church, led by Jaime Cardinal Sin, played an important role supporting and legitimizing the protest against the dictator. When Benigno Aquino, Jr., the principal opposition leader, was assassinated in August 1983, the nation mourned, and the population became mobilized. The guerrillas profited from the polarization. Marcos became the target of the guerrillas' wrath as well as the cause of their successful recruitment. The communist New People's Army, which numbered in the hundreds when Marcos declared martial law in 1972, would increase to over 20,000 armed men by the time Marcos quit power.[40]

Marcos tried to use the American media to warn of "a second Nicaragua."[41] When asked by *Newsweek* reporters how he would respond if the United States asked him to resign, Marcos boasted: "I think your leaders are wiser than that. I don't think they would dare. . . . They know how I would react. . . . I would immediately tell the whole world about it."[42]

Reagan initially broke from Carter's human rights-oriented policy and identified with Marcos. Vice President George Bush was sent to the Philippines in July 1981 where he complimented Marcos, saying "we love your adherence to democratic principles and democratic processes."[43] The next year Reagan warmly welcomed Marcos on a state visit to Washington.

The killing of Benigno Aquino and the growing power of the insurgents finally impelled the Reagan administration to distance itself from Marcos and press him for reforms. President Reagan's planned state visit to the Philippines in November 1983 was canceled. A State Department policy paper written in November 1984, and leaked to the press five months later, warned: "An overriding consideration should be to avoid getting ourselves caught between the slow erosion of Marcos's authoritarian control and the still fragile revitalization of democratic institutions." It recommended economic aid and diplomatic pressure to persuade Marcos to accept a democratic political succession.[44] Marcos accepted some of the minor U.S. demands, but blasted the United States for interfering in Philippine politics.[45] American conservatives grew uneasy about the insurgency, while liberals demanded that Reagan "repudiate any notion of propping up Ferdinand Marcos."[46]

The Reagan administration was divided on what to do. The president viewed Marcos as a friend; having criticized Carter for abandoning America's friends, he was loath to do the same thing. The Defense Department was "impressed with Marcos's grit" and anxious about its largest military complex outside U.S. territory. The CIA and the State Department were convinced that Marcos's continuance in power would lead to another Nicaragua.[47]

The administration resolved its bureaucratic conflict by encouraging Marcos to hold a free election before 1987. First CIA Director William Casey and then Senator Paul Laxalt, a close friend of President Reagan, flew to the Philippines to deliver messages from Reagan and to talk about elections.[48] Apparently believing he would win the election either freely, or by manipulation as he was believed to have done with the numerous referenda and elections since the imposition of martial law, Marcos announced on U.S. television that he would schedule a new election. Unlike in Nicaragua, the Philippine opposition never seriously considered supporting the guerrillas against Marcos. Though initially divided, it eventually united behind the candidacy of Corazon Aquino, the widow of the slain leader. The Philippines had experience with free elections, and the National Citizens

Movement for Free Elections (NAMFREL), an independent pollwatching organization, had the capability of finding fraud and the courage to publicize it.

The elections were held on February 7, 1986. Marcos manipulated the results, but he was caught and denounced by NAMFREL, the international press, and a U.S. delegation led by Senator Richard Lugar. Corazon Aquino then launched a non-violent protest to be recognized as president. Marcos, having lost the support of the Church, independent businessmen, and the united political opposition, finally lost the loyalty of key elements of the army. On February 22, Defense Minister Juan Ponce Enrile and Vice Chief of Staff General Fidel Ramos announced their support of Aquino and called on Marcos to resign.

Did the United States encourage the military to rebel? Available sources do not offer a clear answer. Given President Reagan's affinity to Marcos, he is unlikely to have approved such contacts. On February 11, Reagan still equivocated, blaming "both sides" for electoral fraud, to the embarrassment of the U.S. ambassador and Aquino, both of whom knew that Marcos alone was responsible.[49] Nonetheless, by the time of the military defection on February 22, Reagan apparently was convinced to withdraw support from Marcos. U.S. officials contacted by the military coup-plotters had reportedly told them that they would not condone a military coup, but they also did not discourage it.[50]

On February 24, 1986, army rebels, surrounded by the civilian opposition and a group of nuns, approached the presidential palace. Marcos faced the choice of whether to order his soldiers to fire into the crowd or resign. The White House issued a statement urging Marcos not to attack the rebel forces: "A solution to this crisis can only be achieved through a peaceful transition to a new government." Marcos then phoned Paul Laxalt to ask whether that statement "was genuinely from President Reagan" or just reflected the views of the State Department, which he did not trust. Laxalt said that it was from Reagan. Then Marcos asked Laxalt if Reagan wanted him to resign. Laxalt called Reagan, who told the senator that Marcos "would be welcome to come to the United States," but did not answer the question whether he wanted Marcos to resign.[51] Reagan was no more prepared to ask Marcos to resign than Carter had been to ask Somoza. But neither was he prepared to defend a declining dictator.

In his next conversation with Marcos, Laxalt therefore answered the question about Reagan's view on resignation indirectly: "I indicated that I wasn't prepared to make that kind of representation." Then, Marcos asked Laxalt's own views, and as Laxalt recalled: "I wasn't bound by diplomatic niceties. I said, 'Cut and cut cleanly. The time has come'."[52] Marcos decided to leave.

The economic situation that Corazon Aquino inherited was catastrophic, and the political panorama threatening. Nonetheless, she managed to assemble a government, negotiate with the guerrillas, and maintain control of the armed forces. The democratic transition in the Philippines was one of the two most successful of these succession crises.

Chile, 1988–89

As it had with the Philippines, the Reagan administration at first repudiated Carter's human rights policy, and sought warm relations with the dictatorship of General Augusto Pinochet, who had held power since 1973. Nearly four years later in 1984, the administration returned to a policy similar to that of Carter's for three reasons: violence by the extreme left; intensified demands for a return to democracy by the moderate opposition; and the desire to demonstrate that the administration's commitment to democracy was not just a ploy for obtaining aid for the *contras* in Nicaragua. The administration decided to show it was serious about democracy in Nicaragua by supporting it in Chile.

The *New York Times* reported on December 2, 1984, that: "Mediation in Chile Termed Essential by U.S. Officials: Review Produces a Consensus for a Major Effort to Avoid 'Another Nicaragua'." Like Marcos, Pinochet tried to turn the same analogy in his favor by arguing that it was his opponents who wanted to turn Chile into "another Nicaragua." The administration began to vote against loans to Chile or to abstain in the international development banks, and it urged reforms and a democratic transition, although it was unwilling to consider overthrowing Pinochet.[53] Indeed, the consensus in the policy review was that the United States should not even "take sides"; rather it should be an impartial mediator between Pinochet and the opposition.

Chile's succession crisis was the most gradual and controlled of all cases examined here, perhaps because of Chile's virtually unbroken 140-year democratic and constitutional tradition before Pinochet's 1973 coup.[54] The polarization during the Allende government (1970–73) and the resulting coup were traumas that the majority of the Chilean public had no desire to repeat. Initially intimidated by Pinochet, the opposition finally decided to unite and participate in the plebiscite on Pinochet's tenure scheduled for October 5, 1988.

With U.S. encouragement, the opposition succeeded in negotiating the conditions necessary to assure that the election would be free. One important reason was that Pinochet thought he could win a free election and wanted to ensure that it would not appear tainted. His confidence was based on the country's prosperity, and polls that showed it was a close contest. International observers were invited, and with the eyes of the world focused on the election, it would have been very costly to rig the vote count or disregard the outcome.[55]

On October 5, 1988, nearly four million Chileans voted, representing 97 percent of the registered voters. They rejected Pinochet by 54 to 43 percent, and although there was some reluctance on Pinochet's part to accept the results, the other military members of the junta issued an immediate and clear statement that the opposition had won. This cleared the way for a presidential election on December 14, 1989, with the victor to take office on March 11, 1990.

In the debate on constitutional reform, the military junta, led but no longer controlled by General Pinochet, demonstrated that it was prepared to overrule its leader in order to keep the electoral process on track. In addition both the opposition, representing sixteen center-left political parties, and the conservative parties showed considerable patience and pragmatism in their campaigns, which augured well for the consolidation of the democratic process.

Bad and Good Outcomes:
Internal and External Explanations

Three of the crises culminated with non-democratic anti-American revolutionary regimes—the worst outcome from the perspective of the United States and local democrats. Two of the cases ended with democracies—the best outcome. Two led to military take-overs. How can the different outcomes be explained? Although the U.S. presidents were very different, U.S. policies toward these crises were quite similar. In Haiti, the Kennedy administration tried harder but with less success to persuade the elder Duvalier to leave in the earlier phase than the Reagan administration did during the second phase. These examples as well as the other cases make it clear that U.S. policy alone cannot explain the different outcomes.

First, I will summarize the stages of the succession crises, then discuss explanations for the different outcomes, looking at internal explanations first, then reviewing their relationship to U.S. policy. (See Table 1). I conclude with an analysis of past and future options available for U.S. foreign policymakers.

In these cases, when a broad-based opposition movement identified the United States with the dictator, the U.S. president tried to alter that perception and gain leverage on the dictator by distancing and eventually dissociating from him. Dissociation was a tactic to try to persuade the dictator to accept a transitional arrangement. A free election was the vehicle the United States preferred for steering between the unacceptable options of defending or overthrowing the dictator, or accepting the revolutionaries. When the crisis worsened and the worst-case scenario became more likely, the United States searched frantically to assemble a third force—a moderate, perhaps even democratic alternative to the dictator and the revolutionaries.

This was the sequence—identification, distancing and dissociation to encourage a free election, and the search for a third force—in every case, except, partially, in Iran. The president viewed his policy as one of support for the Shah to the end, but Carter's own comments on human rights were perceived as a distancing policy, and at the operational level, the ambassador also distanced himself from the Shah and searched for a third force.[56] This was the only case in which the pattern of U.S. policy was ambiguous.

The middle sector played the pivotal role in every case. All or most of the middle sectors dissociated themselves from the dictator; indeed the crisis could be said to have begun, at least from the U.S. perspective, when middle class defection became apparent. In three cases, the decision by centrist groups and democratic governments to support a violent overthrow of the regime provided legitimacy to the revolutionaries and neutralized a U.S. role. In Cuba and Nicaragua the center, supported by democratic governments in the region, aligned with the guerrillas. In Iran, the moderate National Front aligned with Khomeini, and expelled Bakhtiar when he entered the Shah's government.[57] The middle sectors chose the risky option of supporting the revolutionaries out of frustration with the intransigence of the dictator and in hope that they could moderate the revolutionaries if they helped them. Squeezed between an illegitimate dictator and anti-American revolutionaries, the United States would not support the dictator, but it could not intervene against the revolutionaries since the latter had the support of the middle classes.

In two successful cases—the Philippines and Chile—the middle sectors did not ally with the guerrilla insurgency, and the guerrillas did not enjoy any support from democratic governments. In the Dominican Republic and Haiti, the middle sectors were relatively weak, and there was no insurgency. This eliminated the prospect of a worst-case scenario from the U.S. perspective, but it meant that the military filled the power vacuum after the dictators departed.

The role of the military also had important effects on the outcomes. The military remained loyal to the dictator in the cases of Cuba, Nicaragua, and Iran, and all three militaries collapsed when the dictators left. In Nicaragua, some thought that the Guard's disintegration was due to the lack of assurances of aid by the United States, but such assurances had been given in Cuba and in Iran with no effect. The military defection from the dictator in the Dominican Republic, Haiti, the Philippines, and (to a limited extent) in Chile permitted non-revolutionary successor regimes to emerge.

The elections were important to success in the Philippines and Chile. The opposition negotiated conditions that permitted a vote in which fraud could be detected. In these two cases, last-minute efforts to manipulate the vote or the count failed. Whether or not the dictator was prepared to accept his loss initially, the election denied him legitimacy more effectively than all the demonstrations or strikes. Thus, elections served as the best vehicle for peaceful change, even for countries emerging from long periods of tyranny.

The United States was important in encouraging elections in these cases, but it had encouraged free elections unsuccessfully in Cuba, Nicaragua, and Haiti. The reason for the policy's success or failure had less to do with the United States than with the history of the target country. Nicaragua and Haiti had never had a free election, and Cuba's experience with democracy was negligible. In these countries, the opposition was divided into small fractions, many of which preferred to withdraw under protest rather than participate in the elections. In contrast, both the Philippines and Chile had had many free elections, and the opposition was willing to risk participation. In both cases, the dictator had also convinced himself that he could win the election, either honestly or with minimal, undetectable fraud. Negotiating the terms for free elections proved more effective than negotiating transitions. In Nicaragua, a transitional arrangement was negotiated, but it fell apart within one day of Somoza's exit. The negotiated exit of the Shah also failed within days of the arrival of the Ayatollah. Only where elections legitimized a successor regime did pre-arranged transitions work.

A final factor explaining the different outcomes was the influence of recent similar experiences on decision-makers. The trauma of Castro's victory impelled both local and international actors to try to precipitate regime changes in the Dominican Republic and Haiti in order to preempt revolution. Similarly, two decades later, the Nicaraguan trauma had a profound influence on the crises in Chile and the Philippines. The moderate sectors appeared to have learned the principal lesson of the Nicaraguan revolution—unite, participate in elections, and resist the siren calls of the insurgents. From the outside, efforts to encourage and monitor elections seem to offer the most promise for a graceful and successful exit from succession crises, although local actors and experiences remain the principal cause of the success or failure of elections. . . .

Future Choices

In considering future U.S. policies, then, the only real choices are within the parameters . . . of promoting liberalization. Because military intervention is ruled out, the United States cannot control or even manage a succession crisis. The issue for U.S. policymakers is how to influence the crisis from the margin of events. The outcome will depend, first and last, on the decisions of local actors—on the dictator, the military, the moderate opposition, and the radicals—but U.S. influence and timing can have important influences.

Although crises of political succession have a number of common elements that permit a single recommended strategy, each has unique national characteristics. To assist U.S. policymakers in understanding the differences and similarities between current and past succession crises, . . . a more systematic support system is needed. Currently, the State and Defense Departments have historical offices, but these concentrate more on writing diplomatic or military history than on preparing historical background information useful to the policymaker. The White House, which lacks an historical office, needs one.

The cases demonstrate that the best outcomes occurred when dictators agreed to elections and were forced to accept their results, and a united opposition chose to participate and could negotiate the terms for free elections. The United States needs better information on the actors than it has had in past succession crises in order for it to contribute to an environment that fosters this outcome. The dictator's personal needs and weaknesses should be the objects of intense and continuing study. The United States should pursue contacts with the military at all levels and ensure that they understand how the United States views the crisis.

The most delicate and important relationships are with the moderate opposition and the insurgents. Here, the history of past succession crises ought to have the most impact. When moderates divided and allied with the insurgents, they forfeited their future. The United States has not tended to establish contacts with insurgents, mainly for fear that this would undermine its relationship with the moderates. The best way to serve the goals of contacting the rebels without hurting other relationships is to do so through intermediaries—Congressmembers, private citizens, foreigners. Procedurally, these strategies should only be pursued after fully consulting with friendly regional governments.

As a succession crisis approaches, the United States should develop a comprehensive strategy aimed at all four stages of the crisis: (1) isolate the dictatorship through a clear, multilateral human rights policy; (2) facilitate the dictator's exit through negotiations that reflect a subtle understanding of his weaknesses and needs; (3) assist in the transition toward free elections through the international mediation of elections, as occurred in Nicaragua from July 1989 through April 1990, and in Haiti from July 1990 through February 1991; . . . and (4) aid the consolidation of democracy. . . .

But by the time the dictator has fallen into a succession crisis, the boundaries of U.S. influence have already narrowed. Before that happens the United States should use the full panoply of American resources, including non-governmental groups and quasi-governmental organizations, like the National Endowment for Democracy and the party institutes, to aid democratic institutions and establish contacts with more groups across the political spectrum. Other like-minded nations could assist the effort. The United States can only expand those boundaries if it develops a longer-term strategy for fostering and consolidating democracy.

NOTES

1. Cited in Elaine Sciolino, "Panama's Chief Defies U.S. Powers of Persuasion," *New York Times*, January 17, 1988, p. E3.

. . .

3. Jeane Kirkpatrick, "U.S. Security and Latin America," *Commentary*, January 1981, p. 36.

4. William LeoGrande, "The Revolution in Nicaragua: Another Cuba?" *Foreign Affairs,* Vol. 58, No. 1 (Fall 1979), p. 28. . . .

5. For a critique of those who rely solely on either the international or the internal perspective, and a discussion of the "interactive perspective," see Robert Pastor, "Explaining U.S. Policy Toward the Caribbean Basin: Fixed and Emerging Images," *World Politics,* Vol. 38, No. 3 (April 1986), pp. 483–515.

6. See, for example, "Forum: Why Are We in Central America? Can the U.S. Live with Latin Revolution?" *Harper's,* June 1984, pp. 35–48; and Morris J. Blachman, William M. LeoGrande, and Kenneth Sharpe, *Confronting Revolution: Security Through Diplomacy in Central America* (New York: Pantheon, 1986).

7. Cited by Arthur M. Schlesinger, Jr., *A Thousand Days: John F. Kennedy in the White House* (Boston: Houghton Mifflin, 1965), p. 769.

8. These regimes are quite different and not equally hostile to the United States, but common to all three is deeply-ingrained anti-Americanism.

9. Figueres's involvement is documented in a hearing of the U.S. Senate, Committee on the Judiciary, *Communist Threat to the U.S. Through the Caribbean: Hearings before the Subcommittee to Investigate the Administration of the Internal Security Act and Other Internal Security Laws, Part 8,* January 22–23, 1960, pp. 447–454. Pérez acknowledged his help in an interview with WGBH Public Television (Boston), in New York, May 2, 1984.

10. Cited in Hugh Thomas, *Cuba: The Pursuit of Freedom* (New York: Harper and Row, 1971), pp. 1015–1016.

11. Thomas, *Cuba,* p. 1018.

12. Thomas, *Cuba,* p. 1028.

13. The quotation and conclusion are from Secretary of State Dean Rusk, testimony before the U.S. Senate. *Alleged Assassination Plots Involving Foreign Leaders,* an interim report of the Select Committee to Study Governmental Operations with respect to Intelligence Activities, November 20, 1975, pp. 191–192; hereafter cited as Senate Report on Assassinations (1975).

14. Bernard Diederich, *Trujillo: The Death of the Goat* (Boston: Little, Brown, 1978), p. 41.

15. The citation is from a memorandum from Secretary of State Christian Herter to the president, April 14, 1960. Presidential approval was indicated in a letter from Herter to the secretary of defense, April 21, 1960. *Senate Report on Assassinations* (1975), p. 192.

16. Cited in Stephen G. Rabe, *Eisenhower and Latin America: The Foreign Policy of Anticommunism* (Chapel Hill: University of North Carolina Press, 1988), p. 156.

17. *Senate Report on Assassinations* (1975), pp. 197–205, 257.

18. *Senate Report on Assassinations* (1975), p. 209. Record of Actions by National Security Council, May 5, 1961; approved by the president, May 16, 1961. Emphasis added.

19. *Senate Report on Assassinations* (1975), p. 212.

20. Theodore Sorensen noted that the assassination of Trujillo "introduced an atmosphere of revolt and unrest into the Dominican Republic that is continuing as of this writing." Sorensen, *Kennedy* (New York: Bantam Books, 1966), p. 328. Kennedy escaped blame because his role was not disclosed for more than a decade.

21. In its analysis of this final cable, the Senate Committee addressed the question whether it was "designed to avoid a charge that the United States shared responsibility for the assassination." The Committee concluded that the cable's "ambiguity illustrates the difficulty of seeking objectives which can only be accomplished by force—indeed, perhaps only by the assassination of a leader—and yet not wishing to take specific actions which seem abhorrent." *Senate Report on Assassinations* (1975), pp. 212–213, 263.

22. Cited by Schlesinger, *A Thousand Days*, pp. 770–771.

23. Edwin Martin, "Haiti: A Case Study in Futility," *SAIS Review*, Vol. 1, No. 2 (Summer 1981), p. 66. A similar plan with a similar result was formulated regarding Haiti during the Carter administration.

24. Edwin Martin, "Haiti," p. 63.

25. Georges Fauriol, "The Duvaliers and Haiti," *Orbis*, Vol. 32, No. 4 (Fall 1988), p. 601.

26. President Reagan's press conference of February 11, 1986, reprinted the next day in *The New York Times*, p. 10. Others, including Georges Fauriol, "The Duvaliers and Haiti," and Elizabeth Abbot, *Haiti: The Duvaliers and Their Legacy* (New York: McGraw-Hill, 1988), have written that the U.S. embassy played a much larger role in Duvalier's departure; if true, this would mean that President Reagan was either misleading the American people in his answer or did not know what his administration had done in Haiti.

27. This entire section borrows from my book *Condemned to Repetition: The United States and Nicaragua* (Princeton, N.J.: Princeton University Press, 1987).

28. The two ambassadors were Joseph Whelan (1951–61) and Turner Shelton (1969–75). . . .

29. Author's interview with Alfonso Robelo, July 29–30, 1983, San Jose, Costa Rica.

30. On the tenth anniversary of the revolution, the Sandinistas published the transcripts of the exchange in which Humberto Ortega, then head of the Sandinista army, demanded the surrender of Federico Mejia, the Guard commander, making clear his intention to capture Managua regardless of the previous agreement. "Las Ultimas Horas de la Guardia Somocista: El Frente Jamas Detuvo Avance Hacia Managua," *Barricada* (Managua), July 19, 1989, pp. 6–7.

31. During a National Security Council (NSC) discussion of General Julio Gutiérrez as a possible head of Nicaragua's Guard after Somoza's departure, Defense Secretary Harold Brown and Deputy NSC Adviser David Aaron reminded each other that he was the Nicaraguan equivalent of General Fereidoun Jam, who had been considered to head the Iranian armed forces after the Shah left. See Pastor, *Condemned to Repetition*, p. 117.

32. Author's interview with former President Jimmy Carter, November 12, 1987, Atlanta, Georgia.

33. Zbigniew Brzezinski, *Power and Principle: Memoirs of the National Security Advisor, 1977–1981* (New York: Farrar, Straus, Giroux, 1983), p. 354.

34. For Iranian perceptions, see Gary Sick, *All Fall Down: America's Tragic Encounter with Iran* (New York: Random House, 1985), p. 7. . . .

35. In 1976, the Inspector General of the Foreign Service concluded in a confidential report: "The government of Iran exerts the determining influence" in the relationship with the United States. Sick, *All Fall Down*, p. 20.

36. Jimmy Carter, *Keeping Faith: Memoirs of a President* (New York: Bantam, 1982), p. 437.

37. Sick, *All Fall Down*, p. 34.

38. Carter, *Keeping Faith*, p. 440.

39. Carter, *Keeping Faith*, pp. 442–443.

40. Theodore Friend, "Marcos and the Philippines," Orbis, Vol. 32, No. 4 (Fall 1988), p. 572.

41. "Marcos Warns of Philippines Becoming a Second Nicaragua," *Mexico City News*, December 21, 1985, p. 2.

42. "Interview with Ferdinand Marcos," *Newsweek*, January 30, 1984, p. 36.

43. "In Toast to Marcos, Bush Lauds Manila Democracy," *Washington Post*, July 1, 1981, p. A20.

44. Don Oberdorfer, "U.S. Pressing for Democratic Succession in Philippines," *Washington Post*, March 12, 1985, p. A11.

45. "Marcos Faults U.S. Role in Philippine Politics," *New York Times*, March 19, 1984, p. A7.

46. Stephen J. Solarz, "Last Chance for the Philippines," *The New Republic*, April 8, 1985, pp. 12–17.

47. This summary of the bureaucratic division is from various newspaper accounts, but especially useful was an article by Fred Barnes, "White House Watch: Civil War," *The New Republic*, March 10, 1986, pp. 8–9.

48. Paul Laxalt, "My Conversations with Ferdinand Marcos: A Lesson in Personal Diplomacy," *Policy Review*, Summer 1986, pp. 2–5.

49. For an account of the conversation between the U.S. ambassador and Aquino based on interviews with both, see Sandra Burton, *Impossible Dream: The Marcoses, the Aquinos, and the Unfinished Revolution* (New York: Warner Books, 1989), pp. 361–363, 371.

50. Gerald Boyd, "U.S. Had Warnings of Manila Revolt," *New York Times*, February 25, 1986, p. 6. . . .

51. Laxalt, "My Conversations with Marcos," pp. 2–5.

52. For Laxalt's comments, see Charles Mohr, "Laxalt Says Marcos Vote Was Suggested by CIA," *New York Times*, July 18, 1986, p. 5; for the White House statement and background comments, see Seth Mydans, "Marcos Ignores Plea by U.S. and Vows to Stay in Office: Rebels to Swear in Aquino," *New York Times*, February 25, 1986, pp. 1, 5; Bernard Gwertzman, "Reagan Sent Marcos Secret Message 12 Hours Before White House's Plea," *New York Times*, February 28, 1986, p. 6.

53. Bernard Gwertzman, "Mediation in Chile Termed Essential by U.S. Officials: Review Produces a Consensus for a Major Effort to Avoid `Another Nicaragua'," *New York Times*, December 2, 1984, pp. 1, 4; Joel Brinkley, "U.S. to Abstain on Loan to Chile to Protest Human Rights Abuses," *New York Times*, February 6, 1985, p. 4; "Pinochet Charges Opponents Want Another Nicaragua," *Mexico City News*, July 5, 1986, p. 6.

54. See Arturo Valenzuela, "Chile: Origins, Consolidation, and Breakdown of a Democratic Regime," in Larry Diamond, Juan J. Linz, and Seymour Martin Lipset, eds., *Democracy in Developing Countries*, Volume IV: *Latin America* (Boulder, Colo.: Lynne Rienner, 1989), especially pp. 159–161.

55. An excellent study is "The Chilean Plebiscite: A First Step Toward Redemocratization," report by the International Commission of the Latin American Studies Association to Observe the Chilean Plebiscite, *LASA Forum*, Vol. 19, No. 4 (Winter 1989), pp. 18–36.

56. Carter did not distance himself officially from the Shah for several reasons: the Shah was viewed as a modernizer; democratic groups were weak; the major threat came from anti-democratic anti-American clergy; and Iran was a major oil-producer in a strategic location on the periphery of the Soviet Union. For a description of the overall ambiguity of the policy, see Sick, *All Fall Down*.

57. See Gholam R. Afkhami, *The Iranian Revolution: Thanatos on a National Scale* (Washington, D.C.: The Middle East Institute, 1985), pp. 180–191; Sick, *All Fall Down*, pp. 162–172.

. . .

8

Guerrillas and Elections: An Institutionalist
Perspective on the Costs of Conflict and Competition

Matthew Soberg Shugart

*Matthew Shugart is an expert on issues of constitutional design and
electoral rules. He is the coauthor of* Seats and Votes: The Effects and
Determinants of Electoral Systems *(1989) and* Presidents and Assemblies: Constitutional Design and Electoral Dynamics *(1992).
In this selection, he examines the conditions under which governments
as well as guerrilla movements fighting against them agree to cease their
military conflict and compete via elections instead. After developing a
theoretical model about the conditions under which agreement is
reached, he examines several case studies: Colombia, Nicaragua,
Venezuela, and Zimbabwe.*

*Shugart observes that an "electoral exit" to conflict is unlikely to
occur if just one side has an incentive to pursue this end. In order to
achieve such a settlement, the costs of participating in elections must be
lower than the costs of continued fighting for both sides. External actors
can play a key role in lowering the cost of the former or raising the cost
of the latter.*

*Shugart argues that in order for such a peaceful settlement of a revo-
lutionary conflict to occur, there must be institutional reform that allows both the ruling and the revolutionary parties to participate freely*

Matthew Soberg Shugart, "Guerrillas and Elections: An Institutionalist Perspective on the Costs
of Conflict and Competition," *International Studies Quarterly* 36, no. 2 (June 1992): 121–139,
141–151. Copyright © 1992 International Studies Association. Reprinted with permission of Blackwell Publishers.

Author's note: Much of the research, including trips to Colombia, Nicaragua, and Venezuela, needed
to complete this paper was funded by the Graduate School of International Relations and Pacific
Studies at the University of California, San Diego (UCSD) and the Tinker Foundation. I am grateful to Gail Sevrens and Daniel Nielson for research assistance, and to the UCSD Committee on
Research and the Graduate School of International Relations and Pacific Studies for making their
employment possible. Thanks to Maxwell Cameron, Tom Grant, Bernie Grofman, Evelyne Huber,
Caesar Sereseres, Goldie Shabad, and the anonymous reviewers . . . for comments on earlier drafts.

in elections and that guarantees that the winners will not be able to eliminate the losers. *External actors can also play an important role in facilitating institutional reform.*

Critical Questions

1. *What do governments typically demand from guerrillas before agreeing to an electoral settlement of a conflict?*

2. *What do guerrillas typically demand from governments?*

3. *What do external actors need to do to facilitate this process?*

4. *What are the prospects for applying Shugart's model to revolutionary struggles currently taking place?*

Of cases of democratization, those that involve the cessation of armed revolutionary conflict appear especially vexing as well as theoretically challenging. Where a conflict has raged over the very nature of the state and fundamental ideological disputes and where many have died in battle, how can we expect an electoral settlement, in which rebels exchange their warmaking for votes? The task of this paper will be to seek understanding of the process by which former rebels become significant players within electoral institutions.

Despite the frequency with which guerrilla conflicts became subject to democratization in the late 1980s, the topic remains poorly developed in the literature, with a few important exceptions (Chernick, 1988; Licklider, 1990; Stedman, 1991). My analysis will proceed within a theoretical framework based in what has been called the "new institutionalism" (March and Olsen, 1984; Grofman, 1990). As such it suggests that the decisions by regime and rebel leaders alike to seek a democratic "exit" from a conflict are based upon rational calculations of the possibilities and limitations inherent in playing the competitive electoral game versus continuing the armed conflict.

Definition of the Problem and Scope of the Analysis

To define the problem we need to consider what would constitute "success" in the democratization of guerrilla conflict. For this purpose, Giovanni Sartori's concept of a *relevant party* is instructive. To Sartori (1976), a party is relevant when it has either coalition or blackmail potential. Coalition potential refers to a party's ability to participate in executive power. A party has blackmail potential if, by the votes it receives, it can deny another party's obtaining executive power when that party will not join a coalition with it. Whereas the term *relevant party* was developed with parliamentary systems in mind, it can also be adapted to presidential systems. A presidency, being an indivisible office, sometimes can be denied to one party by the entry of a "spoiler" candidate from some minor party. Even if a party—for our purposes, a party of ex-guerrillas—should be unable to play that role, it may be able to influence legislative coalitions by participating in congressional elections.

We thus have already arrived at a point at which we see that institutional choices can make a difference in a party's relevance. Such institutional choices include the basic choice between presidential and parliamentary regimes. Additionally, there are many variations on the relative powers of executives and assemblies in presidential systems, as well as ancillary features to both basic regime types, that affect political leaders' strategies and electoral payoffs (Strom, 1990; Shugart and Carey, 1992). The electoral system—whether it is proportional representation (PR) or not, and if so, to what degree—certainly affects the relevance of some parties (Taagepera and Shugart, 1989).

Institutional change may lower barriers to entry for new participants in the political market; therefore, negotiations over the institutional rules of the game are usually crucial components of any electoral settlement. Government and guerrilla leaders alike must weigh the costs of continued warfare against the possible benefits of competing with each other in elections. This calculation is affected by the institutional context in which such competition takes place.

Institutions themselves may be changed as part of a settlement. Why do institutional reforms take place? One possibility is precisely to lower the barriers to opponents and lure them into the system. Another is to provide institutional guarantees to pro-regime forces, thus making competition with opponents less costly. Di Palma (1990) has referred to the latter as *garantismo*. To understand why institutional changes occur as part of a settlement, we shall need to look at the overall context in which the revolutionary conflict takes place.

One obviously important—but not sufficient—aspect of the context is the military nature of the struggle and the political support an army has. *Ceteris paribus,* neither side can be expected to settle for negotiating terms of electoral competition if it anticipates improving its position by continued warfare. It seems likely as well that a government or rebel group that had placed all its eggs in the one basket of military power to the neglect of political mobilization would view elections as setting back a struggle for which, militarily, it was well equipped. These characteristics of the conflict are intertwined with bargains struck over institutional reforms in such a way as to critically affect the kinds of ceasefires that can be negotiated. Not all ceasefires are created equal; some grant greater advantage to one side or the other when considered alongside the rules of the game for the emerging electoral competition. Thus the paper develops a theory of the relation of ceasefire terms to the costs of electoral competition.

Another critical component of the context—and one that might alter the role of military and (domestic) political factors—consists of the international constraints within which government and rebels operate. The international environment structures the menu of choices from which the players may choose, reducing or enhancing actors' maneuverability. Changes in international support for one side or the other may affect the perceived costs and payoffs of particular strategies.

The cases to be considered all involve conflicts in which governments confronted guerrillas whose goal was to overthrow and assume the power of the whole state. Thus secessionist and irredentist conflicts—the Basque problem in Spain, the Tamil separatists in Sri Lanka, or the Yugoslav civil war, for example—are outside the scope of the present analysis. It is likely that attempted resolutions of such conflicts will follow similar dynamics. However, separatist conflicts are perhaps even more intractable, since they involve fundamental questions about what constitutes the boundaries of the state. Moreover, being defined by territorial and cultural exclusivity, a separatist movement cannot even pretend to be an equal competitor across the whole country. On the other hand, a leftist (ex-) insurgency and a rightist governing party theoretically at least can appeal across the whole population for electoral support, given the right conditions.

A further limitation on the scope of this analysis is to exclude those cases in which a major foreign troop deployment is made to assist one side or the other. Without defining what constitutes a "major" deployment, let us leave aside for now cases such as Afghanistan, Angola, and Cambodia, in which day-to-day combat operations were conducted by a foreign army on behalf of a beleaguered government.[1] In the conclusion, I shall have a few words to say about why these cases are exhibiting a different pattern of settlement. The conclusions of this paper can be extended to such cases, but it is preferable at this preliminary stage to focus principally on the relatively simpler cases where foreign involvement, although important, was more limited.

Democratization and Rebels

In his classic statement of the conditions for democracy, or "polyarchy," Dahl (1970) postulated that the chances for electoral incorporation of a regime's opponents would increase as the costs of tolerance came to be lower than the costs of continued suppression of opposition. The form of conflict under consideration in this paper offers especially challenging tests for the axiom, as suppression takes the form of armed counterinsurgency and almost inevitably has involved human rights abuses and heavy casualties. The costs of toleration are also presumably extreme when the conflict takes the form of guerrilla violence and the most fundamental rejection of the regime by its armed opponents. We shall explore the ways in which the axiom of Dahl may prove a useful heuristic for understanding the emergence of rebels as significant players via democratic elections.

In a vein similar to Dahl's, Rustow (1970) considered democracy to be a potential second-best solution once actors had failed to establish hegemony for themselves. This perspective is enlightening in two respects. First, it alerts us to the possibility that "democratic ideals" are not necessary for a democratic exit to be sought to a conflict. This view has recently been expressed even more forcefully by Di Palma (1990). In cases studied herein, leftist rebel propaganda specifically rejected "bourgeois" democracy in favor of "popular democracy" and a one-party state. Where rebels have fought leftist regimes, the basis of rebel propaganda has been a rejection of the very possibility of the government's offering free competition, given its ideology and structure.

Closely related to the notion that democracy need not rest upon widespread commitment to democratic values is the question of the rebels' goals. At no point should the argument be construed as implying that participation in the existing (albeit reformed) political system must ultimately be a goal of the rebel leadership. A rebel group such as Sendero Luminoso in Peru or Cambodia's Khmer Rouge, both of which emerged out of doctrinaire Maoist parties, may appear *a priori* to be less inclined to reach a settlement than Colombia's M-19 or Venezuela's FALN, both of which broke from far less doctrinaire reformist parties. However, the model to be developed here is based solely on the constraints and opportunities afforded by the prospect of continued war on the one hand and the prospect of electoral competition on the other hand. . . . By implication, even Sendero Luminoso, if one day confronted by a calculus of the constraints and opportunities similar to that confronted by other rebel groups explored here, will enter into electoral competition, its vaunted "fanaticism" notwithstanding.[2]

A Theoretical Framework for Analysis

Approaches to the study of democratization have been carried out at levels of both macro-determinants and micro-choices (for a review, see Przeworski, 1986). The approach to be used here will be explicitly micro-level and rational choice. That is, objective factors should be seen as, at most, constraints, with leadership exercising a considerable degree of room for maneuver (O'Donnell and Schmitter, 1986; Przeworski, 1986). When regimes are in flux, leaders' behavior becomes crucial in accounting for the transformation from one regime to another (cf. Linz, 1978).

Let us start from Dahl's axiom that democratization depends upon the relation between cost of suppression and cost of toleration. Since these terms imply a focus based upon the perceptions and preferences of regime elites and we also need to consider the rebels' costs, let us generalize Dahl's concepts into costs of armed *conflict* versus costs of electoral *competition* for each side. Our first step thus is to hypothesize what, based upon the type of revolutionary crisis being experienced, would be the relative magnitude of each of the following costs:

Cost	For Regime	For Rebels
Conflict	Suppression	Resistance
Competition	Toleration	Participation

Costs of Conflict

For theoretical purposes let us take the costs of conflict for both sides to be determined by the scope of the war, including international support and the kinds of war-related resources that each side can command. If a regime or rebel movement has been dependent upon foreign sponsors, an electoral settlement may offer the foreign sponsor a way out of a conflict in which its costs have become unacceptable. Such an interpretation is consistent with the series of settlements or movements toward settlements in the so-called regional conflicts involving clients of the U.S. and Soviet Union in the late 1980s: e.g., Afghanistan, Angola, Cambodia, and Nicaragua. If a patron abandons its client in a conflict, the client's cost of conflict has increased and it may become less resistant to seeking a settlement.

Resources in these conflicts typically depend heavily upon foreign supporters, but domestic political factors are relevant, too. For example, a rebel movement that has focused upon cultivating a mass base may have better resources for extracting sacrifice from its supporters and thereby continuing the war than a rebel movement that lacked such a committed, reliable following.[3] The important point here is that costs of conflict, although subject to some degree to leadership flexibility, are largely outside leaders' direct, immediate control. A decision at an earlier date to rely on a particular foreign patron or a particular strategy of warfare is a decision that "locks in" one or the other party and minimizes its flexibility when the patron cuts off aid or the other side obtains new armaments.

Domestic actors do have some freedom to escalate or reduce fighting and thereby alter the other side's costs of conflict, but such moves are usually tactical. If we assume that, aside from tactical considerations—scoring propaganda points, retreating to reconsolidate forces, etc.—each side would prefer to induce the other's surrender, then we must look for factors that constrain a party's pursuit of this goal. For instance, a rebel movement might be warned by its foreign backers that it will lose aid if it does not agree to a peaceful solution. Unless the rebel group possesses under its control sufficient resources to continue the conflict alone, it may look for ways to participate in elections. It may even appeal to foreign supporters of the government to provide security guarantees, in the form of observers or peacekeeping forces, when it sees the government as not having sufficient credibility. Similarly, the government, driven by economic pressures, may seek accommodation in order to make up for shortfalls in military aid by its patron or to pacify the country as a prerequisite to investment from abroad. Seeking accommodation may mean making unilateral institutional reforms to entice the rebels or signalling a willingness to negotiate such changes.

In the scenarios just broached, international pressures would have raised the costs of conflict for each side in ways that neither side could control directly, moving matters into the realm of domestic institutions. These institutions, on which the costs of competition depend to a considerable degree, are much more directly in the hands of the actors, especially and ultimately the government, to adjust.

Costs of Competition

Understanding changes in the costs of conflict might be sufficient if all we sought to account for were the factors compelling governments or rebels to seek settlement of conflicts. But the dependent variable in this study is more demanding; we want to understand not only when rebels come to terms with governments but also how they become *relevant participants* in the electoral process. No understanding is complete, therefore, without a consideration of electoral institutions.

Let us then take the costs of competition to depend principally on institutional variables. Without electoral institutions with low barriers to the rebels' electoral relevance, the incentive for the rebels to incorporate will be low unless compelled by other factors such as unsustainable military burdens or severe international pressures on themselves. Institutional change can lower barriers to entry for the rebels, thereby lowering the costs of participation for them. On the other hand governing parties surely would be unwilling to change rules that currently favor them to rules that might favor the armed opposition unless they are compelled to do so under severe pressures—i.e., increases in the cost of suppression. Institutions can be designed to provide guarantees that lower the costs of tolerating competition with the rebels. Relative to the conflict variables, the variables that affect competition are much easier to manipulate through what Sartori (1968) called "political engineering." Political institutions may be seen as "bargains among self-interested politicians" (Geddes, 1990); indeed, the extent to which such bargains affect the rebels' opportunities in elections is a critical factor in negotiating cease-fire terms, as we shall explore below.

From War to Settlement

What we have, then, is the plausibility of a settlement resulting from, and only from, the situation below:

$$T < S \text{ and } P < R$$

That is, the regime's costs of toleration must be lower than its costs of suppression, *and* the rebels' costs of participation must be lower than their costs of resistance. The circumstances under which these two conditions will be met may be better understood in terms of figure 1. For sake of simplicity, let us assume four possible outcomes of the interaction of costs between the two sides. In the lower left corner, the costs of electoral competition outweigh the costs of armed conflict for both sides, resulting in internal war. However, if for one side (but only for one side) the costs of competition should become lower than the costs of conflict, then the struggle enters a phase of *stalemate* in which a settlement is not yet near, but one side now might be willing to contemplate settling, owing to a shift in its incentives.[4]

There are two logical types of stalemate. In a "Type 1" stalemate, the government's costs of suppression are already greater than its costs of tolerating the rebels as electoral competitors. What holds the key to a settlement is bringing the rebels' cost of participation down below their cost of continued resistance. The result may be a reformed electoral law or credible institutions for providing security and fraud prevention in elections. These kinds of reforms provide new participants with a stake, or "equity," in the institutions of the political system (cf. Strom, 1989), lowering their incentive to remain outside or to defect at a later date. I shall call reforms that lower barriers to rebel participation Type 1 institutional reforms.

Now let us consider "Type 2" stalemates. Here a point has already been reached at which the rebels' cost of participation is lower than their cost of resistance. What is needed to produce settlement is for the regime's cost of toleration to be brought below its cost of continued suppression. A means of exit thus becomes what I shall call Type 2 institutional reforms, those that provide guarantees to the governing parties that their interests will be protected in the new electoral competition. Type 2 institutional reforms might include extraordinary majorities or built-in protection for the government that certain posts will not be up for competition immediately or that certain issue areas will not be addressed in the short run (cf. Przeworski, 1986). Such institutional rules, according to Buchanan and Tullock

Figure 1. Possible Outcomes of the Interaction
of Costs of Conflict and Competition

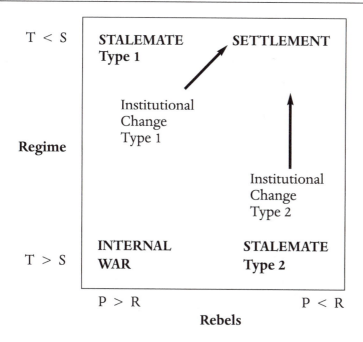

T < S | **STALEMATE**
Type 1 | **SETTLEMENT**

Institutional
Change
Type 1

Regime

Institutional
Change
Type 2

T > S | **INTERNAL WAR** | **STALEMATE**
Type 2

P > R | P < R

Rebels

(1962), require a larger investment in bargaining to reach decisions, but also carry the risk of increasing the incentive for some groups, *viz* the larger ones, to defect. This trade-off between expanding the coalitions necessary to reach decisions (i.e., raising *transaction costs*) and the risk of giving key sectors the incentive to defect (through increasing *external costs*) will be addressed in the discussions of some individual cases that follow.

Even in conditions of stalemate Type 2, in which the guerrillas have the upper hand militarily and it is the governing parties for whom institutional guarantees are *desiderata,* we must not lose sight of one important fact: the governing parties still have control over the electoral apparatus itself. Thus there are also guarantees needed for the opposition, but these are less likely to be of the purely institutional variety. Rather, they typically involve the use of international observers and possibly an international police force to provide security and signal the government's commitment to accepting the rebels as electoral competitors.

Finally, it is at least feasible that a conflict could move along the diagonal in figure 1, that is, directly from Internal War to Settlement. This is unlikely, however, as the costs to both sides would be high, given the uncertainty inherent in either side's making a first move, let alone getting simultaneous moves, to lower the other side's cost of competition. It is more likely that each side will remain committed to the conflict until some reversal or the loss of foreign support changes the calculus. Still, if a settlement were to occur out of Internal War, it would presumably involve a mix of the two types of institutional reform. That such reforms would have to be negotiated simultaneously and in great complexity only decreases further the likelihood that a full-blown and inconclusive war could provide the opportunities necessary for a settlement.

Ceasefires and Institutional Reforms:
Breaking the Stalemate

In discussing the cases, we shall see that negotiations over terms of ceasefires are closely related both to the nature of the stalemate that must be broken and to the process of institutional reform. Not surprisingly, rebels resist ceasefire terms that require their demobilization or confinement to bases outside the country. The resistance to such terms is greater when the rebels, during the war, have relied extensively on outside sanctuary, as we shall see in the cases of Namibia and Nicaragua. For such rebels, the costs of participation in the absence of their armed force are high; they lack the political support needed to dominate elections without their soldiers. On the other hand, rebels who have sustained a high degree of mass mobilization can afford more easily to demobilize, as they have a network of cadres upon which they can rely in the coming electoral campaign.

In the realm of institutional reforms, a great degree of Type 1 reforms (lowering barriers to rebel participation) or low degrees of Type 2 reforms (guarantees to the regime) are conditions that provide for a low cost of participation for the rebels. On the other hand, great Type 2 reforms or low Type 1 reforms make the cost of rebel participation higher. Institutional reform is a two-edged sword, however. A reform that decreases the rebels' cost of participation may also enhance the regime's fears of a large rebel showing in elections, thereby maintaining the regime's cost of toleration at a relatively high level. Similarly, providing guarantees to the regime may make the rebels' electoral prospects dimmer. What level of reform of either type will obtain depends on each side's bargaining strength. Although no theory of bargaining will be supplied here, the discussion here has already foreshadowed how the nature of the conflict affects the whole process. An ascendant rebel movement (Type 2 stalemate) will compel the regime to seek Type 2 reforms to protect itself. One means might be raising transaction costs in an assembly to be elected with rebel participation. However, doing so is sure to make the rebels resist a ceasefire in which they must demobilize or leave the territory, especially if their political support is questionable. An ascendant regime (Type 1 stalemate) may offer liberalized electoral competition (Type 1 reforms), but only under the condition that the rebels disarm first. Whether they will do so depends upon their calculation of how liberalized the competition is and whether they have sufficient resources to continue fighting and thereby obtain either more favorable ceasefire terms or still lower institutional barriers, or both. The key to success, therefore, is to strike a balance between each side's transaction and external costs. Raising transaction costs to provide the weaker party with guarantees may raise external costs by giving the larger party incentive to defect. Near the end of this paper, we shall see how the balance was struck in several cases—sometimes in ways that threatened the settlement—and how the factors of the nature of the conflict, ceasefire terms, and institutional reform were intertwined in particular cases.

What Happens to the Armies?

One of the most contentious issues in resolution of these conflicts is the question of how to dispose of the military force of each side now that each side is committing itself to nonviolent competition. It is unlikely that either side will be willing to disarm totally, as trust is not sufficiently high. Each side wants to retain the option of militarily punishing the other for reneging, even if it does not wish to retain the option of offensive action. (That the latter condition may not always be met only complicates the issue further.) Although this paper will not undertake a detailed discussion of the matter of disposing of each side's military capability, some general tendencies cannot be overlooked. First, rebels often demand that they be included in a new government prior to elections and that one task of this government is to develop a new national army in which the rebels are treated as equal professionals alongside the existing military. Until the transition is complete the rebels expect to retain their weapons and any territory that they (claim to) control. Thus, during the transitional phase of the ceasefire, the rebels seek to maintain their forces as "insurance" against reneging, while seeking an integration of forces as a signal of the government's commitment to accepting the rebels as equals not only in elections but also in state institutions.

Governments, on the other hand, typically demand that no transfer of power be made to the rebels and that the latter must disarm immediately. For the government, gaining the demobilization of the rebels is insurance that the rebels cannot reignite the war, while keeping the integrity of the existing army is a sign of the rebels' commitment to existing (or reformed) state institutions.

What we can say about the disposition of forces is that, in each successful case, *the rebels were demobilized prior to elections.* Moreover, no integration of the two sides' armies has taken place prior to the election of a new government. The conclusion will take up briefly Angola and other cases where foreign combat troops played a role, as these appear to be outside the basic pattern. For cases of entirely or mostly internal warfare, however, even when the rebels "win" in the sense of constituting the post-electoral government, they lose on their demands for keeping their forces in reserve and for creating a new army.

Attempted Incorporations: Cases

We now turn to some brief case studies. Venezuela and Zimbabwe are two well-established cases of ex-rebels as relevant electoral players. Colombia, Nicaragua, and El Salvador* also represent important cases for developing theory.

Venezuela

The Venezuelan guerrilla conflict was generally confined to small-scale terrorism and the rebels never achieved a large mass base. Yet, as we shall see, the case is important for developing some generalizations about settlements to Type 1 stalemates. A party of ex-rebels sometimes has held the

---

* Editor's note: The Salvadorean conflict was still ongoing when this article was written, and so the author's discussion of it has been omitted here.

balance of power in congress and, in 1989, it won the governorship of an important state in the country's first-ever direct gubernatorial elections. The conflict was brought to an end by an amnesty granted by the government of President Rafael Caldera, elected in 1968 (Ellner, 1988). For the regime, the costs of toleration were low because the guerrillas had been isolated politically and militarily. For the rebels, the costs of participation were lowered by no concessions beyond the legalization of their parties, but had there not already been in place an electoral system conducive to representing small parties, a mere amnesty may not have been sufficient.

The Conflict.   The first major Venezuelan guerrilla group formed as a breakaway from the then-dominant political party, Acción Democrática (AD), and as a response to that party's rightward drift stipulated by the Pact of Punto Fijo (Levine, 1973; Ellner, 1980; Karl, 1986a). In that pact, AD and two other parties, including the Christian Democratic COPEI, agreed on a common program of government meant to reassure capitalist and Church interests about the moderate scope of policy in a new democratic regime. The parties also agreed to share power, but to exclude the Communist party. A militant faction of the AD, joined later by the Communists themselves, then opted for guerrilla warfare.

However, because of the organizational penetration of the AD, the rebels were unable to win much sympathy among the rural population (Harding and Landau, 1964). It was partly for this reason and partly because of U.S. counterinsurgency assistance to the Venezuelan military that the guerrillas' cost of resistance was very high. Failing to mobilize a popular movement or to provoke an insurrection, the guerrillas isolated themselves from the population. They were snubbed by the failure of their call for a boycott of the 1963 elections, and by 1968 many of their leaders had been jailed, the organizations had split, and the armed networks had been "virtually liquidated" (Levine, 1973:53). By 1969, the guerrillas were ready to accept an amnesty offered by the first non-AD government to those not directly implicated in terrorist actions. The ex-guerrillas were allowed to form their own political parties (Ellner, 1980).

Accounting for the Settlement.   The Venezuelan settlement was not a case of negotiated institutional change, but it shows the conditions (1) that make conflict desirable to some actors, and (2) that make resolution leading to the guerrillas' becoming a relevant party feasible. Because of the pact that accompanied the re-establishment of democracy in 1958, the regime had a certain exclusionary character, a factor without which the decision of some elites to opt for guerrilla warfare would have been less likely. But the regime against which the guerrillas were fighting was indeed democratic and rather favorable to minority parties: it used closed-list proportional representation (PR), including a very low barrier to representation of small parties,[5] and an impartial board for conducting and certifying elections (Penniman, 1980). The closed-list system means that parties competed on the basis of party platforms, unlike systems in which candidates within parties must compete with one another. In systems with intra-party competition, the individual candidate needs access to "pork" funds to deliver to organized followings who provide votes to that candidate instead of to another of the same (or other) party (Geddes, 1991; McCubbins and Rosenbluth, 1991). Venezuela's closed-list electoral system, coupled with the low barriers to new parties, permitted policy-based alternatives, including exrebels, to find a niche without needing prior access to budgetary largess.

Whereas the presidential form of government may seem to imply a winner-take-all concentration of power (Linz, 1984; Lijphart and Rogowski, 1991), this tendency was mitigated in part by the ease of access for small parties and even more by the lack of a presidential veto (Shugart and Carey, 1992). Thus it was possible for small parties to hold the balance of legislative power, especially in the early 1970s, when no party approached a majority in congress, but also after AD and COPEI emerged as the two dominant parties. Finally, it is also significant that the deal granting amnesty was made after the alternation in executive power from AD to COPEI, thus allowing the rebels to deal with a party other than that from which they had split. COPEI's dealings with the erstwhile guerrillas proved to have a long-term payoff for COPEI as well. The Movement toward Socialism (MAS), formed by ex-guerrillas, became an anti-AD coalition partner for mayoral and gubernatorial positions that were subject to popular vote for the first time in 1989. These alliances built upon years of cooperation in congress.

In Venezuela by 1968, then, the regime's cost of toleration was lower than its cost of suppression. The rebels' cost of participation was certainly lower than their cost of resistance, but not only because of the military situation. The regime already offered Type 1 institutions, because the 1961 constitution required representation of minorities. Without this feature (whether already existing or resulting from negotiations), coupled with an amnesty, the rebels might simply have refused as "crumbs" the government offer to rejoin the electoral game. After all, the Greek guerrillas in 1949 refused to settle for competition on the government's terms (there was no

Venezuela-style provision for minor parties) and remained an illegal party for some time even after the end of the war (Ikle, 1971:95). Thus the institutional incentives for the guerrillas in Venezuela made their emergence as relevant electoral actors possible.

Zimbabwe

Zimbabwe's story is rather different, in that the guerrillas were clearly ascendant over the regime. When elections were finally held with rebel participation, the parties formed by the rebels won overwhelmingly. We might think that the rebels' costs of participation would have been quite low, given that the dominant guerrilla force, the Zimbabwe African National Union (ZANU, led by Robert Mugabe), had achieved mass commitment from a sizeable portion of the population. Wide areas of the country were effectively off limits, especially at night, to the regime's army because the rebels and their civilian networks functioned as a rival societal and governmental structure (Gregory, 1981). However, their ascendancy should also have made the cost of resistance low. So why did they settle? Although the rebels would have preferred that elections take place only after rebel participation in a provisional government, pressure from their international allies was crucial in raising their cost of resistance, as we shall see. For the white minority Rhodesian government, obviously the cost of tolerating a black Marxist competitor in elections was extremely high. The settlement was ultimately achieved, therefore, only when agreement was reached on a constitution that entrenched certain guarantees, including overrepresentation in parliament for whites. The conflict thus moved from a stalemate to settlement by means of Type 2 institutional reforms.

The International Environment and the Cost of Conflict. The rebels originally demanded a share of power including control over the state police and a transitional period of up to six months before elections. Yet what resulted was a much shorter transition during which there was *no transfer of even a share of state power to the rebels.* Critical to the rebels' acceptance of these seemingly unfavorable conditions were changes on both sides of the ledger: the guerrillas' Mozambican allies "put the screws on Mugabe" (Stedman, 1990:143) to accept the settlement,[6] meaning that the potential loss of support would raise the rebels' cost of resistance. On the other hand, guarantees of electoral fairness lowered the cost of participation. The outside mediator, the British government, realized that "some military element, apart from the Rhodesian police and the opposing armies, would be necessary to ensure impartiality" (Davidow, 1984:73). Thus a force of armed Commonwealth monitors was deployed to oversee the transition.[7] During this period the rebels were to assemble at designated points under Commonwealth supervision.[8]

International factors also accounted for the shifting calculations on the government side. The rebels were nearing an overthrow of the regime, having mobilized much of the population for protracted guerrilla warfare. This warfare was sufficiently strong and effective to compel the Rhodesian regime's primary external backer (South Africa),[9] and later its *de facto* colonial master (the U.K), to seek accommodation with the black majority, increasing the cost of continued suppression. After the independence of the former Portuguese colonies of Mozambique and Angola, the value of a white-ruled ally in Rhodesia was no longer perceived as worth the cost to the South African regime (Martin and Johnson, 1981). Perhaps the most critical source of international pressure that pushed the Rhodesian regime toward compromise were the international sanctions. The government's need for renewed trade with countries upholding the sanctions (all the more important if South African assistance were cut) gave it little choice but to seek a negotiated solution, particularly after a so-called internal settlement boycotted by the guerrillas had failed to impress Commonwealth and other countries of the government's worthiness of recognition.

Accounting for the Settlement.   That over 22,000 guerrillas arrived at the assembly points (about 16,500 of them from ZANU) shows how successful the movement had been in mobilizing fighters, as the figure was far higher than almost anyone had anticipated (Davidow, 1984:91). During the election campaign, ZANU had no need to convert people to its cause; it simply had to ensure that its civilian militants got to the polls the great numbers of rural Zimbabweans who already supported Mugabe (Gregory, 1981:67). This condition certainly made the cost of participation relatively low for ZANU, once it had received both assurances that the elections would be fairly monitored and warnings that it could not count on continued external support if it resisted the concessions implied by accepting its forces' removal from the field.

Whereas ZANU was feared by the British and the Rhodesian government as being the more radical group, the existence of another group, the Zimbabwe African People's Union (ZAPU), and the specific institutional rules adopted, served to lower the government's cost of toleration. Twenty out of one hundred assembly seats were set aside to represent (i.e., overrepresent) the white minority in the assembly—a Type 2 institutional guarantee for the government—and the government would depend on the confidence of that assembly.

Although ZANU and ZAPU were formally united in a Patriotic Front and did not split into separate electoral organizations until shortly before the elections, it is plausible that Joshua Nkomo, leader of ZAPU, suspected that Mugabe would jettison his "less powerful" partner (Stedman, 1990:202); therefore, both ZAPU and the Rhodesian government had the option of forming a coalition cabinet to exclude ZANU, if ZANU failed to win a majority (Davidow, 1984:59). ZAPU, the group that had paid less attention to mass mobilization during the war, was considered less of a threat than ZANU; yet it was precisely the group that had mobilized a great mass of the peasantry during the war that proved to be in the best position to draw votes. ZANU's cost of competing was low as long as the voting was open and fair. On the other hand, the costs for ZAPU and the Rhodesian government (including the white minority and its black allies) were low enough to encourage electoral competition given the prospects of post-election coalition-building. These calculations of the costs within the institutional system (parliamentarism, *garantismo* for whites, and election monitoring) were made possible in the first place by the changing costs of the conflict for each side. The cost to South Africa of the war in Rhodesia, coupled with the search by the Rhodesian regime for international recognition and the lifting of sanctions, raised the cost of suppression. For the rebels, the cost of continued resistance was increasing even as they were winning the war, as friendly governments sought a way out.

Colombia

The Colombian case consists of two distinct phases. In both we have a version of the Type 1 stalemate. However, in the phase of the early 1980s, no significant institutional reforms were offered by the government and the rebels did not disarm, resulting in failure. In the second phase, Type 1 reforms were offered, including the "carrot" of rebel participation in a constituent assembly *if they first disarmed*. With this concession, the rebels' cost of participation was dramatically lowered. At that point, several rebel groups agreed to the government's offer, most prominently the M-19. Two other groups stayed outside. After discussing the nature of the conflict and the failure of the first settlement to lure any of the groups into permanent peace, I shall discuss the successful accord with the M-19 and contrast it with the continued failure to incorporate another group.

The Conflict.   Near the end of the decade of Liberal versus Conservative warfare in Colombia, known as "La Violencia," some of the Liberal party bands became organized into self-described revolutionary peasant "self-defense" forces, often under the influence of Colombia's Communist party. This manifestation of violence, although geographically isolated, spread in the aftermath of the Cuban revolution and the articulation of the *foco* theory of insurgency (Gott, 1970; Chernick, 1989:292–96). The legacy of this period may be seen in one of Colombia's major guerrilla groups, the Revolutionary Armed Forces of Colombia (FARC). This group continued to reject the National Front, in which Liberal and Conservative parties each received half of each district's congressional seats regardless of the votes' distribution, and alternated the presidency, with both parties supporting a common official candidate at each presidential election (Hartlyn, 1988). A second important group, the April 19th Movement (M-19), took its name from the date of a supposedly fraudulent election in 1970 under the National Front, when a populist candidate backed by the left was narrowly defeated by the official candidate.

The first major effort to resolve the guerrilla problem followed the election of Belisario Betancur by less than a majority of votes in 1982. Betancur was the first Conservative to be elected in competition with Liberals since the end of the National Front. Thus, with Betancur seeking a way to mobilize support for new policies (Archer and Chernick, 1989:56–7), there is a resemblance to the Venezuelan opening: an alternation of the executive to the second party in a close election, leading the president to seek new coalitional possibilities.

Early failures of an amnesty to provide a way out of the violence led to calls for a ceasefire and negotiated end to the war as further conditions for peace. Thus Betancur formed a Peace Commission charged with direct negotiations with rebel leaders. As this Great National Dialogue continued, more and more elite opinion in Colombia became convinced of the need for breaking with the traditional two-party-dominated political system (Chernick, 1988; Archer and Chernick, 1989). The goal of a more modern or "efficient" state would later be echoed in the government's own document, justifying a constitutional revision.[10]

The Failed Settlement.   As part of the ceasefire that was eventually agreed upon,[11] the government's army was withdrawn from areas of guerrilla operation, and offensive activities were to be ceased. The agreement went so far as to grant belligerent status to the guerrillas, meaning that they were granted official legitimacy by the state as an armed opposition with control over territory and population. Unfortunately, the peace process did not lead to peace, as private armies were formed by those who had reason to fear the presence of armed irregular forces. These vigilantes served to replace the official army in areas from which it had been withdrawn. Moreover, the rebels themselves did not cease military operations—indeed, they expanded their operations into areas abandoned by the government's army. Thus a cycle of violence resulted and the terms of the "peace process" are largely to blame, as we shall see (Beaufort, 1989).

The peace process did lead to the formation of a political party, the Unión Patriótica (UP), which subsumed the old Colombian Communist party, whose army is the FARC. This party first participated in elections in 1986 and won 4.4 percent of the vote for congress. The percentage was disappointing, but the absolute number of votes (nearly 300,000) represented substantial growth for the left.[12] The UP's presidential candidate received 4.5 percent, the highest ever for a leftist (Hartlyn, 1988:148–51, 229). Even so, the UP's showing fell far below that which might represent a real break with traditional bipartism.

One successful result of the dialogue was the initiation of direct elections for mayors. The UP in 1988 elected mayors in several municipalities. However, most of the areas of UP success have been areas of FARC activity, which in turn are often areas of long-standing activity by the Communist party (Pinzon de Lewin, 1989).[13] Thus, outside of areas of "traditional" Communist domination, the UP did not provide much of an alternative. Moreover, inside its own areas, the FARC's continued (legal) carrying of arms led to charges that the UP won elections by campaigning with weapons, or *proselitismo armado* (a point to be discussed below). The situation had to be called a failure as long as the FARC remained armed (cf. Archer and Chernick, 1989:75).

The failure of the peace effort of the early 1980s may be explained by its specific terms. Ironically, for the rebels the terms of the ceasefire only minimally lowered their cost of participation, while simultaneously *lowering* the cost of continued resistance. The cost of resistance was reduced simply because of the withdrawal of government troops from regions of guerrilla influence. The cost of participation was not much changed, because no major reforms were made to the electoral process, which consisted of intense intra-party competition and in which election depended on the ability to deliver private goods to constituents (Archer, 1989, Shugart and Fernandez, 1992). At the municipal level, the creation of directly elected mayors was an incentive to participate, but for national elections, there was little "carrot" offered the rebels. The pro-rebel candidates could not expect to compete on an even plane in congressional elections (let alone for president) as long as elections to congress depended mainly on the provision of favors for which access to the national treasury was essential. Thus the rebels took best advantage of what was offered them: participation in mayoral elections under the banner of the UP in 1988 and continued guerrilla activity in the absence of a governmental presence or a requirement for a demobilization.

Another question that arises is why would a government make a deal legalizing rebels' carrying of weapons. For the Colombian government, the repression of the 1970s had become costly, with charges of human rights abuses in an era of considerable inter-American concern over such issues. The Colombian government, through its participation in the Contadora group, was seeking to accommodate the forces of revolutionary change symbolized by the Sandinista regime in Nicaragua. To accommodate these forces would buy breathing space for the government at home, since the home-grown rebels also received aid from Nicaragua and Cuba.[14] At the same time that the cost of suppression was thus rising, the cost of tolerating rebel participation in elections under existing rules was not great, given the rebels' isolation. After all, Communists had been running in and winning elections in (mostly remote) regions of guerrilla influence for decades (Pinzon de Lewin, 1989). The cessation of hostilities and recognition of a new party that purported to incorporate more diverse elements of the left than traditional Communism offered minimally a respite and maximally a respectable end to the violence. As we have seen, however, this "peace process" failed.

Accounting for Success: The Deal with the M-19. A very different process ensued later with another major Colombian guerrilla group, the M-19. This group surrendered its arms in March 1990, days before a congressional/local election in which it participated by presenting lists of candidates in some regions. It then fielded a presidential candidate for the first time in May 1990. Its original candidate was assassinated, but his replacement, Antonio Navarro Wolff, won 13 percent of the vote. The process of incorporating the M-19 into elections took place simultaneously with a process of major institutional changes, including a constituent assembly to rewrite the country's constitution.

The first institutional reform to benefit the former guerrillas was a change in the electoral system that lowered barriers to new participants (Shugart, 1992). Through the congressional election of 1990, a voter received from a particular local leader's campaign workers a slip of paper with the candidates' names on it to deposit at the polling place. There was no "official ballot" containing names of the several contending candidates or parties from which to choose while in a booth. This old system, moreover, entailed several factions of each traditional party competing against one another as well as against other parties in local multi-seat districts. The effect of the system was to perpetuate a politics based upon clientelism and the provision of services in exchange for votes (Archer, 1989). Only on such personalistic exchanges could candidates differentiate themselves and win the votes needed to beat other competitors, including co-partisans, and only with access to the public coffers could candidates provide the demanded services. Thus new entrants and anyone offering policy alternatives, let alone ex-guerrillas, were at an electoral disadvantage.[15]

The 1990 presidential election was the first Colombian election to give voters an official multi-party ballot. For the election of a Constituent Assembly in December 1990, the ballot provided for choice among several lists of candidates competing in a single *nationwide* district. Such an electoral system dramatically lowered the barriers to new participants since it eliminated the special advantage to locally based party factions in the congressional electoral system. The M-19 list received more votes (27% of the total) than any other single list, putting the ex-guerrillas and their allies in a position to have a strong influence over the future shape of Colombian political institutions.

The success of the M-19 is powerful testimony to the effects of institutional change that lowers barriers to the entry of new competitors—Type 1 reforms—in bringing about conditions under which guerrillas not only will disarm but also will become relevant electoral players. For whereas the government military campaigns against the guerrillas had sharply raised the cost of resistance, the cost of participation could have remained high had the M-19's prospects not been relegated to a minor role. Instead, the promise of a voice in reconstructing the country's basic institutions gave the guerrillas a stake in participating.

For the government and its constituency, the cost of toleration might seem to have been high, given that it was handing to ex-rebels an opportunity to reshape the political system. In other words, there were high "external" costs (Buchanan and Tullock, 1962). However, helping make them lower was another political-economic feature of the Colombian situation in the late 1980s. The Colombian government sought to carry out structural reforms in the political system in order to bring about a more "efficient" state that would better link Colombia's economy with the rest of the world (Shugart and Fernandez, 1991). From the perspective of a government seeking constitutional reform for reasons of its own, and seeking opportunities for new alliances with forces not tied to existing entrenched political and economic interests because of their previous marginalization, the cost of tolerating the ex-rebels' participation was indeed low. Once again, then, we see an alternation in power—this time to a "technocratic" and outward-oriented faction of the Liberal party—and the executive's seeking new alliances as factors aiding the incorporation of a formerly armed minority.[16]

Despite the successful process with the M-19 and despite ongoing negotiations in 1990–91, the other principal guerrilla movement, the FARC, chose not to participate. Its incentives to participate would seem to be the same as those of the M-19, since the use of a nationwide district to elect a constituent assembly would ensure it a role in redesigning the country's institutions that was proportional to its support. The FARC, as mentioned, has had long-term control over regional bases. This, especially when coupled with its related involvement in cocaine trafficking, gives it a resource for continued conflict that the M-19 and other groups lacked. The group is so marginal on the national scene, yet so dominant in its isolated areas, that it is difficult to imagine what institutional reforms would entice it. To demobilize and parlay its local support into national votes would be to give up the power that it holds in its base areas without a commensurate share of national power. Thus the FARC more closely resembles separatist movements than national contenders for power and, correspondingly, the government's attempts to bring about a settlement have focused on local-level concessions: directly elected mayors, regional autonomy, and local control over police forces. Since the FARC can already elect mayors responsive to it, it can take advantage of most of the new constitution's provisions for devolving power without having to surrender any of its military resources. Thus the situation remains akin to that of the mid-1980s: low cost of resistance and little to gain from participation at the national level.

Nicaragua

In Nicaragua in 1990, the rebels did not become a political party, but supported a candidate for the presidency and a congressional slate that won majorities of the vote. As in Zimbabwe, the main guarantees for the opposition were in the form of international mediation, not institutional reform, although government concessions on the composition of the electoral council (under the Nicaraguan constitution a fourth branch of government) do constitute a Type 1 reform. Unlike Zimbabwe, and more like Venezuela and Colombia, the regime does not appear to have been in danger of being overthrown. The Sandinista government, confident that its revolutionary program could carry the day in elections, saw the cost of tolerating the opposition sufficiently low that it could afford to grant concessions to opposition parties. For both the Sandinistas and the alliance of opposition parties, the negotiations on electoral conditions were linked to bringing about a ceasefire with the rebels. Of course, as it turned out, the concessions and ceasefire led inexorably to the Sandinistas' electoral defeat. On the other hand, the process did not result in the rebels' direct participation, partly, I shall argue, because institutional concessions were not offered to them, but only to their non-armed allies.

The Conflict.   Attempts to use elections to bring about an end to guerrilla conflict in revolutionary Nicaragua passed through two phases. In the first, in 1984, the guerrillas were never a party to negotiations. In the second, there were successful negotiations, even though the guerrillas did not form a political party. That the Sandinistas seized power in the midst of a multi-class insurrection not (entirely) the product of FSLN-led mobilization explains in large part the ability of a serious opposition challenge to the new regime to emerge. Labor unions and producer associations maintained ties to pre-revolutionary political and social movements, including factions of the Liberal and Conservative parties that broke with the Somoza-dominated regime, Social Christians, and Marxist groups whose organizing predates the formation of the Sandinistas (Walker, 1970; Booth, 1985:97–126). These sectors constituted the social base for many of the opposition parties which emerged to challenge the new regime. In the countryside there were areas that remained relatively untouched by revolutionary activity against Somoza and areas where the revolution came only after 1979 as an outside force, regions where Somoza's regime still had a social base (Radu, 1986). In such regions, old patron-client ties remained powerful and served as a base for much of the contra movement (Cruz, 1987).

Reinforcing these tendencies were the many international constraints upon the Sandinistas which inhibited their drive for consolidation of power, a process which would have required foreign backing beyond the commitment that the Sandinistas received from the Soviet bloc (even before, but especially after, the rise of Mikhail Gorbachev) to carry out a major confrontation with rivals. In other words, the cost of suppressing the insurgency was high enough to induce the regime's leaders to seek electoral toleration of opposition. However, at least in the first post-revolutionary elections of 1984, the cost was not high enough for them to entertain negotiations directly with the guerrilla opposition.

The FSLN intended, by holding elections in 1984, to induce potential supporters of the armed opposition to remain within the legal structure of a still unconsolidated regime (Booth, 1985:210; Christian, 1985:171). Additionally, elections could help the regime regain international aid and halt the increasing dependence upon the Soviet bloc. What is important for our purposes here, however, is that although the guerrilla war was a crucial factor in bringing about the elections, direct negotiations with those guerrillas never played a role. The elections of 1984 therefore were not seen as a way of incorporating insurgents into democratic institutions but rather as a way of legitimizing a regime that was simultaneously seeking the defeat of an insurgency. The situation was rather different in the run-up to the elections of 1990. Still, the elections were not part of a process of directly incorporating insurgents into elections. They differed from 1984 in that negotiations with the insurgents did play a major role in some institutional changes designed to make the electoral process fairer, as well as in advancing the date of the elections by over a year.

Accounting for Success, with Reservations.   As a result of the negotiations leading to the elections and ceasefire in 1990, parties were given access to state-run television, censorship was lifted, a new electoral council was created, and observers were invited to oversee the voter and candidate registration and the campaign as well as the election itself. These negotiations took place under the auspices of a regional Peace Process under the inspiration of Costa Rican president Oscar Arias, who won a Nobel Peace Prize for his efforts. Whereas the Sandinistas were under immense pressure to hold these elections and to make them fair, the regime's basic survival was not jeopardized to the same degree as was that of Rhodesia, for example. Without Rhodesian-style acquiescence to an international military peace-keeping presence on the part of the regime, and without the total military defeat of the rebels, a rebel force is unlikely to accept terms requiring it to disarm in advance of elections. A rebel force in such a setting has little incentive to disarm, lacking the kind of guarantees of fairness that were made possible by external involvement in the process of settlement in Rhodesia (and also in Namibia).

The Nicaraguan case is made still more problematic because the opposition that challenged and defeated the Sandinistas in the elections of 1990 was a separate entity from the guerrillas. This fact helps explain the delicate nature of the transition, including the contras' reluctance to disarm and continuing tensions with a government whose election they helped bring about. The reason the settlement was so tenuous was that the elections had not given the movement a direct stake in representative institutions.

To understand why the rebels did not participate directly, . . . let us consider the institutional setting in which the 1990 elections took place. Elections were for a six-year term for both president and congress, with the presidency elected by plurality and the congress by PR. However, ironically, the form of PR used in 1990 was less favorable to small parties than that of 1984, which had barriers as low as Venezuela's.[17] Moreover, because of the plurality rule for presidential elections the only effective way to beat the Sandinistas was by forming a large center-oriented ticket. With congressional elections held at the same time as presidential, the large-bloc advantage would be strong in the congressional as well as presidential campaign (Shugart and Carey, 1992). Thus the rebels themselves (as opposed to some of their exiled civilian leadership) were excluded from direct participation in the alliance. If there had not been such an overwhelming desire to defeat the FSLN, the contras might not have had an incentive to support the elections at all, given their own lack of direct office stakes. On the other hand, had they not agreed to negotiate a ceasefire, the elections might have been a repeat of 1984, with the FSLN beating a disorganized and probably boycotting opposition. It was thus the concessions won by the war that made removing the FSLN possible. . . .

Ceasefire Terms and Relation to Costs of Competition

The character of the ceasefire itself is one of the most critical components of the whole process. Ceasefires may take the form of a ceasefire in-place, in which the rebels are allowed to keep their weapons, with at least implied territorial concessions. Or a ceasefire might involve the surrender of arms by the rebels or, identical in its effects, the removal of rebels to camps whether inside or outside the country. Since the ceasefire alters the shape of the struggle, from one of armed conflict to one of electoral competition, the cost of toleration or participation will be influenced by the terms of the ceasefire. Moreover, assessments by each side of the kinds of ceasefire it can accept are bound to be influenced by the nature of the guerrilla war itself, as we shall see.

We have already seen the extent to which international guarantees were crucial to the kind of ceasefire obtained in Zimbabwe. The rebels were removed from the battlefield, so they could not via their arms influence the electoral outcome. This form of ceasefire was possible because of its strong element of mutuality: government forces were to be confined to barracks as well. By the time the resident British governor consented to allowing Rhodesian forces back in the field, the process was already well underway. More important, both sides' compliance was monitored by outside forces.[26] The rebels' attention to the cultivation of a mass base and their success in gaining such support was what gave them the confidence to accept terms seemingly less favorable to themselves—no transfer of power before elections, and the requirement of rebel disarmament—than those they had been demanding.

In Namibia, a ceasefire on terms somewhat akin to those in Zimbabwe—in that the rebels were to be confined to camps and an international force was to monitor the process—almost broke down. In April 1989, the SWAPO rebels undertook a large-scale invasion of the territory from bases in neighboring Angola. Perhaps because SWAPO throughout much of the guerrilla war had relied on Angolan sanctuary, its leaders might have feared that a ceasefire in which so few of their forces were proven to be inside the territory would harm their electoral prospects. Indeed, having been proclaimed by the United Nations General Assembly the "sole legitimate representative of the Namibian people," SWAPO perhaps saw little need for extensive political work. Yet even more critical to understanding the rebels' invasion just as the ceasefire was to take effect is an institutional factor: under the UN accord, a two-thirds vote was required for the constituent assembly to approve the constitution. Therefore, SWAPO had reason to worry about the elections and ceasefire terms that called for its effective demobilization prior to elections. The invasion may have been a last effort to avoid having to bargain with other forces after the elections. By its association with Ovambo nationalism, SWAPO was able to garner about 90 percent of the Ovambo vote (Ovambos generally live close to the Angolan border). However, elsewhere in the territory, SWAPO won less than 50 percent of the vote, and its overall countrywide share was 57 percent (Potgieter, 1990). For SWAPO, high transaction costs made the constitutional procedures undesirable because they threatened to take away some of the victory they thought was theirs by virtue of their battlefield strength. However, those same guarantees were crucial for reducing the external costs to other sectors represented by the government of the territory.

The case of Nicaragua in the late 1980s highlights again some of the important issues which surround the relationship between ceasefires and elections, and contains a parallel with Namibia: the rebels' crossing the border in advance of an electoral campaign despite ceasefire terms that required the bulk of their forces to remain outside. Unlike the other cases considered here, no important rebel leaders entered the campaign as candidates for Nicaragua's 1990 elections.[27] Indeed, the Nicaraguan Resistance (contras) were not even an armed wing of the United Nicaraguan Opposition (UNO), headed by presidential candidate Violeta Chamorro. Still, the contras and UNO did have one overriding objective in common: remove the Sandinista party and President Daniel Ortega from power. Having failed on the battlefield to oust the regime, some of the contras hoped to turn their supporters inside the country into voters for UNO. Indeed, many of the contras who were infiltrating back into Nicaragua, just prior to Ortega's announcement in November 1989 of the end to a ceasefire originally negotiated in March 1988, said that their purpose was not to carry out military campaigns but rather to join the political campaign of UNO (Boudreaux, 1989).

That the Nicaraguan rebels should have undertaken such actions was linked to the winner-take-all nature of the electoral process. Whereas PR was used for the congressional election, the stakes were very high as a result of the election's being a "referendum" on FSLN rule. The institutional rules were low on *garantismo,* as Di Palma (1990:68) suggests is likely wherever the revolutionary left, ill disposed to compromise with "moderates," has been in power. As a result, external costs were high for the rebels, whoever won: they were extreme should the FSLN win, but they were also high should the opposition win, since the rebels could not be sure of having a continuing voice in an UNO government in which they would lack elected positions. Thus the contras hedged their bets, using their arms both to help prevent the worst possible outcome for them, a democratic legitimation of the FSLN, and to provide their only means of ensuring themselves of continuing political "voice."

What the Nicaraguan Resistance was doing, then, was engaging in what in the discussion of Colombia was referred to as *proselitismo armado*. Such tactics involve using the presence of armed guerrillas to encourage the joining and supporting of the guerrillas' favored political cause and to provide an implied threat to those who might otherwise resist. It is interesting that in two cases, Namibia and Nicaragua, in which the ceasefire terms provided for the confinement of much of the rebel force across an international border, the rebels themselves began crossing the border in advance of the opening of the electoral campaign. In both cases, whatever other significant differences there may be, this action indicates the rebels' insecurity over their ability to play an important electoral role. That is to say, the terms of the campaign—a two-thirds majority barrier to clear in Namibia and neither low barriers to minority representation nor a neutral peacekeeping force in Nicaragua—had not lowered the cost of participation decisively below the cost of resistance. Rebels thus undertook operations on the eve of elections in an effort to alter the balance more to their favor. . . .

The lesson in the events of these several cases is that we cannot draw a neat separation between the real power exercised by forces in the field and the political sphere of electoral campaigns. Indeed, it is questionable how truly "free" elections can be unless both sides are effectively withdrawn from the battlefield. The battlefield situation—whether one army or another is present in a given area even in the absence of combat—is bound to have political repercussions. Ceasefires are not devoid of political content: the form the ceasefire takes will affect the parties' fortunes in the elections and thus shape each side's cost of competition. A recognition of these considerations explains why questions of disarmament versus cease-fire in-place are so contentious, once both sides have agreed in principle on the desirability of a negotiated, electoral way out of the conflict.

Transaction Costs and Institutional Reform

Institutional reform is a two-edged sword. A reform that decreases the rebels' cost of participation by lowering barriers to their entry into the system may also increase the government's cost of toleration simply because it enhances the rebels' chance of becoming a large party. The key, particularly when the rebels are a formidable force (stalemate Type 2), is to build in guarantees to the government that increased rebel participation will not jeopardize the government's political standing (beyond what it might expect to achieve or maintain by continued suppression). This implies that a situation may also occur in which the building in of guarantees to the government weakens the rebels' prospects, thus raising their cost of participation. Such a scenario is a plausible interpretation of events in Namibia. Since that case illustrates some important points about the role of constitutional procedures in settlements, let us return to it.

The Namibian settlement required a two-thirds vote of an elected constituent assembly to pass a constitution for the new state. The two-thirds rule, plus the extreme form of nationwide PR employed in the elections, served to provide guarantees to the government and its constituency of white and non-Ovambo blacks against possible dominance by SWAPO. In doing so, however, it may have contributed to SWAPO's decision to infiltrate troops into the territory, as was discussed above, in order to make the securing of a two-thirds majority more likely. Thus the two-thirds rule kept the cost of participation higher than a simple majority rule would have. On the other hand, with majority rule, SWAPO could have dictated the constitutional outcome, had it wished to do so. Most likely the resulting constitution would not have had the restraints on SWAPO leader Sam Nujoma's control of the executive presidency that stemmed from the need to clear the two-thirds hurdle: a two-term limit on presidential tenure, a cabinet requiring the confidence of the assembly, and a territorially based upper house. Thus the two-thirds rule, increasing transaction costs, was crucial for lowering the cost of toleration for the territorial government (and its South African patron) by also serving to lower its external costs.

The importance of providing the rebels a means to influence the rules of the game in which the new democratic order will be carried out is demonstrated by Colombia as well as Namibia. In both cases, rebels participated in elections for an assembly to write a new constitution. This factor surely accounts for SWAPO's willingness to participate despite the two-thirds rule and despite the exclusion of SWAPO delegates from the negotiating process that set up the elections. In Colombia, too, the constituent assembly was an irresistible carrot for the M-19 and other groups. The decision rule for the new Colombian constitution was a simple majority within the constituent assembly, meaning low transaction costs. This would appear to raise the external costs, that is, the risk of outcomes unfavorable to some key actors. However, the important distinction between Colombia and

Namibia is that the decision rule that was chosen in each case depended upon the type of stalemate being broken by institutional reform. In Namibia, there was an ascendant guerrilla group, thus the two-thirds rule provided guarantees that the guerrillas would not dominate and that the bargaining power of minorities, including the government's constituents, would be enhanced. In Colombia, the guerrillas were a diminishing threat; giving them voice in the system was the carrot, but to have opted for extraordinary majority rule would have simply enhanced the rebels' bargaining power. . . .

The Nicaraguan story is somewhat similar to that of El Salvador in that an election in 1984 to determine an assembly for the drafting of a new constitution was held in a context of a rebel force having external support for continued resistance. Even in 1990, the rebels themselves did not participate, leaving the new government with a difficult process of reincorporating its (supposed) allies into the system, but unable to offer them political positions that had already been filled.

Sequences and Conditions in Producing Settlements

We have now arrived at a point at which we can bring together the many strands of the preceding discussion and see how the type of stalemate, institutional reforms, and ceasefires are intertwined in the process of settlements in which guerrillas emerge as relevant electoral competitors. The discussion of cases and the consideration of ceasefire terms have demonstrated the following conclusions about the sequencing of events. In Type 1 stalemates, those in which the government is ascendant militarily over the rebels, the typical pattern is that the ceasefire precedes the negotiation of institutional reforms, or else the reforms are offered as part of a package in which the rebels must accede to their demobilization beforehand. In Type 2 stalemates, those in which the rebels are ascendant, institutional reforms precede the ceasefire. We can better understand the sequencing when we remember that institutional reforms are ultimately a move made by the government; even where negotiated, it is the government that, short of overthrow, decides to replace its existing constitution or electoral law with one more conducive to reaching a settlement. The ceasefire, on the other hand, is more of a mutual move than institutional reform, yet is principally a move made by the rebels. It was the rebel leadership that originally chose to raise arms against the government and it is the rebel leadership that ultimately decides whether or not the terms are right for ending the rebellion. The sequencing also can be understood with reference to Internal Wars, where neither side is clearly ascendant militarily. In Internal Wars, . . . simultaneous moves by each side are necessary.

The observed difference in sequencing relates directly to each side's costs of conflict and competition. The descriptions of scenarios that follow are meant to be abstract and not pure representations of empirical cases, which of course are affected by numerous idiosyncrasies. The purpose is to construct a schema that might guide further theorizing on this topic and help us understand when settlements can be expected and what kinds of ceasefire terms and institutional reforms are necessary to resolve a particular given case of guerrilla conflict.

In Type 1 stalemates, the government's cost of toleration already is less than its cost of suppression and it therefore has the incentive to seek a settlement. But the rebels' cost of participation remains above its cost of resistance, unless institutional reforms give it the chance to become potentially a relevant political party. In such a calculus of costs, a government nearing military victory would not be expected to offer unilateral concessions which the rebels might treat as a sign of political weakness. Thus the government allows reforms to be negotiated or allows rebels to participate in electoral institutions on the grounds that a demobilization of rebel forces take place. The empirical cases that most fit this scenario are Colombia's deal with the M-19 and Venezuela.

In Type 2 stalemates, the ascendancy of the rebels means that the government's cost of tolerating the rebels as electoral competitors exceeds the cost of suppression, whereas the rebels' cost of participation is lower than the cost of resistance. The only way the government can afford electoral competition with its rivals is to obtain prior agreement on institutional reforms that protect its (minority) position: increasing transaction costs by requiring extraordinary majorities or over-representing the interests of the regime's constituency. Only with such assurances will the government contemplate a ceasefire as a first step toward electoral competition. The empirical cases that typify this scenario are Namibia and Zimbabwe.

Table 1 summarizes the sequence of events entailed in reaching settlements of various kinds. The top of the table, part 1A, concerns Type I stalemates. The first step is the ceasefire, which may take one of two forms. If the government's cost of tolerating the rebels is already quite low, it may accede to a ceasefire in-place, in which the rebels keep their arms. Such a ceasefire lowers the rebels' cost of participation, since they obtain a concession in the form of cessation of hostilities and are granted recognition as an electoral competitor. Since the rebels do not relinquish their arms, the government's cost of toleration may actually increase (from an already low level), such that no institutional reforms will be offered. Such a settlement is unlikely to be successful, but is an option that a government facing isolated pockets of resistance might attempt, as in Colombia in the 1980s.

If the rebels are demobilized first or at least removed from the territory in question during the process, the government's cost of toleration is lowered, since the armed threat is removed. As a result, the rebels' cost of participation is likely to increase, if they are asked to participate in elections under existing institutions with relatively high barriers to their entry as relevant competitors. Thus institutional reforms may be offered as a means to lower the cost of participation. As we saw in case discussions, governments that made such offers (in Colombia, El Salvador, and Venezuela) sought the rebels' participation in a future alliance against existing electoral rivals.[29] If the government does not foresee an alliance with a party of ex-rebels, it is unlikely to offer reforms. As in Nicaragua in 1990, such a settlement may be unstable, since the rebels' stake in the institutional rules is weak. The tendency of governments to offer incentives to rebel electoral participation when they are seeking alliance partners is a finding with considerable implications for more general theories of democratization. Przeworski (1986:55–6) argued that the primary moving force that leads to democratization is a decision by some sectors within the ruling coalition to seek allies on the outside. That this condition holds true even in many cases in which the "outsiders" have been fighting the government should strengthen theorists' willingness to see this factor as crucial.

Table 1, part 1B, summarizes the conditions of settlements resulting from Type 2 stalemates. As mentioned previously, institutional reform (Type 2) precedes the ceasefire, as the government seeks *garantismo* as protection from what is sure to be a very large rebel representation after anticipated elections. Combined with rebel demobilization or the rebels' confinement to camps outside the disputed territory, these moves obviously decrease the government's cost of toleration, but they increase the rebels' cost of participation. The institutional rules make the prize to be won in elections less tempting and the disposition of their forces decreases their

Table 1. Moves and their effects in settlements of guerrilla conflicts

Move	Effect of Cost on Participation	Effect on Cost of Toleration	Conditions	Examples
1A: Type 1 Stalemate				
1) Ceasefire				
a) Armed, in-place	Lowering	Increasing (from already low level)	Institutional reforms unlikely. Unsuccessful settlement	Colombia 1980s
b) Demobilized or removed from territory during process	Remain high; may increase	Lowered further		See 2) below
			i) If rebels are potential coalition partners for government, institutional reforms offered. See 2) below.	
			ii) If coalition not viable, no reforms. Unstable settlement	Nicaragua 1990
2) Institutional reforms (Type 1)	Lowering	Kept acceptable	Rebels form party or parties	Colombia (M-19) Venezuela (Type 1 institutions in place)
1B: Type 2 Stalemate				
1) Institutional reforms (Type 2), and	Increasing (from low levels); raises transaction costs	Lowering	Peacekeeping and observers counteract increasing cost to rebels	
a) rebels demobilized			i) Stable if rebels have political networks	Zimbabwe
			ii) Unstable if rebels' political networks weak	Namibia
b) ceasefire in-place, armed	Lowering, but Type 2 reforms may counteract	Increasing significantly	Untenable for government	None
1C: Internal War				
Ceasefire in-place, armed	Lowering	Increasing significantly	Untenable for government	None
Demobilization	Increasing significantly	Lowering	Untenable for rebels	None
Institutional reform (Type 1 and Type 2)	Uncertain	Uncertain	Difficult, owing to needed simultaneity	El Salvador 1990s?

confidence in the result. However, their cost of participation is already low relative to their cost of resistance, mainly because of international pressures upon them to end the war. Their willingness to acquiesce ultimately requires appropriate guarantees, which can be provided in the short-term by the introduction of international observers and peacekeepers. Examples include Zimbabwe, where the settlement was relatively stable, owing to the rebels' extensive political networks which functioned in lieu of their armed guerrilla cadres. In Namibia, the settlement was unstable, nearly breaking down when the rebels reinfiltrated the territory, in part, as I have argued, because they could not count on their political networks to overcome the high transaction costs of the settlement. The table also shows the hypothetical process of a Type 2 stalemate being settled by means of a ceasefire in-place. As indicated, such a settlement would be untenable for the government, and there are no such cases.

Finally, part 1C of Table 1 considers the cases of Internal War. A ceasefire in-place is untenable for the government because it lowers the cost of rebel participation, allowing them to use their armed cadres to influence elections during the ceasefire, and, for the same reason, increases the cost to the government of tolerating rebel participation in elections. A ceasefire involving rebel demobilization has the exact opposite effects. Not surprisingly, neither of these scenarios exists empirically. . . . It is uncertain what the consequences of institutional reform, which must incorporate elements of both Types 1 and 2, would be, since the consequences depend in large part on the ceasefire terms. The complexity of Internal Wars thus requires simultaneity of moves, unlike the two types of stalemate identified here. . . .

Wrapping Up

The cases suggest that when rebels are permitted to keep their weapons (Colombia in the 1980s) or do not participate directly in elections (Nicaragua, El Salvador 1989–91), even the formation of new political parties and their contesting elections will leave the rebels little stake in the electoral outcome. However, for rebels to enter electoral competition in a context of their own disarmament requires low barriers to their ability to become a relevant party and thus their opportunity to achieve more political power through the electoral system than through continued conflict. Hence the negotiation with rebel participation of a new constitution for Zimbabwe, the election of constituent assemblies in Colombia and Namibia, and the deployment of international monitors in several cases were crucial for lowering the rebels' costs of participation. Leaving aside Nicaragua, in which . . . the ex-rebels are not a relevant party[,] . . . in each successful case, the rebels were demobilized prior to the elections. This demobilization must be taken as a crucial element of successful emergence of (former) rebels as relevant players in elections.

A final set of points to be made concerns the restructuring of the regime's army and government. In no case were these the kinds of institutional changes that were meant to lure in the rebels. . . . Not even in Zimbabwe, where the rebels were arguably on the verge of smashing the army militarily, was the old army dismantled or the two armies merged prior to elections. Indeed, the temporary British governing authority relied on much of the Rhodesian security apparatus during the campaign. Why any government would accept a fusion of the armies prior to elections is puzzling. . . . Such a concession seemingly would raise the cost of toleration by giving the regime's opponents a foothold in state institutions. . . . Each government with rebel participation emerged only out of the electoral institutions offered the rebels as terms of the settlement. Notwithstanding the typical rebel demand for a provisional government, a general conclusion is that these tough conditions fade rather quickly when the government offers a significantly liberalized electoral process with international monitoring and, typically, constitutional reforms to make rebel participation in governing coalitions more feasible. This point thus highlights an overriding theme of this paper on which it shall conclude: institutions matter, even to guerrillas!

NOTES

1. There were South African troops deployed in one of the cases discussed here, Rhodesia (Zimbabwe), but these forces primarily were guarding a small number of fixed strategic sites rather than playing a leading role in combat operations, in the sense of, for example, the Cuban forces in Angola.

2. A factor considered in this paper that may lead one to predict that Sendero would be less likely to settle at some future point is the extent of international pressure. The Peruvian rebels appear to be unusually free from international leverage, unlike most of those in the cases discussed herein. Note, however, that such a prediction would be fully consistent with the theoretical argument developed below concerning a rational calculus of costs and does not require resort to the group's special ideology, goals, or style.

3. On the other hand, such a movement would also be able to count on its supporters to vote for it in elections.

4. I use the term *stalemate* not in its literal sense of a draw, which would imply two roughly equal forces opposing each other, but to signify a conflict in which neither side is strong enough to eliminate the other (through military victory), even though one side may be ascendant strategically over the other.

5. With as little as 0.55% of the nationwide vote, a party is guaranteed a seat in the Chamber of Deputies. See Shugart (1992).

6. According to Stedman's account, the warning by Samora Machel, leader of Mozambique, was blunt and colorful: he indicated that he would he happy to give Mugabe a nice home on the beach in Mozambique if he were to walk away from the settlement! In turn, Mozambique's incentives were altered by Rhodesian military actions against Mozambican territory.

7. I do not see the provisions for international observers as Type I institutional reforms, although they have a similar effect. They do not, however, constitute an institution, as the monitoring affected only the period of the campaign and voting. The institutions of the electoral system and constitutional structure of the government could have been more favorable, especially to ZANU, than what was employed. Confident of being the largest party, ZANU would have been served best by not using PR and a parliamentary system, both of which could have meant coalition government had ZANU fallen somewhat short of a majority of votes. Indeed, the ZANU government replaced PR with a one-seat district plurality system and subsequently introduced an elected presidency. Thus, although monitors reduced the costs of participating in elections that the guerrillas could not control, they did not consist of a concession designed to help the rebels win an acceptable share of seats or executive power, as are Type 1 institutional reforms.

8. Originally, the armed forces of the regime were to be confined to barracks, also under Commonwealth supervision.

9. It may seem ironic to maintain that South Africa "pressured" the Rhodesian government into seeking an exit from the conflict, given that South African troops remained inside Rhodesian territory until formal independence was granted Zimbabwe. However, there are numerous examples that South Africa wished to rid itself of the burden of backing the Rhodesian exclusionary government. For example, Martin and Johnson (1981) devote an entire chapter to the effect that the Portuguese coup, leading to Mozambican independence, had on official South African thinking about the viability of white rule in a Rhodesia that now had over 1,000 miles of frontier with a black, Marxist-ruled Mozambique. That the South Africans would seek a way out of their commitment to Rhodesia does not, however, indicate that they countenanced a Marxist-ruled Zimbabwe, but only that South African reaction changed the parameters of the game.

10. "Reflexiones para una Nueva Constitucion," *El Espectador,* November 25, 1990.

11. The text of the agreement between Betancur's government and the FARC is printed in Pinzon de Lewin, 1986.

12. The figure includes joint lists presented by Liberals and the UP in some regions.

13. In Colombia, it is often said, one is born either a Liberal or a Conservative. What is less often recognized is that the same sort of regional and familial base of partisanship applies to the Communists as well.

14. Proof of military support is difficult to come by, although it is widely accepted as fact in Colombia. Proof of "solidarity," however, was quite open: the Colombian rebels' international publications justifying their cause were produced in and mailed from Managua.

15. The similar political consequences of a similar electoral system in Japan are developed theoretically by McCubbins and Rosenbluth (1991). Shugart and Fernandez (1992) extend the analysis to the Colombian case.

16. The government was vindicated when Navarro deemed the president's reform proposals "excellent" and spoke in favor of capitalism, but "democratic capitalism." The example of the M-19 also spurred negotiations with other guerrilla groups whose disarmament was crucial to the government's hopes of attracting increased foreign investment. The FARC and the National Liberation Army, however, remained on the outside. For the FARC, because of its isolated regional bases (see above), and for both groups because of their minuscule potential for a national base, it may be impossible to make institutional reforms that would entice them.

17. The larger opposition parties' interests were served by an electoral system that took away the incentives for fragmentation in the 1984 rules. A minority like the armed resistance, if it were to form a political party, would have been better served by the 1984 rules.

. . .

26. Indeed, a critical reason for the decision to permit security operations by Rhodesian forces was allegations of intimidation by ZANU. Such intimidation could hardly have been an issue had there not been a ceasefire in the first place, leading to ZANU's entry into electoral competition.

27. Although one, an ex-Sandinista as well as ex-contra, Eden Pastora, returned briefly to campaign for the Social Christian party and then went back into exile.

. . .

29. In the Venezuelan case, institutional reforms were not necessary. Still, the settlement fits in the pattern: the rebels were not permitted to participate freely in electoral institutions until they had been definitively disarmed.

. . .

REFERENCES

Archer, R. P. (1989) "The Transition from Traditional to Broker Clientelism in Colombia: Political Stability and Social Unrest." Paper presented at the annual meeting of the Latin American Studies Association, Miami, Florida.

Archer, R. P., and M. Chernick (1989) "El Presidente frente a las Instituciones Na-
cionales." In *La Democraácia en Blanco y Negro: Colombia en los Años Ochenta,* edited
by P. Vasquez de Urrutia, pp. 31–80. Bogotá: Fondo Editorial CEREC.

Beaufort, E. de (1989) *Observaciones Críticas a la Concepción y a los Métodos del Proceso de Paz
de Belisario Betancur 1982–1986.* MA thesis, University of the Andes, Bogotá, Colombia.

Booth, J. A. (1985) *The End and the Beginning: The Nicaraguan Revolution.* Boulder, CO:
Westview Press.

Boudreaux, R. (1989) "War Shadows Campaign." *Los Angeles Times,* November 9, pp.
A16–A17.

Buchanan, J. M., and G. Tullock (1962) *The Calculus of Consent: Logical Foundations of
Constitutional Democracy.* Ann Arbor: University of Michigan Press.

Chernick, M. W. (1988) Negotiated Settlement to Armed Conflict: Lessons from the
Colombian Peace Process. *Journal of Interamerican Studies and World Affairs* 30, 4
(Winter):53–88.

Chernick, M. W. (1989) "Reforma política, aperture democrática y el desmonte del
Frente Nacional." In *La Democrácia en Blanco y Negro: Colombia en los Años Ochenta,*
edited by P. Vasquez de Urrutia, pp. 285–320. Bogotá: Fondo Editorial CEREC.

Christian, S. (1985) *Nicaragua: The Revolution in the Family.* New York: Random House.

Cruz, A., Jr. (1987) "One Hundred Years of Turpitude." *The New Republic,* November 16,
pp. 26–36.

Dahl, R. A. (1971) *Polyarchy: Participation and Opposition.* New Haven, CT: Yale University Press.

Davidow, J. (1984) *A Peace in Southern Africa: The Lancaster House Conference on Rhodesia,
1979.* Boulder, CO: Westview Press.

Di Palma, G. (1990) *To Craft Democracies.* Berkeley: University of California Press.

Duarte, J. N., with D. Page. (1986) *Duarte: My Story.* New York: G. P. Putnam's Sons.

Ellner, S. (1980) Political Party Dynamics in Venezuela and the Outbreak of Guerrilla
Warfare. *Interamerican Economic Affairs* 34, 2 (Autumn):3–24.

Ellner, S. (1988) *Venezuela's Movimiento a Socialismo: From Guerrilla Defeat to Innovative Politics.* Durham, NC: Duke University Press.

Garcia, J. Z. (1989) "El Salvador: Recent Elections in Historical Perspective." In *Elections
and Democracy in Central America,* edited by J. A. Booth and M. A. Seligson, pp.
60–92. Chapel Hill: University of North Carolina Press.

Geddes, B. (1990) "Democratic Institutions as a Bargain among Self-Interested Politicians." Paper prepared for presentation at the annual meeting of the American Political Science Association, San Francisco.

Geddes, B. (1991) A Game Theoretic Model of Reform in Latin American Democracies.
American Political Science Review 85:371–392.

Gott, R. (1970) *Guerrilla Movements in Latin America.* London: Nelson.

Gregory, M. (1981) Zimbabwe 1980: Politicisation through Armed Struggle and Electoral Mobilisation. *Journal of Commonwealth and Comparative Politics* 19, 1
(March):63–94.

Grofman, B. (1990) "Will the Real 'New Institutionalism' Please Stand up and Take a Bow." Unpublished paper.

Harding, T. F., and S. Landau. (1964) "Terrorism, Guerrilla Warfare and the Democratic Left in Venezuela." *Studies on the Left*, 4, 4 (Fall):118–128.

Hartlyn, J. (1988) *The Politics of Coalition Rule in Colombia.* Cambridge: Cambridge University Press.

Ikle, F. (1971) *Every War Must End.* New York: Columbia University Press.

Karl, T. (1986a) "Petroleum and Political Pacts: The Transition to Democracy in Venezuela." In *Transitions from Authoritarian Rule,* edited by G. O'Donnell, P. Schmitter, and L. Whitehead. Baltimore: Johns Hopkins University Press.

Karl, T. (1986b) "Imposing Consent? Electoralism vs. Democratization in El Salvador." In *Elections and Democratization in Latin America, 1980–1985,* edited by P. Drake and E. Silva. San Diego: Center for Iberian and Latin American Studies.

Levine, D. H. (1973) *Conflict and Political Change in Venezuela.* Princeton, NJ: Princeton University Press.

Licklider, R. (1990) "How Civil Wars End: Preliminary Results from a Comparative Project." Paper prepared for presentation at the annual meeting of the American Political Science Association, San Francisco.

Lijphart, A., and R. Rogowski (1991) "Separation of Powers and the Management of Political Cleavages." In *Do Institutions Matter? Comparing Government Capabilities in the U.S. and Abroad,* edited by K. Weaver and B. Rockman. Washington, DC: Brookings Institution.

Linz, J. J. (1978) *The Breakdown of Democratic Regimes: Crisis, Breakdown, and Reequilibration.* Baltimore: Johns Hopkins University Press.

Linz, J. J. (1984) "Democracy—Presidential or Parliamentary: Does It Make a Difference?" Prepared for the workshop, "Political Parties in the Southern Cone," World Peace Foundation of the Woodrow Wilson International Center for Scholars.

March, J. C., and J. P. Olsen (1984) "New Institutionalism: Organizational Factors in Political Life." *American Political Science Review* 78:734–749.

Martin, D., and P. Johnson (1981) *The Struggle for Zimbabwe: The Chimurenga War.* London: Faber and Faber.

McCubbins, M. D., and F. M. Rosenbluth (1991) "Electoral Structure and the Organization of Policymaking in Japan." Unpublished paper.

Norton, C. (1989) "Salvadoran Rebels Woo Peasants." *Christian Science Monitor,* February 7, p. 3.

O'Donnell, G., P. C. Schmitter, and L. Whitehead, eds. (1986) *Transitions from Authoritarian Rule: Tentative Conclusions about Uncertain Democracies.* Baltimore: Johns Hopkins University Press.

Pastor, R. A. (1987) *Condemned to Repetition: The United States and Nicaragua.* Princeton, NJ: Princeton University Press.

Penniman, H., ed. (1980) *Venezuela at the Polls.* Washington, DC: American Enterprise Institute.

Pinzon de Lewin, P., ed. (1986) *La Oposición en Colombia: Algunas Bases para su Discusión.* Bogotá: FESCOL.

Pinzon de Lewin, P. (1989) *Pueblos, Regiones y Partidos: La Regionalización/Atlas Electoral Colombiano.* Bogotá: Fondo Editorial CEREC.

Potgieter, P. J. J. S. (1990) "The Resolution 435 Election in Namibia: Format and Outcome." Paper prepared for presentation at the annual meeting of the American Political Science Association, San Francisco.

Przeworski, A. (1986) "Some Problems in the Study of the Transition to Democracy." In *Transitions from Authoritarian Rule: Tentative Conclusions about Uncertain Democracies,* edited by G. O'Donnell, P. C. Schmitter, and L. Whitehead. Baltimore: Johns Hopkins University Press.

Radu, M. (1986) The Origins and Evolution of the Nicaraguan Insurgencies. *Orbis* 29, 4 (Winter):821–840.

Rustow, D. (1970) Transitions to Democracy. *Comparative Politics* 2:337–363.

Sartori, G. (1968) "Political Development and Political Engineering." In *Public Policy,* Vol. 17, edited by J. D. Montgomery and A. O. Hirschman. Cambridge: Cambridge University Press.

Sartori, G. (1976) *Parties and Party Systems.* Cambridge: Cambridge University Press.

Shugart, M. S. (1992) Leaders, Rank and File and Constituents: Electoral Reform in Colombia and Venezuela. *Electoral Studies* 11, 1.

Shugart, M. S., and R. Fernandez (1991) "Constitutional Reform and Economic Restructuring in Colombia." Paper presented at the meeting of the North American Association of Colombianists, Ibagué, Colombia.

Shugart, M. S., and R. Fernandez (1992) "Economic Adjustment and Political Institutions: Foreign vs. Domestic Constituents in Colombia." Work in progress.

Shugart, M. S., and J. M. Carey (1992) *Presidents and Assemblies: Constitutional Design and Electoral Dynamics.* Cambridge: Cambridge University Press.

Stedman, S. J. (1990) *Peacemaking in Civil War: International Mediation in Zimbabwe, 1974–1980.* Boulder, CO: Lynne Rienner.

Strom, K. (1989) "A Behavioral Theory of Competitive Political Parties." Unpublished paper.

Strom, K. (1990) *Minority Government and Majority Rule.* Cambridge: Cambridge University Press.

Taagepera, R., and M. S. Shugart (1989) *Seats and Votes: The Effects and Determinants of Electoral Systems.* New Haven, CT: Yale University Press.

Walker, T. W. (1970) *The Christian Democratic Movement in Nicaragua.* Tucson: University of Arizona Press.

IV

The Transformation of Revolution

The Chinese Revolution of 1949 brought to power a communist government that was virulently hostile to capitalism. Over half a century later, that government's greatest accomplishment has been presiding over China's successful transition to capitalism.

Egypt's 1952 revolution brought to power an Arab nationalist regime that was virulently hostile toward the West, Israel, and the conservative Arab monarchies. Beginning in the 1970s, this government established—and has since maintained—good relations with all three.

Iran's 1979 revolution gave birth to an Islamic fundamentalist regime that was also extremely hostile toward the United States and the West. That same government now has friendly relations with most Western states, except the United States. A rapprochement between Washington and Tehran, though, appears to be in the making.

The selections in Part I observed that relations between status quo powers and revolutionary regimes usually are highly contentious when the latter first come to power. Sometimes they remain contentious for decades. Sooner or later, though, status quo powers and revolutionary regimes usually achieve some sort of modus vivendi. Revolutionary regimes that once set out to transform the existing international system often end up not just accepting it, but working to uphold it. Status quo powers sometimes become their partners or even close allies. Ironically, revolutionary regimes often become status quo powers, which then oppose new forms of revolution.

There is, however, no uniform manner in which revolutionary regimes become integrated into the existing international system. Some integrate quickly, whereas others do so only slowly. Furthermore, improved relations between status quo and revolutionary powers are not certain to remain friendly. Their relations can also deteriorate, as did U.S.-Soviet ties following their alliance during World War II and their détente of the 1970s. Once-friendly Sino-American relations have also deteriorated in recent years.

Different views of how and why relations evolve between status quo and revolutionary regimes are presented here in selections by David Armstrong and Mark N. Katz. Armstrong sees this evolution occurring as revolutionary regimes realize that they cannot alter the existing international system to their liking but that they can make use of it, like other states, to pursue their interests.

I, on the other hand, argue that revolutionary regimes move out of their early anticapitalist, anti-Western phase as a result of their normal internal political evolution. Over time, revolutionary regimes focus less on difficult-to-achieve international goals, such as spreading revolution to other countries, and more on prosaic domestic ones, such as economic development. As this transition occurs, revolutionary regimes—often under successor leaders, as in the Chinese, Egyptian, and Iranian cases—come to see the West less as a hated enemy and more as a necessary partner.

9

Revolution and World Order: The Revolutionary State in International Society

David Armstrong

David Armstrong is the author of Revolution and World Order *(1993)—a book that examines the long-term evolution of relations between revolutionary states and status quo powers. In the following selection, which is drawn from the book's conclusion, Armstrong observes that in the immediate aftermath of overthrowing the old regime, new revolutionary regimes typically seek the radical transformation of the existing "Westphalian" system of international relations.*

Westphalia is the German city in which the peace treaty of 1648 ending the Thirty Years War between Catholic and Protestant forces on the European continent was signed. Armstrong defined "the Westphalian conception of international society" as a society of individual states possessing sovereignty—supreme authority within their territory. This system of international relations was first established in Europe and then spread to the rest of the world through the process of decolonization.

As in any society, the international society of states has a set of prevailing norms regulating the behavior of the individual members. Also as in any society, these norms change and evolve over time. The basic norm of Westphalian international society has been the inadmissibility of forcefully destroying the sovereignty of any state recognized by other states. The international society of states, of course, has not always acted to prevent or reverse the destruction of sovereignty. However, when a revolutionary regime emerges that does not recognize the legitimacy of other governments and seeks their overthrow, the latter have usually put aside their differences and banded together against what they perceive as a common threat.

New revolutionary regimes that seek to radically transform the West-
phalian system of international relations eventually discover that they
cannot succeed against such a coalition and that just trying to do so is
extremely costly as well as fruitless. In time, they come to abandon these
efforts and to grudgingly accept the existing Westphalian system. "So-
cialization" is the term that Armstrong uses to describe this process
through which revolutionary regimes adjust their behavior to existing
international norms.

Critical Questions

1. Why do some revolutionary regimes become socialized into the ex-
isting system of international relations quickly, whereas others do so
much more slowly?

2. If revolutionary regimes accept the existing system of interna-
tional relations only grudgingly, do they truly become socialized? Does
it matter that their acceptance is grudging?

3. Have revolutionary states ever succeeded in transforming the ex-
isting system of international relations? To what extent?

4. At what point do revolutionary regimes become status quo powers?

. . . The root cause of the problem that revolutionary states pose for order
is that international order requires some measure of consensus as to the assumptions, rules, and practices by which international society conducts its
affairs. Revolutionary states are by nature consensus breakers. This study
has considered their particular objections to three of the main foundations
of international order: international law, diplomacy, and the balance of
power. It has suggested that a common sequence, although one that has
manifested itself in different ways, is for an initial hostility towards these institutions of international society to give way to a grudging acceptance of
their value, albeit sometimes coupled with a desire to reform them. This
process, along with other adjustments in the behaviour of revolutionary
states to accord more with the normal patterns of international conduct,
has been defined as a process of "socialization."

The experience of socialization has not been uniform for all revolutionary
states. The United States was, by and large, anxious to gain rapid acceptance

as a "respectable" state, although it retained a sense of its particularity and an intermittent reformism that continued to set it apart to some degree from other established states. The French moved to disown some of the internationally objectionable aspects of their revolution as early as 1793, but by then events had acquired an unstoppable momentum. The Soviets adapted some of their international behaviour quite quickly to the requirements of membership of the society of states, although their ideologues encountered enormous difficulties in their search for doctrinally acceptable explanations of this. However, the Soviet Union maintained a dual identity until the Gorbachev era, when its decision to opt for respectability as a state helped to untie the bonds that had held both the Soviet Union and the socialist camp together.

Many factors have combined to impel states towards socialization. The need to gain access to the international trading and financial system, the need for allies and more generally for greater security, and even an appreciation of the possibility of exploiting the conventional structures and processes of international society for revolutionary purposes have all played a part. But the deeper forces at work in the socialization process all revolve around one central fact. Whatever the larger and longer-term aspirations of victorious revolutionary leaders, after the revolution they were no longer merely directing a revolutionary movement, but had assumed control over a determinate territorial unit which had been a state and which, short of global revolution, they had no option but to continue to manage as a state. Indeed, the internal policies of the revolutionaries were normally directed towards transforming it into a stronger, more efficient state and to harnessing all of its latent power. Yet statehood had external as well as internal aspects, and here the will of the revolutionary elite was not the only variable that counted. The external dimension of statehood involved rules, practices, norms, and institutions whose legitimacy derived from the will of the society of states as a whole. Full statehood meant not only the effective exercise of power internally but international conduct that conformed to these externally determined prerogatives and responsibilities. Achieving the highly desirable goal of statehood, therefore, entailed a high degree of socialization.

The fact that so many revolutionary states were obliged to adapt their behaviour to the Westphalian conception of international society is some testimony to the durability of that conception. But although the essential elements of the Westphalian structure remained in place, the system was far from changeless. Developing ideas about the state itself, direct attempts to reform the institutions of international order, and the great increase in the number of states after 1945 have all contributed to the evolution of international society since 1648. Since revolutionary states played a part in all three of these forces for change it is clear that the interaction between revolutionary states and international society was far from being a one-way process.

Taking each of these three forces in turn, changes in conceptions of the state have, at one level, involved a continual expansion in the functions performed by the state, and correspondingly in the expectations of citizens about what their state can and should do on their behalf. From another perspective, these changes have involved an evolution in the collective judgement of international society about what constitutes a legitimate state. The Westphalian judgement was simple enough—any entity exercising sovereignty that happened to be in existence at the time could qualify, whether it was a dynastic state, a constitutional monarchy, or even, in one or two cases, a republic. The American Revolution indirectly, and the French Revolution directly challenged this *laissez-faire* position with their new ideas of national self-determination and constitutional (ideally republican) government reflecting the popular will. Although many states that failed to meet these criteria remained in being, it became increasingly difficult after 1919 and even more so after 1945 for states to refuse at least to pay lip service to the new values. As the Cold War ended and a new world order has begun to emerge in the 1990s, a liberal polity and national self-determination have appeared to be becoming even more entrenched as yardsticks of legitimacy in late twentieth-century international society. The general understanding of what the idea of a liberal state encompassed has become ever broader through the nineteenth and twentieth centuries. To the original requirement of a democratic constitution has been added the need to meet increasingly demanding norms of internal governance, including the "standard of civilization," the protection of human rights, and the rule of law. International society itself has developed a range of devices through which its collective judgements on such matters could be made known. International organizations like the League of Nations and the United Nations have played an important part in this process. By the early 1990s the leading Western powers, which had achieved a preponderance in international society with the collapse of the Soviet Union, appeared to be moving towards a loose great power concert based on numerous formal and informal mechanisms like the Group of Seven meetings and the UN Security

Council. They also seemed to be engaging in a form of piecemeal international social engineering by linking aid to Third World and Eastern European states to firm commitments by those states to social, political, and economic reform. Statecraft was no longer simply a matter of manipulating the balance of power through a foreign policy whose imperatives were paramount, as in the original post-Westphalian international society. Now domestic policy had primacy and international society had adjusted to reflect this change.

The instruments of international order had also experienced change. The unmanaged power politics of the eighteenth century gave way to a more controlled balance of power system in the nineteenth. The great power concert of the nineteenth century was given institutionalized form (the League Council and the UN Security Council) in the twentieth century, while attempts were made to replace the discredited balance of power system with a "community of power" in the shape of the collective security provisions of the Covenant and Charter. By the 1990s new concepts of "cooperative security" were being mooted as international society sought to reflect the extraordinary changes that had taken place since 1989. The idea of an equilibrium of forces had not vanished from international discourse, and indeed it remained a crucial element in the international politics of certain regions. But the pessimistic assumptions about human nature that had seemed to make a balance of power system, however disguised, an inevitable part of the institutions of order in the Westphalian international society, appeared to be yielding at least some ground to the idea that international relations could develop in more harmonious directions than the balance of power allowed.

Equally striking developments had occurred in the other institutions of international society. "Parliamentary" and other forms of public diplomacy, together with a great increase in "summit" diplomacy, had not entirely replaced traditional diplomacy by the 1990s. But their growth, like the changes in the balance of power system, could be seen as evidence both of an increasing sense of dissatisfaction with traditional diplomacy within international society, and of the way in which the greater openness and democratization inside many states was being reflected in the conduct of international relations.

Similarly, the prodigious growth of international law after the eighteenth century brought with it some subtle amendments to the implicit Westphalian premiss that the sole purpose of international law was to protect and preserve sovereignty. Sovereign equality was still the central legal norm, but the rules that states were prepared to accept had come gradually to reflect a concern with other objectives than the preservation of the society of states and the sovereign rights of its members. This change may, very broadly, be characterized as a shift from rules that promoted *order* towards rules and practices that served the purpose of, first, a system of international *governance,* and later the direct *regulation* of certain aspects of international life. Promoting international order, it will be recalled, involved devising means of ensuring regularity and stability in the pattern of rules, assumptions, and practices that prevailed in international society. Diplomacy, a balance of power, and rules of coexistence were the principal devices employed by states towards these ends. All three could function with only a minimal degree of conscious manipulation by states. When the great powers undertook the role of management of international order in the nineteenth century, they were not challenging the essential principle of sovereignty, except to the limited extent that the conservative powers were able to obtain international support for their interventions against revolution. But they were implicitly acknowledging that membership of international society entailed responsibilities and duties as well as rights, and also that some measure of direct and deliberate involvement in the processes of rule formation in international society and of supervision of Europe's political equilibrium was needed if the goal of order were to be achieved. Later, in the nineteenth century, and even more in the twentieth, special institutions were set up separately from the great power concert to provide for the direct regulation of numerous functional areas of international intercourse. At first these were concerned with matters that aroused little controversy among states, such as postal services, telecommunication, and the control of epidemic diseases. After 1945 more sensitive issues, such as monetary relations, refugees, and, to a very limited degree, human rights, came to be the subjects of international regimes.

The third major factor contributing to the evolution of international society was the great expansion in its membership after 1945. Since the vast majority of new states were relatively poor, non-white former colonies, their concerns diverged sharply from those of the European great powers who had dominated international society until the Second World War. Issues such as colonialism, racism, and Third World poverty were placed on the international agenda, and new international norms emerged which made imperialistic or racialistic practices internationally reprehensible.

Limited international sanctions were brought to bear against the racist regime of South Africa, and the use of violence in the cause of national liberation received at least some degree of international legitimation through resolutions in the United Nations and other fora.

It is impossible to measure with any accuracy the precise contribution of revolutionary states to this evolution of international society. In some cases they were the principal catalysts of change, as in the emergence of new principles of international legitimacy. They also played a critical part in promoting the demands for new international norms after 1945. In other cases change occurred as a consequence of the reaction of established powers to revolutionary states, as in 1814–15. On balance, the Westphalian conception of international society has proved more durable than revolutionary internationalism, so the impact of international society on revolutionary states through the socialization process may be judged to have been stronger than the reverse interaction. But there can be no doubt that both entities have influenced each other. . . .

A very different perspective from that of the international society . . . is the world system approach of Wallerstein and others.[5] This asserts that there is indeed an international society, or, more accurately, a world social system, but, far from reflecting a consensus about underlying values, it comprises an exploitative hierarchical system that developed alongside the emergence of capitalism in Europe. In this world system, economic processes are the main determinants of events, with the state (conceived as a pluralist conglomerate, not a unitary actor) defined by its economic role rather than, as in this study, in juridical terms. The principal feature of the world system is a global division of labour which produces a structure of dominance by a small, capitalist "core" over a large, underdeveloped "periphery." The periphery remains economically dependent on the core because this suits the interests of world capitalism. Institutions such as international law and diplomacy serve, in effect, as tools of the dominant international capitalist class.

This analysis, which, of course, has much in common with several revolutionary ideologies, implies that the confrontation that has been portrayed in this study as one between the Westphalian conception of international society and the revolutionary state is, in truth, part of a global class struggle. It declares, in effect, that the revolutionary critique of international society is essentially correct. Here is not the place for a detailed rebuttal of the world system thesis. Its focus on economic processes involves a very different level of analysis from the legal-political framework that has been employed in this study. Whether it is more fruitful to depict economic processes as taking place within a legal-political structure that is an important determinant of their outcome, or vice versa, will doubtless continue to be a subject of heated speculation. To those who remain sceptical about the prospects for an all-encompassing general theory of international relations, it seems reasonable to suppose that significant phenomena may be discerned that belong primarily to one level of analysis rather than the other, and that both perspectives may afford valuable insights. It is also safe to assume that whichever of these two frameworks dominates at any time will depend upon the kinds of issues involved. In the case of international response to revolutionary states, it would be difficult to sustain an argument that economic considerations have been more than secondary factors. In the domestic politics of long-established states, fundamental constitutional issues, on the rare occasions when they arise, tend to dominate political debate, leaving questions of economic costs and benefits on the sidelines. A similar phenomenon appears to occur when there is a fundamental challenge to the international "constitution"—the Westphalian social contract. International concern about the conduct of revolutionary France, Cuba, China, Libya, or even Iran or the Soviet Union bore little relation to the position of those states in the world economic system. Moreover, the response of established states was essentially the same, regardless of whether the revolutionary state concerned was a great power or a small, Third World nation.

Social order over any lengthy period of time does not depend simply upon the capacity of a society's institutions to maintain stability and regularity, but upon their ability to change in response to new circumstances. International society has shown itself to be adaptable, but all too often change (usually of a very limited nature) has taken place only after the extreme violence of war and revolution. This has been accepted by states because the foundation of their association has been the common defence of sovereignty. Their social contract has been a pact of association—an agreement to consider themselves members of a society—rather than a contract of government, or an agreement to surrender their independence in return for the benefits deriving from the acceptance of a central authority. There are no signs that states are any readier today than in the past to move towards some kind of world government, nor indeed would such a development necessarily be desirable. But such negative consequences of the division of the world into competing sovereign states as an extreme inequality in the apportionment of the world's material and non-material goods are still much in evidence, even if the incidence of major wars has decreased. Historical experience of the interaction between revolutionary states and international society has shown that, while fundamental change in the Westphalian international society is unlikely, none the less the basis of association among states may broaden and some change may be accommodated. Disaffected and alienated states still exist in large numbers and there is a long way to go before a true "end of history" is reached with the universal triumph of the liberal state. It is safe to assume, therefore, that the dialectic between revolutionary states and international society has not yet concluded. There can be no doubt that the collapse of the Soviet Union has brought the world to a remarkable juncture at which the West has achieved a moment of ascendancy, to be used wisely or foolishly. While the lessons of the past cannot dictate the construction of the future, they may at least help to identify mistakes that do not need to be repeated.

NOTE

. . .

5 I. Wallerstein, *The Modern World System* (New York, 1974), 1–13, 132–63, 346–57; B. Andrews, "The Political Economy of World Capitalism: Theory and Practice," *International Organization, 36*/1 (1982), 135–63; J. Caporaso, "Dependence, Dependency, and Power in the Global System: A Structural and Behavioural Analysis," *International Organization, 32*/1 (1978), 13–44.

10

The Embourgeoisement of Revolutionary Regimes: Reflections on Abdallah Laroui

Mark N. Katz

The following selection, drawn from my Reflections on Revolutions *(1999), analyzes the evolution of revolutionary regimes. In that book, I argue that the theory of revolution advanced by the Moroccan scholar Abdallah Laroui in the 1960s and 1970s is useful for understanding their evolution. Unlike classic Marxism and the many "Marxian" interpretations of revolution drawing inspiration from it, Laroui's theory of revolution holds that the embrace of capitalism and the West by revolutionary regimes is, far from being aberrant behavior, the logical consequence of a normal process of "embourgeoisement" in revolutionary states. Indeed, the fact that most revolutionary regimes have embraced embourgeoisement in recent years while only a handful have failed to do so indicates that the latter are abnormal cases.*

Unlike Armstrong, who sees revolutionary regimes adapting to the established international system due to the external constraints that the system imposes on them, Laroui and I see the embourgeoisement of revolutionary regimes as primarily the result of internal political evolution. This difference in interpretation has important international implications. If a revolutionary regime comes to accept established international norms mainly because of external constraints, its continued adherence to these norms may not last if the external constraints are relaxed. On the other hand, external constraints may not be necessary for maintaining the continued adherence to established international norms of a revolutionary regime that has undergone embourgeoisement. There is no guarantee, however, that all revolutionary regimes that embark upon embourgeoisement will actually achieve it.

Critical Questions

1. Why do revolutionary regimes decide to pursue embourgeoisement?

2. How does their decision to do so lead them to alter their view of the
West?

3. What role does the West play in the embourgeoisement of revolutionary regimes?

4. What appears to account for the resistance of some revolutionary
regimes to embourgeoisement?

With the downfall of almost all communist governments and the whole-
hearted adoption of capitalism by most of the few remaining ones, Marxist
class analysis and theories of revolution have, to put it mildly, fallen into dis-
favor. Few now predict that the proletariat or the peasantry will anywhere
rise up to overthrow the bourgeoisie and establish socialism. And those
who do predict this are not taken seriously.

Revolutionaries, however, are active in many countries. Some, such as
the Zapatistas in Mexico as well as Sendero Luminoso and Tupac Amaru in
Peru, are Marxists of one variety or another. These groups, though, appear
to have little prospect of leading a successful revolution, and no prospect of
"building socialism" even if they do (Palmer 1996; Dresser 1997). By contrast, religious fundamentalist revolutionary groups are active in many
countries and appear to enjoy much greater prospects for leading successful
revolutions than do the few remaining Marxist revolutionary groups (Juergensmeyer 1993). This is especially true in the Muslim world, where Islamic
revolutionary groups have already come to power in three countries (Iran,
Sudan, and Afghanistan), and are actively attempting to do so in many others (Roy 1994).

In classic Marxism, feudalism is replaced by capitalism, which is in turn
replaced by socialism. But the Islamic revolution in Iran defied Soviet observers as it appeared to be neither capitalist nor socialist (Papp 1985,
59–61). Nor, obviously, did classic Marxism predict the downfall of socialism and its replacement by capitalism in the late twentieth century.

Yet virtually all the revolutions of the twentieth century—Marxist-Leninist, Arab nationalist, Islamic fundamentalist, or other religious and/or

nationalist varieties—had or have a highly important class element. These were all conflicts in which the struggle between the "haves" and the "have-nots" played an important role. A theory of revolution needs to account for the class factor in order to understand this phenomenon fully, even after the downfall of communism.

It will be argued here that the theory of revolution advanced by the Moroccan scholar Abdallah Laroui in the 1960s and 1970s is especially useful for understanding revolution in the post–Cold War era. Unlike classic Marxism and the many "Marxian" interpretations of revolution drawing inspiration from it, Laroui's theory of revolution provides an explanation of how the embrace of capitalism and the West by revolutionary regimes, far from being aberrant behavior, is the logical consequence of the normal process of embourgeoisement in revolutionary states.

In this study, I will (1) examine the inadequacy of Marxist and "Marxian" theories in explaining the evolution of revolutionary regimes occurring in recent years; (2) outline Laroui's theory of revolution and discuss how it differs from Marxist and "Marxian" theories; (3) analyze the extent to which Laroui's vision appears applicable at present; and (4) discuss the implications of Laroui's theory for the future.

Marxist and "Marxian" Theories

During the nineteenth and twentieth centuries, there have been a wide variety of viewpoints held by, and disputation among, thinkers who considered themselves to be Marxist. Marxist thinking, then, was not a uniform phenomenon, and portraying it as such must be avoided. Nevertheless, Marxist thinkers as a whole shared certain basic assumptions about history and what its direction was. For Marxists, the nineteenth and twentieth centuries was the era in which the main focus of history was the struggle between the bourgeoisie on the one hand and the proletariat and/or the peasantry on the other—the struggle between capitalism and socialism. Marxists also believed that they knew the outcome of this struggle: capitalism would inevitably lose out to socialism, which would then reign triumphant.[1]

There was a great divide in the Marxist tradition between those who believed that the triumph of socialism could occur peacefully and democratically (the social-democratic tradition) and those who believed it could only occur through violent revolution (the communist tradition). Among the latter, there were differences over the precise means by which they envisioned revolution occurring. But in whatever manner it occurred, all believed that socialism was the "end of history." And once the revolution succeeded, the worker and/or peasant solidarity that was one of the most important ingredients of that success would remain strong as it faced the task of "building socialism."

Socialist revolutionary regimes would, of course, be threatened by the capitalist imperialists externally and "class enemies" internally; this was a basic tenet of Marxism-Leninism. Marxist-Leninists, however, did not expect that the workers and peasants in whose name the revolution had been made would seek to dismantle socialism (anyone who sought this was, by definition, not a worker or peasant). Even less did they expect that Marxist-Leninist ruling parties would seek to dismantle socialism or their own monopoly on power.

Throughout much of the twentieth century, Marxist-Leninists seemed to believe that the most likely way in which a revolutionary socialist government could be overthrown was through a successful "imperialist" invasion. However, the deployment of a powerful nuclear arsenal by the USSR from 1949 on made such an invasion increasingly risky for the imperialists, and hence unlikely. The frustration of the American effort to halt the spread of Marxist revolution in Indochina and the development of the "Vietnam syndrome" made imperialist invasion against aspiring Marxist revolutionaries, much less an established Marxist-Leninist regime, even less likely. By 1980, Moscow appeared to be calling for an extension of the Brezhnev Doctrine (the justification for the Soviet use of force to prevent the downfall of communist regimes in Eastern Europe) to Third World Marxist states (Katz 1982, 114–15).

Marxists, of course, were not the only ones to write about revolution. Theories of revolution—often more sophisticated than Marxist-Leninist ones—were advanced by several non-Marxist Western scholars such as Barrington Moore (1966) and Theda Skocpol (1979). Ironically, while these non-Marxist as well as anti-Marxist thinkers often took issue with it, they usually accepted key elements of Marxism-Leninism with regard to revolution. Leftist but non-Marxist scholars seemed to agree (though for different reasons) with Marxist-Leninist predictions about socialist revolution being inevitable, at least in the Third World. Nor did they challenge the notion that such revolutions were irreversible. Anti-Marxist theorists tended to see such revolutions as not necessarily inevitable, but definitely irreversible once they occurred (Kirkpatrick 1979; Wiles 1985).

To the extent, then, that non-Marxist and even anti-Marxist thinkers and policymakers accepted certain Marxist or Marxist-Leninist assumptions about revolution, they can be described as "Marxian." And like their Marxist brethren, these "Marxian" theorists did not predict the downfall of communism, or explain it after the fact.

Laroui's Theory of Revolution

Abdallah Laroui did not set out to write a general theory of revolution, but sought instead to explain why Arab nationalist revolutions occurred and how Arab nationalist regimes evolved after coming to power. He published two books on this subject: *L'idéologie arabe contemporaine* (1967), and *The Crisis of the Arab Intellectual: Traditionalism or Historicism?* (1976).

In these books, Laroui could be seen as someone attempting to apply Marxist analysis to the Arab world. Laroui made frequent reference to Marx and accepted Marx's notion that class struggle was the predominant feature of politics. However, he felt that Marx, and Western Marxist analysis generally, did not accurately describe the nature of class conflict in the Arab states of the mid-twentieth century before the success of Arab nationalist revolution. Like the Marxists, Laroui saw the bourgeoisie as one of the two principal protagonists in the class struggle. Unlike the Marxists, however, he saw both the proletariat and the peasantry as being too weak to challenge the bourgeoisie. In the Arab states, however, there was another class that was strong enough to do so: the petite bourgeoisie (1976, 162–3).

In Laroui's terms, the Arab petite bourgeoisie has the following characteristics:

- It represents the majority of the urban population, so that town life is synonymous with petit-bourgeois life, above all when the economically or politically dominant class is a foreign one.
- It indeed represents a minority in relation to the mass of peasants; but these, insofar as they leave the communal framework to enter a cash economy, transform themselves into small independent landholders before social differentiation reinforces the large and middling properties and increases the number of agricultural workers and landless peasants; they consolidate the power of the urban petite bourgeoisie

since both classes share an attachment to independence and to private property (1976, 163).

Unlike the glowing terms in which most Marxists (or the hysterical terms in which most anti-Marxists) described how the revolutionary proletariat and/or peasantry sought to "build socialism," Laroui portrayed the "revolutionary" petite bourgeoisie as possessing a mundane "attachment to . . . private property." Indeed, he characterized the petite bourgeoisie as seeking immediate access to the high-consumption lifestyle that it sees the bourgeoisie enjoying.

In its consumerist aspirations, the Arab petite bourgeoisie is "modern"— even "Western." On the other hand, it is also extremely traditional. It fears that Westernization will destroy Arab culture and identity, and thus seeks to halt the Arab bourgeoisie's seeming collaboration in this process by isolating the Arab world from the West through the assertion of an anti-Western Arab nationalism. There is an inherent duality, then, in how the Arab petite bourgeoisie views the West: it seeks to emulate the West in some ways, but also rejects it. Laroui "argues that it is the culture of this class, rather than anything inherently Islamic or Arab, which leads to the rejection of the dialogue with the West" (Binder 1988, 337).

In class terms, Laroui saw Arab nationalist revolution as the overthrow of the bourgeoisie by the petite bourgeoisie. The petite bourgeoisie's success was due largely to the small size and relative weakness of the bourgeoisie at the time of its overthrow. In Laroui's theory, then, [Jamal] ʿAbd al-Nasir's "petit bourgeois Egyptian state represents not a transition to bourgeois domination, but a premature overthrow of the bourgeois state in Egypt. It was premature because the process of embourgeoisement . . . had not yet been achieved when the bourgeois state of pre-1952 Egypt was overthrown" (Binder 1988, 332).

But in addition to examining what led up to Arab nationalist revolution, Laroui also theorized about what happened afterward. While Arab nationalist revolution brought the petite bourgeoisie to power, the new regime did not represent that class as a whole. It was only a small part of the petite bourgeoisie that ruled over the rest of the nation, including the rest of the petite bourgeoisie.

The Arab nationalist regimes that arose in the 1950s and 1960s had many ambitions: to bring about "revolutionary socialism," to "stand up to" Israel and its Western backers, to overthrow "backward" Arab monarchies, and most ambitiously, to unite the Arab world into one great state (Nasser 1955; Kerr 1971, 1–7). But the petit bourgeois Arab nationalist regime placed the highest priority on one goal: remaining in power. All other ambitions were subordinate to this overriding ambition, and indeed, were only pursued insofar as the regime believed (sometimes mistakenly) they supported it. And the petit bourgeois regime sought to take full advantage of modern technology (such as sophisticated weapons) in order to remain in power (Laroui 1976, 165–6).

To do this, the petit bourgeois regime seeks to promote modernization and traditionalism simultaneously: "On the one hand it profits from modern culture . . . by economically and militarily consolidating its power; on the other hand it profits from its fidelity to traditional culture by legitimizing an exclusive authority" (Laroui 1976, 163–4). The authoritarian aspects of traditional culture, then, are utilized by the regime to justify not allowing the political modernization or Westernization that could lead to its authority being challenged.

The regime's desire to foster some aspects of modernization while retaining some aspects of traditionalism required a dualistic educational policy:

> The scientific, technological, commercial, and other institutes, which prepare students for service in the modern sector, offer (frequently in a foreign language) the most advanced programs and methods. Thus is educated, on a pattern different from that of the nation at large, a bureaucratic elite that is detached from the population and committed to the service of the State. . . . As for the other educational institutes . . . either they remain faithful to the traditional methods or they are dedicated to defending the same values in a slightly updated manner (Laroui 1976, 165).

What happens, though, is that the bureaucratic elite that receives a modern higher education gradually changes its mind about some of the most firmly held beliefs and policies of the petit bourgeois regime when it first came to power. For example, while the original petit bourgeois leadership saw nationalization as an economic panacea, the bureaucratic elite increasingly comes to see the disadvantages of a state-run economy and the advantages of free enterprise. While the initial revolutionary leadership seemed to delight in "confronting" the West when it first came to power, the bureaucratic elite it raises up finds this counterproductive to cooperation with the West, which it values more and more.

In short, while it might not necessarily value democracy, the educated bureaucratic elite does become embourgeoised. Its plan of action increasingly becomes the embourgeoisement of society as a whole—a task that the prerevolutionary bourgeoisie signally failed to accomplish before it was overthrown.

And as far as Laroui is concerned, this is a highly positive development. For, as Binder put it, Laroui "believes that the establishment of a bourgeois state is a prerequisite to the achievement of an Islamic-Arab cultural authenticity, which can then enter into a conversation with the West on the basis of cultural equality" (1988, 338). The tragedy of Arab nationalist revolution is that it unnecessarily delays this realization: "Laroui seems to think that a traditional monarch can do a better job of completing the 'bourgeois revolution' and constructing a bourgeois state than can a Bonapartist ruler such as Nasser" (Binder 1988, 337). This, of course, is a highly prudent point of view for a scholar making his career in the Kingdom of Morocco to espouse, but if embourgeoisement is the eventual fate of nations, a government that sets about this task calmly is clearly superior to one that insists on first going through a destructive and futile revolutionary attempt to avoid it.

The Applicability of Laroui's Vision

Important aspects of Laroui's theory appear to be validated by the research findings of other scholars as well as by events. Others have noted the leading role of the petite bourgeoisie in several revolutions. In her comparative study of the Iranian and Nicaraguan revolutions, Farideh Farhi noted that the "polar" classes (proletariat, peasantry, bourgeoisie) played a less important role than the "intermediate" classes (educated but impecunious professionals as well as the "petty [sic] bourgeoisie" (1990, 16–17, 37–41). In both cases, she notes, there were multiclass alliances that supported revolution. Forrest Colburn cited Cape Verde as a typical example of a Third World country that underwent Marxist revolution; the peasantry was not particularly revolutionary while in the cities there was no real bourgeoisie or proletariat, but there was a large petite bourgeoisie that supplied the revolutionary leadership (1994, 43–4).

Nazih Ayubi similarly argued that the main support for Islamic revolution in the Middle East does not come either from workers or peasants, but from intermediate classes, including the petite bourgeoisie, the " 'new' middle strata," and students (1991, 158–63). He noted in particular that the " 'virtually proletarianized members of the state-employed petite bourgeoisie, the under-employed intelligentsia, and the larger student population' are the main sponsors of the most militant of the Islamic tendencies" (161).

And just as Laroui did with regard to Arab nationalist regimes, others have observed the process of embourgeoisement occurring in other types of revolutionary regimes. Jerry Hough has described how Leninism appealed to the "half-peasants, half-workers of Russia" frightened of "westernization and those promoting it" in 1917. Over time, however, "the Westernized elite of Peter the Great" was recreated, resulting in the formation of a "huge middle class" that had "very different values from the peasants and workers who were its fathers and grandfathers" (1990, 10). By the 1980s,

> The broad educated public—the bureaucrats and the professionals— were eager for a relaxation of the dictatorship and an opening to the West. They were able to say that the closed nature of Soviet society was a central cause of the country's backwardness and a major threat to long-term defense. They could convincingly urge that what they wanted for themselves personally was absolutely necessary for the achievement of the most basic national goals (Hough 1990, 12).

Although he does not use this term, Hough described a process of gradual embourgeoisement of young Soviets from the 1950s onward. Far from being the initiator of embourgeoisement, Gorbachev (one of the 1950s youths) represented the culmination of pent-up demand for it.

Ervand Abrahamian observed this process at work shortly after the success of the Iranian revolution. He noted that during the early years of the revolution, Ayatollah Khomeini's populist rhetoric aroused anger "against the propertied middle classes" (1993, 51). Later, though, Khomeini emphasized that the middle class was, in fact, the backbone of the regime. On one occasion, for example, he stated that while parliamentary deputies "should always help" the lower class, they "must come predominantly from" the middle class: " 'The revolution will remain secure,' Khomeini concluded, 'so long as the Parliament and the government are manned by members of the middle class' " (1993, 53). Abrahamian concluded that, "Although Khomeini has often been hailed as the champion of the deprived masses, his own words show him to be much more the spokesman of the propertied middle class" (1993, 58). Since the death of Khomeini, Iran's embourgeoisement has only accelerated as a result of the Rafsanjani government's emphasis on private investment and the overwhelming voter preference for a perceived moderate and liberal, [Mohammad] Khatami, over a hard-line revolutionary purist, [Ali Akbar] Nateq-Noori, in the 1997 presidential elections ("Islam and the Ballot Box" 1997).

Indeed, the past decade in particular has witnessed the rapid embourgeoisement of a remarkable number of revolutionary regimes. Several countries in Eastern Europe that had previously been ruled by hard-line Marxist-Leninist regimes have firmly embraced both liberal democracy and a free-market economy: Poland, the Czech Republic, Hungary, Romania, Slovenia, the Baltic states, and most dramatically, former East Germany and its voluntary absorption into a united Germany dominated by the former West. Indeed, the embourgeoisement of these countries has been so all-pervasive that in some of them, former communists have been elected back into office who, far from seeking to reverse this process, have sought to enhance and even accelerate it (Gebicki and Gebicki 1995).

It is hardly surprising, of course, that the embourgeoisement of Eastern Europe would occur so rapidly. Except for Yugoslavia and Albania, these nations did not experience indigenous Marxist-Leninist revolutions, but had Marxist-Leninist regimes imposed upon them by the USSR. For East Europeans—even former communists—getting rid of Marxism-Leninism was part and parcel of getting rid of foreign domination. Yet embourgeoisement has also proceeded rapidly in the former USSR—particularly Russia—where the original Marxist-Leninist revolution took place.

Unlike most of Eastern Europe, some of the strongest Russian political parties—including the communist one—are openly hostile to democracy. Boris Yeltsin—widely touted as a democrat in the period just before and after the collapse of the USSR—resorted to the use of force against his political opponents on more than one occasion. Nevertheless, contested elections and a free press have become an established feature of post-Soviet Russian politics (White *et al.*, 1997). And while the commitment of the former communist economic elite to democracy may be questionable, their commitment to capitalism is not. It is the former communist enterprise managers—not the dissidents—who have overseen the considerable (though far from complete) capitalist transformation in Russia. These managers have, of course, used their position to acquire for themselves much of the equity in these privatized state enterprises. Having done so, however, it is these embourgeoised former communists who now have the greatest stake in the development of a capitalist economy domestically as well as collaboration with Western multinational corporations ("In Search of

Spring" 1997). However much or little democratization has occurred elsewhere in the former Soviet Union, the ex-communist rulers of most former Soviet republics have also embraced—and personally benefited from—embourgeoisement.[2]

Chinese society has experienced a rapidly expanding embourgeoisement ever since Mao's successor, Deng Xiaoping, initiated capitalist economic transformation in the late 1970s. The Marxist leadership has been unwilling to allow democratization, but, as in Russia, it has a large personal stake in the continuation and expansion of a capitalist economy and trade with the West (Overholt 1996; Chan and Senser 1997). A similar process has been launched by the Marxist rulers of Vietnam (Elliott 1995). Whether or not they have made any progress toward democratization, most other former Marxist states in the Third World have also embarked on the path of embourgeoisement (Colburn 1994, 89–96). Indeed, there are only a handful of Marxist regimes that have not.

As Laroui himself noted, embourgeoisement has occurred—at least at the elite level—in some Arab nationalist revolutionary regimes. Egypt has advanced the farthest along this route: while its process of privatization has been relatively slow, this has accelerated in recent years ("The Retreat of Egypt's Islamists" 1997). And no matter how anti-Western oil-rich Arab nationalist regimes have been, none of them has been unwilling to sell their oil to the West—though certain Western countries (most notably the United States) have been unwilling to buy it.

Another example of an embourgeoised revolutionary regime is Mexico. After decades of maintaining a policy of nationalization of major industries and economic isolation from the United States, a new leadership generation in Mexico's ruling party—educated largely in the United States—began in the 1980s to pursue a policy of privatization and economic integration with the United States, culminating with Mexico joining the United States and Canada in the North American Free Trade Agreement (NAFTA), and an increasing degree of democratization (Castañeda 1996; Dresser 1997).

The near universality of revolutionary regimes embracing embourgeoisement in recent years suggests that this process is part of their normal evolution and not something exceptional. Indeed, the fact that there are only a handful of revolutionary regimes that have failed to undergo embourgeoisement indicates that these are somehow abnormal cases. These include, to a greater or lesser extent, Cuba, North Korea, Cambodia, Iraq, Libya, Sudan, Afghanistan, Tajikistan, and Belarus.

How have these states managed to avoid embourgeoisement, at least so far? Some have been unable to pursue it due to chronic civil war severely limiting private investment and consuming most government resources in military expenditures, such as in Cambodia, Sudan, Afghanistan, and Tajikistan. It is not clear, however, that all revolutionary regimes experiencing civil war at present would pursue embourgeoisement even if they succeeded in defeating their domestic opponents. And some not experiencing civil war have basically refused to permit embourgeoisement (Cuba, North Korea, Iraq, Libya, and Belarus). In most of these cases, a very strong leader—often the initiator of the revolution—has remained faithful to what Laroui would call his original petit bourgeois revolutionary vision, and strong enough to enforce it. Such has been the case with Fidel Castro in Cuba, Kim Il Sung (before his death) in North Korea, Saddam Hussein in Iraq, Mu'ammar al-Qadhafi in Libya, and Hasan Turabi in Sudan. This is significant, because in virtually all cases where revolutionary regimes have embraced embourgeoisement, this has not been done by the initial revolutionary leadership, but by its successors. Whether or not the successors to Castro, Hussein, al-Qadhafi, or Turabi pursue embourgeoisement—assuming that their regimes survive to be passed on to successors—remains to be seen.

Two cases appear somewhat anomalous. Although a successor leader, North Korea's Kim Jong Il has not retreated from his father's revolutionary fervor or permitted embourgeoisement. This may be because he is fearful that any change along these lines might unleash political forces he cannot control (Noland 1997).

Belarus's Alexander Lukashenka is hardly the originator of a revolution or a figure with any sort of charisma at all. Unlike virtually all other post-Soviet leaders, however, he has been adamantly unwilling to allow embourgeoisement to proceed in his society. His goal appears to be to keep himself as well as Belarus's uncompetitive Soviet-era economic managers in power through convincing Russia to underwrite them financially. But as the Russian government has demonstrated its unwillingness to do this, and as Belarus becomes increasingly impoverished while its neighbors prosper (Markus 1996), it appears that Lukashenka—or more probably, a successor to him—will have to change course.

Revolutionary regimes that have not experienced embourgeoisement, then, seem to be special cases. There appears to be no permanent obstacle to their eventually embarking along this route once their civil wars come to an end, successor leaderships come to power, or a sufficient amount of time passes necessary for disillusionment with the original revolutionary vision to develop.

Implications of Laroui's Theory

Laroui's theory indicates that "petit bourgeois" revolutionary regimes eventually embrace embourgeoisement in the sense that they come to see privatization of their economies and cooperation with the West as being in their interest. Although embourgeoisement does not necessarily imply democratization, the former can precede or even be accompanied by the latter. The fact that most revolutionary regimes that were once hostile to the West and to market economics are now, irrespective of the extent to which they have democratized, pursuing cooperation with the West and marketization suggests that Laroui's theory is a powerful explanation of the evolution of revolutionary regimes.

What Laroui's theory implies is that, just as previous revolutionary regimes have done, revolutionary regimes that are now extremely hostile to the West will eventually embrace embourgeoisement and cooperation with the West. This would suggest, then, that we may look forward to the day when the Islamic Republic of Iran will drop its anti-American stance and seek cooperation with the United States instead. Indeed, Iran can already be said to be in the process of embourgeoisement, since the private sector plays an important role in the Iranian economy, Tehran cooperates with virtually all Western states except the United States, and competitive (if not completely free) elections play an increasingly important role in Iranian politics.

Further, Laroui's theory implies that anti-Western "petit bourgeois" revolutions occurring in the future will also experience embourgeoisement eventually. The one country in which Western governments as a group fear the consequences of revolution the most is Saudi Arabia. An anti-Western revolutionary regime here could limit Western access to Saudi petroleum, thus dramatically driving up the price of oil and seriously damaging Western economies. Laroui's theory, however, would indicate that no matter how anti-Western a revolutionary regime overthrowing the Saudis might be at first, it will eventually see cooperation with the West as being in its interests. Indeed, the fact that such vehemently anti-Western revolutionary leaders as Mu'ammar al-Qadhafi, Saddam Hussein, and the Ayatollah Khomeini

Khomeini were always willing to sell oil to the West suggests that a revolutionary regime in Saudi Arabia would too; it would, after all, need the money.

Laroui's theory further implies that permanent hostility on the part of Western states toward revolutionary regimes—such as the United States has shown to Iran—may actually be counterproductive. While revolutionary regimes are likely to be highly anti-Western in their early, petit bourgeois phase, Western governments need to be aware that the embourgeoisement of such regimes is part of their natural evolution. Implacable Western hostility to such regimes may unnecessarily delay or prolong this process. This is the gist of the argument currently being made by some former American foreign-policymakers criticizing the U.S. government's continuing hostility toward Iran despite numerous signs of that country's retreat from revolutionary fervor (Brzezinski *et al.* 1997; Murphy 1997).

Nevertheless, Laroui's theory does not imply that the West should be complacent about anti-Western petit bourgeois revolutions, since they are destined to evolve into embourgeoised pro-Western regimes in the long run. There are two problems with Laroui's theory that unsettle this optimistic conclusion. First, Laroui does not indicate whether there is any particular time frame in which the embourgeoisement of revolutionary regimes can be expected to occur. And as the actual experience of such regimes shows, this process can take a very long time indeed—seven decades in the case of the Soviet Union. The status quo Western powers can hardly be expected to forgo trying to stop a revolutionary regime from attempting to export anti-Western revolution (if that is what it is trying to do) due to the conviction that it will eventually abandon such efforts as it undergoes embourgeoisement. Indeed, Western efforts to frustrate the attempt to export revolution may play an important role in convincing revolutionary regimes to abandon this and other revolutionary goals as well as embark upon embourgeoisement.

The fact that the embourgeoisement of a revolutionary regime may not begin, much less be completed, for a relatively long period of time poses a problem for Western foreign-policymakers. They will oppose revolutionary regimes that, in their petit bourgeois phase, seek to export revolution. On the other hand, they should be prepared to collaborate with revolutionary regimes embarking upon embourgeoisement. These phases, however, may overlap, such as when a "moderate" faction in a revolutionary regime embarks on embourgeoisement domestically while an "extremist" faction continues the policy of attempting to export revolution—as appears to be occurring in Iran. Such a situation calls for a nuanced policy on the part of the West that demonstrates its determination to thwart the export of revolution but also encourages embourgeoisement so that the "moderates" within the revolutionary regime can credibly argue that the West is not implacably hostile and that cooperation with it is possible. Such a policy, of course, is extremely difficult to devise and sustain, especially when there are strong domestic political pressures favoring one policy extreme. While American foreign-policy-makers and businessmen may increasingly favor a friendlier U.S. policy toward Iran, the Republican-controlled Congress and American public opinion in general is unprepared to pursue anything except a hard-line policy toward that country at present (Morgan and Ottaway 1997).

The second problem with Laroui's theory is a more important one. Laroui appears to suggest that once a revolutionary regime embraces embourgeoisement, then embourgeoisement will occur. But while this might be a necessary condition for embourgeoisement to take place, it is not a sufficient one. In order for this project to succeed, society in a revolutionary regime must be willing to embrace embourgeoisement despite the economic hardships it inevitably gives rise to. And experience has shown that not all societies are as willing to do this as others.

The societies that have most enthusiastically embraced embourgeoisement are those in most of the Eastern European nations as well as China. And in these countries, embourgeoisement appears to be secure; it seems highly unlikely that forces seeking to destroy free-market economies will rise up in these nations, despite the significant economic dislocations they have experienced.

Mexican society has exhibited a somewhat lesser degree of enthusiasm for the rigors of the free market. One of the political parties that did especially well in the 1997 parliamentary and Mexico City mayoral elections was the leftist Party of the Democratic Revolution. Its egalitarian and nationalistic economic policies appeal to many of those who have been hurt by Mexico opening itself to economic competition from the United States and Canada through NAFTA. Should this party's candidate win the presidential elections, it is not clear that Mexico would remain as committed to NAFTA as the recent reformist Institutional Revolutionary Party (PRI) governments have been. On the other hand, Mexico's other leading opposition party, the National Action Party, appears to be at least as committed as the

PRI to open markets and free trade with the United States ("Mexico Enters the Era of Politics" 1997).

A country in which a wide gap has developed between the government's and a significant segment of society's degree of commitment to embourgeoisement is Russia. There are powerful communist and nationalist parties that have vociferously denounced the extent to which the Yeltsin government has pursued economic privatization and cooperation with the West. If either of these parties captured the Russian presidency, they may well attempt not just to halt but to reverse what progress has been made toward embourgeoisement. Survey research, however, shows that attitudes toward the free market and cooperation with the West tend to divide along generational lines in Russia. It is primarily the older generation that opposes and the younger generation that supports embourgeoisement (Dobson 1996, 10). Assuming that the younger people in Russia now embracing embourgeoisement do not renounce it as they grow older, the passage of time should lead to steadily decreasing support for political parties opposed to it.

The countries where there appears to be an especially wide gap between the government's and society's commitment to embourgeoisement are the postrevolutionary Arab nationalist states—especially Egypt. This is ironic, because it was Egypt in particular where Laroui expected embourgeoisement to proceed as the government became increasingly committed to it. But in Egypt and most other postrevolutionary Arab nationalist regimes, there have arisen powerful Islamic fundamentalist groups generally opposed to embourgeoisement. As noted earlier, several observers have described the main supporters of these movements as hailing from the petite bourgeoisie—the group that supported Arab nationalist revolution to begin with. And unlike in Russia, the younger generation is the basis of support and leadership for these opposition movements in the Arab world (Roy 1994, 49–55).

There are several possible explanations as to why some societies are extremely willing to embrace embourgeoisement while others are resistant to it. Some might cite complex cultural and historical factors. Others might see a society's level of education as having a strong impact on both its willingness and its ability to embrace embourgeoisement. Others still might see the manner in which the government pursues embourgeoisement as being the primary determinant of society's reaction to it: if embourgeoisement is carried out inefficiently and appears to benefit only certain privileged groups, it should hardly be surprising if society as a whole does not support it. Jack Goldstone has suggested that population pressures may impede even good-faith efforts by developing countries to promote prosperity, thus leading to the revolutionary situations they seek to avoid (Goldstone 1997).

Discovering precisely why some societies are not amenable to embourgeoisement at present, though, is less important for purposes of this study than the observation that their being so—for whatever reason—can have consequences that Laroui did not anticipate. In Laroui's terms, a petit bourgeois revolutionary regime that itself becomes embourgeoised but that fails to embourgeoise the petit bourgeois society it rules over may find itself the target of revolutionary forces arising from that society. Instead of merely postponing embourgeoisement, the original petit bourgeois revolution may eventually lead to yet another petit bourgeois revolution—which in turn must go through the time-consuming process of becoming embourgeoised itself before it too can try (and possibly fail) to embourgeoise society.

Thus, in Egypt and Algeria, embourgeoised Arab nationalist regimes that have failed to embourgeoise society are being challenged by "petit bourgeois" Islamic fundamentalist revolutionaries. If these groups come to power and also fail to embourgeoise society, they too may eventually discredit themselves and be opposed and even overthrown by another generation of revolutionaries. It is also possible that Islamic fundamentalist regimes may prove more successful at embourgeoising countries than the Arab nationalist regimes they might overthrow. And it is even possible that the present Arab nationalist regimes that have so far failed to embourgeoise their societies may somehow succeed in doing this—though as Islamic fundamentalist opposition to them mounts, this appears to be increasingly unlikely.

Laroui's theory of revolution does not foretell which—if any—of these alternatives will occur in postrevolutionary states. His theory, though, is useful for understanding how the decision by revolutionary regimes to embark on embourgeoisement is a normal part of their postrevolutionary evolution. The problems with his theory examined here, however, illustrate how the decision by a revolutionary regime to pursue embourgeoisement may not necessarily be successfully implemented.

NOTES

1. Leszek Kolakowski (1978) authored a massive study examining the breadth of nineteenth- and twentieth-century Marxist thought.

2. See, for example, Aslund (1995) on Ukraine; Geller and Connor (1996) on Uzbekistan; Jones (1996) on Georgia; Haghayeghi (1997) on Kyrgyzstan; Dudwick (1997, 99–101) on Armenia; Altstadt (1997, 137–41) on Azerbaijan; Olcott (1997, 216–18) on Kazakhstan; and Ochs (1997, 340–6) on Turkmenistan. Three successive visits to Almaty during the early 1990s demonstrated to me just how rapidly and enthusiastically the ex-communist leadership of Kazakhstan was embracing capitalism.

REFERENCES

Abrahamian, Ervand. 1993. *Khomeinism: Essays on the Islamic Republic.* Berkeley: University of California Press.

Altstadt, Audrey L. 1997. "Azerbaijan's Struggle toward Democracy." In *Conflict, Cleavage, and Change in Central Asia and the Caucasus,* edited by Karen Dawisha and Bruce Parrott. Cambridge: Cambridge University Press.

Aslund, Anders. 1995. Eurasia Letter: Ukraine's Turnaround. *Foreign Policy,* no. 100 (Fall):125–143.

Ayubi, Nazih. 1991. *Political Islam: Religion and Politics in the Arab World.* London: Routledge.

Binder, Leonard. 1988. *Islamic Liberalism: A Critique of Development Ideologies.* Chicago: University of Chicago Press.

Brzezinski, Zbigniew, *et al.* 1997. Differentiated Containment. *Foreign Affairs* 76 (May/June):20–30.

Castañeda, Jorge G. 1996. Mexico's Circle of Misery. *Foreign Affairs* 75 (July/August):92–105.

Chan, Anita, and Robert A. Senser. 1997. China's Troubled Workers. *Foreign Affairs* 76 (March/April):104–117.

Colburn, Forrest D. 1994. *The Vogue of Revolution in Poor Countries.* Princeton: Princeton University Press.

Dobson, Richard B. 1996. "Is Russia Turning the Corner? Changing Russian Public Opinion, 1991–1996." U.S. Information Agency, Office of Research and Media Reaction, Russia, Ukraine, and Commonwealth Branch. R-7-96.

Dresser, Denise. 1997. Mexico: Uneasy, Uncertain, Unpredictable. *Current History* 96:49–54.

Dudwick, Nora. 1997. "Political Transformations in Postcommunist Armenia: Images and Realities." In *Conflict, Cleavage, and Change in Central Asia and the Caucasus,* edited by Karen Dawisha and Bruce Parrott. Cambridge: Cambridge University Press.

Elliott, David W. P. 1995. Vietnam Faces the Future. *Current History* 94:412–419.

Farhi, Farideh. 1990. *States and Urban-Based Revolutions: Iran and Nicaragua.* Urbana, IL: University of Illinois Press.

Gebicki, Wojciech, and Anna Maria Gebicki. 1995. Central Europe: "A Shift to the Left?" *Survival* 37 (Autumn):126–138.

Haghayeghi, Mehrdad. 1997. Privatization Process in Kyrgyzstan. *Caspian Crossroads. 3* (Winter):24–26.

Hough, Jerry. 1990. *Russia and the West: Gorbachev and the Politics of Reform,* 2nd ed. New York: Simon & Schuster.

"In Search of Spring: A Survey of Russia." 1997. *The Economist,* July 12, S1-S18.

"Islam and the Ballot Box." 1997. *The Economist,* May 31, 41–42.

Jones, Stephen E. 1996. Georgia's Return from Chaos. *Current History.* 95 (October):340–345.

Juergensmeyer, Mark. 1993. *The New Cold War? Religious Nationalism Confronts the Secular State.* Berkeley: University of California Press.

Katz, Mark N. 1982. *The Third World in Soviet Military Thought.* Baltimore: Johns Hopkins University Press.

Kerr, Malcolm H. 1971. *The Arab Cold War: Gamal ʿAbd al-Nasir and His Rivals, 1958–1970,* 3rd ed. London: Oxford University Press.

Kirkpatrick, Jeane. 1979. Dictatorships and Double Standards. *Commentary* 68 (November):34–45.

Kolakowski, Leszek. 1978. *Main Currents of Marxism,* 3 vols. Oxford: Oxford University Press.

Laroui, Abdallah. 1967. *L'idéologie arabe contemporaine.* Paris: Francois Maspero.

_____. 1976. *The Crisis of the Arab Intellectual: Traditionalism or Historicism?* Berkeley: University of California Press.

Markus, Ustina. 1996. Imperial Understretch: Belarus's Union with Russia. *Current History* 95:335–339.

"Mexico Enters the Era of Politics." 1997. *The Economist,* July 12, 27–28.

Moore, Barrington, Jr. 1966. *Social Origins of Dictatorship and Democracy: Lord and Peasant in the Making of the Modern World.* Boston: Beacon Press.

Morgan, Dan, and David B. Ottaway. 1997. U.S. Won't Bar Pipeline Across Iran. *Washington Post,* July 27, pp. A1, A27.

Murphy, Richard W. 1997. It's Time to Reconsider the Shunning of Iran. *Washington Post,* July 20, pp. C1, C6.

Nasser, Gamal Abdul. 1955. *Egypt's Liberation: The Philosophy of the Revolution.* Washington, D.C.: Public Affairs Press.

Noland, Marcus. 1997. Why North Korea Will Muddle Through. *Foreign Affairs* 76 (July/August):105–118.

Ochs, Michael. 1997. "Turkmenistan: The Quest for Stability and Control." In *Conflict, Cleavage, and Change in Central Asia and the Caucasus,* edited by Karen Dawisha and Bruce Parrott. Cambridge: Cambridge University Press.

Olcott, Martha Brill. 1997. "Democratization and the Growth of Political Participation in Kazakstan." In *Conflict, Cleavage, and Change in Central Asia and the Caucasus,* edited by Karen Dawisha and Bruce Parrott. Cambridge: Cambridge University Press.

Overholt, William H. 1996. China after Deng. *Foreign Affairs* 75 (May/June):63–78.

edited by Karen Dawisha and Bruce Parrott. Cambridge: Cambridge University Press.

Overholt, William H. 1996. China after Deng. *Foreign Affairs* 75 (May/June):63–78.

Palmer, David Scott. 1996. "Fujipopulism" and Peru's Progress. *Current History* 95:70–75.

Papp, Daniel S. 1985. *Soviet Perceptions of the Developing World in the 1980s: The Ideological Basis.* Lexington, MA: Lexington Books.

"The Retreat of Egypt's Islamists." 1997. *The Economist,* July 26, 37–38.

Roy, Olivier. 1994. *The Failure of Political Islam.* Cambridge, MA: Harvard University Press.

Skocpol, Theda. 1979. *States and Social Revolutions: A Comparative Analysis of France, Russia, and China.* Cambridge: Cambridge University Press.

White, Stephen, *et al.* 1997. *How Russia Votes.* Chatham, NJ: Chatham House Publishers.

Wiles, Peter. 1985. Irreversibility: Theory and Practice. *The Washington Quarterly* 8 (1):29–40.

V

The Future of Revolution

There have been many revolutions since the late eighteenth century, but will there be many more in the future? It is impossible to predict confidently where, or how many, revolutions will succeed. There is, however, no shortage of revolutionary activity at the dawn of the twenty-first century. Islamic fundamentalist revolutionaries are active in North Africa, the Arabian Peninsula, Central Asia, and elsewhere in the Muslim world. Although communism collapsed between 1989 and 1991, Marxist revolutionaries are active in several countries, including Colombia, Mexico, Nepal, and Peru. Although usually termed secessionists by outside observers, those fighting for their independence consider themselves to be nationalist revolutionaries. Many such struggles are now taking place in Asia, Africa, and even Europe. There is also the prospect of peaceful, democratic revolution, as occurred in most East European countries in 1989.

In addition to many revolutions, the twentieth century also witnessed widespread democratization. Many people have observed that the spread of democracy has had a profound effect on international relations, since democracies seldom (some say never) go to war with one another. Democratization has had a similar effect on revolution: revolutions have succeeded mainly against authoritarian regimes, not democratic ones.

Why has this been true? Will it continue to be true in the future? These questions are the focus of a debate about the future of revolution in the selections presented here by Jeff Goodwin and Eric Selbin.

Goodwin and Selbin agree that democracy and revolution are inversely related. The more democratic a state is, the less susceptible it is to revolution. The less democratic a state is, the more susceptible it is to revolution. They disagree, though, about how democratic the world's democracies—especially the newer ones—actually are. Goodwin's view that democracy has been securely established in most (though not all) of the world is the basis for his prediction that the age of revolution is over. By contrast, Selbin's view that democracy has not been securely established, particularly in Latin America and other regions where it has arrived only recently, is the basis for his prediction that revolutions will continue to occur.

These two arguments appear to be diametrically opposed to each other. If one is right, it would seem, then the other must necessarily be wrong. The question is which one is right? Is the age of revolution over or not?

11

Is the Age of Revolutions Over?

Jeff Goodwin

Jeff Goodwin is the author of States and Revolutionary Movements, 1945–1991 *(forthcoming), from which the following selection is drawn. In it, he argues that, whereas the cold-war era (1945–1991) was an age of revolution, the post–cold war era will not be. Some revolutions may still occur, but he believes that they will be much less common, for two reasons: democracy is inhospitable to revolution, and democratization has been spreading to many regions of the world in recent years.*

Goodwin sees democracy and revolution as inversely related: only when democracy is absent can revolution be present. Goodwin observes, "No popular revolutionary movement . . . has ever overthrown a consolidated democratic regime." He further argues that "even imperfect and poorly consolidated democracies tend to diffuse revolutionary pressures." Goodwin discusses why democracy is so inhospitable to revolution.

Since democracy prevents revolution, the spread of democratization must necessarily result in the decline of revolution. This decline in revolution can be reversed only if the trend toward democratization falters. Goodwin, though, thinks that democratization is unlikely to falter, thus making revolution in the future unlikely.

Critical Questions

1. *Why does Goodwin see democracy as being inhospitable to revolution?*

Jeff Goodwin, *States and Revolutionary Movements, 1945–1991* (Cambridge: Cambridge University Press, forthcoming 2000). Cambridge University Press. Reprinted with permission of Cambridge University Press.

Earlier versions of this paper were presented at the panel on "Revolution in the Post–Cold War Era" at the 1998 annual meeting of the International Studies Association, March 17–21, Minneapolis, Minnesota, and at the twentieth international congress of the Latin American Studies Association, April 1997, Guadalajara, Mexico. My thanks to Walter Goldfrank for his comments.

2. How firmly entrenched is democracy in those states to which it has recently spread or appeared to spread?

3. How would Goodwin's theory be affected if a democracy were to be replaced by authoritarian rule?

Between the incineration of Hiroshima in 1945 and the disintegration of the Soviet Union in 1991, dozens of revolutionary conflicts shook the world. Most revolutionary movements of the cold war era (1945–1991), including several powerful ones, were defeated. However, many successfully seized state power, remaking large parts of the globe and, in the process, the international balance of power. In East Asia, revolutionaries seized power in China, Indochina, and North Korea and challenged imperial and neoimperial rule in several other countries, including Burma, Malaya, and the Philippines. French Algeria and Portugal's African colonies (Angola, Cape Verde, Guinea-Bissau, Mozambique, and São Tomé) violently threw off imperial rule, and popular revolts in Kenya, Namibia, South Africa, and Zimbabwe hastened the demise of white-supremist regimes on that continent. In Latin America, revolutionaries seized power in Bolivia, Cuba, and Nicaragua, nearly triumphed in El Salvador, and powerfully shook Colombia, Guatemala, Peru, and Venezuela. Finally, a series of popular rebellions in 1989 finished off the communist regimes of Eastern Europe, which had been fatally weakened by Mikhail Gorbachev's "reforms from above" in the Soviet Union. All told, the revolutions of the cold war era helped destroy European colonialism, toppled some of the century's most ruthless dictators, and humbled the superpowers themselves, contributing in the end to the demise of the weaker one, the Soviet Union. The period from 1945 to 1991—the cold war era—was indeed an age of revolutions.[1]

The End of a Revolutionary Era

With the demise of the Soviet bloc, the question is raised: Is this age of revolutions now over? I believe that it probably is, although not for the reasons that some have proposed. To be sure, some revolutions will continue to occur during the post–cold war era, and revolutionary movements and popular insurgencies will persist in a number of countries and are likely to burst forth in still others. We have already witnessed the violent demise of the Mobutu Sese Seko dictatorship in Zaire (now renamed the Democratic Republic of the Congo) and a popular revolt against the Suharto dictatorship in Indonesia, and revolutions may yet occur in the remaining occupied territories, military dictatorships, and patrimonial regimes sprinkled around the globe—perhaps in Burma, Iraq, Kashmir, Kurdistan, or Tibet. Popular movements may also challenge the communist regimes that remain in China, Cuba, North Korea, and Vietnam—although these regimes are themselves the products of popular revolutions and retain considerably more nationalist legitimacy than did those in Eastern Europe, which were more or less imposed (outside of Yugoslavia and Albania) by the Soviet Union. Several of these regimes, moreover, have initiated market reforms that may result in a peaceful transition toward a type of capitalist economy.

Revolutionary movements, moreover, may continue to thrive—or at least survive—in the peripheries that lie beyond the reach of authoritarian states, as in Algeria, Burma, Colombia, Mexico, and Peru.[2] However, revolutionary movements in these countries currently exhibit little strategic threat to the incumbent regimes. In several of these countries, the rebels are feared and disliked by broad social sectors, not just elites. These movements may be able to exert pressure on the incumbent regimes but seem incapable of seizing state power. In fact, some of these movements may be important mainly for their so-called radical-flank effects. At a national level, that is, these movements may be politically significant to the extent that they open up greater political space for other, more moderate political movements and organizations.[3] Moreover, in the unlikely event that one of these movements actually seizes state power, it seems unlikely that it would seriously challenge the remaining superpower or radically alter global politics, as did many revolutions of the cold war era. The recent revolution in Zaire is a case in point.

My principal claim, however, is that revolutionary movements are less likely to arise and revolutions are less likely to occur during the contemporary period than during the cold war era—especially, but not exclusively, movements and revolutions that would seriously challenge the capitalist world-system. As both a motivating ideal and a modular "repertoire of contention" (Tilly 1978, ch. 5; Tarrow 1994), revolution has lost much of its popular appeal and influence. Why is this so? Why has an age of revolutions—an era marked by several waves of widespread revolutionary conflict—now passed? And might another return?

Two possible keys to our nonrevolutionary times may be the process of "globalization" (that is, the increasingly transnational character of capitalism) and the demise of Soviet communism. Some have suggested that "globalization" has destroyed the very rationale for revolutions. According to this perspective, state power—the traditional prize of revolutionaries—has been dramatically eroded by the growing power of multinational corporations and by the increasingly rapid and uncontrollable movements of capital, commodities, and people. These realities, according to Charles Tilly, "undermine the autonomy and circumscription of individual states, make it extremely difficult for any state to carry on a separate fiscal, welfare or military policy, and thus reduce the relative advantage of controlling the apparatus of a national state" (1993, 247). In other words, as globalization diminishes and hollows out state power, the less rational becomes any political project aimed at capturing state power, including revolution.

I believe that globalization has indeed made revolutions less likely, but not for this dubious reason. Rather than uniformly diminishing states, globalization has been just as likely to spur attempts to employ and, if necessary, expand state power for the purposes of enhancing global competitiveness. Historically, in fact, there has been a strong correlation between a country's exposure to external economic competition and the size of its public sector (Evans 1997). Some have argued that, to a significant extent, globalization is itself a *project* of strong states (Weiss 1997). Popular support for revolutionaries, at any rate, is not usually based on estimations of their likely success in enhancing anything quite so rarified as the autonomy of a country's fiscal policy or even its long-term global competitiveness. Rather, ordinary folk have typically supported revolutionaries because the revolutionaries have spoken up for them when no one else would, protected them from state violence, provided for their subsistence, and defended their traditional rights. I see no reason to believe that in the future people will accept the depredations of authoritarian states and shun revolutionaries on the grounds that state power "ain't what it used to be."

Another, and perhaps more obvious, explanation for the declining prospects for revolution is the collapse of the Soviet bloc. Many revolutionaries of the cold war era were emboldened by the existence of a powerful noncapitalist industrial society, one that was itself dependent and "backward" in the not-too-distant past. The appeal of Soviet communism was all the greater because the Soviets were the self-proclaimed foes of the capitalist powers (above all the United States), which perversely provided aid and

276 THE FUTURE OF REVOLUTION

comfort—in the name of anticommunism—to many a brutal and authoritarian regime. Yet I would argue that it was precisely the brutality and authoritarianism of so many states during the cold war era—including the Soviet-backed regimes in Eastern Europe—that provided the seedbed for widespread revolutionary conflicts (Goodwin 2001). For much of the cold war era, vast tracts of the globe suffered violent and exclusionary forms of colonial rule, imperial domination, military occupation, or postcolonial despotism. In these political contexts, popular rebellions, usually armed and necessarily violent, were often the only practical or even sensible repertoire of political contention. Moderates and reformists, by contrast, seemed utopian or even suicidal.

Democratization and Revolution

Today, however, this seedbed for revolution is virtually desiccated, thanks in no small measure, ironically, to the revolutions of the cold war era: colonialism is all but dead; Soviet domination of Eastern Europe is no more; and U.S. hegemony in the developing world—even in its Central American "backyard"—is increasingly challenged by rival powers (Coatsworth 1994). Most important, and partly because of these very developments, a transnational "wave" of democratization has swept across large parts of East Asia, Eastern Europe, Latin America, and (to a lesser extent) Africa over the past decade or two (Markoff 1996, Huntington 1991). Whereas there were precious few democratic regimes in South America in 1980, for example, transitions to democracy were under way virtually everywhere on that continent just fifteen years later. Thanks in large part to revolutionaries themselves, moreover, democratic transitions are now also under way in Central America; however, with democracy, of course, has also come the pacification of these revolutionaries (Dunkerley 1994, Paige 1997).

In my view, the coming decades are unlikely to exhibit the same scale of revolutionary conflict as the cold war era precisely because of this striking and widespread political transformation. For while we may debate the underlying causes of democratization, and of the most recent wave of democratization in particular, it seems difficult to deny democracy's predominantly *counterrevolutionary* consequences. *No popular revolutionary movement, it bears emphasizing, has ever overthrown a consolidated democratic regime.*[4] The great revolutions of the cold war era toppled exclusionary colonial regimes (as in Algeria and Vietnam), personalist dictatorships (as in Cuba, Iran, and Nicaragua), and the Soviet-imposed communist regimes of Eastern Europe. However, none overthrew a regime that even remotely resembled a democracy. And no institutionalized democracy (including the most developed capitalist societies) is today even remotely threatened by revolutionaries—not western Europe, Japan, North America, India, Costa Rica, Australia, or New Zealand.

Why is democracy so inhospitable to revolutionaries? First and foremost, democracy pacifies and institutionalizes—but does not eliminate—many forms of social conflict. Lipset (1960, ch. 7) has aptly referred to elections as a "democratic translation of the class struggle." Indeed, democracy "translates" and channels a variety of social conflicts—including, but not limited to, class conflicts—into party competition for votes and the lobbying of representatives by "interest groups." Of course, this "translation" has sometimes taken violent forms, especially when and where the fairness of electoral contests was widely questioned. But the temptation to rebel against the state—which is rarely acted upon without trepidation, given its life-or-death consequences—is partly quelled under democratic regimes by the knowledge that new elections are but a few years off and with them the chance to punish incumbent rulers. In addition, democracies have generally provided a context in which ordinary people, through popular protest, can win concessions from economic and political elites, although this often requires a good deal of disruption, if not violence (Gamson 1975, Piven and Coward 1977). As Che Guevara (1985) understood, armed struggles that are aimed at overthrowing fairly elected governments rarely win much popular support unless such governments (or the armies that they putatively command) push people into the armed opposition by indiscriminately repressing suspected rebel sympathizers (Goodwin 1993). By and large, to paraphrase Alan Dawley (1976, 70), the ballot box is the coffin of revolutionaries.

Does the foregoing mean that political radicalism and militancy go unrewarded in democratic societies? Hardly. Democracy, to repeat, does not eliminate social conflict; in fact, in many ways democracy encourages social conflict by providing the institutionalized "political space" or "political opportunities" with which those groups outside ruling circles can make claims on political authorities and economic elites (Tarrow 1994).[5] Not just political parties, then, but a whole range of interest groups, trade unions, professional associations, transnational networks, and social movements become the main organizational vehicles, or "mobilizing structures," of political life in democratic polities. These institutions of "civil society" are generally just that—civil. Their repertoires of collective action include electoral campaigns, lobbying, petitions, strikes, boycotts, peaceful demonstrations, and civil disobedience—forms of collective action that may be undertaken with great passion and militancy, and sometimes for quite radical ends but are not aimed at bringing down the state. Nor are riots, from which democracies are not immune, revolutionary in this sense. So, whereas radicals and militants may survive and even thrive under democracy, or at least some democracies, true revolutionaries seldom do.

Democracy, then, dramatically reduces the likelihood of revolutionary change, but not because it necessarily brings about social justice (although justice *is* sometimes served under democracies). Formal democracy is fully compatible with widespread poverty, inequality, and social ills of all sorts, which is why Karl Marx criticized "political emancipation" and so-called bourgeois democracy in the name of "human emancipation." The prevalence of poverty and other social problems is precisely why extra-parliamentary movements for social justice so often arise in democratic contexts, but these movements almost always view the state as an instrument to be pressured and influenced, not as something to be seized or smashed. To be pessimistic, then, about the likelihood of revolutions during the current period is not at all to be pessimistic about the likelihood of struggles of social justice. And we should recall that the record of past revolutions in achieving social justice is mixed at best.

Even imperfect and poorly consolidated democracies tend to diffuse revolutionary pressures. The neglected case of Honduras illustrates this point well (Booth and Walker 1993, ch. 8). During the 1980s, violent conflicts raged in neighboring countries, but Honduras remained relatively quiescent. No significant revolutionary movement challenged the Honduran state, despite poverty and inequalities that rivaled those of its neighbors. Although several elections took place in Honduras during the 1980s, the democratic regime in that country was (and remains) deeply flawed. A special battalion in the armed forces "disappeared" more than a hundred actual or suspected radicals. The two dominant political parties were and remain virtually indistinguishable. Still, the government generally tolerated and occasionally granted concessions to trade unions and peasant organizations. Dissident intellectuals and human rights activists spoke out against the government, and the armed forces in Honduras never indiscriminately attacked peasant villages or popular organizations in the manner of their Salvadoran or Guatemalan counterparts. As a result, Hondurans never felt the need to join or support revolutionaries in order to defend themselves or to improve their welfare. So, although Honduras's quasi-democracy did few things well, it was effective at preventing the emergence of a revolutionary movement.

The recent wave of democratization, although uneven and incomplete, has largely destroyed the basis for widespread revolutionary conflicts in those societies that it has reached. Yet some scholars insist that the "new world order" has not at all diminished the likelihood of revolutions and, at least in certain respects, may even have made them more probable, at least in developing societies, in the years ahead (Walt 1996, 349–351; Foran 1997a; Selbin 1997). These scholars point out that many countries remain impoverished, dependent upon and subordinate to the wealthy "North," and vulnerable to external economic downturns. They also suggest that, despite the collapse of communism, a range of dissident ideologies and "cultures of opposition" remain available to would-be revolutionaries, including radical nationalism and religious fundamentalism.

Their points are indisputable. Yet, while these factors may generate widespread popular grievances, history tells us that these grievances are not sufficient to cause revolutions or even to generate significant revolutionary movements or popular rebellions. After all, revolutionary movements develop not simply because people are angry, but because the state under which they live provides no other mechanism for social change, violently repressing those who peacefully seek incremental reforms. As Leon Trotsky once put it, people only make revolutions when there is "no other way out" of dire circumstances. Moreover, revolutionary movements, even those with strong popular support, rarely succeed in seizing power unless the authoritarian states that they confront are very weak or suddenly weakened (through war, for example).

John Foran, who is well aware of this line of reasoning, still maintains that the prospects for revolutions have not decreased appreciably in the post–cold war era. He bases his view on the claim that "exclusionary, personalist states, while out of vogue in the post–1980 movement towards formally democratic polities in much of the world, are still an option for dependent developers (and this global democratisation process remains fragile)" (1997a, 814). Foran is right to claim that personalist dictatorships have proven particularly vulnerable to revolutionary overthrow (see, for example, Dix 1984, Farhi 1990, Wickham-Crowley 1992). However, I believe that the personalist dictatorship is an increasingly rare and anachronistic state form that seems headed for extinction. The soil in which such dictatorships sunk their roots—weak elites, demobilized masses, and patrimonial armies—has all but dried up. Revolutions may yet topple dictators like Saddam Hussein in Iraq, but few other personalist dictatorships remain.

Foran and Eric Selbin (1997) also suggest that the end of the cold war has opened more geopolitical space for revolutionaries. By this, they seem to mean that the United States will no longer intervene against democratic revolutionaries. However, with the demise of the countervailing power of the Soviet bloc, geopolitical space has surely *contracted* for those revolutionaries, democratic or otherwise, who threaten the interests of the United States. Witness the growing intervention of the United States in the counterinsurgency in Colombia.

More serious is Foran's warning about the fragility of the recent global process of democratization. Indeed, a new era of widespread revolutionary conflict will dawn, if my analysis is right, if this most recent wave of democratization recedes. Revolutionary conflict will most certainly reappear if the nascent democracies in Eastern Europe, East Asia, Latin America, and Africa are replaced by violent, authoritarian regimes. Fortunately, however, this scenario strikes me as rather unlikely because economic and political elites, including even armies, have become aware of the increasing economic costs of political violence and disorder. Here is where "globalization" may truly matter. The unprecedented speed and mobility of financial resources in the current era hang like the sword of Damocles over those on both the left *and* right who would disrupt predictable business climates and "investor confidence." Under the new world order, the fear of capital flight or boycott may stay the hand of would-be Napoleons or Lenins. Globalization, notwithstanding its often disastrous socioeconomic effects, may help preserve democratic and quasi-democratic regimes and undermine the most brutal forms of authoritarianism. As a political project of the most advanced capitalist countries, especially the United States, globalization seeks to undermine all forms of economic nationalism, whether of the left or right, and to foster the type of free trade that powerful multinational banks and corporations will inevitably dominate. Globalization thus abhors the autocratic and oligarchic forms of patrimonialism or "crony capitalism" that have nurtured so many revolutionary movements during the past century.

History admittedly provides little room for optimism about the permanency of democracy. Past waves of democratization, alas, have been regularly followed by antidemocratic waves. Yet this pattern should give little comfort to revolutionaries, for "the overwhelming majority of [past] transitions from democracy" were not the result of popular revolts, but "took the form of either military coups . . . or executive coups in which democratically chosen chief executives effectively ended democracy by concentrating power in themselves" (Huntington 1991, 291). Needless to say, very few people would welcome such coups today, even if, in the long run, they make revolutions more likely. In fact, the left as a whole (including former revolutionaries), perhaps more than any other segment of the political spectrum in newly democratic countries, has come through hard experience to value bourgeois democracy and the rule of law. The left generally is keen these days on avoiding actions, including armed rebellions, that might provide a pretext for, or unintentionally legitimate, antidemocratic coups. In Latin America, the left's aversion to any actions that might provoke an antidemocratic coup means that it has returned—with some exceptions, of course—to the outlook that prevailed prior to the Cuban Revolution, which leftists initially denounced as "putschist" and "adventurist." The left, in short, today stands as an important obstacle to one of the most basic and necessary preconditions for revolution, namely, authoritarianism. History, of course, is full of such paradoxes.

NOTES

1. The Marxist historian Eric Hobsbawm (1962) has described the period from 1789 to 1848 as "the age of revolution," at least in Europe, although the revolutionary movements that swept across that continent in 1848 were largely defeated.

2. See Foran (1997a, 1997b) for a discussion of the likelihood of revolution in some of the aforementioned countries.

3. In authoritarian contexts, civil society often benefits from the presence of a strong "radical flank" of revolutionaries. The guerrilla movements in El Salvador and Guatemala of the 1980s, for example, although unable to seize state power, had important radical-flank effects, thereby contributing both directly and indirectly to the process of democratization in those countries.

4. Rightist movements did destroy democratic regimes in Germany, Italy, and Spain, but those regimes were of relatively recent vintage, which is to say, they were not fully consolidated.

5. Unfortunately, the "political opportunities" concept has been defined and operationalized so as to include virtually every environmental factor that facilitates political protest. See Goodwin and Jasper 1999.

REFERENCES

Booth, John A., and Thomas W. Walker. 1993. *Understanding Central America.* 2d ed. Boulder: Westview Press.

Coatsworth, John H. 1994. *Central America and the United States: The Clients and the Colossus.* New York: Twayne.

Dawley, Alan. 1976. *Class and Community: The Industrial Revolution in Lynn.* Cambridge: Harvard University Press.

Dix, Robert. 1984. "Why Revolutions Succeed and Fail." *Polity* 16:423–446.

Dunkerley, James. 1994. *The Pacification of Central America.* London: Verso.

Evans, Peter. 1997. "The Eclipse of the State? Reflections on Stateness in an Era of Globalization." *World Politics* 50: 62–87.

Farhi, Farideh. 1990. *States and Urban-Based Revolutions: Iran and Nicaragua.* Urbana and Chicago: University of Illinois Press.

Foran, John. 1997a. "The Future of Revolutions at the *Fin-de-siècle.*" *Third World Quarterly* 18: 791–820.

_____. 1997b. "The Comparative-Historical Sociology of Third World Social Revolutions: Why a Few Succeed, Why Most Fail." In *Theorizing Revolutions,* ed. John Foran, 227–267. London: Routledge.

Gamson, William A. 1975. *The Strategy of Social Protest.* Homewood, Ill.: Dorsey Press.

Goodwin, Jeff. 1993. "Why Insurgencies Persist, or the Perversity of Indiscriminate Violence by Weak States: A Qualitative Comparative Analysis." Paper presented at the 1993 meeting of the American Sociological Association, Miami Beach.

_____. 2001. *No Other Way Out: States and Revolutionary Movements, 1945–1991.* Cambridge: Cambridge University Press.

Goodwin, Jeff, and James M. Jasper. 1999. "Caught in a Winding, Snarling Vine: The Structural Bias of Political Process Theory." *Sociological Forum* 14: 27–54.

Guevara, Che. 1985. *Guerrilla Warfare.* Lincoln: University of Nebraska Press. Originally published in 1960.

Hobsbawm, E. J. 1962. *The Age of Revolution, 1789–1848.* New York: New American Library.

Huntington, Samuel P. 1991. *The Third Wave: Democratization in the Late Twentieth Century.* Norman and London: University of Oklahoma Press.

Lipset, Seymour Martin. 1960. *Political Man: The Social Bases of Politics.* Garden City: Doubleday.

Markoff, John. 1996. *Waves of Democracy: Social Movements and Political Change.* Thousand Oaks: Pine Forge Press.

Paige, Jeffery M. 1997. *Coffee and Power: Revolution and the Rise of Democracy in Central America.* Cambridge: Harvard University Press.

Piven, Frances Fox, and Richard A. Coward. 1977. *Poor People's Movements: Why They Succeed, How They Fail.* New York: Vintage.

Selbin, Eric. 1997. "Magical Revolutions: The Future of Revolution in the Land of Magical Realism." Paper presented at the twentieth International Congress of the Latin American Studies Association, Guadalajara, Mexico.

Tarrow, Sidney. 1994. *Power in Movement: Social Movements, Collective Action and Politics.* Cambridge: Cambridge University Press.

Tilly, Charles. 1978. *From Mobilization to Revolution.* Reading: Addison-Wesley.

_____. 1993. *European Revolutions, 1492–1992.* Oxford: Blackwell.

Walt, Stephen M. 1996. *Revolution and War.* Ithaca: Cornell University Press.

Weiss, Linda. 1997. "Globalization and the Myth of the Powerless State." *New Left Review,* no. 225: 3–27.

Wickham-Crowley, Timothy P. 1992. *Guerrillas and Revolution in Latin America: A Comparative Study of Insurgents and Regimes Since 1956.* Princeton: Princeton University Press.

12

Same as It Ever Was:
The Future of Revolution at the End of the Century

Eric Selbin

Eric Selbin is the author of Modern Latin American Revolutions
*(1999). The following selection is a revised version of a paper he first
presented at the 1998 International Studies Association annual convention. In it, Selbin disagrees with those who argue that the spread of democratization makes revolution less likely in the future.*

*Looking primarily at Latin America, Selbin notes that the already
huge number of poor people in the region has swollen even larger over
the past two decades, contemporaneous with the latest wave of democratization there. Selbin sees this growing impoverishment as being due
primarily to the rapid free-market transformations that Latin American
governments have pursued at the behest of the International Monetary
Fund and the West in general. Although democratization did not cause
the negative consequences that so many Latin Americans suffered as a
result of economic dislocations, it has not served to protect them, either.
Nor can it protect them where the "democratization" acclaimed by the
West is highly corrupt and where the military is often still the final arbiter in the political realm.*

*In such circumstances, it is not surprising that democracy is becom-
ing increasingly unstable in several Latin American countries and that
revolutionary activity is occurring in some of them, including Colombia, Mexico, and Peru. Since the circumstances giving rise to such activity are unlikely to be ameliorated, more—not less—revolutionary
activity appears to be in store for Latin America.*

Acknowledgements: My thanks to Helen Cordes, John Foran, Mark Gasiorowski, Jeff Goodwin,
Michael Hickey, Karen Kampwirth, Misagh Parsa, Timothy Powers, Annie Richard, Ken Roberts,
Sidney Tarrow, and Timothy Wickham-Crowley. Some of these people will be underwhelmed by
my interpretations or disagree with them; I am most appreciative of their efforts to show me the
error of my ways, and thus these fine folks are obviously not responsible for my bad judgement in
ignoring their wisdom and sage advice.

Critical Questions

1. Does Selbin disagree with Goodwin that democracy is inhospitable to revolution?

2. To what extent must democratization advance in order to be a barrier to revolution?

3. Are the conditions that Selbin identifies as making Latin America ripe for revolution present in other regions of the world?

"It's the end of the world as we know it" seems to be the mantra of a variety of folks declaiming, among other things, "the end of history," meaning the triumph of liberal democracy and free-market principles;[1] the looming clash of civilizations;[2] the demise of liberal democracy;[3] and, not surprisingly, the end of revolutions,[4] their "vogue" passed,[5] not least in their twentieth century bailiwick, Latin America and the Caribbean.[6] The extent of these presumptions is significant if not entirely intuitive. For example, the "loose talk of 'democratic capitalism' conceals the contradictory forces at work in liberal democracies that have opted for free markets. Democratic institutions and free markets are not, in any broad historical perspective, natural allies."[7] Nonetheless, these folks would have us believe that the triumph of some sort of (liberal) democratic capitalism has led to the retirement of noncapitalist ideologies or systems and to the demise of principled attacks on the status quo, certainly the demise of phenomena such as revolution; henceforth, revolutions will serve as footnotes in capitalism's victorious march since supplanting feudalism. To the extent that revolutions continue to exist, they have been consigned to the margins of history, the province of only a very few and recalcitrant hardliners—the Cubans, the North Koreans, assorted Islamic fundamentalists—who dare resist the inevitable "neo-liberal" tide.[8] In Latin America and the Caribbean, we are assured, neo-liberalism holds sway, and revolution is a thing of the past; any apparent instances representing either inexplicable remnants of the cold war or historical relics fallen into the hands of nefarious drug traffickers.

This chapter will not address some of the larger issues alluded to above—the "end of history," the fearsome coming clash of civilizations, the tragedy of "illiberal democracy." The contention here is that with regard to revolution, things are the same as they ever were. I argue that revolution is as likely, perhaps even more likely, than ever before. As global gaps between the haves and the have-nots increase and neo-liberalism fails to deliver on its promise, revolution will become more likely; the advent of the "New World Order" (which is neither new nor particularly orderly; the former refers to globalization, which appears strikingly similar to what was once called "imperialism") will likely offer more space for such activities rather than diminish their likelihood due to a lack of funds and support from the now defunct communist bloc. All that has changed is the perception of such possibilities among policy makers and academics, both inclined to trendiness, the former to wishful thinking (we want these things to go away), and the latter to fanciful thinking (ah, remaking the world).[9] Real people in the real world will continue to struggle for justice and dignity regardless of whether we choose to recognize it as such, whether we define it as revolution. The question that remains is whether it is still useful to define these struggles for justice as revolutions, not whether we will continue to encounter them.

Canon, Tradition, Revision

For the immense majority of humanity—the billions of poor and exploited—history conceptualized as a march toward liberal democracy and free-market principles has not even begun. The intensity and immediacy of our age has resulted in the failure to appreciate the long term, a point we will return to later. And the notion that the demise of the Eastern bloc between 1989 and 1991 represents some sort of endpoint for a process that began with the French Revolution in 1789 is hard to justify; since the end of World War II, there has not been a single day in which an armed revolutionary process was not under way somewhere, many of them wars of independence or regional autonomy, or contention for state power. A Dutch study found that in 1995, of the 58 significant armed conflicts under way, 57 were internal.[10] And in many cases these groups—and others like them, perhaps as many as 268[11]—share the sort of radical visions, the dramatic notions of fundamentally transforming their societies that we associate with revolution. For these people and others, revolution remains a meaningful and powerful option by which to reshape their world, which leads to the next point: John Foran, Karen Kampwirth, and I are doing our best to suggest that the reports of the death of revolution as a theoretical construct of use to social scientists have been greatly exaggerated, and a spate of forthcoming books and articles, including some by those who now proclaim the death of the concept, suggest we might be right.[12]

Revolutions are distinct processes. This observation is not meant to deny the importance or significance of related phenomena such as cycles of protest, social movements, coups d'état, or rebellions. Such events and processes clearly result in significant sociopolitical change and often leave lasting legacies within their community and, on occasion, their society. The term *revolution* implies that revolutionaries acquire control of the state structures and, in the period thereafter, seek to transform in a fundamental way at least some major facet of society. It is the latter, the devotion to the creation of a new orientation for society, rather than the former, acquisition of state power, that defines the "great revolutions."[13] Social revolution refers to those relatively rare cases that include conscious efforts—which is not to deny the profusion of concomitant unintended consequences as well—by at least an active minority of the participants to transform profoundly the entire society.[14] People believe themselves presented with what seem like boundless opportunities to reshape their world, and by extension themselves, and who among us is really prepared to claim that people will no longer seek to transform themselves and their world?

Hence my contention is that the long term—perhaps even the short term—prospects for revolution are as strong today as ever before. Although there may be less international support for revolutionaries now than there was during the cold war (the level of international support has always been heavily overestimated, as documents now available from the former East bloc states make clear[15]), there is more space for revolution without the intense bipolarity of the cold war years and therefore more "permissiveness" (not that revolutionaries ever sought permission). Moreover, the primary causes of revolution, in most every conceptualization of the term, remain widespread: we live in a time of great global change (replete with potential for systemic upheaval), people are hungry and resent the widening gap between the rich and the poor, and people are confronted by the failed promises of neo-liberalism and liberal democracy. Furthermore, these same people, overflowing with historical narratives of rebellion and revolution and the possibilities inherent in creating a new world, have a model of revolution and an opportunity to exercise it, as everyone struggles to define and decipher the (not so) new world (dis)order.

A surprising number of people under an array of circumstances have left the private space of their homes to fight in public space for public goods in pursuit of private desires.[16] How and why they cross that threshold from the inside to the outside in an effort to transform their world remains the central puzzle for us all. Students of revolution need to take seriously the notion that theories of revolution are rooted in and driven by individuals and the culture that they create and transmit. This transmission occurs primarily through the mechanisms of collective memory, symbolic politics, and the social context of politics that they create.[17] As long as people who face profound inequities and are unable to redress their grievances through the system extant articulate compelling stories with engaging and empowering plots, revolutions will be made.

If You Have Ghosts, Then You Have Everything

Collective memory, symbolic politics, and the power and potential of that tool kit in the social context of politics are critical to our understanding of the state and future of revolution. "We moderns," Michael Mayerfeld Bell has suggested, "despite our mechanistic and rationalistic ethos, live in landscapes filled with ghosts."[18] Although Mayerfeld Bell has a slightly different notion of ghosts—"the sense of the presence of those who are not physically there"[19]—than I mean to employ here, there are critical meeting points. The first is that the way in which we construct history, and our understanding of it is heavily peopled, populated by the constructs we put there and how we understand them; places both real and imagined are "personed."[20] People tell and retell stories of resistance and rebellion, stories that are imbued with great meaning, freighted with import, and full of ghosts of the past who still haunt—and perhaps interact with—our present. For example, people outside Cuernavaca, Morales, Mexico still speak of revolutionary leader Emiliano Zapata—murdered in 1919—in the present tense, which relates to the second meeting place. Mayerfeld Bell cites Wendy Griswold's compelling estimation that "the meanings attributed to any cultural object are fabrications, woven from the symbolic capacities of the object itself and from the perceptual apparatus of those who experience the object."[21] I think Griswold captures something profound and important. Griswold's perception is illustrated quite well by the following:

> [There is] an old Andean tradition, specifically female, which conceives of history as a woven cloth; it consists in recognizing the warp and weft, the texture, the forms of relationships, in knowing the back from the front,

the value and significance of the detailed pattern, and so on. In other words, we are trying to read in the book of life that which has never been recorded in written form; we are attempting to capture the image brought to mind and revealed in the moment of the interview before it is lost again to silence.[22]

The point is that all of our understandings are derived from who and what we are, particularly as revealed by the stories we tell and the ideology and ideas that they reflect, facets deeply embedded in the culture we create.

Both of these elements mean that we have to pay attention not only to people and the stories that they tell, but also to the context in which they tell them. They also imply that many of the world's people live in a time of their own—a time that is far more mythological than chronological.[23] Nowhere is this more evident than when the Commandante Ramona of the EZLN (Ejército Zapatista de Liberación Nacional, or Zapatista National Liberation Army) notes that her people have struggled for more than five hundred years and will think nothing of struggling for five hundred more, or longer. Although many people would view such phrasing as little more than rhetoric, I would contend that it reflects a different understanding of time and place, that it reflects a world that is, perhaps, just outside of our usual social science and rationalistic realm. It is in this sense, as I will touch on below, that an "alien" concept such as "magical realism"—a literary concept commonly associated with some Latin American and Caribbean literature—may be of some use in understanding revolutions that, in the context of the New World Order, might seem "magical."

Although Algeria may be the most compelling revolutionary situation, we need look no further than Latin America and the Caribbean, which have a nearly five-hundred-year-old tradition of rebellion and revolution.[24] Guerrilla movements are operating in at least Bolivia, Colombia, Mexico, and Peru, and more might arise in the future, especially since the increasingly undemocratic procedures used to implement "neo-liberal reforms" have done little to promote the social welfare of profoundly impoverished populations. More people in Latin America and the Caribbean live in poverty today than did twenty years ago. According to the executive secretary of the United Nations Commission on Latin America and the Caribbean, "the levels [of poverty] are still considerably higher than those observed in 1980, while income distribution appears to have worsened in virtually all cases."[25] The numbers remain staggering: nearly half of the region's 460 million people are poor—an increase of 60 million in one decade. Meanwhile, the number of Latin American billionaires rose from six in 1987 to forty-two in 1994, a figure that is widely reported and resented.[26] The social and economic deprivation is stultifying. And political "reforms" not only have failed to make meaningful differences in the material conditions of people's everyday lives but have failed to transform their ideological conditions either, and as a result the reforms undercut the very democratic processes they are claimed to portend.

It is important not to exaggerate. Democracy—specifically Western democratic procedure—has been far more successful recently in Latin America and the Caribbean than ever before; democracy is certainly wider—if not necessarily deeper—than in any of the previous cycles of democratization. During the 1980s the trend toward democracy was strong and steady; almost every country in the region had a free, open, and fair election, a norm that held firm through the 1990s. Although one election does not a democracy make, most of these countries have had more than one election and have even witnessed the peaceful transfer of power between opposing parties. In a region notoriously cool toward democratic procedures and the relinquishment of office, elections and transitions are no small feats. Equally striking has been the attention to, if not respect for, human rights and dignity, and some tangible efforts have been made in these areas.

Yet even a cursory examination of the state of the hemisphere shows that meaningful democratic practices remain weak. Few of these democracies are inclusive; they are based instead on elite pacts and the continued marginalization of the region's indigenous population, and there have been notable setbacks over the last ten years: the 1992 *autogolpe,* dubbed a "Fujicoup," in Peru; the 1992 coup in Haiti; the two popularly supported coup attempts in Venezuela in 1992, and the ambiguous role of current President Hugo Chavez Frias—a former coup plotter—and the constitutional convention he has convened to circumvent the nominally democratic institutions; Paraguay's "non-coup" in 1996 and coup attempt in May 2000;[27] Ecuador's constitutionally dubious "congressional coup" of 1997 (in which the military served as final arbiter and king maker); repeated popular calls for a coup in Panama since the U.S. invasion of 1989; the role of Guatemala's military in first supporting and then destroying a 1993 effort to emulate the "Fujicoup" with a *Serranazo;* intimations of *continuismo* by Fujimori in Peru and Menem in Argentina; and the occasional ominous noises from the military and its partisans in both Brazil and Chile. *Continuismo* is particularly evident in Chile, where Gen. Augusto Pinochet moved into the

Senate and is claiming immunity as a senator from prosecution for crimes he may have committed while president. As for human rights, although the generals are out of political office and back in their barracks, they have left their legacy and retain their minions. A palpable sense of justice has not yet taken hold in much of the region, and death squads remain active in a number of countries, most notably Brazil, El Salvador, Guatemala, and Peru. Although democracy in Latin America and the Caribbean is arguably institutionalized, countries across the region have corrupt and ineffective judiciaries, weak and often aimless political parties, subservient legislatures, and militaries that remain out of the reach of civilian control. Democratic consolidation remains elusive.[28]

The ever more apparent failure of neo-liberalism to redress the grievances of the region's poor and dispossessed and the resurgent death squads of the right present the region's progressive forces a historical moment into which they might step. Again, it is important not to exaggerate. The advent of neo-liberalism was driven at least in part by the paucity of credible alternatives for solving the widespread economic failures that had become endemic to Latin America and the Caribbean. Just as neo-liberalism failed to deliver on its promise, so too the region's revolutionaries have not produced a markedly better record for confronting the monumental inequities that are commonplace throughout the region. Profound political, economic, or social transformation anywhere in the region has remained elusive for all sides. But if revolutions have not created the utopia that some dreamed of, neither did they leave the world unchanged. Although armed revolution has declined for the moment, it seems premature to sound the death knell for either the concept of revolution or the revolutionaries of Latin America and the Caribbean.

But will revolution as we have known it be the path they take? Social movements seem to have center stage at this point, enabled and ennobled by transnational issue networks that have had real influence on individuals, local groups, and governments at home and abroad. And communalism, especially related to indigenous peoples, continues to expand. Associations around gender, ecology, and religion appear vibrant. But successes at ameliorating social ills to date are shallow and few, and frustration seems to be mounting. The potential and possibility of people taking up revolutionary activity to redress the grievances of millions of people in the region remain real. Real, too, is the extent to which the modern revolutionary mythos— the commitment to political, economic, social, psychological, and cultural justice—resonates with embattled and embittered populations whom the global tide of neo-liberalism is drowning, driving and inspiring people to change the material and ideological conditions of their everyday lives.

It strikes me as extremely unlikely that the current lull (in relative terms) in what might be considered revolutionary activity will last. Although very uncomfortable with its deterministic undertones, I am reminded of Thomas Jefferson's dictum that revolutions are as inevitable in the political world as storms in the natural; the people of Latin America and the Caribbean will create their future with the tool kit their culture provides them, and revolution remains a ready tool.

Conclusion: Same as It Ever Was?

The end of the twentieth century, often referred to as the century of revolutions, finds us at a time and in a place redolent of a magical realist novella replete with forking paths, mystical spirits, and things not what they seem: the co-occurrence of realism with the fantastic, the mythic, and the magical seems commonplace. And it is the commonplace that most merits our attention. As John Markoff suggests, "if we are to seize the moments of social creativity, we need to study the messy details of historical processes and not just the grand trends."[29] We may have seen the last revolutionary conflict of the cold war era—an era opened in some sense by the Allied invasion of Russia during its revolution.[30] Arguably, we may have witnessed the end of a cycle of at least nominally Marxist-Leninist (and Maoist) revolutions that began in October 1917 (if not 1871 or 1848; how do we date this and what does it mean that such groups are still extant?). Nonetheless, does anyone really believe that the events and processes identified by three generations of scholars of revolution and innumerable generations of revolutionaries will disappear? While Túpac Amaru, the last Inca slaughtered by the Spanish in 1572, may reappear from the dead in various guises, from the mists of the jungle and time, a different person or persons occupying the same space, echoing Zapatista leader Marcos's contention that behind the ski masks are different Marcoses (Marcoses creating neuroses for the Mexican government?)—reality for most remains largely the same.

Alejo Carpentier, a Cuban author who is generally acknowledged to have brought magical realism into Latin America and the Caribbean, suggested that "in the cultural universe of Latin America the prevalence of myth, magical practices and diverse cosmogonies facilitate the expression of 'the marvelous' in everyday life."[31] Replace "Latin America" with almost any other region of the world and you capture the feel of the new century. What must seem more magical, more marvelous, than the possibility of creating a new life, a new world? Often imbued with a mythic resonance, the story of most revolutionary processes bears a highly fanciful semblance to reality and is matched by a marked, if vague, feeling of surrealistic authenticity.

Are we at the end of revolutions as we know them? Perhaps, certainly if by revolution we mean a process that accords neatly with the "great" revolutions of the past two hundred plus years.[32] But the pronouncement of the end of revolutions might be news to those in the mountains of Latin America and the Caribbean as well as parts of Africa, Asia, and Oceania. I concur here with Walter Goldfrank, who has argued that we are clearly "in a period in which the century-plus of Marxism [I would amend to Marxism-Leninism] as a world movement and a set of world parties has ended, and the new overarching vision has barely begun to be enunciated. [Yet] Earth-destroying, militaristic, patriarchal, racially inflected capitalism continues to generate mind-numbing inequalities and dangers to human livelihood."[33] There is every reason to think that revolutions will persist, as real people living in a real and at times surreal world continue to resist inequality and seek to rework and reform their lives.

NOTES

1. Francis Fukuyama, "The End of History." *National Interest* 16 (summer 1989); see also Francis Fukuyama, *The End of History and the Last Man* (New York: Avon Books, 1993). The "end of history," Fukuyama proclaims, is denoted by the triumph of liberal democracy and free-market principles, not necessarily in that order.

2. Samuel Huntington, *The Clash of Civilizations and the Remaking of the New World Order* (New York: Simon and Schuster, 1996).

3. Fareed Zakaria, "The Rise of Illiberal Democracy." *Foreign Affairs*, 76 (November–December 1997): 22–34.

4. Robert Snyder, "The End of Revolution?" *Review of Politics* 61 (winter 1999); Arthur Gilbert, "Revolution, War, Genocide: The Assault on the Idea of Revolutionary Progress" (Toronto: International Studies Association, 1997); Jeff Goodwin, "Is the Age of Revolution Over?" (Minneapolis: International Studies Association, 1998).

5. Forrest Colburn, *The Vogue of Revolution in Poor Countries* (Princeton: Princeton University Press, 1994).

6. Carlos Figueroa Ibarra, "Shipwreck and Survival: The Left in Central America." *Latin American Perspectives* 24 (January 1997); Michael Powelson, "The Failed Promise of Guerrilla War in Latin America" (New Orleans: Southwestern Social Science Association, 1997).

7. John Gray, "Global Utopias and Clashing Civilizations: Misunderstanding the Present." *International Affairs* 74 (January 1998), 154.

8. Some U.S. conservatives, bizarrely, include the Clinton administration among these recalcitrant few. For a fairly coherent example of a fairly wacky argument, see John Gray, "The Left's Last Utopia: Amerika (sic) the Beautiful." *National Review* 45 (July 19, 1993): 30–35.

9. With regard to North American academics and their romanticization of revolution and revolutionaries, see Mongo Sánchez Lira and Rogelio Villarreal, "Mexico 1994: The Ruins of the Future." In *First World, Ha, Ha, Ha! The Zapatista Challenge,* ed. Elaine Katzenberger (San Francisco: City Lights, 1995), 223.

10. A. J. Jorgeman, "Contemporary Conflicts: A Global Survey of High and Lower Intensity Conflicts and Serious Disputes." *PIOOM Newsletter and Progress Report,* no. 7 (Leiden: PIOOM Foundation, Leiden University, the Netherlands), 22–23, cited in Ted Robert Gurr and Will Moore, "Ethnopolitical Rebellion: A Cross Sectional Analysis of the 1980s with Risk Assessments for the 1990s." *American Journal of Political Science* 41 (October 1997), 1079.

11. Gurr and Moore, "Ethnopolitical Rebellion," 1079.

12. These include Jeff Goodwin, *No Other Way Out: State and Revolution 1945–1991* (Cambridge: Cambridge University Press, forthcoming); Robin Wright, *The Last Great Revolution: Turmoil and Transformation in Iran* (New York: Alfred Knopf, 2000); Fred Halliday, *Revolution and World Politics: The Rise and Fall of the Sixth Great Power* (Durham: Duke University Press, 1999); Mark N. Katz, *Reflections on Revolutions* (New York: St. Martin's, 1999); Alexander Motyl, *Revolutions, Nations, Empires: Conceptual Limits and Theoretical Possibilities* (New York: Columbia, 1999); Eric Selbin, *Modern Latin American Revolutions,* 2d rev. ed. (Boulder: Westview Press, 1999); Cynthia McClintock, *Revolutionary Movements in Latin America: El Salvador's FMLN and Peru's Shining Path* (Washington, D.C.: USIP, 1998); Edward McCaughan, *Reinventing Revolution: The Renovation of Left Discourse in Cuba and Mexico* (Boulder: Westview, 1997); and Jeffrey Paige, *Coffee and Power: Revolution and the Rise of Democracy in Central America* (Cambridge: Harvard University Press, 1997). Chapters and articles include Michael Walzer, "Intellectuals, Social Classes, and Revolutions." In *Democracy, Revolution, and History,* ed. Theda Skocpol (Ithaca: Cornell, 1998); John Foran, "The Fin-de-Siècle Revolution in Latin America: Predicting the Future from the Lessons of the Past." *Third World Quarterly* 18 (December 1997); and Doug McAdam, Sidney Tarrow, and Charles Tilly, "Towards an Integrated Perspective on Social Movements and Revolution." In *Comparative Politics: Rationality, Culture, and Structure,* ed. Mark Lichbach and Alan Zuckerman (Cambridge: Cambridge University Press, 1997). Edited volumes include Daniel Castro, ed. *Guerrilla Warfare in Latin America* (Wilmington: Scholarly Resources, 1999), John Foran, ed., *Theorizing Rev-*

olutions (New York: Routledge, 1997), and Richard Fox and Orin Starn, eds., *Between Resistance and Revolution: Cultural Politics and Social Protest* (New Brunswick: Rutgers, 1997).

13. The French, Russian, and Chinese revolutions, almost all agree, are the "great revolutions." Too rarely does this list include the first great social upheaval of the twentieth century, Mexico. On occasion it might include Cuba or even Iran, which at least one book has recently dubbed the "last" such phenomenon; see Robin Wright, *The Last Great Revolution: Turmoil and Transformation in Iran* (New York: Alfred Knopf, 2000). A nice, brief summation of the "France, Russia, China" perspective can be found in Michael Walzer, "Intellectuals, Social Classes, and Revolutions." In *Democracy, Revolution, and History*, ed. Theda Skocpol (Ithaca: Cornell University Press, 1998), 128.

14. Thus, Hannah Arendt argues, the course of history "suddenly begins anew, that an entirely new story, a story never known or told before, is about to unfold." People, she avers, believe "that they are agents in a process which spells the end of the old order and brings the birth of the new world"; Hannah Arendt, *On Revolution* (New York: Penguin, 1965), 28. In the estimation of Randall Collins, "the rare elation that accompanies a revolutionary uprising is probably due to there being no apparent boundary between one's own micro-situation and that prevailing anywhere else"; Randall Collins, *Weberian Sociological Theory* (New York: Cambridge University Press, 1986), 261. As William Sewell said of France for the period July 12 to 23, 1789, this is "an extraordinary period of fear, rejoicing, violence, and cultural creativity that changed the history of the world"; William Sewell Jr., "Historical Events as Transformations of Structures: Inventing Revolution at the Bastille." *Theory and Society* 25 (December 1996), 845. In seeking to explain what was so revolutionary about the French Revolution, Robert Darnton refers to the "possibilism"; Robert Darnton, "What Was Revolutionary about the French Revolution?" *New York Review of Books* (January 19, 1989), 17. In so doing, Darnton evokes the nineteenth-century French historian Jules Michelet, who said of France in 1789: ". . . everything was possible . . . the future was present . . . that is to say time was no more, all a lightning flash of eternity"; Michelet is quoted in Michael Kimmel, *Revolution: A Sociological Interpretation* (Philadelphia: Temple University Press, 1990), 186.

15. Classic examples of the Soviet–Cuban export model of Latin American and Caribbean revolution include Mark Falcoff, "Struggle for Central America." *Problems of Communism* 33, no. 2 (1984), 63–66; Georges Fauriol, *Latin American Insurgencies* (Washington, D.C.: Georgetown University Center for Strategic and International Studies, 1985); Henry Kissinger, *Report of the National Bipartisan Commission on Central America* (Washington, D.C.: U.S. Government Printing Office, 1984); Michael Radu and Vladimir Tismaneau, *Latin American Revolutionaries* (Washington, D.C.: Pergamon-Brassey's, 1990); William Ratliff, *Castroism and Communism in Latin America, 1959–1976* (Washington, D.C.: American Enterprise Institute, 1976); and Howard Wiarda, ed., *Rift and Revolution: The Central American Imbroglio* (Washington, D.C.: American Enterprise Institute, 1984).

16. Eric Selbin, "Revolution in the Real World: Bringing Agency Back In." In *Theorizing Revolutions*, ed. John Foran (New York: Routledge, 1997), 129.

17. Selbin, "Revolution in the Real World," 123, 130–132.

18. Michael Mayerfeld Bell, "The Ghosts of Place." *Theory and Society* 26 (December 1997), 813.

19. Ibid., 813.

20. Ibid., 813.

21. Ibid., 831; he cites Wendy Griswold, "The Fabrication of Literary Meaning." *American Journal of Sociology* 92 (May 1987). The actual title is "The Fabrication of Meaning: Literary Interpretation in the United States, Great Britain, and the West Indies"; this particular quote is drawn from page 1079.

22. Andean Oral History Workshop (THOA)/Silvia Rivera Cusicanqui, "Indigenous Women and Community Resistance: History and Memory." In *Woman and Social Change in Latin America,* ed. Elizabeth Jelin (London: Zed, 1990), p. 180.

23. Paul Mojzes, *Yugoslavian Inferno: Ethnoreligious Warfare in the Balkans* (New York: Continuum, 1994), p. 40. Mojzes defines mythological time as when "concepts of the past and present are so intermixed that a grievance of long ago is perceived as a present affliction. Likewise . . . a present action may not only vindicate but actually eradicate and reverse a past defeat."

24. In 1519 on the island of Hispaniola native chieftain Enriquillo took up arms against his *encomendero* (colonial landlord) and the colonial authorities. Castro, *Guerrilla Warfare in Latin America,* p. ii.

25. Gert Rosenthal, quoted in David Schrieberg, "Dateline Latin America: The Growing Fury." *Foreign Policy* (spring 1997), 165.

26. Ibid., 165–166.

27. Arturo Valenzuela, "Paraguay: The Coup That Didn't Happen." *Journal of Democracy* 8 (January 1997), 43–55.

28. For a more in-depth exploration of this issue, see Jennifer Mathews and Eric Selbin, "The Generation of Darkness: The Failure of Democratic Consolidation in Chile," paper presented at the 1995 Southern Political Science Association, Tampa, Fla. *Democratic consolidation* has become a popular catchphrase, used knowingly—if vaguely—by students of transitions and transformations to democracy to cover a multitude of contexts and processes. Most often, consolidation is used as synonymous or conflated with institutionalization, that is, "consolidation" of the state apparatus and state power. This misuse is a serious mistake and fails to recognize that in any transition to democracy there are at least two analytically distinct processes: institutionalization and consolidation. Institutionalization is a familiar concept, a process that may be readily measured by such factors as the changing status or function of key government structures. Consolidation is an elusive concept related to people's perceptions of the material and ideological conditions of their everyday lives and their relationships with each other, with the new government, even with the democratic process itself, and consolidation is not as easily measured as institutionalization. Democratization would seem to demand more than simply reinvigorating, reordering, and reconstructing moribund institutions. Deepening democracy requires that people make a commitment to democracy, a commitment that

they are likely to make only if democratization is reflected in their lives and the society around them—a popular political culture of democracy. This is where the concept of consolidation comes into play. The distinction between institutionalization and consolidation was first proposed in the context of social revolutionary processes in Selbin, *Modern Latin American Revolutions,* 12–25.

29. John Markoff, "Peasants Help Destroy an Old Regime and Defy a New One: Some Lessons from (and for) the Study of Social Movements." *American Journal of Sociology* 102 (January 1997), 1139.

30. Tens of thousands of troops from Canada, Czechoslovakia, France, Great Britain, Italy, Japan, Poland, the United States, and elsewhere spent some three years supporting the efforts of the sundry White armies to unseat the revolutionary government; the Allied intervention in Russia was one of the major multinational military operations of this century.

31. Quoted in William Rowe and Vivian Schelling, *Memory and Modernity: Popular Culture in Latin America* (London: Verso, 1991), 89. It is interesting to note that "the marvelous, on which twentieth-century magical realism is based, has its origins in the colonial period, and was transmitted above all by women. The transmission occurred in the gap between tactical obedience and pragmatic evasion, *obedezco pero no complo* ("I obey but I do not accept"). . . ." (Ibid., 23). From such subversive notions much may follow.

32. But see the increasingly active and powerful Maoist revolutionary movement in Nepal.

33. Walter Goldfrank, "Praxis, Shmaxis: Commentary on Wagar," *Journal of World Systems Research* 2 (1996), 4. *(http://csf.colorado.edu/jwsr/archive/vol2/v2_n2-e.htm)*

Suggestions for Further Reading

In addition to the full versions of the selections reprinted in this volume, the following works are especially recommended on each of the topics covered in this reader.

Introduction

Brinton, Crane. 1965. *The Anatomy of Revolution.* 3d ed. New York: Vintage Books. (A depiction of how events unfold in revolution that has proven remarkably prescient with regard to subsequent revolutions.)

Foran, John. 1993. "Theories of Revolution Revisited: Toward a Fourth Generation?" *Sociological Theory* 11 (March): 1–20. (An excellent discussion of the theoretical literature on revolution published during the 1980s and early 1990s.)

———, ed. 1997. *Theorizing Revolutions.* London and New York: Routledge. (Leading scholars analyze several approaches to revolution, including state-centered, structural, elite conflict, demographic, agent-centered, gender, racial, cultural, and comparative-historical approaches.)

Goldstone, Jack A. 1980. "Theories of Revolution: The Third Generation." *World Politics* 32 (April): 425–453. (An excellent discussion of twentieth-century theoretical literature on revolution through the late 1970s.)

Goodwin, Jeff, and Theda Skocpol. 1989. "Explaining Revolutions in the Contemporary Third World." *Politics & Society* 17 (December): 489–509. (An analysis of why some types of nondemocratic regimes are more vulnerable to revolution than others.)

Part I: Revolution and International Conflict

Brzezinski, Zbigniew, et al. 1997. *Differentiated Containment: U.S. Policy toward Iran and Iraq.* New York: Council on Foreign Relations. (A discussion of the pros and cons of, as well as alternatives to, the U.S. government's containment policy toward revolutionary regimes in Iran and Iraq.)

Calvert, Peter. 1996. *Revolution and International Politics.* 2d ed. London: Pinter. (Useful chapters on force in the international system, wars of national liberation, different forms of revolutionary action, aid and intervention, and counterinsurgency.)

Conge, Patrick J. 1996. *From Revolution to War: State Relations in a World of Change.* Ann Arbor: University of Michigan Press. (Like Walt's *Revolution and War,* this book analyzes the circumstances in which revolution has or has not led to international war. Conge emphasizes different factors than Walt.)

Katz, Mark N. 1997. *Revolutions and Revolutionary Waves.* New York: St. Martin's Press. (An analysis of relationship patterns among revolutionary actors espousing the same or similar ideologies.)

Skocpol, Theda. 1982. "Social Revolutions and Mass Military Mobilization." *World Politics* 40 (January): 147–168. (Skocpol argues that new revolutionary regimes can increase their domestic support through military mobilization against a foreign opponent. The selection by Snyder reprinted here builds on Skocpol's article.)

Part II: Counterinsurgency and Revolution

Akehurst, John. 1982. *We Won a War: The Campaign in Oman, 1965–1975*. Salisbury, Wiltshire: Michael Russell. (The British have generally been more willing and able than the Americans to undertake long-term counterinsurgency efforts against revolutionary movements. This book describes how they did so in Oman.)

Bennett, Andrew. 1999. *Condemned to Repetition? The Rise, Fall, and Reprise of Soviet-Russian Military Interventionism, 1973–1996*. Cambridge: MIT Press. (A comparison of Soviet counterinsurgency efforts in Afghanistan and Russian counterinsurgency efforts in Chechnya.)

Jentleson, Bruce W. 1992. "The Pretty Prudent Public: Post-Post-Vietnam American Opinion on the Use of Military Force." *International Studies Quarterly* 36 (March): 49–74. (An influential analysis of American public support for military intervention abroad in the post–Vietnam era.)

Lomperis, Timothy J. 1996. *From People's War to People's Rule: Insurgency, Intervention, and the Lessons of Vietnam*. Chapel Hill: University of North Carolina Press. (A comparative analysis of why some large-scale counterinsurgency efforts against revolutionary movements have succeeded whereas others have failed.)

Rodman, Peter W. 1994. *More Precious than Peace: The Cold War and the Struggle for the Third World*. New York: Charles Scribner's Sons. (An excellent account of the Soviet-American competition in the Third World during the latter part of the cold war.)

Part III: Democratization and Revolution

Arendt, Hannah. 1963. *On Revolution*. London: Penguin Books. (An analysis of, among other subjects, why the American Revolution resulted in democracy whereas the French Revolution did not.)

McClintock, Cynthia. 1998. *Revolutionary Movements in Latin America: El Salvador's FMLN and Peru's Shining Path*. Washington, D.C.: U.S. Institute of Peace Press. (A comparative analysis of the rise and fall of revolutionary movements seeking to overthrow two "democratizing" governments at the dawn of the post–cold war era.)

McDaniel, Tim. 1991. *Autocracy, Modernization, and Revolution in Russia and Iran*. Princeton: Princeton University Press. (McDaniel argues that rapid economic modernization without democratization led to revolution against these two autocratic governments.)

Moore, Barrington, Jr. 1966. *Social Origins of Dictatorship and Democracy: Lord and Peasant in the Making of the Modern World*. Boston: Beacon Press. (A classic—and controversial—attempt to explain why some revolutions result in democracy whereas others result in dictatorship.)

Skocpol, Theda, ed. 1998. *Democracy, Revolution, and History.* Ithaca: Cornell University Press. (Several leading scholars re-examine Moore's *Social Origins* in light of subsequent events.)

Part IV: The Transformation of Revolution

Brooker, Paul. 1997. *Defiant Dictatorships: Communist and Middle-Eastern Dictatorships in a Democratic Age.* New York: New York University Press. (An examination of why and to what extent eight different revolutionary regimes have avoided socialization so far.)

Colburn, Forrest D. 1994. *The Vogue of Revolution in Poor Countries.* Princeton: Princeton University Press. (An analysis of the failure of socialist revolutionary regimes in the Third World to foster economic development.)

Halliday, Fred. 1994. "An Elusive Normalization: Western Europe and the Iranian Revolution." *Middle East Journal* 48 (spring): 309–326. (An examination of why the Islamic Republic of Iran's efforts to befriend West European governments have met with only limited success.)

Hough, Jerry F. 1997. *Democratization and Revolution in the USSR, 1985–1991.* Washington, D.C.: Brookings Institution. (An analysis of Gorbachev's efforts to transform a revolutionary state.)

Rajaee, Farhang. 1999. "A Thermidor of 'Islamic Yuppies'? Conflict and Compromise in Iran's Politics." *Middle East Journal* 53 (spring): 217–231. (On the embourgeoisement of Iran's younger leadership generation.)

Part V: The Future of Revolution

Goldstone, Jack A. 1995. "The Coming Chinese Collapse." *Foreign Policy,* no. 99 (summer): 35–52. (A prospective application of Goldstone's theory of revolution to China.)

Keddie, Nikki R., ed. 1995. *Debating Revolutions.* New York: New York University Press. (Section 1 of *Debating Revolutions* contains articles by Keddie, Goldstone, and Timur Kuran on whether revolutions can be predicted.)

Simon, Jeffrey D. 1989. "Revolutions without Guerrillas." R-3683-RC. Santa Monica: RAND Corporation. (Simon sees modern revolutions occurring more through rapid urban action than through drawn-out rural insurgency.)

Snyder, Robert S. 1999. "The End of Revolution?" *Review of Politics* 61 (winter): 5–28. (Snyder argues that the causes of revolution in the recent past have either declined or been eliminated, and that the spread of liberalism makes revolution unlikely in the future.)

Zunes, Stephen. 1994. "Unarmed Insurrections against Authoritarian Governments in the Third World: A New Kind of Revolution." *Third World Quarterly* 15 (September): 403–426. (Zunes argues that unarmed insurrection has become a common type of revolution in the Third World.)

INDEX

Aaron, David, 195
Aaron, Harold R., 152
Abbot, Elizabeth, 195
Abrahamian, Ervand, 258, 267
Acheson, Dean, 47
Adams, Richard N., 150
Adams, Thomas, 165
Adelman, Jonathan R., 23, 29, 57, 61, 106
Afghanistan
    antiregime coalition, 202
    embourgeoisement, 260–261
    Islamic revolution, 4, 251
    revolution, 3
    Soviet Union and, 8, 93, 114
Afkhami, Gholam R., 197
Africa, 273, 276
African National Congress, 6
Albania, 3, 259
Algeria, 3, 26, 167–168, 266, 289
Allardt, Erik, 57
Allemann, Fritz René, 122, 145–146, 150, 152, 153
Allende, Salvador, 188
Alliance for Progress, 54
Altstadt, Audrey L., 267
Amann, Peter, 56
Amaru, Túpac, 251, 292
American Revolution
    effects of, 2
    French and British in, 7
    Seven Years War and, 68
    state reconstruction following, 24, 26
    war and, 70
American Socialist, The, 59n32
Andrews, B., 249
Anglo-American war of 1812–1813. See War of 1812
Angola, 1, 3, 214, 224. See also Front for the National Liberation of Angola; Popular Movement for the Liberation of Angola
April 19th Movement (M-19; Colombia), 203, 216, 218–220, 227
Aquino, Benigno, Jr., 185, 186
Aquino, Corazon, 186, 187, 188
Arab countries
    alliances, 4
    education in, 256
    embourgeoisement, 265

nationalism, 255, 256
    Westernization, 255
Arab revolutions
    class issues, 254–258
    countries of, 3
    goals of, 3–4, 255–256
    Laroui's theory, 254–266
    support for, 257–258
Arana Osorio, Carlos, 125
Arbenz, Jacobo, 48, 125, 126
Archer, R. P., 216, 217, 218, 219, 235, 236
Arenas, Jaime, 153
Arendt, Hannah, 295
Argentina, 90
Arias, Jorge, 132
Arias, Oscar, 222
Arizmendi Posada, Octavio, 152
Arjomand, Said Amir, 18, 19, 29, 94, 108
Arms race. See Cold war
Arms sales
    counterinsurgency and, 114–115
    Great Britain, 101
    Nicaragua, 96
    Soviet Union, 101
    United States, 92, 103, 127–133
Armstrong, David, 62, 240, 241, 250
Aron, Raymond, 74
Artola Azcarate, Armando, 153
Asia, 4, 273, 276
Aslund, Anders, 267
Atkinson, Rick, 165
Avant, Deborah, 157
Ayoob, M., 107
Ayubi, Nazih, 257, 267

Bailey, Jennifer, 61
Bakhash, S., 94, 108
Bakhtiar, Shahpour, 185, 190
Balance, offense-defense, 34
Balance-of-power issues
    effects of revolution, 36, 42, 45, 273
    international institutions and, 245
    theoretical basis, 34
Balance-of-threat issues, 32, 33–34
Baltic states, 259
Banisadr, Abol Hasan, 94
Banzer, Hugo, 150n19
Barnes, Fred, 196

Barquín, Ramón, 144, 150n14, 153, 177
Barrientos, René, 123, 140, 152n56
Batista, Fulgencio, 86, 121–122, 127, 150n14, 176–177
Bazargan, M., 85, 92, 94
Beaufort, E. de, 217, 236
Belarus, 260, 261
Belgium, 145
Benford, Robert D., 58
Benjamin, J., 89, 108
Berejikian, Jeffrey, 58
Berman, K., 108
Betancourt, Rómulo, 124
Betancur, Belisario, 216
Bill, James A., 61, 92, 108
Binder, Leonard, 255, 257, 267
Blachman, Morris J., 106, 194
Blackey, Robert, 56, 58
Blackmail, 200
Blanchard, George S., 138, 151
Blasier, C., 106
Boletín del Ejército, 120–121
Bolger, Daniel P., 166
Bolivia. See also Latin America
    armed forces, 123, 126t
    Cuban training for, 143, 147
    Green Berets in, 137, 152n56, 153n77
    guerrilla forces, 289
    Guevara, Ché, and, 62n56, 137, 140, 147, 152n56
    as illiberal revolutionary state, 79–80
    military coup d'état, 150n19
    military size and spending, 118, 119–120
    political factors, 140
    U.S. military aid and training, 123, 127, 128, 129t, 130, 132, 133, 134t, 135–136, 137, 138–139, 140, 148
    USSR and, 103
Bolsheviks, 6, 18, 22, 39, 57n12, 66. See also Russian Revolution
Bond, James E., 153
Bonsal, P., 87, 90, 108
Booth, John A., 221, 222, 236, 278, 282
Borge, Tomas, 58
Borkenau, Franz, 60
Bosch, Juan, 179
Boudreaux, R., 225, 236
Bourgeoisie
    Arab states, 254–255
    in the class struggle, 254
    Cuba, 83–84, 85, 87, 91
    embourgeoisement, 250–266
    Iran, 83–84
    Nicaragua, 83–84, 85

petit bourgeoisie, 254–255, 262, 263, 265, 266
Bowles, Chester, 179
Boyd, Gerald, 196
Bravo, Douglas, 145, 152, 153
Brazil, 135
Brezhnev Doctrine, 253
Brinkley, Joel, 196
Brinton, Crane, 20, 21, 29
Brown, Archie, 165
Brown, Harold, 195
Brownlee, Romie L., 166
Bryant, Louise, 61n42
Brzezinski, Zbigniew, 92, 183, 195, 263, 267
Buchanan, J. M., 206, 220, 236
Bueno de Mesquita, B., 107
Builder, Carl H., 161, 165
Burton, Michael G., 12, 29
Burton, Sandra, 196
Bush, George, 186
Business and corporate issues, 48

Caldera, Rafael, 211
Calhoun, Craig, 18, 29
Cambodia, 3, 260–261. See also Khmer Rouge
Canada, 2
Caporaso, J., 249
Carazo, Rodrigo, 182
Carey, J. M., 200, 212, 223, 238
Carillo, Justo, 177
Carpentier, Alejo, 292–293
Carr, Edward Hallett, 59
Carter, Jimmy
    citation to, 196
    Council of Freely Elected Heads of Government, 182
    human rights policies, 91–92, 190
    Iranian revolution, 93–94
    Nicaraguan revolution, 95, 97, 171, 184–185
    shah of Iran, 184, 185, 190, 197n56
    U.S. policies in Nicaragua, 183
Carter (Jimmy) administration
    Haiti plans, 180, 195n23
    Iranian hostage crisis, 93–94
    Iranian revolution, 92, 93, 183
    Nicaraguan revolution, 95, 96
    U.S. policies in Nicaragua, 182
Case histories
    democratization and revolution, 210–223
    revolution and international conflict, 86–101
    succession crises, 175–189

Case histories—by country
  Chile, 188–189
  Colombia, 215–220
  Cuba, 86–91, 176–177
  Dominican Republic, 177–179
  Haiti, 179–181
  Iran, 91–95, 183–185
  Nicaragua, 95–99, 181–183, 221–223
  Philippines, 185–188
  United States, 86–106
  Venezuela, 210–213
  Zimbabwe, 99–101, 213–215
Casey, William, 186
Castañeda, Jorge G., 260, 267
Castaño, Camilo, 152
Castro, Daniel, 294
Castro, Fidel. See also Cuba
  armed forces and, 126
  Batista government and, 86, 176
  battlefield experience, 64
  communists and, 86, 87–88, 89
  domestic opposition to, 87–88
  embourgeoisement and, 261
  as nationalist, 109n35
  Sandinistas and, 39
  Soviet Union and, 88, 90, 91
  U.S. and, 47, 48, 86–87, 88, 89, 90, 91,
    108n19, 192
  view of revolutions, 117
Castro, Raúl, 88
Cataldi, Milton Delfin, 151
Ceasefires. See Military issues
Central Intelligence Agency (CIA)
  Barquín, Ramón, 177
  Castro, Fidel, 89, 90
  estimates of Cuban training,
    142–143
  Mossadegh, Mohammed, 184
  Nicaraguan exiles, 97
Chaliard, Gerard, 74
Chamberlin, William Henry, 57, 58, 61
Chamorro, Pedro Joaquín, 182
Chamorro, Violeta, 85, 96, 225
Chan, Anita, 260, 267
Chapelle, Dickey, 144
Charles X, 12
Chavez Frias, Hugo, 290
Chechnya, 4
Chehabi, H. E., 91–92, 108
Chen, J., 102, 103
Chernick, M. W., 199, 216, 217, 236
Chile
  case history, 188–189
  continuismo, 290–291

crisis of succession, 172, 173, 175,
    188–189, 191
  elections, 189, 191
  military, 191
  U.S. and, 173, 188
China
  alliances, 3, 103
  Communist Party, 103, 239, 260
  economic issues, 260
  embourgeoisement, 260, 264
  foreign policies, 145, 260
  international power of, 3
  Manchu dynasty, 3
  Nationalist government, 3
China—revolution (1949)
  effects of, 2–3, 239
  export of, 3
  internal enemies, 25
  international conflict, 30
  Korean War and, 30, 71
  purges, 49
  relations with U.S., 102
  social class and, 5
  state reconstruction following, 24
  U.S. view of, 52
  view of the U.S., 103
  violence in, 56n10
Chinese Communist Party, 6
Chong, Dennis, 60
Chorley, Katherine C., 57
Christensen, T., 102
Christian, S., 96, 97, 222, 236
CIA. See Central Intelligence Agency
Civil rights, 17–18. See also Human rights is-
  sues
Civil war. See Wars
Cliffe, J. T., 22, 29
Coalitions
  breakdown of, 75, 77
  Colombia, 216
  democratization and, 230, 233
  international conflict and, 82–83, 241–242
  Iran, Cuba, and Nicaragua, 78, 83–84,
    95–96
  organization of, 21–22
  relevant parties and, 200
  revolutionary regimes and, 6, 19, 20, 24,
    27, 207
  role of elites, 13, 20
  Third World countries, 82
  Venezuela, 212
  Zimbabwe, 215
Coatsworth, John H., 276, 282
Cohan, A. S., 56

Cohen, Eliot, 166
Cohen, W., 102
Colburn, Forrest D., 257, 260, 267, 293
Cold war. *See also* Soviet Union; United States
  Angola, 1
  arms race, 68
  China, 3
  colonial rule during, 276
  Cuba, 91
  illiberal revolutions during, 79–80, 103, 107n3
  international society, 244
  Iran, 91
  post–World War II period, 68
  revolutions, 3, 272, 273–277, 280
  Russian Revolution and, 30
  status quo powers, 7
  Soviet Union, 68
  U.S. foreign policies, 106
Collins, Randall, 295
Colombia. *See also* Latin America; April 19th Movement
  antiguerrilla warfare, 120, 123
  armed forces, 122, 123, 126t, 232
  case history, 215–220
  constitution, 216, 218–219, 227
  Contadora group, 218
  Cuban and Nicaragua aid and training for, 143, 144, 146–147, 148, 218
  guerrilla forces, 289
  La Violencia, 120, 122–123, 216
  military experience, size, and spending, 118, 119–120, 141
  political issues, 229, 230, 235n13
  Revista de las Fuerzas Armadas, 120
  revolution and conflict, 4, 216–219
  theory of guerrilla warfare, 120
  U.S. military aid and training, 128, 129, 130, 132, 134t, 138, 140, 141, 148
Communism and communist parties. *See also* Marxism; Marxism-Leninism
  Colombia, 216, 217, 218
  downfall of, 251, 254, 274
  embourgeoisement, 259–260
  Nicaragua, 221
  socialism and, 252–253
  Soviet Union, 6, 275
  spread of, 2, 6, 47
  U.S. view of, 52
  Venezuela, 124, 211
Conflict. *See* Guerrillas and guerrilla warfare; International issues; Wars

Congo. *See* Democratic Republic of the Congo
Connor, John T., Jr., 267
Conservative Party (Colombia), 216
Contras. See Nicaragua
Corruption, 11, 16
Coser, Lewis A., 59
Costa Rica, 182–183
Costs. *See* Guerrillas and guerrilla warfare
Cottam, R., 92, 93, 94, 108
Coubre incident, 89, 90
Counterinsurgency, 114, 135–141
Counterrevolutions
  difficulties of, 53–54
  fear of, 51, 52
  status quo powers and, 73
  successful, 62n60
  war and, 70, 71, 73
Coups d'état
  Arab nationalist revolutions, 5
  Chile, 188
  definition and significance, 114, 172, 281
  Dominican Republic, 178
  Guatemala, 48, 125
  Iran, 91
  Latin America, 290
  Portugal, 234n9
  role of elites in, 12
  U.S.-backed, 62n60, 91
  Venezuela, 124
Coward, Richard A., 277, 282
Crises of succession. *See* Succession crises
Crisis of the Arab Intellectual, The: Traditionalism or Historicism? (Laroui), 254
Cromwell, Oliver, 26
Cruz, A., Jr., 221, 236
Cuba. *See also* Batista, Fulgencio; Castro, Fidel; Guevara, Ché; Latin America
  armed forces, 121–122, 123, 126, 144
  case histories, 86–91, 176–177
  crisis of succession, 172, 173, 175, 176–177, 191
  democracy in, 191
  domestic conflict, 87–89
  embourgeoisement, 260, 261
  emigration to Venezuela, 146
  explosion, 108n20
  guerrilla movement, 148
  Latin American aid and training, 142–143, 148
  military experience, size and spending, 118, 119, 120–121
  nationalization of U.S. property, 90, 91
  political factors, 190

relations with the Soviet Union,
88–91
relations with the U.S., 79, 84, 86–91
revolution, 3, 54, 71, 78, 84, 85, 105, 144,
172, 175
support for the Sandinistas, 183
theory of guerrilla warfare, 120
training of Latin Americans,
142–144
troops sent to Angola, 1
U.S. military assistance to, 127, 130, 132,
134t, 135
U.S. rights in, 173
U.S. view of, 52, 79, 177
violence in, 56n10
weapons, 144
Cultural issues, 256, 257, 288–289
Czech Republic, 259

Dahl, R. A., 202, 203, 236
Dance, E. H., 61
Darnton, Robert, 295
Davidow, J., 100, 101, 214, 215, 236
David, S., 107
Dawisha, Karen, 267, 268
Dawley, Alan, 277, 282
Dearborn, Henry, 178
Deas, Malcolm, 150
Debating Revolutions (Foran), 9
Debray, Regis, 62
Democracy and democratization. *See also*
Electoral systems; Guerrillas and guerrilla
warfare—incorporation
abandonment or destruction of, 167,
281n4
class conflicts, 277
consolidation, 296n28
costs and, 202, 203, 214–215
crisis of succession and, 174, 191
democratic values, 202–203
economic factors, 284
elections, 191–192
embourgeoisement and, 262
establishment of, 270–271
forces leading to, 230
forestalling revolution, 167, 270, 272,
276–279
globalization and, 280
permanence of, 280–281
political factors, 277–278
revolutions and, 270, 276–281
as second-best solution, 202
transitions to democracy, 296n28
U.S. role in, 191

Democracy and democratization—by
country
Chile, 188–189, 191
Colombia, 215–220
Dominican Republic, 170, 179
El Salvador, 281n3
Guatemala, 281n3
Haiti, 180, 181
Latin America, 276, 290
Nicaragua, 188
Philippines, 186, 191
Venezuela, 211–213
Zimbabwe, 213–215
Democratic Republic of the Congo, 3, 274
DeNardo, James, 57, 60
Deng Xiaoping, 260
DePuy, William E., 162, 166
Developing countries. *See* Third World
countries
Diamond, Larry, 197
Dictatorships. *See also* individuals and indi-
vidual countries
crises of succession, 172–174
personalist, 279–280
in revolutionary process, 23, 170, 175,
279–280
view of U.S. foreign policies, 173
Diederich, Bernard, 194
Dilemmas, 45, 61n44, 73
Di Palma, G., 200, 225, 236
Diplomacy, 245
Diplomatic History, 102
Dissociation. *See* International issues
Diversionary theory, 82–83
Dix, Robert, 102, 105, 107, 279, 282
Dobson, Richard B., 265, 267
Domínguez, J., 84, 86, 87, 88, 90, 91, 108,
151
Dominican Republic
assassination of Trujillo, Rafael, 170,
194n20
case study, 177–179
crisis of succession, 172, 175, 177–179,
191
Cuban military assistance, 144–145
elections in, 179
military, 191
U.S. military assistance, 135
U.S. rights in, 173
Dower, John, 59
Downie, Richard, 159, 165
Drake, P., 237
Draper, T., 86, 108
Dresser, Denise, 251, 260, 267

Duarte, J. N., 236
Dudwick, Nora, 267
Dulles, John Foster, 176
Dunkerley, James, 276, 282
Dunn, John, 57
Duvalier, François "Papa Doc," 179
Duvalier, Jean-Claude "Baby Doc,"170, 195n26
Dynamics of Doctrine: The Changes in German Tactical Doctrine During the First World War (Lupfer), 157
Dyson, James, 164

Eckstein, H., 107
Economic issues. *See also* individual states
    capitalism, 251, 252, 293
    class struggle, 247–248
    embourgeoisement, 264
    free markets and free trade, 280, 285
    globalization, 275, 280, 286
    inflation, 15
    international trends, 16, 247
    Marxism, 252–254
    postrevolutionary reconstruction, 24, 25, 36
    poverty, 284
    redistribution of assets, 22
    revolution and, 285
    role in state breakdown, 11–12, 16, 18, 27
    socialism, 252–253
    socialization and, 243
    state control, 256
Ecuador, 290
Edwards, Lyford P., 56
Egypt
    Arab nationalist revolution, 3, 5, 239, 255
    embourgeoisement, 260, 265, 266
    radical elites, 13
Eisenhower, Dwight D., 178
Eisenhower (Dwight D.) administration
    U.S. policy in Cuba, 47, 87, 89–90, 91, 177
    U.S. policy in Iran, 91
Electoral systems. *See also* Democracy and democratization
    class struggle and, 277
    electoral competition, 203, 206
    institutional rules and reforms, 200, 206–207, 208, 214–215, 219, 226–228
    proportional representation, 200
    withdrawal and disarmament of military, 226, 232
Electoral systems—by country
    Colombia, 216, 217–220
    Latin America, 290

Namibia, 224–225, 226, 227–228
Nicaragua, 182, 191, 221, 222–223, 225, 226
Venezuela, 211–213
Zimbabwe, 214–215, 224
Elites
    anti–Western, 78
    coalition building, 20, 27
    ideological progression, 21
    marginal, 25, 28, 35
    motivations of, 86
    postrevolutionary reconstruction, 24, 25, 36, 42
    post–World War I, 72
    spirals of suspicion and, 46–47, 55
    state breakdown and, 11–13, 16, 18–19, 27, 35, 42
    use of international conflict, 82
    war and, 71, 72
Elites—by country
    Colombia, 216
    France, 12
    Iran, 92
    Latin America, 290
    Prussia, 12
    Russia, 258
    Soviet Union, 108n16
    Third World countries and, 102
Elliott, David W. P., 260, 267
Ellis, John, 57
Ellner, S., 211, 236
El Salvador. *See also* Farabundo Marti National Liberation Front
    arming of rebels, 96–97
    attacks by armed forces, 278–279
    civil war, 71
    constitution, 228
    effects of guerrilla movement, 281n3
    Reagan administration, 98–99
    rebel political participation, 230, 232
Enders, Thomas O., 98, 99
English Revolution, 12, 21, 24, 26, 70. *See also* United Kingdom
Enrile, Juan Ponce, 187
Ethics. *See* Moral issues
Ethiopia, 1, 3, 6, 101
Ethnic issues, 16
Europe, Eastern
    communist regimes, 2, 5, 274, 276
    democratization of, 259, 273
    embourgeoisement, 264
    hostility to the U.S., 79
    international social engineering, 245

Europe, Western
  colonialism, 4
  fears of Jacobin conspiracy, 52
  international society and, 246
  state-building in, 81
Evans, Peter, 275, 282
Everingham, M., 108
Exiles and sympathizers
  counterrevolution and, 54
  portrayal of revolutionary regimes, 44,
    48–49, 51, 52–53
  returning to homeland, 60n41
Externalization
  China, 102–103
  Cuba, 88–89, 105–106
  Iran, 93, 105–106
  Nicaragua, 96–97, 105–106
  theory, 81–87, 91, 101–102, 105, 107n10
  Zimbabwe, 99–100

Falcoff, Mark, 295
Farabundo Marti National Liberation
  Front, 6. See also El Salvador
FARC. See Revolutionary Armed Forces of
  Colombia
Farhi, Farideh, 107, 257, 267, 279, 282
Farland, Joseph, 178
Farrell, Theo, 164
Fauriol, Georges, 195, 295
Feinberg, R., 80, 106
Fernandez, Orlando, 152
Fernandez, R., 218, 220, 238
Figueres, José, 176–177, 194n9
Figueroa Ibarra, Carlos, 294
Fisher, F., 107
Foran, John, 9, 279, 280, 281, 282, 286, 294,
  295
Ford (Gerald) administration, 182
Foreign policies. See International issues;
  individual countries
Fox, Richard, 295
France, 2, 20, 68, 243. See also Military is-
  sues
France—Revolution (1789). See also Ja-
  cobins
  calling of French Estates General, 12
  effects of, 2
  international conflict, 6, 30
  radicalism, 18, 22
  social issues and, 5, 13, 295n14
  state reconstruction following, 24
  violence in, 56n10
  war and, 64, 68, 70
Franklin, Billy J., 149

Friend, Theodore, 196
Fronde, 20
Front for the National Liberation of An-
  gola, 6
Fujimori, Alberto, 290
Fukuyama, Francis, 293
Fulbrook, Mary, 21, 29
Fursenko, A., 86, 88, 89

Gaddis, J., 106
Galeano, Eduardo, 151
Gall, Norman, 143, 150, 152, 153
Gamson, William A., 277, 282
Gann, L., 108, 118
Garantismo (Nicaragua), 200, 215, 225, 230
Garcia, J. Z., 236
Gardner, Arthur, 176
Garratt, Bob, 165
Garver, J., 102, 103
Gasiorowski, M., 108
Gebicki, Anna Maria, 259, 267
Gebicki, Wojciech, 259, 267
Geddes, B., 205, 212, 236
Geller, Tatyana S., 267
Gellner, Ernest, 62
Gensler, Martin D., 153
George, Alexander, 79, 107, 165
Germany, 20, 72, 259
Geyer, Georgie Anne, 151
Gilbert, Arthur, 293
Gilbert, Dennis, 59, 61, 96
Gilmore, Kenneth O., 153
Glaser, Charles L., 61, 107
Goffman, Erving, 150
Goldfrank, Walter, 293, 297
Goldman, Emma, 61n42
Goldstone, Jack
  breakdown of revolutionary coalition,
    75
  citations to, 9, 11, 29, 59, 60, 266
  embourgeoisement, 265–266
  process model of revolution, 9–10
Gonzalez, Luis J., 150
Goodwin, Jeff, 108, 167, 270–271, 272, 276,
  277, 281, 282, 293, 294
Gorbachev, Mikhail, 165, 222, 243, 258, 273
Gorman, S., 108
Gott, Richard, 149, 151, 152, 153, 216, 236
Governments. See States
Granovetter, Mark, 60
Gray, John, 294
Great Britain. See United Kingdom
Greece, 212–213

Green Berets. *See* Military issues—United States
Greer, Donald, 56
Gregory, M., 213, 214, 236
Grenada, 3, 101
Griswold, Wendy, 288, 296
Grofman, B., 199, 237
Group of Seven, 244–245
Grove, Eric, 166
Guardia, Sara Beatriz, 151
Guatemala. *See also* Latin America
   armed forces, 123, 125, 126
   coups d'état, 48, 125, 290
   Cuban training and support for, 143, 144–145, 146, 148
   guerrilla forces, 123–124, 125, 141, 281n3
   land reforms, 48
   military size and spending, 118, 119–120
   political factors, 140, 278–279
   U.S. military aid and training, 127–128, 130, 132, 133, 134t, 137, 138–140, 141, 148
   U.S. relations with, 88, 116
Guerrillas and guerrilla warfare. *See also* Military issues; Wars; individual countries
   antiguerrilla warfare, 120, 125
   costs of conflict and tolerance, 200, 202, 203, 204–209, 213, 214–215, 217–218, 229
   democracy and, 202
   external aid, 117–118
   finances, solidarity, and external aid, 142–148, 204
   foco theory, 50–51, 62n56, 216
   goals of, 202–203
   Guevara, Ché, and, 38, 64
   military size and spending, 118–120
   political issues, 232–233
   revolutionary movements and, 65
   success or failure of, 117, 141, 142
   U.S. military aid and training, 123, 125, 134–135, 136–141, 142
   use of term, 74n3
   weapons, 144
Guerrillas and guerrilla warfare—incorporation. *See also* Democracy and democratization
   costs of conflict and incorporation, 204–209, 211, 212, 213, 218, 219–220, 222, 225, 226–228, 229, 230, 232–233
   end to conflict, 198–199, 207, 208–210, 218–219, 233
   moves and effects, 231–232
   sequences and conditions, 228–232

Guerrilla/rebel groups and armies
   April 19th Movement (M-19; Colombia), 218–220
   contras (Nicaragua), 71, 98–99, 221, 223, 225–226
   Farabundo Marti National Liberation Front (El Salvador), 6
   Front for the National Liberation of Angola, 6
   Movement toward Socialism (MAS; Venezuela), 212
   Popular Front for the Liberation of Oman, 6
   Popular Movement for the Liberation of Angola, 6
   Revolutionary Armed Forces of Colombia (FARC), 216, 217, 220
   Sandinista National Liberation Front (FSLN; Nicaragua), 6, 39, 95–99, 182–183, 221, 222
   Sendero Luminoso (Peru), 203, 233n2, 251
   SWAPO (Namibia), 224–225, 227
   Tupac Amaru (Peru), 251
   Zapatista National Liberation Army (Mexico), 251, 289
Guevara, Angel Raúl, 150, 151
Guevara, Ché. *See also* Bolivia; Cuba
   Bolivia, 147
   citation to, 282
   execution, 152n56
   guerrillas, 38, 62n56, 137, 152n56
   role in Cuban revolution, 88
   view of revolution, 277
   view of war, 64
Guinea-Bissau, 3
Gulf War. *See* Persian Gulf War
Gurr, Ted Robert, 23, 25, 26, 29, 57, 59, 294
Guthrie, Charles, 161, 165
Gutiérrez, Julio, 183, 195n31
Gutman, R., 98, 108
Gwertzman, Bernard, 196

Haghayeghi, Mehrdad, 268
Hagopian, Mark, 58
Haiti
   case study, 179–181
   coup d'état, 290
   crisis of succession, 172, 173, 175, 189–190, 191
   Duvalier, François "Papa Doc," 179, 180
   Duvalier, Jean-Claude "Baby Doc," 170, 180–181

elections, 180, 181, 191
Marine Corps in, 162
military, 191
U.S. rights in, 173
Halliday, Fred, 30, 31, 63, 294
Halperin, Morton, 59
Hammond, Nancy, 57
Harare. See Zimbabwe
Harding, T. F., 211, 237
Hardin, Russell, 57
Hartlyn, J., 216, 217, 237
Hartz, Louis, 80
Haya de la Torre, Victor, 143
Henriksen, T., 108
Héraud, Javier, 147
Herbst, J., 101, 108
Herman, Charles, 164
Herter, Christian, 89–90, 194n15
Herz, John, 61
Higley, John, 12, 29
Hillen, John, 166
Hiro, D., 93, 94, 108
Hirschman, A. O., 238
History, 294n1, 295n14, 296n23
Hobsbawm, Eric J., 62, 281n1, 282
Holland revolution, 70
Honduras, 97, 278–279
Hough, Jerry, 258, 268
Howard, Alan, 153
Howard, Michael, 161, 165
Human rights issues
    Colombia, 218
    Haiti, 180
    Iran, 91–92, 190
    Latin America, 290, 291
    Philippines, 186
    standards of civilization, 244
Hungary, 259
Huntington, Samuel P., 56, 276, 281, 282, 293
Hunt, M., 80, 103
Hunt, W., 21, 29
Hussein, Saddam, 261, 262–263, 280. See also Iraq

Idéologie arabe contemporaine (Laroui), 254
Ideologies
    definitions, 38
    militaries, 23
    organization and, 21–22, 27
    portrayal of opponents, 39, 40, 44, 59n37
    progression of, 21
    role in revolutionary state, 42–43, 104

role in revolutions, 17–19, 23, 27, 37, 50, 54–55
    themes, 20, 38–41, 44–45, 58n26
Ikle, F., 213, 237
IMF. See International Monetary Fund
Immerman, Richard H., 61
Imperialism (Lenin), 69
India, 4
Indochina, 107n6, 253
Indonesia, 4, 274
Institutional Revolutionary Party (PRI; Mexico), 264
Institutional rules and reforms, 206–207
    costs of participation and toleration, 208, 214–215, 219, 226–229, 230–231
    reasons for, 200–201
Insurgency. See Revolutionaries and revolutionary states
International issues. See also Sovereignty; Westphalian system; Wars; individual countries
    balance of power, 245
    conflict, 82–83
    diplomacy, 245
    dissociation, 190
    effects of revolution, 24, 263
    embourgeoisement, 250, 263
    foreign support of rebel movements, 204–205
    institutional reforms, 201
    institutions of international society, 242, 246
    international law, 245–246
    international norms, 241, 246, 247, 248, 250
    international observers, 204, 207, 214, 232, 233, 234n7
    need for foreign assistance, 24
    offense-defense balance, 49–55
    preemptive strikes, 84–85, 91
    role in revolutionary conjuncture, 15–16
    sanctions, 247
    socialization, 242–249
    stalemate, 234n4
    state reconstruction following revolution, 24
International Monetary Fund (IMF), 284
International organizations, 32, 244. See also United Nations
Iran
    alliances, 4
    in the cold war, 91
    crisis of succession, 172, 173

policies under the shah, 1, 92, 183–184
U.S. and, 183–184, 196n35
Iran—Islamic Republic
    democratization, 168, 262
    embourgeoisement, 258, 262, 263–264
    foreign policies, 46, 94, 103, 239
    postrevolutionary state, 26, 92–93, 94–95
    Rafsanjani government, 258–259
    success of clerics, 94
    support of fundamentalist revolutions, 6,
        265
    U.S. view of, 92
Iran—revolution (1979)
    case histories, 91–95, 183–185
    class issues, 258
    coalition of, 6
    crisis of succession, 175, 184
    domestic factors, 85, 92–93, 184
    effects of, 4
    export of, 4
    fiscal policies and, 17
    foreign policies, 1, 105
    hostage crisis, 93–94
    ideologies, 39, 251
    international conflict, 30
    moral rigor, 18
    policies of, 1, 85
    political factors, 190
    purges, 49
    social issues and, 13, 91–92
    U.S. and, 78, 79, 84
    violence in, 56n10
    war and, 30, 71
Iran-Iraq war (1980–1988), 30, 69, 71
Iraq, 3, 5, 260, 261
Ireland, 2, 69
Islamic fundamentalism, 265, 266, 270
Islamic revolution, 251, 257–258. See also
    Iran—revolution
Italy, 145

Jacobins, 18, 21, 22, 24, 26. See also France—
    Revolution
James II, 12
James, Daniel, 152
Jam, Fereidoun, 195n31
Janowitz, Morris, 149
Jasper, James M., 281, 282
Jelin, Elizabeth, 296
Jenkins, Brian M., 165
Jervis, Robert, 56, 61, 81, 107
Jiménez, Pérez, 123–124
Joes, Anthony James, 57
Johnson, Lyndon B., 179

Johnson, P., 108, 214, 234n9, 237
Jones, Stephen E., 268
Jorgeman, A. J., 294
Juergensmeyer, Mark, 251, 268

Kagan, R., 84, 95, 96, 97, 98, 99, 108
Kahn, E. J., 62
Kampwirth, Karen, 286
Karl, T., 211, 237
Karns, Margaret, 29
Kashmir, 4
Katzenberger, Elaine, 294
Katz, Friedrich, 74
Katz, Mark N., 240, 250, 253, 268, 294
Kautsky, Karl, 39
Keddie, Nikki, 60
Kegley, Charles, 164
Kennedy, John F., 173, 178, 179–180, 194n20
Kennedy (John F.) administration, 177,
    178–179, 180, 189–190
Kennedy, M. L., 22, 29
Kennedy, Paul, 69, 74
Keohane, R., 107
Kerr, Malcolm H., 256, 268
Khatami, Mohammad, 258–259
Khmer Rouge, 3, 203. See also Cambodia
Khomeini, Ayatollah Ruhollah. See also Iran
    class issues, 258
    expectations of, 58n19
    role in Iranian revolution, 92, 185, 258
    view of U.S. and the West, 93, 184,
        262–263
Khrushchev, Nikita, 90. See also Soviet
    Union
Kiessler, Richard, 117, 149
Kim Il Sung, 261
King, G., 107
Kinzer, Stephen, 61
Kipling, Rudyard, 164
Kirkpatrick, Jeane, 171, 193, 254, 268
Kissinger, Henry, 68–69, 74, 104, 295
Kitson, Frank, 163, 166
Klandermans, Bert, 58, 60
Klare, Michael T., 134, 151
Kolakowski, Leszek, 268
Kolko, G., 80, 106
Korea, 260, 261
Korean War, 30, 47, 71
Kriesi, Hanspeter, 58, 60
Kuran, Timur, 43, 60

LaFeber, W., 80, 106
Lake, A., 108
Lake, W. A., 106

Lalman, D., 107
Lamberg, Robert F., 134, 143–144, 151, 153
Lancaster House Agreement, 100
Landau, S., 211, 237
Lando, Barry, 152
Lanz, Díaz, 88, 90
Laos, 3
Laqueur, Walter, 74, 142, 152
Laroui, Abdallah, 250, 252, 254–266, 268
Lartéguy, Jean, 150, 152, 153
Latin America. *See also* individual countries
    Alliance for Progress, 54
    armed forces of, 118–120, 121, 123, 126
    Cuban aid and training, 148
    death squads, 291
    democratization, 276, 290–291
    guerrilla movements in, 289
    magical realism in, 292–293
    neo-liberalism, 291–292
    poverty in, 284, 289–290
    revolutions in, 273, 284, 285–286,
        291–292
    social movements, 291
    U.S. counterinsurgency training,
        135–141, 143
    U.S. direct investment, 151n30
    U.S. Military Assistance Program,
        127–133
    U.S. military intervention, 116, 120
Lauren, Paul Gordon, 165
Lawrence, T. E., 164
Laxalt, Paul, 186, 187–188, 196
League of Nations, 244, 245
Learning theory, 155, 158–162
Lebow, Richard Ned, 61
Leites, Nathan, 152
Lenin, Vladimir Ilich, 74
    Bolshevik rule, 57n12
    citations to, 59
    imperialism, 40
    offensive of world capitalism, 61n46
    power and revolution, 56n4
    Russian Revolution and, 39, 58n19,
        59n36
    von Clausewitz, Carl, and, 65
    war and revolution, 69
Leninism, 258. *See also* Marxism-Leninism
Lentin, Albert-Paul, 152
LeoGrande, William, 106, 171, 194
Levine, D. H., 211, 237
Levy, Jack, 62, 107
Lewis, John Wilson, 57
Lewy, Guenter, 165
Liberal Party (Colombia), 216, 220

Libya, 3, 260, 261
Lichbach, Mark I., 57, 295
Licklider, R., 199, 237
Lieuwen, Edwin, 129, 130, 150
Lijphart, A., 107, 212, 237
Linz, Juan J., 197, 203, 212, 237
Lipset, Seymour Martin, 197, 277, 282
Loftus, Joseph, 118, 149
Lohmann, Susanne, 60
Lomperis, Timothy, 114, 115
Lopez, George A., 29
Louis XIV, 12
Louis Philippe, 12
Lugar, Richard, 187
Lukacs, George, 74
Lukashenka, Alexander, 261
Lupfer, Timothy T., 157
Luxenberg, A., 89

M-19. *See* April 19th Movement
MAAGs. *See* Military Assistance Advisory
    Groups
MacArthur, John, 59
Macdonald, D., 85, 106
Macgregor, Douglas A., 166
Machel, Samora, 234n6
Machiavelli, Niccolò, 60
Malaya, 114, 155, 160, 163
Mandel, Ernest, 74
Manigat, Leslie, 181
Mao Tse-tung
    citation to, 61
    goals, 102–103
    reactionaries, 39–40
    spread of revolution, 50
    suspicions of the U.S., 46
    view of imperialism, 59n35
    view of war, 64
MAP. *See* Military Assistance Program
March, J. C., 199, 237
Marcos, Ferdinand, 170, 185–188, 196n41,
    196n45, 196n52. *See also* Philippines
Markoff, John, 276, 282, 292, 297
Markus, Ustina, 261, 268
Martin, D., 108, 214, 234n9, 237
Martin, Edwin, 179, 195
Marxism. *See also* Communism and com-
    munist parties
    in China, 260
    ideologies and theories, 39, 251, 252–254
    Laroui and, 254
    present-day, 251, 270
    revolutions, 3, 4, 252
    in Russia, 260

view of U.S., 80
as a world movement, 293
Marxism-Leninism, 253, 259, 293
Marx, Karl, 278
MAS. *See* Movement toward Socialism
Maspero, François, 152
Mathews, Jennifer, 296
Matos, Húbert, 85, 88
Maullin, Richard L., 150, 151, 153
May, Earnest R., 165
Mayer, Arno, 67, 71–72, 74, 107
Mayerfeld Bell, Michael, 288, 296
McAdam, Doug, 60, 294
McCaughan, Edward, 294
McClintock, Cynthia, 294
McCubbins, M. D., 212, 235, 237
Menem, Carlos, 290
Mensheviks, 6
Mercado, Rogger, 151–152
Methodologies, 78–80, 200–202, 203
Metz, Steven, 166
Mexico
    embourgeoisement, 260
    free market, 264
    guerrilla forces, 289
    nationalization of industry, 103
    North American Free Trade Agreement, 260, 264
    political issues, 264
    suspicions of the U.S., 46
    U.S. military assistance, 136
    Zapatistas, 251
Mexico—revolution, 4
    crisis of succession, 172
    effects of, 2–3
    international military actions, 71
    U.S. relations with Mexico, 103
    violence in, 56n10
Michelet, Jules, 295
Middle East, 1, 3–4. *See also* individual countries
Migdal, Joel S., 57
Mikoyan, Anastas I., 89, 90
Milani, M., 93, 108
Milgram, Stanley, 150
Military Assistance Advisory Groups (MAAGs), 138
Military Assistance Program (MAP), 127–133
Military issues. *See also* Coups d'état; Guerrillas and guerrilla warfare; Wars
    adaptability, 156, 158–159, 163–164
    armies, 150n17
    authority, 150n27

in Bolivia, 152n56, 153n77
ceasefires, 201, 205, 208–210, 216–217, 223–226, 228, 229–230, 231
corruption, 11
costs of war, 201
disarming, 209–210, 232–233
in France, 162
innovation, 156–158
internal military resources, 117–121
leadership, 122
loyalty of armed forces, 116, 121–122, 125–126
military assistance, 127–141
military size and spending, 118–120
military solidarity, 121–126
offense-defense balance, 49–55
organizational culture, 156, 158–162
postrevolutionary regimes, 24–26, 36
power and, 34
revolution in military affairs, 163–164, 166n37
role of armed forces in revolutions, 14, 23, 35, 57n14, 191
stalemates, 206, 208–210, 226–227, 228, 229–230, 231, 234n4
Military issues—United Kingdom. *See also* Malaya
    adaptability, 156, 157–158, 161, 163
    leadership, 160
    organizational culture, 155, 160, 161, 162, 163
    Persian Gulf War, 162
    political factors, 157, 160
Military issues—United States. *See also* Vietnam War
    adaptability, 156, 157–159, 161, 163
    Green Berets, 125, 137, 138–139, 152n56, 153n77
    leadership, 160
    low-intensity conflict, 159, 162
    organizational culture, 155, 159, 160, 161, 162, 165n25, 166n41
    political factors, 157, 162
    primary mission, 154, 161, 162
Millett, Alan R., 165
Millett, R., 108
Miranda, R., 98, 108
Mobile Training Teams (MTTs), 138
Mobutu Sese Seko, 274
Mohr, Charles, 196
Mojzes, Paul, 296
Monarchies, 3, 7, 13, 21
Montgomery, J. D., 238
Moore, Barrington, Jr., 121, 149, 253, 268

Moore, Will, 294
Moral issues, 38, 39
Morgan, Dan, 264, 268
Morley, M., 87, 89, 108
Mossadegh, Mohammed, 91, 184
Moss, Richard, 61
Motyl, Alexander, 294
Movement toward Socialism (MAS;
  Venezuela), 212
Mozambique, 3, 213, 214, 234n6, 234n9
MTTs. *See* Mobile Training Teams
Mugabe, Robert. *See also* Zimbabwe
  as avowed Marxist, 99, 101, 109n35
  as leader of Zimbabwe, 100, 214
  Machel, Samora, and, 234n6
  Nkomo, Joshua, and, 215
  Zimbabwe African National Union, 213
Mullahs. *See* Iran
Mullen, William J., Jr., 166
Muller, Edward N., 57
Munson, Donn, 150, 152
Murphy, Richard W., 263, 268
Murray, Williamson, 158, 163, 165, 166
Mydans, Seth, 196

NAFTA. *See* North American Free Trade
  Agreement
Naftali, T., 86, 88–89
Nagl, John A., 115, 154
Namibia, 223, 224–225, 227–228, 229,
  232–233
Namphy, Henri, 181
Napoleon, 65
al-Nasir, Jamal 'Abd (Gamal Abdul Nasser),
  255, 256, 268
Nateq-Noori, Ali Akbar, 258–259
National Action Party (Mexico), 264
National Front (Colombia), 216
Nationalism
  in Arab states, 255
  professed nationalists, 109n35
  role in revolutionary process, 23, 24, 27,
    28, 42
  state stability, 16
Nationalist revolutions, 4
Navarro Wolff, Antonio, 218, 235n16
Neorealist school, 34
Nepal, 4
Neustadt, Richard E., 165
New People's Army of the Philippines, 6
New York Times, 188
Nicaragua. *See also* Sandinista National Lib-
  eration Front
  aid to, 95, 96, 97

armed forces, 121–122
case histories, 95–99, 181–183, 221–223
conflict, 221
constitution, 221
contras, 71, 98–99, 221, 223, 225–226
crisis of succession, 172, 173, 181–183,
  190, 191
elections, 182, 191, 221, 222–223, 225
foreign policy, 98, 105
international factors, 221, 222–223
military, 191
political factors, 190, 221, 222–223, 230,
  232
relations with the U.S., 46, 79, 84,
  108n29, 182–183
revolution, 3, 71, 78, 84, 95, 172, 175
U.S. military assistance to, 135, 162
U.S. rights in, 173
U.S. view of, 52, 95
violence in, 56n10
Nichol, D., 101
Nixon, Richard, 176, 184
Nkomo, Joshua, 100, 215
Noden, Edward C., 166
Noland, Marcus, 261, 268
North American Free Trade Agreement
  (NAFTA), 260, 264
North, Douglass C., 38–39, 58, 59
Norton, C., 237
Nujoma, Sam, 227

OAS. *See* Organization of American States
Obando y Bravo, Archbishop, 97
Oberdorfer, Don, 196
Ochs, Michael, 268
O'Donnell, G., 203, 237, 238
Olcott, Martha Brill, 268
Olsen, J. P., 199, 237
Olson, Mancur, 57
Oman, 114
Opp, Karl-Dieter, 57
Organski, A. F. K., 104
Organizational learning theory. *See* Learn-
  ing theory
Organization of American States (OAS),
  182
Origins of Alliances, The (Walt), 32
Ortega, Daniel, 58n19, 225. *See also*
  Nicaragua; Sandinista National Liberation
  Front
Ortega, Humberto, 58n24, 195n30
Osborne, Harold W., 149
Osorio, Arana, 139
Ottaway, David B., 264, 268

Overholt, William H., 260, 268
Oye, K., 80, 106

Pact of Punto Fijo, 211
Page, D., 236
Pahlavi, Mohammed Reza (shah of Iran), 91, 93, 183, 191–192, 197n56
Paige, Jeffery M., 276, 282, 294
Paine, Thomas, 61n42
Palestine Liberation Organization (PLO), 6
Palmer, David Scott, 251, 269
Panama, 123, 124, 134–135, 290
Papp, Daniel S., 251, 269
Paraguay, 290
Parker, Jay M., 159, 165
Parrott, Bruce, 267, 268
Party of the Democratic Revolution (Mexico), 264
Pastora, Eden, 235n27
Pastor, Robert
    citations to, 58, 95, 96, 97, 106, 108, 169, 194, 195, 237
    National Security Council staff, 169
Paterson, T., 89, 108
Patriotic Front (Zimbabwe), 215
Pawley, William, 177
Paynton, Clifford, 56
Peace, 73
Peceny, M., 106
Penniman, H., 212, 237
People's Republic of China (PRC). See China
Pérez, Carlos Andres, 176, 182, 194n9
Persian Gulf War (1990–1991), 162, 163, 166n26
Peru. See also Latin America; Sendero Luminoso
    armed forces, 122, 123, 126t, 140
    coup d'état, 290
    Cuban aid and training for, 143, 147, 148
    guerrilla forces, 289
    military size and spending, 118, 119
    radical elites, 13
    rebels, 233n2
    revolutions, 4
    theory of guerrilla war, 120
    U.S. military aid and training, 127–128, 129t, 130, 132, 134t, 138, 140, 148
Petkoff, Teodoro, 153
Petras, James, 149, 151
Petroleum, 262–263
Pettee, George, 61
Philippines
    case history, 185–188

communists, 185
    crisis of succession, 172, 173, 175
    democracy and democratic tradition, 168, 185, 188
    elections, 186–187, 191
    fiscal policies, 17
    human rights, 186
    Marcos, Ferdinand, 170
    military, 191
    political factors, 191
Pinochet, Augusto, 188, 189, 290. See also Chile
Pinzon de Lewin, P., 217, 218, 238
Piven, Frances Fox, 277, 282
Platt Amendment, 86
PLO. See Palestine Liberation Organization
Poland, 70, 259
Political factors. See also individual countries
    in ceasefires, 205, 208
    concept of "political opportunities," 281n5
    costs of violence and disorder, 280
    in democracy, 277–278
    international conflict, 82–83
    military innovation and, 157
    offensive power and, 34
    political engineering, 205
    regime differences, 200
    regional conflicts, 204
    in revolutions, 35, 40–41, 50, 72, 226, 276–281
    in stalemates, 206, 229
    in succession crises, 190, 193
    U.S. control in Third World countries, 173
    U.S. view of revolutionary states, 103
    in wars, 72–73
Political Institutions and Military Change: Lessons from Peripheral Wars (Avant), 157
Political parties, 200
Political parties—by name
    Acción Democrática (AD; Venezuela), 211, 212
    AD (Colombia), 124
    Christian Democratic COPEI (Venezuela), 211, 212
    communist (Colombia; Venezuela; Nicaragua; Russia; Soviet Union), 6, 124, 211, 216, 217, 218, 221, 259, 275
    Conservative Party (Colombia; Nicaragua), 216, 221
    Institutional Revolutionary Party (PRI; Mexico), 264

Liberal Party (Colombia; Nicaragua),
216, 220, 221
National Action Party (Mexico), 264
National Front (Colombia), 216
Party of the Democratic Revolution
(Mexico), 264
Patriotic Front (Zimbabwe), 215
Social Christian (Nicaragua), 221
Unión Nacional para la Independencia
Total de Angola, 101
Unión Patriótica (Colombia), 217, 218
United Nicaraguan Opposition (UNO),
225
Zimbabwe African National Union
(ZANU), 100, 213, 214–215, 234n7
Zimbabwe African People's Union
(ZAPU), 214–215
Popkin, Samuel L., 57
Popular Front for the Liberation of Oman,
6
Popular groups, 14, 20
Popular Movement for the Liberation of
Angola, 6
Population issues, 9, 15
Portugal, 234n9
Posen, Barry R., 164
Potgieter, P. J. J. S., 225, 238
Powell, Charles, 164
Power. *See also* Balance-of-power issues;
Status quo powers
Arab nationalist regimes, 256
China, 3
France, 2
globalization and, 275
military and political issues, 34, 200, 212
offensive, 34
power and revolution, 56n4
Russia, 2
of states, 34, 36, 37, 44
PRC (People's Republic of China). *See*
China
PRI. *See* Institutional Revolutionary Party
Prío Socorras, Carlos, 144
Prosletitismo armado (Colombia), 226
Prussia, 12
Przeworski, A., 203, 206, 230, 238
Puerto Rico, 144–145
Pumaruna, Américo, 152
Purges, 49
Puritans, 18, 21, 22
Purkitt, Helen, 164

al-Qadhafi, Mu'ammar, 261, 262–263
Quester, George, 56

Rabe, Stephen G., 194
Race, Jeffrey, 57
Radicals and radicalism. *See also* Revolutionaries and revolutionary states
bourgeoisie and, 105
conservative, 18
in Cuba, 83–85
in Iran, 92–93, 94–95
in Nicaragua, 97, 99
postrevolutionary state and, 27
revolutionary drift toward, 21–22
Soviet Union and, 84
suppression of, 22
United States and, 83–84, 104
in Venezuela, 124
in Zimbabwe, 99, 100, 101
Radu, Michael, 221, 238, 295
Ramazani, R. K., 108
Ramos, Fidel, 187
Ratliff, William, 98, 108, 152, 295
Ray, Michèle, 152
Reagan, Ronald
Haiti, 181, 195n26
Marcos, Ferdinand, and, 187,
196n52
Nicaragua, 97, 98–99
Philippines, 186
Sandinista fear of, 96
Zimbabwe, 101
Reagan (Ronald) administration
Chile, 188
citations to, 195
Ethiopia, 101
Haiti, 180, 189–190
Iran, 94, 103
Nicaragua, 97–99, 103, 188
Philippines, 186
Soviet Union, 103
Zimbabwe, 101
Realism, magical, 292–293
Realist school, 32, 85, 103, 104, 297n31
Rebels. *See* Guerrillas and guerrilla warfare
Reed, John, 61n42
Reflections on Revolutions (Katz), 250
Reforms. *See* Institutional rules and re-
forms
Reiter, D., 84
Revista Militar del Peru, 120
Revolución, 145
*Revolution and Rebellion in the Early Modern
World* (Goldstone), 9
Revolution and War (Walt), 32
Revolution and World Order (Armstrong),
241

Revolutionaries and revolutionary states.
See also Counterrevolutions; Radicals and radicalism
class issues and, 247–248, 254, 257
Cuban, Iranian, and Nicaraguan, 83–84
democratization and, 276, 277–278, 279
domestic policies, 77–78
embourgeoisement, 250, 252, 255, 256–266
evolution of, 239–240, 279
exiles and sympathizers, 44, 48–49, 51, 52–53
expectations and suspicions, 58n19, 61n53, 104, 107n8
foreign policies, 83
free-rider effect, 37, 38, 40
goals, externalization, and defense of the revolution, 81–86, 287
illiberal revolutionary states, 79–80
insurrection, coup d'état, and insurgency, 114
integration of, 239–240
international conflict and, 104–105, 242
reasons for joining movements, 37–38
religious fundamentalists, 251, 279
shifts in alliances, 76
socialist, 253
socialization and, 242–249
spread of revolutions and, 43–44, 50, 51
support for, 275
Third World countries, 82, 102
view of U.S. and the West, 80, 81, 83, 84–85, 262–266
war and, 64–65, 73
Western hostility towards, 263
Revolutionary Armed Forces of Colombia (FARC), 216, 217, 220
Revolutions. *See also* Coalitions; Ideologies; States; individual revolutions
ages of, 281n1, 295n14
anticolonial, 26
bourgeoisie and, 105
causal models of, 9, 10–11, 14, 27
causes of, 287–288
class issues, 251–252
cold-war era, 273, 287
conflicts in, 45–55, 66
definitions, 5–7, 10, 34–35, 42
differences in, 9, 35, 114
elites in, 12–13, 14, 17, 20, 42
exiles and sympathizers, 44, 48–49
forces for revolutionary conjuncture, 15–18, 26–27

forecasting and strategies to avoid, 16–17, 27
free-rider effect, 37, 38, 40
future of, 270–281, 284–293
government overthrow, 167
"great revolutions," 287, 295n13
honeymoon period, 20
illiberal, 107n3
internal transformations of, 81–82
leaders, 25–26, 35, 51
militaries, 23, 82
nationalism in, 23, 73
offense-defense balance and, 50
patterns and processes, 7–8, 9, 10, 19–26, 34–45, 59n37, 65–66
revolutionary movements, 5–6, 25–26
revolutionary regimes, 6, 7, 8, 25–26
social programs, 19, 287
success of, 37
terrorism and violence, 22–23, 25, 27–28, 35–36, 37, 42, 56n10, 56n11, 59n27, 60n38, 65
theories of, 252–266, 274–281
Revolutions—international relations. *See also* Wars and revolutions
basic effects, 1–2, 4, 7, 30, 45–55
causes of, 30–31
crises of succession and, 174–175
in divided revolutionary movements, 62
export and spread of, 3, 6, 43, 50, 53–54, 73, 263
foreign policies and, 42–43, 76–77
globalization, 275
status quo powers, 7–8, 9–10, 114
universalism, 40–41, 42, 50, 54–55
Westphalian system of, 241
Rhodesia, 100, 213–215, 222–223, 233n1, 234n9, 235n26. *See also* Zimbabwe
Rivera Cusicanqui, Silvia, 296
Robelo, Alfonso, 96, 97, 182, 195n29
Rochford, E. Burke, Jr., 58
Rockman, B., 237
Roeder, Philip G., 57
Rogowski, R., 212, 237
Romania, 259
Rose, G., 104
Rosenau, James, 164
Rosenbluth, F. 212, 235, 237
Rosen, Stephen P., 156–157, 164, 165
Rosenthal, Gert, 296
Rowe, William, 297
Roy, Olivier, 251, 265, 269
Rubin, B., 108
Rule, James B., 58

Rusk, Dean, 62n59, 194
Russell, Diana E. H., 121, 149, 150
Russia. *See also* Bolsheviks; Soviet Union
  Afghanistani Taliban revolution, 4
  allied intervention, 297n30
  Belarus and, 261
  capitalism, 259–260, 265
  democracy in, 259
  elites in, 72
  embourgeoisement, 259, 265
  international power of, 2
  Leninism, 258
  political issues, 265
  radicalization in, 22
  tsarism, 39
Russian Revolution (1917). *See also* Bolsheviks; Communism and communist parties; Marxism; Marxism-Leninism; Soviet Union
  effects of, 2
  internal enemies, 25
  international conflict, 30
  radicalism, 18, 22
  social class and, 5
  state reconstruction following, 24
  violence in, 56n10
  war and, 64, 70–71
  World War I and, 63, 67, 69
  World War II and, 71
Rustow, D., 202, 238

Sacasa, Juan, 181
Salazar, Evelio Buitrago, 150
Salazar, Gustavo A. Sanchez, 150
Salazar, Jorge, 97
Sánchez Lira, Mongo, 294
Sandinista National Liberation Front (FSLN; Nicaragua), 6, 39, 95–99, 182–183, 221, 222–223. *See also* Nicaragua
Santo Domingo, 162
Sartori, G., 200, 238
Saudi Arabia, 262
Scarritt, J., 108
Schaller, Michael J., 62
Schelling, Vivian, 297
Schlesinger, Arthur M., Jr., 194, 195
Schlesinger, Stephen, 61
Schmitter, P. C., 203, 237, 238
School of the Americas, 135
Schram, Stuart, 74
Schweller, R., 104
Sciolino, Elaine, 193
Selbin, Eric, 270, 271, 279, 280, 283, 284, 294, 295, 296

Seligson, M. A., 236
Sendero Luminoso (Peru), 203, 233n2, 251
Senge, Peter M., 166
Senser, Robert A., 260, 267
Seven Years War, 68
Sewell, William, Jr., 295
Shah of Iran. *See* Pahlavi, Mohammed Reza
Shain, Yossi, 60
Sharpe, Kenneth, 106, 194
Shaw, W., 101
Shelton, Ralph "Pappy," 137
Shelton, Turner, 195
Sheng, M., 102
Shiʿites. *See* Iran
Shugart, Matthew Soberg, 107, 198, 200, 212, 218, 219, 220, 223, 234, 235, 238
Shultz, George, 171, 180–181
Shy, John, 165
Sick, Gary, 92, 93, 108, 195, 197
Silva, E., 237
Silver, Morris, 57
Singer, J. David, 56
Sin, Jaime Cardinal, 185
Sinn Fein, 69
Skocpol, Theda
  citations to, 14, 24, 25, 56, 57, 59, 62, 82, 107, 108, 269, 294, 295
  military mobilization in revolution, 82
  revolutionary governments, 56n6
  state-building, 77
  theory of revolution, 253
Slovenia, 259
Small, Melvin, 56
Smith, Earl, 176
Smith, Ian, 100
Smith, W., 87, 90, 91, 108
Snow, David A., 58
Snyder, Robert, 30, 31, 75, 293
Social Christian Party (Nicaragua), 221
Socialism. *See* Economic issues
Social issues
  classes, 5, 20, 24
  of complex societies, 20
  ideology and, 19
  mobility, 12–13
  nationalism, 53–54
  poverty, 278, 284, 289–290
  postrevolutionary reconstruction, 24, 25, 28, 55, 56n9
  revolutionary response to, 18, 22, 35
Solarz, Stephen J., 196
Somalia, 1

Somoza Debayle, Anastasio, 95, 181–182, 184, 191, 221
Somoza Garcia, Anastasio, 121–122, 181
Sorensen, Theodore, 194n20
South Africa
    African National Congress, 6
    Angola and, 1
    Rhodesia/Zimbabwe and, 214, 215, 233n1, 234n9
    social issues, 13, 247
South America, 276. *See also* Latin America; individual countries
South West Africa People's Organization of Namibia, 6
Sovereignty, 73–74, 241, 244, 245–246, 248–249
Soviet Union (USSR). *See also* Cold war; Russia
    Castro, Fidel, and, 88
    collapse of, 275–276
    communism, 6, 275
    downing of South Korean airliner 007, 101
    Eastern Europe and, 79, 259
    effects of cold war revolutions, 273
    embourgeoisement, 259, 263
    nuclear weapons, 253
    socialization, 243
    use of force, 253
Soviet Union—foreign policies
    Afghanistan invasion, 93
    alliances, 1, 3, 239–240
    capitalist powers, 275–276
    Cuba, Iran, and Nicaragua, 84, 86, 222
    effect of cold war, 68–69
    Iran, 1
    military aid, 131
    settlements of regional conflicts, 204
    Third World countries and, 78, 80, 106
Spain, 65
Special Action Forces, 138
Spiral models. *See* States
Sri Lanka, 4
Stalemate. *See* Military issues
Starn, Orin, 295
States. *See also* Balance-of-power issues; Wars; Wars and revolutions
    capabilities and power, 34, 36, 37, 44
    communications between, 44
    conditions of state breakdown, 11–14, 17–19
    decline of, 69
    elites and, 13, 18–19
    ethnic and nationalist issues, 16

European state-building, 81
export of revolution to, 53–54, 73
functions of, 244
liberal, 244
models of state behavior, 156
offense-defense balance, 49–55
perceptions of, 34, 42–43
power of, 56
radical ideologies, 19
realist theories of, 32, 34
relationship patterns of, 32–33, 45–55
revolutionary outcome and state recon-struction, 23–28, 34–35, 36, 42, 55, 56n9, 77
security of, 33–34, 45–46
social forces of, 53–54, 243, 278
spiral models, 45–55, 75, 76–77, 81, 88, 91, 96, 104
terrorism and violence, 22–23, 37
threats to, 32, 34, 42
war and, 63, 67, 68, 69–70, 73
States and Revolutionary Movements (Good-win), 272
Status quo powers. *See also* Democracy and democratization; individual countries
    authoritarian, 168
    cold war, 7
    counterinsurgency, 114–115
    counterrevolutions, 73
    democratic, 168
    political issues, 248
    revolutions and, 7–8, 9–10, 71, 114, 167, 239
    United Kingdom and United States, 7
    war, 63
Stedman, S. J., 199, 213, 214, 215, 234, 238
Stein, A., 107
Stein, Nancy, 151
Stohl, Michael, 29, 107
Strom, K., 200, 206, 238
Stycos, J. Mayone, 132
Succession crises. *See also* individual countries
    case histories, 175–189
    explanations of outcomes, 189–192
    problems of, 172–173
    stages of, 173–174
    U.S. management of, 192–193
Sudan, 3, 4, 251, 260–261
Sullivan, William, 184
SWAPO (Namibia), 224–225, 227
Sympathizers. *See* Exiles and sympathizers
Syria, 3
Szulc, Tad, 74, 88, 90, 108

Taagepera, R., 200, 238
Tajikistan, 260–261
Taliban, 4. *See also* Afghanistan
Tang Tsou, 59
Tarrow, Sidney, 58, 60, 62, 274, 277, 283, 294
Taylor, A. M., 108
Taylor, Michael, 57
Tekle, A., 108
Templer, Gerald, 162, 166
Terror, 22–23, 25, 27–28
Theorizing Revolutions (Goldstone), 9
Third World countries. *See also* individual countries
    aid to, 245
    bourgeoisie and embourgeoisement, 105–106, 260
    domestic policies, 77, 82, 104
    economic issues, 11
    foreign policies, 77, 82
    revolutions, 9, 100, 101–102, 253–254
    Soviet Union and, 78, 80, 106
    succession crises, 169–175
    U.S. relations with, 75–106
Thirty Years War, 241
Thomas, Hugh, 87, 88, 108, 153, 177, 194
Tilly, Charles
    citations to, 56, 59, 77, 81, 150, 274, 283, 294
    erosion of state power, 58*n*18, 275
    state-building, 77, 81
Time magazine, 143
Tismaneau, Vladimir, 295
Torrijos, Martin, 182
Trimberger, Ellen Kay, 13, 29, 56, 57
Trotsky, Leon, 64, 69, 74, 279
Trujillo, Rafael, 170, 177–179, 194*n*20, 195*n*21
Truman (Harry S.) administration, 103
Tullock, Gordon, 57, 206, 220, 236
Turabi, Hasan, 261
Turcios Lima, Luis, 125, 146
Turkey, 2–3, 13
Turner, Ralph H., 149

Unión Nacional para la Independencia Total de Angola (UNITA), 101
Union of Soviet Socialist Republics (USSR). *See* Russia; Soviet Union
Unión Patriótica (UP; Colombia), 217, 218
UNITA. *See* Unión Nacional para la Independencia Total de Angola
United Fruit Company, 48

United Kingdom. *See also* English Revolution; Malaya; Military issues—United Kingdom
    radical movements in, 22
    Rhodesia / Zimbabwe, 101, 213–214
    as a status quo power, 7
    war with France, 68, 70
United Nations, 101, 224, 244–245, 247. *See also* International organizations
United Nicaraguan Opposition (UNO), 225
United States. *See also* American Revolution; Military issues—United States
    approval of assassinations, 178
    "China Hands," 49, 62*n*54
    economic goals, 76–77
    export of revolution, 2
    military training, 123, 124, 134–138
    "Red scares," 52
    socialization of, 242–243
    as a status quo power, 7
    succession crises, 190–191
    support of national communism, 103–104
United States—Army. *See* Military issues—United States
United States—foreign policies
    alliances, 1, 3, 101, 103–104, 239–240
    arms sales, 92, 103, 127–133
    authoritarian regimes, 275–276
    case histories, 86–106
    crises of succession, 169–175
    Cuba, Iran, Nicaragua, 1, 79, 83–84, 85–86, 170, 263
    direct investment in foreign countries, 151*n*30
    Europe, 106
    foreign aid, 123, 126–139, 151*n*30
    hostility to revolutionary change, 80, 263
    human rights, 180
    Iran, 264
    Latin American guerrilla movements, 116
    relations with dictators, 173, 280
    relations with Third World states, 75–106
    revolutionary change and, 79, 99–100, 103, 106
    settlements of regional conflicts, 204
    Venezuela, 153*n*68
    view of communism, 52
UP. *See* Unión Patriótica
Urcuyo, Francisco, 183
Urrutia Lleó, Manuel, 87
Uzbekistan, 4

Valenzuela, Arturo, 197, 296
Valsalice, Luigi, 153
Vance, Cyrus, 92
van Creveld, Martin, 164, 166
Van Evera, Stephen, 56, 61, 80
Van Ness, Peter, 59
Vasquez de Urrutia, P., 236
Vasquez, Fabio, 147
Venezuela. *See also* Latin America
  aid to, 145, 153n68
  armed forces, 123–124, 126t
  case history, 210–213
  coups d'état, 124, 290
  Cuban emigrants to, 146
  Cuban training and support for, 143,
    144–146, 148
  democracy and constitution, 211–212
  guerrilla warfare, 124, 211
  military size and spending, 118, 119–120
  political issues, 124, 144, 211–212, 229,
    230
  settlement of guerrilla conflict, 210–213
  support for the Sandinistas, 182–183
  theory of guerrilla warfare, 120
  U.S. military aid and training, 128, 130,
    132, 133, 134t, 137, 138–139, 148
Verba, S., 107
Vietnam, 3, 107n6, 114, 260
Vietnam War
  Marine Corps in, 162
  support forces, 138
  United States and, 8, 73, 155, 160,
    161–162
Villa, Pancho, 71
Villarreal, Rogelio, 294
von Clausewitz, Carl, 65, 74

Waghelstein, John D., 152
Walker, Thomas W., 108, 221, 238, 278,
  282
Wallerstein, I., 247, 249
Walt, Stephen
  citations to, 32, 55, 81, 106, 107, 279, 283
  conflict, 30
  research issues, 106n2
  revolutions and war, 31, 56n11
  spiral model, 75, 77, 79, 81, 104
Waltz, K., 104
Walzer, Michael, 18, 29, 294, 295
War and the International, The (Trotsky), 69
War of 1812, 2, 70
Wars. *See also* Guerrillas and guerrilla warfare; Military issues; individual wars
  anticipation of, 156–157, 161
  changes in and military adaptability,
    163–164
  civil war, 36
  control in, 121
  conventional, 163–164
  crisis-generated, 71–72
  effects on states, 63
  external and internal, 164, 229, 231,
    232
  offense-defense balance, 49–55
  of peace, 164
  political issues, 72–73
  propaganda during, 39, 41
  revolution in military affairs, 163–164,
    166n37
  risks of, 55
  states and, 63, 67, 68, 69–70
  status quo powers and, 63
  success in, 161
Wars and revolutions
  balance of threat and, 32
  conflict in, 45–55, 66, 69–70, 71–72
  dilemmas of, 73
  effects of revolution, 24, 32, 36, 42,
    45–55, 66–67, 70–73
  effects of war, 66, 67–70
  foreign policy purposes, 65
  geopolitical shifts and, 24
  pacifism, 64
  processes, 65–67
  similarities and distinctions, 65–67
Watts, Barry, 158, 165
Weaver, K., 237
Weiss, Linda, 275, 283
Welch, Richard, 61, 87, 90
Westad, O. A., 102, 103
Western powers, 244–245
Westphalian system, 241–249
Whelan, Joseph, 195
Whitehead, L., 237, 238
White, Stephen, 259, 269
Wiarda, Howard, 295
Wickham-Crowley, Timothy P., 115, 116,
  279, 283
Wiles, Peter, 269
Williams, W., 80
Wilson, James Q., 165
Wiseman, H., 108
Wolf, Charles, 142, 152
Worden, Steven K., 58
World War I, 63, 67–68, 70, 71
World War II
  German elites, 72
  Marxist revolutionary movements, 63

morale during, 121
nationalist movements during, 69
postwar period, 68
processes of, 74n7
Russian Revolution and, 71, 72
Wright, Robin, 294, 295

Xinjiang, 4

Yemen, 3, 6
Yon Sosa, Marco, 125, 146
Young, C., 102
Yuen Foong Khong, 165
Yugoslavia, 3, 259

Zabih, S., 93
Zaire, 274
Zakaria, Fareed, 104, 293
ZANU. See Zimbabwe African National
  Union
Zapata, Emiliano, 288

Zapatista National Liberation Army (Mex-
  ico), 251, 289
ZAPU. See Zimbabwe African People's
  Union
Zeitlin, Maurice, 149, 151
Zimbabwe. See also Rhodesia
  aid to, 101
  case histories, 99–101, 213–215
  elections, 213, 224
  international pressures on, 213–215, 224
  political issues, 229, 232–233
  relations with U.S., 79–80, 100–101
  USSR and, 103
Zimbabwe African National Union
  (ZANU), 100, 213, 214, 215, 234n7
Zimbabwe African People's Union
  (ZAPU), 100, 214, 215
Zimbardo, Philip G., 150
Zisk, Kimberly Martin, 164
Zonis, Marvin, 58
Zuckerman, Alan, 294

DATE DUE